TREATING ADDICTIONS WITH EMDR THERAPY AND THE STAGES OF CHANGE

Nancy J. Abel, LCSW, LADC, is a licensed clinical social worker and a licensed substance abuse counselor with over 38 years of experience. She is presently in private practice in South Portland, Maine, where she specializes in working with addictions, dual diagnosis, trauma, and EMDR. She is an EMDRIA-approved consultant. She was coordinator of family services at Day One (Drug Rehabilitation, Inc.), a highly reputable agency in Portland, Maine, for adolescents with alcohol and drug problems and their families. She was also director of substance abuse services at Shoreline Community Mental Health Services in Brunswick, Maine. For over 14 years she was an adjunct faculty member in the department of social work at the University of Southern Maine. In addition, she taught in the addiction certificate program at the University of New England. She has extensive experience as a speaker and trainer and presents workshops on addictions and EMDR with John M. O'Brien.

John M. O'Brien, PhD, has been a licensed psychologist in private practice in Portland, Maine, since 1998. He specializes in the treatment of substance abuse, grief, trauma, and gay/lesbian issues. Dr. O'Brien served on the American Psychological Association's Committee on Rural Health and as chair of Sections on LGBT Issues and Independent Practice of Division 17, Counseling Psychology. He is a past president of the Maine Psychological Association and currently serves as the Continuing Education Chair. He is an adjunct faculty member at the University of Maine at Augusta, teaching courses in psychology and addictions since 2000. Dr. O'Brien is an EMDRIA-approved consultant who provides consultation on EMDR, CBT, DBT, and addictions treatment.

TREATING ADDICTIONS WITH EMDR THERAPY AND THE STAGES OF CHANGE

Nancy J. Abel, LCSW, LADC
John M. O'Brien, PhD

SPRINGER PUBLISHING COMPANY
NEW YORK

Springer Publishing Company, LLC
11 West 42nd Street
New York, NY 10036
www.springerpub.com

Acquisitions Editor: Sheri W. Sussman
Production Editor: Shelby Peak
Composition: Newgen Knowledge Works

ISBN: 978-0-8261-9856-3
e-book ISBN: 978-0-8261-9874-7

14 15 16 17 / 5 4 3 2 1

Library of Congress Cataloging-in-Publication Data
Abel, Nancy J., author.
Treating addictions with EMDR therapy and the stages of change / Nancy J. Abel, John M. O'Brien.
p. ; cm.
Includes bibliographical references and index.
ISBN 978-0-8261-9856-3 (alk. paper)
I. O'Brien, John M., author. II. Title.
[DNLM: 1. Eye Movement Desensitization Reprocessing. 2. Case Reports. 3. Substance-Related Disorders—therapy. WM 425.5.D4]
RC451.4.N87
362.2'3—dc 3

2014009299

Printed in the United States of America by Gasch Printing.

To our clients,
who have taught us so much

CONTENTS

PREFACE

NANCY'S STORY

I think I was born to be a social worker. It feels like it is in my blood.

I am one of those unusual people who knew when I was really young what I wanted to do with my life. I remember the exact moment when I knew what my career would be. It was the summer between my junior and senior years of high school. I was doing volunteer work at the Margaret Fuller House in Cambridge, Massachusetts. The "Marga," as we called it, was a settlement house that served as a community center in a low-income neighborhood and offered myriad services. I worked on the playground with the preschool kids. One day, one of the college work–study students was putting a basketball into the closet and said, "Ah, we social workers have a tough life." I had never heard of a social worker but I loved that place and I loved the work. I went back to high school and read about social workers in one of the career books. I knew I would spend my life as a social worker.

I went to college and then right on to graduate school in Boston. Upon receiving my MSW, I moved to Maine, where my first job was at a community mental health center. I had a number of jobs before I opened a private practice in the 1980s. I also continued to work in the public sector and taught for years at two local colleges as an adjunct faculty member.

One of my favorite jobs was serving as the coordinator of family services for a local agency for kids and families dealing with adolescent drug and alcohol abuse. Before that job, I didn't know much about substance use disorders. I received a fast-track on-the-job education. I decided I needed to be more than self-taught and went on to study at the Center for Addiction Studies at Harvard University as a special student. I was lucky enough to have Howard Shaffer as my teacher. He informed my work with and thinking about addiction clients.

My work focused on dealing with addictions and mental health issues. I was fascinated by the challenges of working with this population. I became the director of substance abuse services at a local agency and developed a program for dealing with dual diagnosis.

Meanwhile, I kept hearing about this therapy, Eye Movement Desensitization and Reprocessing (EMDR). Frankly, it seemed like hogwash to me. What kind of therapy had a therapist waving fingers in front of a client's eyes? Despite the rave reviews I heard from people who had done the training, I was a skeptic and I would not recommend it to anyone. Then one day (it is funny how our lives can change in a moment's time!), I was on the phone talking to a managed care clinician about a client who had a fear of dentists. The clinician told me a story about a client who had a serious dental phobia. He had an opportunity to observe an EMDR session where the client's phobia had disappeared.

This got me thinking. What is this therapy? Why is everyone raving about it? I decided to try it out. What better way to see if it worked than to try it myself? I had an old trauma from childhood that had never been resolved. It caused me a great deal of anxiety that would not dissipate, no matter how much I talked about it. In addition, I had a bridge phobia of unknown origin. I was terrified of driving over bridges.

I found a great EMDR therapist, Brenda Sawyer, in Gardiner, Maine, and worked with her on my trauma. Almost immediately, the anxiety around this went away. I felt a weight lift off me. And I started being able to drive over bridges with no problems despite the fact that we didn't target that directly!

I was sold! I signed up for EMDR therapy training and immediately began to use it with clients. I was astounded by the progress made by my clients. Several years before I was trained, I had a client whose house had burned down. She developed posttraumatic stress disorder (PTSD) and was triggered by the sound of fire engines. She felt better after talk therapy but the trigger was still there. While I was in the training, I thought about her and wished I had EMDR skills when I worked with her. Luckily, she returned to treatment and I offered her EMDR therapy. She got better. No more triggers. I am still astounded by how fast people change and how improved the quality of life is following EMDR.

I began to use EMDR with addiction issues: Resource Development, Affect Tolerance, and the Popky/DeTur protocol. I was sitting in Seattle, Washington, at the EMDRIA annual conference, sort of drifting off, when the speaker began to talk about Michael Hase's Memory of Addiction Protocol. She mentioned that he would be speaking about it at the next session. I snapped awake. I had not signed up for it but I ran out during the break and changed sessions. After listening to Michael Hase's talk, I came out of the room and said to my colleagues in attendance, "This is why I came to this conference." I went home and started using it and again was astounded by how helpful it was for clients in recovery who were dealing with urges and cravings. I used it with my client "Margo" that first week home and she felt immediate relief. Margo became the subject of the first article that I coauthored.

EMDR therapy changed my personal and professional life. The integration of EMDR into my work with addictions has enhanced and complemented my work in a way that has been rich and challenging.

This book is an opportunity to share the culmination of my professional work and what I have learned about integrating EMDR into the work with clients with addictions, trauma, and comorbid disorders. I feel tremendous passion about this work. From that first moment in the hall of the Marga when I decided to become a social worker until now, I have loved what I do and I feel enormously grateful for my career. It has been exciting, challenging, intellectually stimulating, frustrating at times, and I cherish every moment. I am excited to share what I have learned with you.

JOHN'S STORY

I first became aware of the critical need for working with clients with addictions and their families when I was a high school guidance counselor in the late 1980s. A colleague and I decided to offer a support group for kids from families where alcohol was a problem. The high school was in a very affluent community and we wondered if any students would be willing to attend. The response was so overwhelming that we had to create a group for each of the two lunch periods to accommodate the students. In addition, some of my students were struggling with addictions of their own. I could see that if I was working in the mental health field, I needed to know more about addictions.

I pursued further graduate training at Michigan State University and completed my internship at the Dallas VA Medical Center, including specialty training in addictions. I wanted to learn as much as I could to be of help to clients, whether the problem with addiction was their own or that of a family member. On the final day of my internship, I was stunned when I heard the director of training say, "Now your learning really begins!" What? I have more to learn?

In my first job out of my doctoral program, I worked in a partial hospital program and I was in charge of the dual diagnosis track. I ran psychoeducational and therapy groups and was a case coordinator for patients. My clients quickly taught me what would and would not work in being of assistance to them. I also noticed in their records that many of them had trauma histories. Although we acknowledged these histories in their treatment, we could not address their trauma in any more than a cursory way, given their lack of stability and average 5-day treatment.

I then went on to work in the outpatient department and had clients with histories of trauma and addiction referred to me. I found myself now struggling with how to best meet their needs that were often intense. Many of them required frequent hospitalizations and struggled with sobriety. I sought out training in Dialectical Behavior Therapy (DBT), Seeking Safety, and other Phase-One trauma.

I then heard about EMDR from a colleague and was drawn to this training, mostly out of curiosity. I tend to be research oriented and I was rather doubtful of what some were touting as a "miracle cure." In the practicum during this training, I decided to choose an old memory that I thought had been fully processed. While targeting this allegedly "resolved" incident, I had a sudden upsurge of affect and found that my resolution of this memory achieved a different level. I was hooked.

Once in private practice, I specialized in treating addictions and trauma. I focused on further developing skills in EMDR. Yet, I wondered how to best integrate EMDR therapy for clients with addictions. I continued my learning process through further professional development and realized that my internship director was right.

My learning goes on. I'm pleased to share with the reader what my clients have taught me so far and offer ideas about areas for further learning. I hope that you find this book to be a helpful resource in your work.

OUR STORY

Nancy worked at a local university in the Addictions Studies Program. John applied for a faculty position in the program and Nancy was asked to interview him. We met at a local coffee shop and the rest is history.

Our first joint effort was the establishment of a special interest group (SIG) on addictions for our local EMDR community. We decided to train to become EMDRIA-approved consultants and we began to co-lead consultation groups that specialized in addiction and trauma issues. We then branched out to do trainings on addiction and trauma in the local area and around New England. Writing articles together about EMDR with trauma and addictions followed.

We have a unique partnership. We have strengths in different areas; we balance each other out. Although we think similarly about many aspects of psychotherapy, we have different styles in our approaches to working with clients.

This book is the next step in our collaboration.

ACKNOWLEDGMENTS

The authors would like to extend their thanks to

- Everyone at Springer Publishing Company, including our editor, Sheri W. Sussman, Katie Moyer, and our entire team
- Francine Shapiro, for inspiration and support
- Our colleagues in the Southern Maine EMDRIA community
- Our professional colleagues in the state of Maine and beyond
- Our families and friends who have given us so much support

INTRODUCTION

The issue of addiction and recovery is a complex one: Each individual is unique and it makes sense that each person's recovery from addiction would also be unique. In addition, the issue of addiction is a serious health concern often overlooked by health practitioners.

SCOPE OF THE PROBLEM

One of the challenges of describing the incidence of addiction in the United States lies in its very definition. There are diverse perspectives on addiction and there is no one agreed-upon way to define it (Juhnke & Hagedorn, 2006). Much of the research about substance use or problem behaviors is based on client self-report (van Wormer & Davis, 2013). These factors affect the research on addiction and thus there may be minimization of addiction's true impact.

Substance Abuse and Mental Health Services Administration (SAMHSA; 2013) National Survey of Drug Use and Health reported that of the population in the United States aged 12 years or older, 22.2 million people were substance abusers or dependent. About 6.5% of Americans reported heavy drinking (5 or more drinks on the same occasion on at least 5 days in the last month), 23.9 million Americans aged 12 years or older were current users of illicit drugs, and 69.5 million Americans aged 12 years or older use tobacco. Approximately, 17.5% of individuals diagnosed with mental illness also met the criteria for a substance use disorder (SAMHSA, 2012). Alcohol, cannabis, and cocaine are the most frequently used substances by individuals with mental illness (Mueser, Noordsy, Drake, & Fox, 2003).

Approximately 50% of all clients who present to mental health professionals have problems related to their own alcoholism or that of a family member (Corrigan, Mueser, Bond, Drake, & Solomon, 2008). These numbers do not incorporate the impact of drug-related or behavioral addictions that would likely increase this percentage significantly. The number of clients affected by other addictions (e.g., gambling, sex, work) is largely unknown due to differences of opinion about how to define these disorders (Tamam, Zengin, Karakus, & Ozturk, 2008).

It is very important that all mental health clinicians have an awareness of addictions and a variety of tools to use to deal with addicted clients. Many traditional treatments created to work with this population have proven effective. In addition, Eye Movement Desensitization and Reprocessing (EMDR), developed in the 1980s by Francine Shapiro, is a newer way to think about dealing with addictions. This book will explore both.

HOW TO USE THIS BOOK

This book is meant to provide a practical and useful guide for both experienced clinicians and those new to the addiction field. It offers many useful and helpful techniques and suggestions as clinicians develop individualized treatment plans for clients. The authors hope to encourage clinicians to address these issues directly and with success. The book is based on the theories of Prochaska and DiClemente, incorporating the Stages of Change Model for assessing client motivation to change (1982, 1992). It includes many practical interventions that are both traditional and EMDR therapy in focus.

The authors first wrote about EMDR therapy, trauma, addictions, and the Stages of Change in 2011 when they proposed a Roadmap Model for treatment (O'Brien & Abel, 2011). At that time, they outlined their basic philosophy:

1. The addictions treatment literature has established that not all treatments work for all clients (NIDA, 2009).
2. Addiction treatment must be individualized.
3. All clients presenting for treatment are not in the same place. In other words, they present at different stages and levels of motivation.
4. Trauma underlies addiction for many individuals. When it does, it must be dealt with to promote good, ongoing recovery. The question becomes when and how to do this.
5. Incorporating EMDR therapy into addictions treatment involves complex decisions.

It behooves clinicians to be thoughtful, educated, and aware of all the options for dealing with these complex issues.

Part I of this book explores the theories applicable to this work, including the scope of the problem. There are chapters on addiction, assessment, trauma, EMDR therapy, and the Stages of Change that provide clinicians with the theoretical material that is the foundation for making sharp clinical decisions.

In Part II, the authors discuss each Stage of Change and offer both traditional and EMDR therapy interventions for each stage. Clinicians may pick and choose from these interventions to develop appropriate treatment plans for clients.

In Part III, several cases are presented as examples of how the work can be accomplished. Finally, resources and protocols are presented for use with clients.

The authors have found that working with this population may be extremely rewarding. Despite its challenges, the work can be very gratifying when clients succeed in getting into healthy recoveries and resolve serious traumas. By the time many clients come to our offices, they feel hopeless and in despair. It is important that we hold hope for all of our clients. Although the relapse rate is high, an individualized approach based on analyzing motivation for change and providing appropriate interventions can give clients an increased chance of succeeding in their recovery.

PART I

RESEARCH FOUNDATIONS AND THEORY

INTRODUCTION

Part I of this book focuses on a review of research and theory regarding eye Movement Desensitization and Reprocessing (EMDR) therapy and addiction. We will examine the current literature on EMDR therapy, addictions, the Stages of Change, trauma, and assessment of both trauma and addiction. Each chapter ends with learning points that provide an overview of the conclusions from the literature.

Many clinicians have a negative view of anything that relates to science or evidence-based practice (EBP). They erroneously believe that it will require them to use a treatment manual that dictates interventions for each session, perhaps even with a script of what to say. This is far from the truth. EBP is defined as "the integration of the best available research with clinical expertise in the context of patient characteristics, culture, and preferences" (American Psychological Association [APA] Presidential Task Force, 2006, p. 273). Research is one important component of effective treatment but the experience and expertise of the clinician are critical, as is incorporating the unique needs and preferences of the client.

Even if we know that research and theory are important, it is difficult for clinicians to stay up to date on the current developments in their specializations. Barriers to adopting EBP include negative beliefs about EBP or inadequate training in EBPs and poor understanding of what changes to make or why these changes are important (Lundgren et al., 2011). Clinicians may not get enough supervision or reinforcement of newly developed skills (Carroll, 2012; Lundgren et al., 2011). Those in private practice are not the only ones struggling to use science as a foundation for their work. Even large, specialty addiction treatment centers are slow to integrate EBPs (Fitzgerald & McCarty, 2009; LaPaglia, 2011).

Despite this resistance to change, the majority of clinicians recognizes the value of research and wants to provide good care to clients. Many of us get trained in EBP in graduate school or through professional development and believe that we integrate them effectively into the treatment.

Even though clinicians believe that they are doing "evidence-based treatments," they engage in more informal discussions with clients than they realize and these discussions may interfere with the application of evidence-based treatment skills (Bamatter et al., 2010; Martino, Ball, Nich, Frankforter, & Carroll, 2009). In one study, 20% of the clinicians engaged in informal discussion with a client for 75% or more of the duration of their sessions (Martino et al., 2009).

So, why are theory and research important? If we want to be effective clinicians, we need to not only believe that we are engaging in effective interventions that are scientifically based but also to actually do them! That is where intentionality comes in. Intentionality is "purposeful behavior toward some conscious outcome" (Owen, 2009, p. 175). As psychotherapists, we need to utilize intentionality to be mindful of what we are doing in sessions with our clients and to integrate the best research into our work. Psychotherapy is both an art and a science; clinicians need to be well prepared in both realms (Friedlander, 1992). Part I of this book provides you with the scientific foundation that you need to artfully provide informed and effective interventions with your clients.

CHAPTER 1

EYE MOVEMENT DESENSITIZATION AND REPROCESSING THERAPY

Eye Movement Desensitization and Reprocessing (EMDR) is a psychotherapy model that was originally developed in the late 1980s by Francine Shapiro for the treatment of trauma. Since its initial creation, EMDR therapy has grown to be a treatment approach that has a wide variety of applications. In this chapter, we examine the origins of EMDR therapy, its theoretical underpinnings, EMDR techniques and protocols, and finally, the current status of the research to support its use.

EMDR clinicians undergo specific, comprehensive training in order to practice this form of treatment. This book is for informational purposes only and should not be viewed as a substitute for that training. Therapists are encouraged to complete EMDR training with the EMDR Institute and to engage in consultation to ensure ongoing fidelity to the model. More information about this can be found in the Resources chapter of this book.

EMDR THERAPY DEVELOPMENT

Dr. Francine Shapiro is the originator of EMDR therapy. In 1987, she was walking in the park near her home and noticed that she was reflecting on some disturbing thoughts about her life. At one point, she noticed that her eyes began to spontaneously move in a diagonal direction. She then found herself refocusing on the disturbing thoughts that she had been experiencing and she noticed that they did not seem to have as much affective potency. She was curious about this effect and tried it several more times. Each time she used this process, she noticed the same effect (Luber & Shapiro, 2009; Shapiro, 2012).

Dr. Shapiro then conducted informal investigations with others and asked them to try this same process, using eye movements, and she found that they experienced similar effects. She discovered that some individuals needed different types of eye movements (diagonal/horizontal) and a varied pace of the movements. Once again she was intrigued by this but remained unclear about what was happening. She decided to try the application of this technique with a volunteer client to see if what she had found might have a clinical application. She tested the procedure with a combat veteran by targeting a single trauma. In one session, she found that the client was able to eliminate the disturbance associated with this memory (Leeds, 2009).

Dr. Shapiro then proceeded to complete a formal study of 22 individuals who were experiencing posttraumatic stress disorder (PTSD) symptoms related to a variety of traumas. She found that this technique reduced the disturbance associated with a target memory significantly. Her initial work was known as eye movement desensitization (EMD; Shapiro, 1989).

This led Dr. Shapiro to study EMDR in more controlled and formulaic ways. She developed a specific protocol that was used to standardize the treatment and began to present her work at professional conferences. In 1991, EMD was renamed EMDR in order to capture the idea that this treatment is about linking traumatic events to other life experiences (Maxfield, 2009a).

Since her original work, the EMDR Institute was established to standardize this treatment. Thousands of therapists have been trained worldwide in EMDR therapy and its applications. Protocols have been developed for many different presenting complaints beyond trauma, including anxiety, performance, and most notably for our purposes, addiction.

WHAT IS EMDR THERAPY?

EMDR is a specific treatment protocol that has been empirically validated for the treatment of trauma. We explore the research that supports its applications later in this chapter.

Specifically, the EMDR Standard Protocol for trauma involves the client holding an image of a trauma, a negative belief about self, the emotions that are stirred up by the trauma, and the location of the trauma in the body while experiencing bilateral stimulation. Initially, the bilateral stimulation was eye movements. The therapist holds his or her fingers in front of the client and moves them back and forth in front of the client's eyes. The client follows the movements with his or her eyes and then reports what images thoughts or feelings occurred during the process. The process repeats until the trauma is desensitized or the client has a neutral reaction (EMDRIA, 2012).

After some initial work, clinicians found that not all clients could tolerate the use of eye movements throughout a session, especially if the individual wore glasses. Some clients' eyes would tire and some would have difficulty staying with the treatment. It was determined that it was bilateral stimulation of both sides of the brain that was the likely underlying mechanism of action as opposed to eye movements specifically. Clinicians started to use bilateral tones in the left/right ears and bilateral left/right tactile stimulation (accomplished by tapping on the client's knees or hands or by using tappers).

EMDR is a treatment that can also be blended with many other theoretical approaches. Clinicians who are oriented to various treatment approaches such as psychodynamic, cognitive, behavioral, humanistic, and existential (as well as many others) can easily integrate this approach into their work with clients. EMDR allows the clinician to maintain his or her primary approach and provides a mechanism to help clients heal from trauma and other presenting complaints (Shapiro, 2001).

EMDR THERAPY: WHAT IT IS NOT

EMDR has been a source of controversy since its original development. Many leaders in the field of trauma treatment were suspicious of this approach. Because EMDR was not developed empirically, these detractors believed that it was akin to "reading tea leaves" and that it was not a valid approach to treatment. There was initially a body of research that disparaged this approach, calling it pseudoscience and indicating that it was not effective (McNally, 1999, 2001; Philip, 1996; Rosen, McNally, & Lilienfeld, 1999). Reports surfaced that EMDR was harming patients (Shapiro, 1991). Proponents of EMDR were dismayed to hear about this research (Greenwald, 1999; Leeds, 2009).

Closer examination of these "treatment failures" showed the reasons for these results. Most notably, the clinicians who were providing "EMDR therapy" had never been formally trained by Francine Shapiro. These clinicians were taught by others who had been through the formal training and who then decided to teach it on their own. These events led Dr. Shapiro to formalize her expectations and initially restrict training to those sessions that she would personally conduct until she was able to publish a text on EMDR that outlined the treatment model (Shapiro, 1995).

Today, the EMDR Institute has very strict guidelines about the definition of EMDR and what constitutes this treatment (EMDRIA, 2012). Without proper training, a clinician may do more harm than good to a client, particularly if the therapist does not know what to do or how to handle the clinical material (intense emotions, distorted cognitions, etc.) that emerges.

EMDR therapy is not simply waving your fingers in front of someone's eyes and seeing what happens. EMDR is not a technique that someone can learn from a 3-hour workshop. In order for a clinician to be minimally trained in EMDR therapy, he or she must attend two trainings provided by the EMDR Institute that are separated by at least 3 months. In between these trainings, he or she must treat clients and receive at least 10 hours of consultation from an Institute-approved consultant. Even after formal training, clinicians benefit from ongoing professional development around EMDR.

EMDR as a treatment approach requires that a clinician have sound clinical training as a foundation. EMDR therapy training does not replace the need for a broad clinical background in how to work as a psychotherapist. Clinicians need to have good judgment and ethical decision-making skills as a precursor to EMDR's use. EMDR training and consultation presupposes that the clinician bring these skills to his or her work with clients. No treatment or technique will provide all of the answers about how to manage clients. The clinician needs to be prepared to stop the use of bilateral stimulation and utilize his or her clinical skills if problems come up for the client with the implementation of EMDR or the processing of specific memories.

Adaptive Information Processing Model

EMDR therapy is based on the Adaptive Information Processing (AIP) Model. This model describes how information is processed in the brain, how disruptions in the processing can affect individuals, and how to resolve these blocks. This model is founded on the following three principles (Leeds, 2009):

1. Humans have an information processing system that allows them to naturally respond to problematic or dysfunctional life experiences and resolve the distress associated with them.
2. A traumatic event may disrupt the usual AIP system and, if this happens, this unprocessed information leads to disturbance.
3. EMDR combines a focus on specific information about the traumatic event with bilateral stimulation to bring resolution to the previously unresolved traumatic event.

All of our experiences are organized in associated memory networks in our brains. As we go through life, the things that we experience that we judge to be important are stored with similar events in metaphoric "files" in the brain. Our perceptions at the time, our behavior and that of others, and our emotions are all linked and stored together. We catalog experiences in our brains in this way and these memory networks are automatically activated as we engage with similar situations in the present (Solomon & Shapiro, 2008).

Disruptions in the usual functioning of AIP are what create symptoms and problems in current life. Shapiro (2001) stated that some experiences may be inadequately processed; some experiences that are distressing are not cataloged in the brain in the usual way. Instead, these memories remain stuck and are stored with the negative affect and perceptions that the person experienced at the time of the incident. The result of this dysfunctional process is that the person will respond to current life situations that are similar to this memory with potentially inappropriate affect, thoughts, perceptions, and behaviors. In this way, previous life events are experienced not as being in the past but rather as being in the present, consciously or unconsciously (Shapiro, 2001).

For example, someone who was driving a car when a car accident occurred may get stuck on the idea that "I am a failure" for not preventing the event. Regardless of the facts of the situation, the person may perpetuate this belief and its associated negative view of his or her behaviors and negative emotions. Driving in a car, being on a highway, or witnessing another accident could all potentially reactivate that belief and associated feelings if the initial event were not adequately processed. Other life events that activate this belief will become stored together in a dysfunctional memory network. Unprocessed events could lead to serious mental health symptoms, including PTSD.

It is these dysfunctional memory networks that EMDR targets with the goal of connecting them with more adaptive memory networks stored elsewhere in the brain. By doing so, the memories that had been dysfunctionally stored are altered and are no longer isolated from more adaptive information and responses to current life events. Memories and information that have been appropriately processed in this model provide the foundation for good mental health (Solomon & Shapiro, 2008).

Bilateral Stimulation

As its name indicates, EMDR was originally developed as a technique that utilized eye movements. Clinicians were trained to have clients follow their fingers as they moved them back and forth in front of the client's eyes. Some clients found that their eyes would quickly tire from the repetitive movement. Clinicians were finding that their arms and shoulders also became tired from the need to maintain these movements throughout the session, especially when they were conducting multiple sessions daily.

Over time, other types of bilateral stimulation were developed. Clinicians were trained to also use bilateral tones and tactile stimulation (tapping on the client's knees or hands) as these forms of stimulation proved to elicit the same response in clients. Machines were developed such as the light bar and Tac/AudioScan that would produce bilateral stimulation in a way that was easier for both clinician and client.

Controversy over EMDR's exact mechanism still exists, especially about whether the eye movement component is necessary at all (Gunter & Bodner, 2009). However, EMDR therapy has been shown to be more effective than no treatment at all (Högberg et al., 2007) and equally as effective and faster than forms of exposure therapy in treating PTSD (Ironson, Freund, Strauss, & Williams, 2002; Rothbaum et al., 2005). Some critics argue that bilateral stimulation is not necessary and that EMDR is simply another form of exposure treatment. However, there is evidence that eye movements do provide a unique component in treating trauma (Nowill, 2010; Schubert et al., 2011). In addition, some evidence suggests that eye movements may provide a superior effect in relation to other forms of bilateral stimulation (Jeffries & Davis, 2013). However, as of this writing, there are no definitive conclusions that one type of bilateral stimulation is more effective than others and more research will be necessary to firmly establish both the necessity of eye movements in EMDR and the relative superiority of types of bilateral stimulation (Nieuwenhuis et al., 2013).

EIGHT-PHASE MODEL

EMDR is an eight-phase model of treatment. Each of the phases has specific goals and tasks that the clinician should accomplish when utilizing EMDR with any client. Each of the eight phases is described in detail below. Please also see Table 1.1 (see Leeds, 2009, p. 42).

TABLE 1.1 Eight Phases of EMDR Treatment

Phase	Goals	Tasks
Phase 1 History Taking	• Establish therapeutic alliance. • Gather psychosocial and medical history. • Develop the treatment plan and case formulation. • Rule out exclusion criteria.	• Obtain narrative or structured history. • Conduct an objective assessment of symptoms. • Identify targets for reprocessing: (a) past events etiological to current symptoms; (b) current triggers, and (c) future goals.
Phase 2 Preparation	• Obtain informed consent to treatment. • Offer psychoeducation. • Practice self-control methods. • Have patient start a weekly log. • Strengthen therapeutic alliance.	• Orient patient to issues in trauma-informed psychotherapy with EMDR. • Provide metaphors for mindful noticing during reprocessing. • Verify from log that patient is helped by methods for self-control.
Phase 3 Assessment	• Access primary aspects of the target selected from treatment plan for EMDR reprocessing. • Obtain baseline measures on SUD and VoC.	• Elicit the image, current negative belief, desired positive belief, current emotion, and physical sensation. • Record baseline measures for SUD and VoC.
Phase 4 Desensitization	• Reprocess the target experience to an adaptive resolution as indicated by a 0 SUD.	• Provide discrete sets of bilateral stimulation and assess changes via brief patient reports. • Return to target periodically to assess gains and identify residual material. • Use additional interventions only when reprocessing is overtly blocked.
Phase 5 Installation	• Continue reprocessing target with overt inclusion of preferred belief. • Fully integrate preferred belief into memory network as indicated by 7 VoC.	• Provide discrete sets of bilateral stimulation while patient holds target in awareness with desired positive belief. • Continue until patient reaches 7 VoC or "ecological" 6 VoC.

Phase 6 Body Scan	• Verify any residual disturbance associated with the target is fully reprocessed. • Allow patient to reach higher levels of synthesis.	• Provide discrete sets of bilateral stimulation while patient focuses on reprocessing any residual physical sensations until there are only neutral or positive sensations.
Phase 7 Closure	• Ensure client stability and current orientation at the close of each reprocessing session.	• Use self-control techniques if needed to ensure stability and current orientation. • Brief patient about treatment effects. • Request patient to keep a log of self-observations between sessions.
Phase 8 Reevaluation	• Verify whether all aspects of the treatment plan are being addressed.	• Adjust treatment plan as needed based on patient reports from log. • Recheck target(s) to ensure stable treatment effects.

EMDR, Eye Movement Desensitization and Reprocessing; SUD, Subjective Units of Disturbance Scale; VoC, Validity of Cognition Scale.

Sources: Adapted with permission from Shapiro (January, 2008 & January, 2005). Copyright 2008, 2005 by EMDR Institute.

Adapted with permission from Shapiro (2007b). Copyright 2007 by Wiley.

Phase 1: History Taking

The initial goal in EMDR therapy is to establish a therapeutic alliance with the client. This should be based on trust and openness, allowing the client to be honest about his or her reactions to the process of EMDR. Without a strong alliance, EMDR therapy is not going to be effective. The client needs to feel safe and protected by the clinician as this is a potentially very difficult and destabilizing process (Shapiro, 2001).

History taking includes gathering information about the client's presenting complaints and goals as well as his or her medical and psychosocial status. The clinician needs to gain a clear understanding of his or her issues in order to formulate an overall treatment plan (Shapiro, 2007a).

Some clients are not appropriate candidates for EMDR therapy. Phase 1 includes screening for these exclusions. Because EMDR is a powerful treatment that must be used with caution, using this treatment with clients who are not stable may result in retraumatization of the client and a treatment failure (Shapiro, 1991).

Clients who are actively dissociating are likely not appropriate for immediate trauma processing. Although some exceptions exist, these clients generally need assistance with skill building and development of strategies to manage dissociation in order to be ready for trauma processing (Forgash & Copeland, 2008; Leeds, 2009).

Those who are actively suicidal are also inappropriate for this treatment. Moving too quickly to process traumatic material in this case can further exacerbate suicidality in the client. Clients may need to be evaluated for psychiatric medication to help to stabilize depression (EMDRIA, 2012; Shapiro, 2001).

Clients who are actively psychotic, with personality disorders, engaged in self-harming behaviors, and those with certain medical conditions may not be appropriate for EMDR treatment. Consultation and/or supervision are essential in considering these cases and deciding the next steps in treatment (Leeds, 2009; Shapiro, 2001).

The Three-Pronged Protocol

Once the assessment of the client is completed, the clinician will develop the treatment plan based on a three-pronged protocol. This protocol utilizes past, present, and future as a way to organize the targets of treatment. The clinician identifies the appropriate memories to process from the past and works with the client to desensitize them. Once these are processed, the focus turns to present triggers that could still activate dysfunctional responses and to skill building for the future to prevent a return to old coping patterns. It is in this initial phase that the clinician can develop a general plan for each of these "prongs."

The clinician develops a plan for each of these prongs using different strategies. Some clinicians arrange the associated memories by age and take a developmental approach. Others may arrange memories based on the unifying cognition or the unifying affect. Many use the approach of "first," "worst," and then all the rest of the memories. Regardless of the model that is used, it is essential to have a map of memories established in preparation for the next phases (Leeds, 2009).

Phase 2: Preparation

Phase 2 of EMDR treatment involves specific strategies to adequately prepare the client for EMDR trauma processing. Appropriate preparation is essential. Clinicians should guard against overlooking the importance of this phase.

Clients need to give informed consent about EMDR treatment and the fact that, like any treatment, it may not help at all and could potentially make the client feel worse. During the desensitization phase, clients may feel quite destabilized. They need to be prepared for this. Clients will also need psychoeducation about EMDR and the AIP model as well as the effects of trauma and the mechanism of PTSD. This helps to orient the client to what he or she is experiencing and what he or she can expect in treatment.

Bilateral stimulation is introduced in this phase. The client is presented with the option for eye movements, alternating tones, and tactile stimulation, depending upon the mechanisms available to the therapist. Client comfort with and preferences for each of these modalities should be explored and documented. If a client becomes stuck in processing a memory while engaged in an EMDR session targeting a trauma with one of these modalities, the clinician may want to shift to another type of processing. Exploration and documentation of bilateral stimulation that works more or less effectively for the client will make those situations much easier to manage.

It is also in this phase that the client is introduced to some essential skills that will be needed in EMDR processing. The clinician ensures that the client has appropriate self-regulation skills. Coping skills are reviewed and the client is taught self-management skills to manage physiological arousal, such as progressive muscle relaxation (Conrad & Roth, 2007), diaphragmatic breathing (Fried, 1999; Nelson, 2012), or grounding, a technique that directs attention away from internal reactions to external stimuli (Forgash & Knipe, 2012; Najavits, 2002). The first EMDR therapy protocol, Safe/Calm Place, is installed with the goal of shoring up the client's coping and assessing the client's response to bilateral stimulation. (See Appendix B1 for a description of this technique.) The client is also taught to think about the trauma processing by using metaphors such as "viewing scenery on a train" or "watching a video on a television screen" in order to provide some distance from the material (Leeds, 2009). The length of time needed for clients to develop these skills will vary based on his or her presentation (Forgash & Knipe, 2012).

The client also learns how to stop the processing at any point by identifying a specific way that he or she will signal the need to do so. It is critical to identify this in advance. Some clients may utter words during processing that are part of reactions to the events being reexperienced (e.g., "Stop!" or "I can't do this") as opposed to a desire to end the processing. The "stop" signal helps to clarify this up front (EMDRIA, 2012; Shapiro, 2001).

Clients are also encouraged to create a weekly log for themselves. This log can take various forms, depending upon client willingness and preference. It can provide an important foundation for awareness of what associations are emerging during EMDR treatment, including old memories as well as the emergence of new, previously repressed memories or other associated reactions. In addition, this provides a way to double-check on previously processed memories to determine if there are any parts of the trauma issues that remain unresolved.

Phase 3: Assessment

In this phase, the clinician and client select a specific memory to be processed. The choice of memory will be guided by clinical judgment as well as client preference.

Once a specific memory is selected, the memory is assessed in preparation for processing. The client is asked to identify the worst or most disturbing part of the incident and an image that best represents it. If a client cannot identify a specific image, the clinician can ask the client to identify a bodily sensation or other sensory experience that occurs when he or she thinks about the incident.

Cognitions that are related to the incident and the disturbing image are then explored. The negative cognition (NC) captures the presently held self-referencing negative belief that this incident activates. Examples of this could include "I am worthless," "I am inadequate," or "I am not good enough." A positive cognition (PC) is also then identified as the belief that the client would like to be able to connect the incident with a more adaptive view of self once desensitization is complete.

The client then rates the PC on the Validity of Cognition (VoC) Scale ranging from 1 to 7; 1 is seen as *completely false* and 7 represents *completely true*. Most often, VoCs will be low in this phase. If a client's VoC is high when thinking about the incident, the clinician should reexamine the cognition and the client's understanding of the process.

While considering the disturbing image and negative belief, the client then reports on other emotions that he or she experiences in thinking about the incident. This is important to understand as the emotions the incident triggers initially may change over time. For example, a client who was abused may experience terror and helplessness when he or she thinks about it initially. Later in the session or in future sessions focused on this memory, the emotions related to the incident may change.

The client then rates his or her level of disturbance on the Subjective Units of Disturbance Scale (SUDS) rating from 0 to 10 where 0 is *neutral or no disturbance* and 10 is the *highest level of disturbance* that the client can imagine experiencing. Use of this scale helps the clinician to track client progress and/or identify when a client remains stuck in processing (EMDRIA, 2012).

The final component of the assessment phase relates to the body. The client is asked to consider the disturbing image, the NC, and the emotions connected to the memory and then identify places in the body that are activated by the memory. Changes in bodily sensations will be another important aspect to track as clients enter the desensitization phase (Shapiro, 2001).

Phase 4: Desensitization

Once the target memory has been assessed, the clinician will proceed to desensitize the memory. As mentioned previously, the clinician may utilize various forms of bilateral stimulation including eye movements, tones, or tactile stimuli (or some combination thereof). The clinician then summarizes the memory components that have been identified for the client to be sure that the memory is activated and asks the client to "just notice what happens" during the bilateral stimulation. It is important to clarify for clients that they should "just let whatever happens happen." Otherwise, some clients can misunderstand the task and may unwittingly hamper processing efforts by remaining focused on the highly disturbing material and not allowing the mind to move to other places. A good number of clients worry about whether or not they are doing the processing correctly. Clients often need to be reassured that there is no wrong way to do this. They may need to be encouraged to relax into the process (if they can) and just let what happens happen. This is an example of why a strong therapeutic relationship is a necessary component of EMDR; the clinician must have a strong alliance with the client in order to provide this reassurance.

The client is then encouraged to focus on the material for a "set" of bilateral stimulation that will vary in its speed and length based on clinical judgment and client preference. At the end of each set, the client is encouraged to take a breath and is then asked, "What do you notice now?" or "What are you getting?" The client is then asked to summarize as best as possible what he or she has experienced with regard to the incident. The goal of these verbalizations is to help the clinician understand where the client is in the processing. Ideally, the clinician stays "out of the way" and lets the client experience associated images, affect, and bodily sensations without interfering. This process continues until the client reports that the incident is no longer disturbing and is rated as a "0" on the SUDS. There are exceptions to this. On rare occasions, a client may not be able to reach a "0" on the SUDS due to the extreme disturbance of the event. Clinicians should get consultation about cases such as this.

Cognitive Interweave

Most issues for clients who are experiencing the effects of unresolved trauma are organized around three issues: safety, responsibility, and choice. As clients process a memory, clinicians may often hear these themes in this order as clients move to resolution. After attributing appropriate responsibility for their part in an event and their feelings about the event, clients can recognize that the event no longer is occurring and that they can be safe now. This will help them choose to move forward in life (Shapiro, 2001).

In some cases, the natural process of healing described previously that underlies EMDR therapy gets stuck. In these instances, the client begins to "loop" in the processing, repeating the same material over and over much like a skipping record. The clinician may offer brief verbalizations designed to help the client access awareness of issues related to responsibility, safety, and choice, depending upon the theme of the client's verbalizations. This will help to jump-start the process and ideally help the client move forward in the processing (Hensley, 2012; Leeds, 2009; Shapiro, 2001).

Phase 5: Installation

In this phase, the client is asked to reevaluate the PC that was identified in the assessment phase. The client is asked to think about the original incident and rate the PC on the VoC Scale (1–7). Bilateral stimulation is utilized while the client holds the original experience and the PC in mind until the client rates the VoC as 7 (or in rare instances, 6).

It is not unusual for the PC to shift as a result of processing. Clinicians should not be surprised if the client spontaneously indicates that a different adaptive cognition has emerged. If this occurs, the new PC is still rated on the VoC scale and processing continues as noted above.

Phase 6: Body Scan

The body scan is the last component of reprocessing. Trauma theorists have posited that "the body keeps the score" (van der Kolk, 1996). The body scan is completed to ensure that the incident is completely processed and that there are no remaining effects of the memory.

The client is asked to close his or her eyes and to focus on the incident with the installed PC. The client is directed to notice any sensations that emerge while scanning the body. If disturbing sensations do emerge, the client is directed to focus on them while additional bilateral stimulation is utilized. This process is continued until the disturbing sensations are no longer present. If, on the other hand, positive sensations emerge, the client may be encouraged to focus on them as bilateral stimulation is utilized. This can be done to further accentuate the positive results of the memory work (Shapiro, 2001).

Phase 7: Closure

If a client is able to process an incident in one session, then the closure process will simply be to direct the client to notice any associated dreams, memories, or other associations that emerge in the week ahead. As noted in Phase 2, clients have been encouraged to keep a weekly log. This log may help clients track any further associations to the target or other information that emerges that may reactivate the disturbance associated with the memory.

In some cases, clients will not completely process a memory in one session. This results in what is known as an "incomplete session." In these instances, the client is guided in closing down the neural network and reorienting him- or herself to the present (EMDR Institute, 2012; Leeds, 2009). Skills that were identified and developed in Phase 2 are called upon to help the client regulate him- or herself. The client is encouraged to contact the therapist if additional disturbance comes up during the week that is unmanageable or to check in with the therapist as needed.

Phase 8: Reassessment

Reassessment is completed when a client returns for the next session. The client is asked about his or her reactions to the processing in the previous week and any new information that has emerged. If the previous session was incomplete, the client is guided in reevaluating the original incident and Phase 4 desensitization continues, following the phases noted.

EMDR THERAPY PROTOCOLS

Over time, many protocols have been developed for use in EMDR processing. As previously mentioned, EMDR applications are being used with a wide variety of presenting complaints. There are a myriad of protocols and treatment options. For our purposes, we will restrict our discussion to the protocols that we have chosen to use in our work with clients presenting with trauma and addiction-related concerns. For further exploration of other protocols and applications, the reader is directed to protocol collections gathered by Marilyn Luber (2009, 2010). In addition to the standard protocol for trauma, the following protocols used in treating clients who present with addictions are reviewed: Safe/Calm Place (Shapiro, 2001); The Two-Handed Interweave (Shapiro, 2005); The Standard Protocol (Shapiro, 1995, 2001); Resource Development Installation (RDI; Korn & Leeds, 2002); Affect Tolerance (York & Leeds, 2001); Desensitization of Triggers and Urge Reprocessing (DeTUR; Popky, 2005); and CRAVEX/Memory of Addiction (Hase, 2010).

The Safe/Calm Place Exercise

The Safe/Calm Place exercise was originally developed to help combat veterans who experienced intense anxiety responses when asked to use relaxation exercises. This activity was originally known as the "safe" place, but because many trauma clients could not imagine any place in the world where they could experience safety, the name was changed to the "calm" place for these clients. A client's lack of positive response to the safe/calm place may indicate that he or she will have a more difficult time with EMDR treatment and require more from the clinician (Leeds, 2009).

In this exercise, the client identifies a safe or calm place in imagination. Once he or she has developed an image and focused on its associated emotions and sensations, the clinician uses bilateral stimulation to strengthen the image. Short sets with a slower pace are used in an effort to minimize the chance for activation of traumatic material (Leeds, 2009). A cue word is identified and paired with the image. This can then be used to help the client access this place to deal with minor disturbances in the past and to deal with future issues.

The Two-Handed Interweave

The Two-Handed Interweave, developed by Robin Shapiro (2005), is an extremely helpful technique to use with clients who are ambivalent or having difficulty making a decision. The client "places" one idea or thought or issue in one hand, then places the other, opposite idea, thought, or issue in the other hand. The client opens one hand, then the other, while focusing on the idea in the open hand. The therapist may use bilateral stimulation, if that is preferred. The processing stops occasionally and the client discusses what has been observed or decided. Traumatic material may surface during this process and the clinician must then make a decision as to whether it is appropriate and timely to use the standard protocol to process what has emerged. Use of this technique usually leads to a fruitful discussion; some clients make decisions about change following the use of this interweave.

Standard Protocol

The standard EMDR protocol (Shapiro, 1995, 2001) is the central component of EMDR treatment. The eight-phase model already described is this protocol. It is critical for clinicians who are being trained in EMDR therapy to become clear about the application of the standard protocol before they expand their expertise to other protocols.

Resource Development Installation

There are many different ways that clients can develop self-regulations skills or enhance ego-strengths and coping mechanisms. The authors utilize the Resource Development Installation (RDI) protocol (Korn & Leeds, 2002) and find it to be quite useful for clients with addictions.

The initial step in the RDI protocol is to have the client identify a challenging present-life situation. The client then rates this stressor using the SUDS (0–10; 0 = *no disturbance*, 10 = *most disturbance*). The client identifies a quality that is needed to deal with the stressor (e.g., strength, centeredness). There are then three ways to create the resource needed. The client may identify a personal situation in which he or she exhibited the quality, a resource figure embodying the quality, or an image or symbol that represents the quality. One or more of these resource exemplars is then further developed by identifying images, sounds, and body sensations that best represent it. Bilateral stimulation is then used to reinforce these representations. The client then returns to the stressor identified at the start of the protocol and imagines using the newly developed resources to cope with it.

Affect Tolerance Protocol

Both addiction and trauma have been identified as disorders of affect and affect regulation (Verdejo-García, Pérez-García, & Bechara, 2006). Cummings, Gordon, and Marlatt (1980) identified poorly managed affect as a primary trigger for relapse. The Affect Tolerance Protocol (York & Leeds, 2001) may be helpful in stabilizing a trauma client in Phase 1 trauma treatment, helping a client to develop the skills to prepare for change, or assisting a client in recovery to prevent relapse. This protocol is especially useful when the client comes to session experiencing an affect that is difficult to manage or manifests the affect in the session as the result of some issue being addressed.

The client identifies a feeling that is distressing and then determines the worst part of it. He or she then develops an image of the worst part of the feeling as well as identifying a negative cognition and positive cognition as well as associated body sensations. The client rates the VoC of the PC and the SUDS level of the worst part of the feeling. The client identifies "feelings about the feelings" and locates the feeling in the body. The overall goal of the protocol is to help the client reduce the level of distress associated with the affect (i.e., increase the ability to cope with/tolerate the feeling).

The clinician uses bilateral stimulation to desensitize the feeling. Ideally, the SUDS will go down either due to desensitization or to the client's spontaneous use of coping skills. The clinician checks the SUDS level after two to three sets. If the distress does not reduce, the clinician helps the client to use other affect management strategies that have been successful for the client in the past (breathing, grounding) or begins to teach new ones. The PC is then installed. No body scan is used at the end of the session.

As noted, Affect Tolerance is an essential skill for those in recovery from addiction and trauma. Other protocols may also be used to help clients develop these skills (e.g., Leeds, 2011).

ADDICTION-SPECIFIC PROTOCOLS

DeTUR Protocol

Popky (2005) developed the DeTUR Protocol to assist clients with addiction. The protocol is used to help clients focus on reinforcing positive coping in recovery and reducing the impact of relapse triggers. The client is encouraged to strengthen motivation for change before tackling the triggers of his or her addiction.

The client initially focuses on the Positive Treatment Goal, that is, the image that represents what life would be like if changes were successful. After identifying in general how much better life will be without active addiction, the client creates a visual representation of life without addiction (or with successful harm reduction). This picture is then enhanced with bilateral stimulation. The client and clinician work together to help the client to develop and/or reinforce both internal and external resources to support behavior change.

Next, the client develops a list of triggers for relapse; each trigger is broken down into its component parts. For example, if the client says that driving home from work is a trigger, the client lists all elements of that experience as part of the triggering event, such as leaving the office, opening the car door, driving on the highways, and so forth. The client is told that the entire process must be desensitized for this to be effective. The clinician then uses bilateral stimulation to desensitize the relapse triggers identified by the client, one at a time. Clients are taught to use bilateral stimulation on their own if urges come up outside of session.

Hase Memory of Addiction/CRAVEX Protocol

Hase (2010) created the Memory of Addiction/CRAVEX Protocol. Each episode of use/addictive behavior is seen as related to an addiction memory (AM). According to this view, addiction is conceptualized as a repetitive activation of the same neural network that relates to the initial reasons that clients became addicted. The goal of the protocol is to desensitize the AM and to link this network with healthier coping.

The client initially identifies his or her last craving, urge, or relapse related to addiction. The standard protocol is a general outline for treatment. Once an image for the urge/relapse is selected, the client then identifies PCs/NCs, the VoC, emotions, and body sensations. Instead of the SUDS, the client rates his or her level of urge (LOU) on a scale from 0 to 10, where 0 is *no urge* and 10 is the *highest urge* that one can imagine. Bilateral stimulation is used and the LOU is tracked until it reduces to a 0. Once the urge/relapse is desensitized (LOU = 0), the PC is installed.

EMDR Research

When EMDR was first introduced in 1989, critics charged that it was nothing more than "finger waving therapy" (Maxfield, 2009b). Despite these critiques, research has been ongoing into the efficacy and effectiveness of EMDR.

Schubert and Lee (2009) provided an overview of the three phases of research on EMDR therapy. Initial research focused on the effectiveness of EMDR as a treatment for PTSD compared to a control group that was placed on a waiting list (Högberg et al., 2007; Jensen, 1994; Rothbaum, 1997). The second wave of research on EMDR focused on its effectiveness in comparison to wait list controls and other treatments for EMDR (Carlson, Chemtob, Rusnak, Hedlund, & Muraoka, 1998; Edmond, Rubin, & Wambach, 1999; Edmond & Rubin, 2004; Scheck, Schaeffer, & Gillette, 1998). In both cases, EMDR emerged as a valid treatment and as equally efficacious as compared to other first-line treatments for PTSD.

EMDR therapy is also being utilized by clinicians for a wide variety of psychiatric symptoms including obsessive-compulsive disorder (Marr, 2012), migraines (Konuk, Epözdemir, Atçeken, Aydin, & Yurtsever, 2011), panic disorder (Leeds, 2012), and grief (Solomon & Rando, 2012). At present, research has established only that EMDR therapy is a valid and effective treatment for PTSD. Other applications of EMDR are still being studied to support their clinical utility for disorders beyond PTSD (Maxfield, 2009a).

Research at present is focused on issues related to exploring the exact mechanisms for EMDR. Although we know that EMDR works, we still cannot determine the exact mechanisms of the change processes that occur during treatment. Current hypotheses about the active mechanism of EMDR include that it is a process akin to REM sleep, that it creates increased hemispheric communication, or that it provides psychological distancing (Gunter & Bodner, 2009). Ongoing research will help clinicians continue to explore whether the change process in EMDR is about REM-related processing of information, increased communication between left/right hemispheres of the brain, or other mechanisms yet to be clarified (Gunter & Bodner, 2009; Schubert & Lee, 2009).

EMDR Therapy and Addiction

Research on the use of EMDR therapy with addiction is limited but growing. The only randomized control trial of the use of EMDR in clients with addiction was published by Hase, Schallmayer, and Sack (2008). The study utilized "treatment as usual" with and without EMDR. Components of the treatment as usual included detoxification, motivational interviewing, assessment of social support/adjustment, relaxation skills, group therapy, and art therapy. Treatment lasted 14 to 21 days and clients were then referred to a rehabilitation program and 12-step meetings.

The experimental group of patients received treatment as usual with the addition of EMDR targeting the "addiction memory," which was viewed as the core of their addiction. Findings indicated that treatment enhanced with EMDR decreased cravings more effectively than treatment as usual. In addition, rates of relapse at 1- and 6-month intervals were lower in the EMDR treated group as compared to the control group. Finally, patients who received the EMDR treatment reported lower levels of depressive symptoms posttreatment, whereas those who received treatment as usual had no such effect.

Cox and Howard (2007) described the use of EMDR therapy to treat a case of sex addiction. They described how early traumas often underlie sex addiction and trigger relapses. They discussed a single case to demonstrate that sex addiction may be effectively treated with EMDR. The client was treated with sex addiction education, 12-step meetings, working with a sponsor, and EMDR therapy that targeted past sexual abuse. Once old traumas were processed, the client was treated with EMDR that targeted current life situations that were triggering shame and urges to act out sexually. Other techniques (letter writing, empty-chair technique, relapse prevention skills) were used to enhance his ongoing recovery. Treatment was successful in helping to resolve the distress associated with his history of sexual abuse and preventing relapse.

Marich (2009) reported on the use of EMDR in treating a cross-addicted female client with a history of sexual assault, who met criteria for alcohol dependence, cannabis dependence, sedative dependence, and PTSD. When this client came for treatment, she had just received her third Operating a Vehicle Intoxicated (OVI) conviction. She had several previous attempts at sobriety, the longest being 4 months, and had tried both inpatient and outpatient treatment over a 12-year period. After the client achieved sobriety, the author used the EMDR standard protocol to target shame-based experiences that were interfering with her recovery. The client was guided in the use of the future template (the third prong of the three-pronged protocol) to enhance PCs in order to reinforce these beliefs to solidify her recovery process. At 18th-month follow-up, the client had maintained sobriety.

Abel and O'Brien (2010) reported on the use of EMDR to treat a female client who presented with PTSD and alcohol dependence. This client could not maintain sobriety without processing an important traumatic event. The standard EMDR protocol was used to help the client to deal with the aftereffects of her husband's suicide. Once this event was processed, the client was able to achieve solid sobriety in a way that she had not previously been able to do. These authors argued that certain clients need to process their underlying traumas in order to achieve and maintain a sober life.

Marich (2010) reported on the potential role of EMDR therapy in continuing care for women in recovery from addiction. Ten women were interviewed about their experiences with addiction and their recovery process. All of the participants described how EMDR therapy contributed to their successful recovery to varying degrees. The author highlighted the critical role that the therapeutic relationship played in successful EMDR treatment.

O'Brien and Abel (2011) presented an outline for intervening with clients who present with addictions. These authors integrated the Transtheoretical Model (Prochaska & DiClemente, 1982, 1992) with EMDR-based interventions used to intervene with clients who present with varying levels of motivation to change behavior. The decisions about if and when to use the standard EMDR protocol to process trauma in clients with addictions and the factors to consider in making this determination were discussed.

Bae and Kim (2012) reported on treatment of Internet addiction utilizing the DeTUR Protocol. A 13-year-old male with Internet addiction and comorbid depression was treated with four sessions using the Popky protocol. Seven triggers of Internet use were targeted. At the end of treatment, the client reduced his Internet use to 1 hour per day and clinical depression was reduced to a subclinical level. These gains were maintained at 6- and 12-month follow-up.

SUMMARY

In this chapter, the authors explored the historical foundations of EMDR therapy harkening back to its beginnings in 1987. EMDR was defined and the AIP model was described. The eight phases of EMDR were discussed in detail. The protocols that the authors have chosen to use to treat addictions and trauma were each described. Finally, we have summarized the current research on EMDR in general as well as the developing literature on EMDR treatment of addiction.

LEARNING POINTS

1. EMDR is a treatment developed to treat PTSD and can be easily integrated into a wide array of theoretical approaches to psychotherapy.
2. There are eight phases that encompass EMDR treatment. In order for this treatment to be successful, clinicians need to follow the standard guidelines of treatment, including the targeting of present and future triggers of traumatic events.
3. A number of protocols may be of use in the treatment of clients with PTSD and addiction. Protocol selection will vary based on client needs and preferences.
4. Extant research has demonstrated that EMDR is an efficacious treatment for PTSD. Research is still developing to substantiate the use of EMDR therapy with addiction and a wide variety of psychiatric diagnoses. The available research on EMDR and addictions treatment was described.
5. The protocols currently being used by the authors to treat addictions were described in detail: Popky/DeTUR, Hase/CRAVEX, RDI, Affect Tolerance, Safe/Calm Place, and Robin Shapiro's Two-Handed Interweave.

CHAPTER 2

ADDICTIONS

In this chapter, the authors explore concepts related to addiction. The difference between addiction and dependence is examined. Several different models of addiction are described and the authors examine the model that they believe to be of primary importance, the Biopsychosocial Disorder Model of addiction. The trauma connection is reviewed. Both substance and process addictions are discussed, including all of the common drugs of abuse.

DEFINITIONS

The word *addiction* is rooted in the Latin word "addicere," meaning "a giving over, surrender" (Dictionary.com). This is the heart of the concept of addiction. The addicted person focuses his or her life around his or her addiction, leaving other life areas (such as work and family responsibilities) unattended (van Wormer & Davis, 2013).

Addiction can be defined in many different ways. Harvard Medical School defines addiction as "a behavioral pattern of compulsive drug use, characterized by overwhelming involvement with the use of a drug, the securing of its supply and a strong tendency to relapse after completion of withdrawal" (Shaffer, 1989). According to the American Society of Addiction Medicine (ASAM), "addiction is a chronic disease of brain reward, memory and related circuitry... (that) leads to characteristic biological, psychological, social and spiritual manifestation" (ASAM, 2011, p. 1). Other elements of addiction include difficulties being able to abstain, problems with craving and controlling one's behavior, relationship difficulties, and problematic emotional responses (ASAM, 2011). In short, an addict has neurobiological, psychological, and social difficulties with behavior that are focused on a substance or a process of choice to the exclusion of all other things.

People have historically thought of addiction as relating to use of alcohol or drugs that has spiraled out of control. However, there is a growing body of evidence to suggest that addiction can also be conceptualized with regard to behaviors such as gambling, sex, and food (Karim & Chaudhri,

2012; Khantzian & Albanese, 2008). Research is supporting the validity of these disorders as addictions (Smith, 2012). There is some controversy about how far to extend the term "addiction" and whether labeling some behaviors as addiction simply gives an excuse for bad behavior (Karim & Chaudhri, 2012).

Diagnostic and Statistical Manual of Mental Disorders, Fifth Edition (DSM-5)

Addiction has been described as being on a continuum from mild to severe. According to the *DSM-5*, these are all called "substance use disorders" (American Psychiatric Association [APA], 2013). The distinction is made between addiction and dependence. Addiction is the compulsive use of the drug such that a person's life is organized around obtaining and using it. Dependence is a physical dependence on the chemical.

Tolerance

Tolerance is a state that occurs as cells in the body adapt to the presence of drugs (Jenkins, 2011; Siegel, 2005). The amount of substance that is used initially by an individual no longer has the same effect (National Institute on Drug Abuse [NIDA], 2007). He or she needs to use more and more of a substance to achieve the desired result (NIDA, 2007). Tolerance is one key factor in the development of dependence and addiction (Siegel, 2005).

Dependence

Dependence is a physiological process through which a person's body becomes accustomed to having a certain amount of the substance in the body. The human body is constantly seeking a state of balance known as homeostasis. If an individual uses a substance regularly, his or her body becomes accustomed to having a certain amount of the substance and is only in physiological balance when that is present. This state of balance is an unhealthy one and is known as allostasis (Allostasis, 2008).

For example, if someone starts to drink, at first the body perceives the alcohol as poison. With continued regular use, the body will become in balance physiologically (e.g., heart rate, breathing) when alcohol is present. This means that when the person does not have alcohol in his or her system, a withdrawal syndrome begins, a sign that the body is now out of balance. The withdrawal process can sometimes be so extreme that it results in a major disruption in a person's physiology and requires inpatient treatment so that the symptoms can be medically monitored.

An individual may be dependent on a substance but not addicted. For example, as the disease of diabetes progresses, a person's pancreas does not produce enough insulin. This requires that a person take a specified amount of insulin every day to keep the blood sugar levels in balance. The person is physically dependent on the insulin but not addicted. The body needs a certain amount of the insulin to function and the body is "dependent" on the insulin to stay in balance. However, this individual does not try to use more and more insulin or change behavior as a result of his or her drug use. Similarly, a person who is prescribed pain medications in order to deal with chronic pain takes them at a prescribed level. The body becomes accustomed to having a certain amount of pain medication in the system and is balanced in this state. In either of these cases, the person's body becomes accustomed to having a certain amount of the substance in it to function. However, if he or she does not take more and more and if he or she does not engage in other addiction-related behaviors, such as secrecy, impairments in functioning, increased relationship/legal/financial problems, he or she does not become addicted.

A person may be addicted to something without physiological dependence. A person may be considered addicted if he or she organizes his or her life around use of the substance. This may or may not include a physiological dependence. One of the hallmarks of addiction is the compulsion to use the substance or engage in the behavior despite its negative consequences (Khantzian & Albanese, 2008).

MODELS OF ADDICTION

There is no one paradigm that can be used to describe addiction. There are many models that are used to identify the etiology, causes, appropriate treatment goals, and most effective strategies for these disorders. Some models are described below:

Moral Model

Addiction is viewed as a result of a lack of will power and moral weakness. Addiction problems stem from intentional action by a person, not the behavior of someone with an illness. The goal of treatment is to help the person strengthen the moral foundation. If the person becomes stronger, then he or she will be able to give up the behavior (Morse, 2004).

Learning Model

Addiction is seen as a bad habit that is learned in a variety of ways. Behaviors may be classically conditioned as automatic responses to stress or be reinforced by others. The goal of treatment is for the person to develop self-control and new habits by learning new ways to manage behavior (Brandon, Herzog, Irvin, & Gwaltney, 2004; Redish, Jensen, Johnson, & Kurth-Nelson, 2007).

Disease Model

From the perspective of the Disease Model, addictions are believed to be biologically based disorders; people are born with genetic predispositions that make normal substance use impossible. The goal of treatment is to abstain from the substance or the behavior and this is seen as the only thing that stops the progression of the disease. The addict is seen as having no control over his or her use. Addictions are chronic, progressive, and fatal processes that can only be managed by abstinence (Cullen, 2011).

Self-Medication Model

When one develops an addiction, it is believed to be a symptom that masks another disorder or underlying issue. A person may be experiencing depression, anxiety, or another symptom that is medicated with the use of substances or behaviors. According to this model, the way to heal addiction is to treat the underlying disorder (Khantzian & Albanese, 2008).

Social Model

Addictions are caused by environmental influences (i.e., family and friends). The individual learns from others in his or her life that substance use is an acceptable way to relax, deal with stress, or push away difficult feelings. To heal the addiction, the person must change social connections and eliminate the influences that have caused the behavior to seem normal (Simons-Morton, 2007).

Biopsychosocial Model

As discussed, there is no one paradigm about addiction. There are many models that conceptualize addiction differently, including seeing it as a moral weakness, a biological or psychological deficiency, a bad habit, or a disease (Shaffer, 1994; van Wormer & Davis, 2013). For the purposes of this book, we will be viewing addiction as a biopsychosocial disorder.

In order to appropriately assess addiction, one must look at the whole person and the biological, psychological, and social issues that impact use. Each person is unique and will therefore have a unique relationship to the object of addiction. Comprehensive assessment of each of these areas is an essential first step in treatment.

The following are areas that need to be explored.

Biological Factors

There is a strong genetic component of addiction; some people may have a biological predisposition (Khantzian & Albanese, 2008). This predisposition can lead to differences in the way that the brain (specifically the reward pathway) responds to substance use. There are biological changes in the brain as a result of sustained addictive behavior, leading to the comment that addiction is a "brain disease" (Leshner, 2001).

Areas to explore include, "What chemical has the person chosen to use?" "What are its properties?" "How would it affect most people?" "How does it affect this person?" "Is there a chance of physical dependency?" "If the person stops the drug or engaging in the behavior, is there a chance of withdrawal syndrome?" All of these issues can help to shed light on how biology is relevant to understanding the person's addiction.

Psychological Factors

Psychology is the study of behavior and mental processes (Myers, 2013). Evaluating the psychological perspective of a client's addiction includes the individual's behavior, emotional functioning, and thoughts. The clinician needs to assess how the person feels about his or her life in general. Lower self-directedness, difficulties with emotions, and distress related to sexual orientation can lead to a greater likelihood of problems (Evren & Evren, 2006; Herrero, Domingo-Salvany, Torrens, Brugal, & Gutiérrez, 2008; Talley, Sher, & Littlefield, 2010).

If the person has a psychological disorder (such as depression or attention deficit hyperactivity disorder [ADHD]), it may or may not be related to his or her use of substances (Rosenthal & Westreich, 1999). Other areas to explore can include, "Does the person currently have significant stress in his or her life?" "Is the source of the stress environmental, the client's perception, or both?" "Is the person using to minimize physical or psychological pain?" "What is the person's basic psychological make-up?"

Social Factors

The sociocultural environment of the individual is another critical component in understanding addiction. The person may be a member of a cultural group for whom substance use plays a central role (e.g., alcohol use in the Irish American population) or a very limited role (e.g., alcohol use among Orthodox Jews). How does this culture view addiction or addiction treatment? How much should culture be integrated into treatment?

The current family environment and family of origin are important to consider. Whom does the person consider to be his or her family? Some people may identify nonblood relatives or "families of choice" (Blumer & Murphy, 2011) as most important to them. Given his or her definition of family, how does this family (and the family of origin) influence the person's choices about substances? What was modeled in the family? What was frowned upon? Is there a family history of addiction?

The influence of peers must also be considered. Who is in the person's social group? How does this group view substance use? Is there peer pressure to use or participate in certain behaviors? One's peer group and its influence are particularly important in adolescence but these issues remain relevant at any age.

In addition, a client's relationship to spirituality could be explored. Does the person have a religion? What impact has religion had on his or her life? Does he or she use the church, mosque, or synagogue for support? Is the person more spiritual than religious? How does the client find or make meaning out of life?

Answering these questions allows a clinician to develop a picture of the individual who presents with a behavioral or a substance addiction or problem. Because each individual is unique and different, the subsequent treatment plan that is developed must also be unique and individualized. We utilize the

Biopsychosocial Model as a foundation for understanding clients and then draw on other models as needed. The authors believe that this is the best and most practical approach for looking at these issues.

THE TRAUMA CONNECTION

Clinicians working in the addictions field need to be prepared to deal with trauma and posttraumatic stress disorder (PTSD), as many clients presenting for addiction treatment have a history of trauma (Jacobsen, Southwick, & Kosten, 2001; McCauley et al., 2012). Two thirds of people seeking treatment for substance use disorders report one or more traumatic life events (Back et al., 2000, 2008; Clark, Masson, Delucchi, Hall, & Sees, 2001; Wasserman, Havassy, & Boles, 1997). Treating patients with comorbid PTSD and substance abuse is often very complicated as these clients often have greater difficulty in maintaining sobriety and in healing their traumas (Ford, Hawke, Alessi, Ledgerwood, & Petry, 2007; Peirce, Kindbom, Waesche, Yuscavage, & Brooner, 2008; Schumacher, Coffey, & Stasiewicz, 2006). Because there is such a strong connection, it is very important for clinicians to have some expertise or knowledge about working with both trauma and addiction.

SUBSTANCE USE ADDICTIONS

Psychoactive drugs act on the nervous system and affect consciousness, perception, and/or mood (Myers, 2013). Substance use has been around since the beginning of time for people to escape reality, relieve pain, or deal with stress (Kinyanjui & Atwoli, 2013; Sreeraj, Prasad, Khess, & Uvais, 2012). As previously noted, the ways that people use drugs and alcohol are affected by cultural norms, expectations, and by what is modeled in the environment by others.

Drug, Set, and Setting

There are many influences on an individual's substance use patterns. Zinberg (1986) concluded that the drug, set, and setting are all important in making an assessment of someone's use. Drug is the chemical the person chooses to use and its qualities as well as the particular impact on the person who is using it. Set is the psychological processes of the individual and how using might impact that person. Setting is the social setting he or she is in, the impact of the environment, and the impact of culture. Setting influences someone's use. For example, on many college campuses one will undoubtedly see individuals abusing alcohol and other drugs. These individuals may look like addicts in terms of the amount used. However, most of these people are going to outgrow this behavior. It is socially acceptable in the United States to have a period of abusive drinking in college; it may even be considered to be a right of passage.

Types of Psychoactive Drugs

Depressants

Depressants are psychoactive drugs that reduce neural activity and slow down mental and physical processes (Myers, 2013). Drugs in this category do not cause depression per se, although that can be an outcome. Instead, this term refers to the biological effect of slowing the body down.

Alcohol

Alcohol is the most widely used psychoactive substance in the United States. One out of every 12 adults meets the criteria for alcohol abuse or dependence (National Council on Alcoholism and Drug Dependence [NCADD], 2013b). Alcohol causes more problems than all illegal substances combined (NCADD, 2013a).

Alcohol impacts brain areas that control inhibition and judgment. It is the leading cause of untimely death in youths in the United States, contributing to unintentional injuries, suicides, homicides, and up to 50% of drownings (Myers, 2013; van Wormer & Davis, 2013). In addition, many health problems such as liver disease, cancer, stroke, and cardiac problems can be directly linked to the effects of alcohol (Anderson, Cremona, Paton, Turner, & Wallace, 1993; Oscar-Berman, Shagrin, Evert, & Epstein, 1997).

Binge drinking (defined as having five or more drinks in a 2-hour period) remains a huge issue on college campuses and is a significant public health concern (Kenji Iwamoto, Corbin, Lejuez, & MacPherson, 2014). Students involved in heavy alcohol use tend to have greater academic difficulties, with one in four college drinkers admitting that poor performance on a test was due to alcohol or drug use and nearly one third of students missing a class for these same reasons (Presley, Meilman, & Lyerla, 1994; Sullivan & Risler, 2002).

Heavy drinking has been defined as exceeding certain amounts of alcohol consumption per day and per week. For men, heavy drinking is defined as alcohol use that exceeds 4 drinks per day or 14 per week, whereas for women, the limit is 3 drinks per day or 7 per week (NIAAA, 2013). In the United States, 5% of the heaviest drinkers consume up to 42% of the alcohol and the top 25% of these drinkers consume 87% (Twitchell, 2003). The best customers of the alcohol industry are the alcoholics.

If a person overuses alcohol on one night, he or she will likely experience a hangover the next day that may include nausea, vomiting, shakiness, and an intense headache (Abadkinsky, 2008). For a person who is physically dependent on alcohol and who suddenly stops using, the withdrawal syndrome can be more extreme and even life-threatening. Symptoms will start within 24 hours after the last drink and can persist for up to 2 weeks. After an initial period of nausea, insomnia, and anxiety, the person can develop hallucinations (mostly likely visual) and then experience delirium, disorientation, and delusions. An individual can develop delirium tremens, leading to an exacerbation of the above symptoms that can potentially be fatal without medical intervention (Abadkinsky, 2008).

Barbiturates

Barbiturates are depressants that slow the sensory cortex, slow motor activity, and alter functioning of the cerebellum, while also creating drowsiness and sedation in the user (Myers, 2013). These drugs are often used to induce sleep for surgery although they do not reduce reactivity to pain and may in fact increase it (Abadkinsky, 2008). Nembutal, Amytal, Seconal, and Phenobarbital are some examples. In years past, this class of medications was often prescribed to induce sleep and to treat anxiety (NIDA, 2011b). Due to the potential for causing overdose either alone or in combination with alcohol, barbiturates are prescribed much less often now than in the past (NIDA, 2011b). Withdrawal from barbiturates falls along a continuum from weakness, dizziness, nausea and sleep disturbance to delirium, convulsions, and even death, depending on the frequency and intensity of use (Abadkinsky, 2008).

Minor Tranquilizers/Benzodiazepines

Benzodiazepines are among the most widely prescribed drugs in the United States (Myers, 2013). These drugs are known as minor tranquilizers and are used to treat anxiety, induce sleep, and as muscle relaxants (Drugs.com, 2013). Valium was the first drug in this class approved by the Food and Drug Administration (FDA) to treat anxiety (Abadkinsky, 2008). Since that time, other drugs in this class, such as Xanax, Klonopin, and Ativan, have been approved and are now prescribed for the same reasons. Long-term use of these medications is not recommended as they lose their effectiveness over time with the development of tolerance (Australian Drug Foundation, 2013). When prescribed for sleep, benzodiazepines can lose their effect after three nights and their benefit for anxiety treatment diminishes after 4 months (Abadkinsky, 2008). Users can also easily develop physical and psychological dependence on these medications. Withdrawal from benzodiazepines can lead to symptoms similar to that of the other depressants: anxiety, insomnia, tremors, muscle twitches, and, at higher doses, hallucinations, grand mal convulsions, and death (Abadkinsky, 2008).

Opioids/Narcotic Analgesics

The substances in this category include heroin, opium, morphine, codeine Oxycontin, Oxycodone, Vicodin, as well as other pain killers. These agents may be either naturally derived from the opium poppy or synthetically manufactured (Stine & Kosten, 1999). Opiates depress the activity of the central nervous system and stimulate endorphin receptors creating a feeling of euphoria and pain relief.

Although medical use of heroin has been banned in the United States since 1924, all of the other drugs in this class are often prescribed to control pain and ease the discomfort associated with surgery (Abadkinsky, 2008). In addition, these drugs are sometimes used to control diarrhea and as cough suppressants. Long-term use of opiates suppresses the body's naturally occurring opiates, the endorphins, making withdrawal from opiates quite painful (Myers, 2013). Withdrawal symptoms can include nausea, vomiting, chills, sweating, loss of appetite, and irritability (Abadkinsky, 2008).

Prescription Drug Abuse

In recent years, there has been increasing attention given to the problem of misuse of prescription medication; it is seen as the nation's fastest growing drug problem (van Wormer & Davis, 2013). It has been defined as "the use of a medication without a prescription in a way other than prescribed or for the experience and feelings elicited" (NIDA, 2011b, p. 1). Although most people who are prescribed medications use them responsibly and appropriately, it is estimated that 52 million people in the United States have used prescription drugs at least once during their lives for nonmedical reasons (NIDA, 2011b). Many first-time drug users (26%) begin their drug use with the nonmedical use of prescription medications (Substance Abuse and Mental Health Services Administration [SAMHSA], 2012). Opioids, depressants, and stimulants are the most commonly abused classes of prescriptions (NIDA, 2011b). Withdrawal from prescription medications will vary depending on the class of drugs and specific drug properties as well as the frequency and quantity of use.

Stimulants

Stimulants are psychoactive drugs that increase central nervous system activity, exciting neural activity, and arousing body functions (Myers, 2013). When used in moderation, they can boost mood, reduce fatigue, and improve concentration (Abadkinsky, 2008). Nicotine and caffeine are two commonly used stimulants.

Amphetamines

Amphetamines are stimulants that activate the sympathetic nervous system and bodily functions (Drug Enforcement Agency [DEA], 2011). These substances increase the release of dopamine, which increases pleasurable feeling, boosting energy level and mood (Greene, Kerr, & Braitberg, 2008). Legally manufactured amphetamines are tablets or capsules, which some abusers may crush to snort or inject intravenously (Abadkinsky, 2008).

Amphetamines have been prescribed in the past to assist with weight loss as they are known to speed up metabolism. However, because appetite returns with greater intensity once someone is no longer taking them, amphetamines are now used only in more extreme cases of weight loss (Abadkinsky, 2008). Amphetamines are also prescribed to treat hyperactivity to improve focus of attention and to treat narcolepsy, a sleeping disorder that can result in episodes of suddenly falling asleep (Berman, O'Neill, Fears, Bartzokis, & London, 2008).

Methamphetamine is chemically related to its parent, amphetamine. However, it provides periods of heightened energy and euphoria that may last up to 8 hours (Myers, 2013). It triggers dopamine and enhances energy and mood. Methamphetamine is the second most abused drug in the world, behind only marijuana (Abadkinsky, 2008). Crystal methamphetamine or "crystal" is a smokeable form of methamphetamine that can lead to hypersexual behavior and loss of inhibitions (Lasting & Charles, 2008).

Withdrawal from amphetamine/methamphetamine tends to produce similar symptoms. These include fatigue, troubled sleep, irritability, intense hunger, and deep depression that may include suicidal thinking (Abadkinsky, 2008).

Cocaine

Cocaine is a crystalline tropane alkaloid obtained from leaves of the coca plant (Andersen, Sawyer, & Howell, 2012). Cocaine hydrochloride is the derivative of coca found on the street in the United States. It is usually cut with other substances, such as sugars, powders, or even rat poison (DEA, 2011). Cocaine that is obtained on the street is typically 20% pure, although some batches may be as high as 50% pure, resulting in many emergency room visits due to accidental overdose (Abadkinsky, 2008).

Snorting cocaine results in an extreme high that peaks within 15 to 20 minutes and lasts up to 60 to 90 minutes (Weaver & Schnoll, 1999). Intravenous use results in a high within 3 to 5 minutes that reduces at 30 to 40 minutes. Users of cocaine have developed ways to heat it and then inhale it ("free basing"); cocaine's chemical instability when heated makes this extremely dangerous and this may result in explosions (Abadkinsky, 2008).

Crack was developed in an attempt to find a way to smoke cocaine in a more stable form. It is made by combining cocaine, baking soda, and water and cooking it. The resulting soap-like substance is smoked and may be the purest form of cocaine found on the street (Foundation for a Drug Free World, 2013). The high from the inhalation of crack takes effect within 5 seconds and typically lasts several minutes. However, the shorter duration of effects results in many users continuing to smoke to achieve the high needed (NIDA, 2013a).

Cessation of cocaine after regular use will produce a withdrawal syndrome. The rush associated with its use depletes the supply of dopamine and norepinephrine in the brain. Symptoms of cocaine withdrawal can include depression, irritability, fatigue, and restless sleep (DEA, 2011).

Caffeine

Caffeine is the world's most widely consumed psychoactive substance (Abadkinsky, 2008). It is a stimulant that activates the pleasure centers of the brain and provides the user with an energy boost.

Caffeine has some medical uses. When combined with painkillers, caffeine is a frontline treatment for migraine headaches (WebMD, 2013). In addition, caffeine is known to improve mental alertness and has been tentatively linked to other physical benefits including the prevention of Parkinson's disease and type 2 diabetes (WebMD, 2013).

Experts state that consuming 200 to 300 mg of caffeine per day is moderate consumption but people can become caffeine dependent on as little as 100 mg per day (Johns Hopkins Medical Center, 2013). When individuals present with anxiety or sleep problems, use of caffeine should be explored in depth. Withdrawal from caffeine can produce mild lethargy, headaches, and difficulty with concentration (Abadkinsky, 2008).

Nicotine

Nicotine is an alkaloid found in tobacco. Nicotine is usually smoked but may also be chewed or used in lozenges. Cigarettes usually contain about 10 mg of nicotine. The average smoker takes in about 1 to 2 mg of nicotine each time he or she smokes (Abadkinsky, 2008).

Nicotine is the leading cause of disease, death, and disability in the United States (NIDA, 2012a). Nicotine accounts for 5.4 millions deaths throughout the world every year, the equivalent of 25 jumbo jets crashing daily (Myers, 2013). By 2030, it is predicted that this will be increased to 8 million deaths per year (Myers, 2013). There are over 440,000 premature deaths connected to nicotine use in the United States per year; 20% of all deaths annually are linked to nicotine and it contributes to one third of all cancers (Abadkinsky, 2008; American Cancer Society, 2012).

Secondhand smoke, or environmental tobacco smoke (ETS) is inhaled when near a lit cigarette or in the presence of a smoker who has just exhaled. ETS causes 53,600 deaths per year in the United States, including 46,000 due to heart disease, lung cancer, and sudden infant death syndrome (American Cancer Society, 2013). In addition, secondhand smoke contributes to bronchitis and pneumonia as well as acting out, hyperactivity, and depression in children (Abadkinsky, 2008).

Thirdhand smoke refers to the effects of lingering pollutants after someone has smoked. Thirdhand smoke may be found on surfaces in a house where someone has smoked or on the smoker's skin or clothes (McBride, 2010). Small children who touch household surfaces coated with smoke particles may be susceptible to carcinogens and experience deleterious effects on brain development although research on the long-term effects of thirdhand smoke is still in its infancy (Fleming, Anderson, Amin, & Ashley, 2012; Hargreaves, 2009).

Symptoms of withdrawal usually start within a few hours of the last cigarette and usually fade within a few weeks although some people experience symptoms for months (Abadinsky, 2008). Common symptoms of nicotine withdrawal include headaches, increased appetite and weight gain, tension, poor concentration, and cravings (Medline Plus, 2012).

Hallucinogens

Hallucinogens are psychoactive drugs that alter perception and mood (Myers, 2013). Effects can include depersonalization (out-of-body experiences), synesthesia (seeing sounds and hearing visual stimuli), and hallucinations of various kinds (sounds, odors, or tactile sensations; Abadkinsky, 2008). Mood effects are mostly euphoric but can also be depressive depending on the individual and other intrapersonal factors. It has not been established if substances in this category have a withdrawal syndrome.

Lysergic Acid Diethylamide

Lysergic acid diethylamide (LSD) or "acid" is a hallucinogen that in low doses produces striking perceptual changes. LSD is usually sold in liquid form, capsules, or tablets but is then divided onto blotter paper for use (NIDA, 2009a). LSD acts on the serotonin and dopamine neurotransmitters and often produces an intense "trip" that may last up to 12 hours although some effects may not fade until after 129 hours (Abadkinsky, 2008; NIDA, 2009a).

Other Drugs

There are other substances that fall into the category of hallucinogens. These substances include phencyclidine (PCP), mushrooms (psilocybin), cactus (mescaline), and dimethyltryptamine (DMT).

PCP was developed as a general anesthetic for surgery. It can create alterations in sights and sounds as well as dissociation (Abadkinsky, 2008). This drug is a white, crystalline powder but it can be mixed with other substances and is sometimes sold in tablets, capsules, or liquid form. The use of PCP causes a very powerful psychotic process similar to schizophrenia and some users have been mistakenly diagnosed with schizophrenia when high (DEA, 2011).

Psilocybin has been used for many centuries by some Native American cultures as part of worship ceremonies. The mushrooms are eaten and have effects similar to those of LSD. They also can affect mood and can alter body image (DEA, 2011).

Mescaline is found in parts ("buttons") of a small cactus called peyote (Abadkinsky, 2008). It produces hallucinogenic effects similar to schizophrenia lasting for 5 to 12 hours. Native Americans in New Mexico have used this drug as part of their religious worship for centuries (DEA, 2011).

DMT is a hallucinogenic substance found in the seeds of certain plants. This drug is commonly found in the morning glory plant and is often a part of the worship of native peoples in the Caribbean and Latin America (Abadkinsky, 2008). DMT is known to provide effects for 45 minutes to an hour and is often called the "business man's trip" (Palo Alto Medical Foundation, 2013).

Marijuana

Marijuana comes from the leaves of the hemp plant. Its active ingredient is delta 9-tetrahydrocannabinol (THC). It may be smoked, inhaled, or orally consumed. Marijuana has mild hallucinogenic effects including distortion of time and increased sensitivity to sounds and colors. The effects of marijuana typically last 1 to 3 hours (Foundation for a Drug Free World, 2013). Marijuana can create euphoria, relaxed inhibitions, and increased appetite (Abadkinsky, 2008). THC remains in the blood stream for a week or more, meaning that regular users achieve a high with a lower dose (Myers, 2013). Marijuana potency today is not the same marijuana of the 1960s or even the 1980s; that marijuana had a THC potency of about 4%. Now its average THC potency is about 15% (NIDA, 2013c). Higher potency marijuana has led to more emergency room visits and the greater likelihood of addiction (NIDA, 2013c).

Daily marijuana users can experience a withdrawal syndrome (Abadkinsky, 2008). Withdrawal from marijuana starts within 1 to 3 days after use, reaches its peak within 2 to 6 days and lasts up to 14 days. Symptoms of withdrawal can include anger, anxiety, decreased appetite, irritability, sleep problems, and stomach pains (Budney, Moore, Vandrey, & Hughes, 2003). As with other substances, withdrawal from marijuana may vary based on the individual.

Inhalants

Inhalants are substances that are commonly found around any home. They are in volatile solvents (such as glue, paint thinner, gasoline, and nail polish remover); aerosols (such as hair spray, spray paint, and deodorant); or anesthetics (found in cans of whipped cream). Many of these substances have similar effects including disinhibition, disorientation, light-headedness, and euphoria (NIDA, 2012b). These effects only last a few minutes and often users continue to inhale the substance for several hours to keep this feeling going. Peak use of inhalants occurs in about eighth grade, primarily by preadolescent and adolescent males (Myers, 2013).

Withdrawal from inhalants does not occur very frequently. However, if a heavy user of inhalants stops using, he or she may experience headaches, muscle cramps, and abdominal pain (Abadkinsky, 2008).

Club/Designer Drugs

"Club drugs" or "designer drugs" are a number of synthetically manufactured drugs that are usually used at bars, nightclubs, or all night "raves" (Abadkinsky, 2008; NIDA, 2010a). They include gamma-hydroxybutyrate (GHB), Rohypnol, Ketamine, and Ecstasy (NIDA, 2012). GHB and Rohypnol are odorless, colorless, and tasteless drugs that can be slipped into alcohol or other beverages, leaving an unsuspecting person under the influence and vulnerable to date rape (NIDA, 2012). Ketamine is a dissociative anesthetic often used by veterinarians for surgery and, depending upon the dosage, can lead to a mellow dreamlike state or an out-of-body, near-death experience (Abadkinsky, 2008). Ecstasy, also known as the "hug drug," has both stimulant and hallucinogenic properties and creates increased feelings of empathy and warmth toward others along with distortions in time and sensations (NIDA, 2013b). Each of the club drugs has its own potential negative consequences.

Withdrawal from club drugs will vary based on the substance. For example, there is no known withdrawal syndrome from Ecstasy, whereas GHB, Rohypnol, and Ketamine each have documented symptoms of withdrawal (Abadkinsky, 2008).

PERSONALITY CHANGE

If an individual has difficulty with regulating emotions, self-esteem, relationships, and self-care, he or she is more likely to develop addiction (Khantzian & Albanese, 2008). Personality changes also occur as an individual becomes more deeply involved in substance abuse and addiction (Caselles, Micó, & Amigó, 2010). Some personality variables that can lead to addiction or that are exacerbated by the use of substances include impulsivity, sensation seeking, negative emotionality (depression, anxiety, neuroticism), and nonconforming behavior (Caselles et al., 2010; Littlefield, Sher, & Wood, 2009). Although these changes can occur at any age, they are more noticeable during the adolescent and emerging adulthood years (Hicks, Durbin, Blonigen, Iacono, & McGue, 2012). Cessation of substance use can result in an elimination of problematic personality patterns (Hicks et al., 2012; Suire & Bothwell, 2006; Sutherland, 1997).

PREVALENCE RATE

The National Institute on Alcohol Abuse and Alcoholism (NIAAA) conducted a comprehensive survey of alcohol and related conditions (Falk, Yi, & Hiller-Sturmhöfel, 2008) examining the rates of alcohol and drug use/abuse in the United States. Data were gathered in two waves, 2001 to 2002 and 2004 to 2005. Results found that 8.5% of adults in the United States met criteria for alcohol use disorder and 2% met criteria for a drug use disorder (NIAAA, 2008; Stinson, Grant, Dawson, Ruan, Huang, & Saha, 2006). Young adults (18–24 years) were found to have highest rates of substance use and men were more likely than women to exhibit problems (Stinson et al., 2006).

The Cost to Society

Chemical and process addictions effect economics, health care, work productivity, family life, crime, social welfare, and mental health (Juhnke & Hagedorn, 2006). Substance abuse and addiction exert heavy costs on our society totaling approximately $559 billion per year in lost worker productivity, crime, incarceration, drug enforcement, and medical costs (NIDA, 2011a). The cost of gambling in the United States, including lost work time, increased crime, and bankruptcies, is estimated to be approximately $54 billion annually (van Wormer & Davis, 2013). Little is known about the economic and societal impacts of other behavioral addictions but they are considered to be a major public health issue in the United States.

BRAIN DIFFERENCES AND GENETICS

There is a genetic component in at least some drug and alcohol addictions. Children of alcoholics are 50% to 60% more likely to develop alcohol use disorders as compared to those without this history (McGue, 1999). Children whose parents abuse illicit drugs are found to be 45% to 79% more likely to engage in problematic drug use (Agrawal & Lynskey, 2006; Kendler, Jacobson, Prescott, & Neale, 2003; Tsuang, Bar, Harley, & Lyons, 2001). In addition, a person's vulnerability to alcohol dependence may also place him or her at risk for other substance use problems and other psychiatric disorders (Dick & Agrawal, 2008; Kendler et al., 2003).

CO-OCCURRING DISORDERS

An individual may have one or more mood disorders and one or more substance-related disorders at the same time; in these situations, the disorders are referred to as "co-occurring disorders" (NIDA, 2010a; SAMHSA, 2006). About 8 million people in the United States with any mental illness also have a substance use disorder and of 11.5 million adults with serious mental illness, 22.6% met criteria in the past year for substance dependence or abuse compared to 5.8% of adults with no history of mental illness (SAMHSA, 2012). Of the eight million Americans with co-occurring disorders, only 6.9% receive treatment for both conditions and 56.6% receive no treatment at all (SAMHSA, 2012). Effective treatment of substance abuse and mental health problems needs to be integrated for both conditions to stabilize. Clinicians must make every effort to provide integrated care for both disorders (Pettinati, O'Brien, & Dundon, 2013).

TRAUMA

A significant relationship exists between trauma/PTSD and abuse of various substances. Researchers have illustrated the relationship between trauma/PTSD and substance use disorders involving alcohol, nicotine, cocaine/crack, opioids, and cannabis as a way to manage symptoms of trauma (Bailey & Stewart, 2013). Estimates are that 22% to 43% of people with PTSD have a substance use disorder at some point in their lives and that this rate may be as high as 75% within the veteran population (Jacobsen et al., 2001).

BEHAVIORAL/PROCESS ADDICTIONS

Behavioral addictions involve a specific action that a person does repetitively, despite negative consequences. According to Karim and Chaudhri (2012), "The use of repetitive actions, initiated by an impulse that can't be stopped, causing an individual to escape, numb, soothe, release tension, lessen anxiety or feel euphoric, may redefine the term addiction to include experience and not just substance" (p. 5). There is a growing body of literature that supports the use of the term addiction to include out-of-control behaviors (Grant, Potenza, Weinstein, & Gorelick, 2010; Grant, Schreiber, & Odlaug, 2013; Karim & Chaudhri, 2012; Khantzian & Albanese, 2008).

Behavioral addictions share many common features with substance addictions.

1. Difficulty resisting the urges to engage in certain harmful behaviors
2. Emotional vulnerability is a key trigger of craving
3. Onset of initial use/behavior in adolescence and higher incidence of problem use in young adulthood as compared to later years
4. Common effects on neurobiology
5. Natural recovery (or sudden cessation of use/behavior without formal treatment) does occur
6. Financial/marital/legal problems are often the result of the use/behavior
7. Reduced pleasure over time. Use becomes an effort to reduce dysphoria
8. Genetic predisposition
9. Positive response to 12-step programs and cognitive behavioral therapy (Black, 2013; Grant et al., 2010, 2013; Karim & Chaudhri, 2012; Khantzian & Albanese, 2008)

There are also unique aspects to behavioral addictions that distinguish them from the substance use disorders. These differences include the following:

1. Although some behavioral addictions do seem to have a withdrawal syndrome associated with them (i.e., gambling), there are no reports of withdrawal that required medical intervention.
2. There are no medications that are currently FDA-approved to treat behavioral addictions.
3. With the exception of gambling, most of the behavioral addictions are not covered in the *DSM-5*.
4. Treatment of behavioral addictions may be "carved out" or not covered by insurance.
5. Some behavioral addictions are more appropriately treated with a "harm reduction" approach automatically (e.g., eating, sex; Grant et al., 2010, 2013).

Some see out-of-control behaviors as symptoms of another disorder (such as bipolar disorder or a personality disorder; Karim & Chaudhri, 2012). Critics do not believe that many of these behaviors should be called addictions at all, arguing that use of the term addiction provides an excuse for bad behavior or is at least an "overmedicalizing" of behavior (Karim & Chaudhri, 2012; Reynaud, Karila, Blecha, & Benyamina, 2010). Some controversy exists regarding these disorders, including whether they are true addictions and whether or not they should be included in the *DSM-5*.

Many of these behaviors may ultimately be categorized as addictions and be incorporated into the diagnostic nomenclature. As Khantzian and Albanese (2008) concluded, "The evidence provides a basis to conclude that these addictive behaviors, much like substances of addiction, serve the need to relieve or change distress associated with enduring painful feelings and problems with self-esteem and interpersonal relationships" (p. 87).

Gambling

Gambling disorder involves the compulsive spending of money in an effort to "win the jackpot," whatever that may be. Gamblers buy scratch tickets, play the lottery, frequent casinos, or participate in the increasing use of gambling options online. In fact, Internet gambling is the fastest growing segment of gambling with 2.5 million Americans playing online poker, wagering $30 million annually (van Wormer & Davis, 2013). Gambling disorder has been renamed and reclassified as an addiction in the *DSM-5* (APA, 2013).

The most serious gambling problems (previously labeled pathological gambling) are estimated to affect about 1% of the U.S. population, whereas problem gambling that is seen as less serious is believed to affect 2% to 3% of the population (van Wormer & Davis, 2013). About 30% to 40% of the revenues of casinos and state lotteries are from problem and pathological gamblers. The financial impact of problem gambling can be devastating; problem gamblers spend $400/month on average and pathological gamblers wager $2,000/month on average (Petry, Weinstock, Ledgerwood, & Morasco, 2008).

Problem gambling has been shown to impact four circuits of the brain: reward, motivation/drive, memory/learning, and control (Iancu, Lowengrub, Dembinsky, Kotler, & Dannon, 2008). Wins and near wins can be experienced somewhat similarly in brain circuitry and psychologically, reinforcing a continuation of the gambling process (Clark, Lawrence, Astley-Jones, & Gray, 2009; Côté, Caron, Aubert, Desrochers, & Ladouceur, 2003; Potenza et al., 2003). Efforts to utilize medications (selective serotonin reuptake inhibitors [SSRIs], naltrexone, antiaddiction agents such as bupropion, and mood stabilizers) to treat gambling disorders have had limited success although this area of research is still in its infancy (Black, McNeilly, Burke, Shaw, & Allen, 2011; Iancu et al., 2008; Pallanti, Bernardi, Allen, & Hollander, 2010).

More men are diagnosed with pathological or problem gambling than women (Petry, Stinson, & Grant, 2005). Women make up about one third of problem gamblers but are only 2% to 4% of the population in treatment (APA, 2004). Gender differences also exist concerning the reasons for gambling, with men seeking "action" and women gambling to "escape" (van Wormer & Davis, 2013).

Gamblers who present with a co-occurring disorder consistently have more severe problems than those without a co-occurring psychiatric disorder. Petry et al. (2005) found that pathological gamblers were six times more likely to have alcohol misuse in their lifetime and a four times more likely to have a substance use disorder as compared to nongamblers. These authors also found that pathological gamblers were eight times more likely to have experienced a manic episode and three times more likely to experience major depressive disorder, dysthymia, generalized anxiety disorder, panic disorder, or specific phobias. Gambling is the addictive disorder with the highest suicide rate, with approximately 20% of addicted gamblers attempting suicide and over 70% reporting that they want to die (National Gambling Impact Study, 1999).

Most insurance companies do not reimburse for treatment of problem gambling. Few pathological gamblers seek treatment; it is estimated that only about 7% to 12% try to get help (Petry et al., 2008), with insurance issues and financial devastation serving as barriers to care. This may change as the *DSM-5* has reclassified gambling as an addictive disorder.

Psychotherapy of individuals who are reporting or questioning their gambling behavior must begin with a good assessment. There are various screening tools that may be helpful (see Appendix A5). Clinicians should also assess for co-occurring disorders and monitor mental status with a specific focus on potential for suicidality. Motivational interviewing, cognitive behavioral therapy, Eye Movement Desensitization and Reprocessing (EMDR) therapy, and psychodynamic therapy can all be useful in addressing both gambling behavior as well as underlying traumas or other psychiatric disorders (Kausch, Rugle, & Rowland, 2006; Najavits, 2011; Petry et al., 2008; van Wormer & Davis, 2013).

Histories of trauma are common in those with pathological gambling with rates as high as 88% (Kausch et al., 2006; Ledgerwood & Petry, 2006; Najavits, 2011). Estimates of PTSD in those with gambling problems range from 12.5% to 29% (Ledgerwood & Petry, 2006). In addition, the severity and frequency of problem gambling has been associated with childhood maltreatment (Petry & Schneider, 2005).

There is a significant overlap between PTSD symptoms and those of pathological gambling (Ledgerwood & Petry, 2006). Individuals with PTSD and/or pathological gambling exhibit impulsivity and dissociation. For those with histories of trauma, gambling may serve as one additional way to numb themselves (Ledgerwood & Petry, 2006).

Food Addiction

Food addictions or eating disorders affect a small percentage of the overall population but are relatively common in girls and young adult women (Hoek & van Hoeken, 2003). Anorexia, bulimia, and binge eating disorder are psychiatric diagnoses that are identified much more often in women (APA, 2013). Men have historically been identified as a small percentage of food addicts but recent research indicates that they may represent up to one quarter of patients affected by anorexia and one quarter of those with bulimia, and that 2% of the men in the United States struggle with binge eating disorder (as compared to 3.5% of women; Hudson, Hiripi, Pope, & Kessler, 2007).

Research on the neurobiological mechanisms of food addictions is still early in its development. Both excitatory and inhibitory brain mechanisms contribute to the motivation to eat, as well as the experience of satiation. Some specific brain areas that contribute to out-of-balance eating include the striatum, hippocampus, amygdala, hypothalamus, and the cerebellum (Kaye, Wagner, Fudge, & Paulus, 2011; Wagner et al., 2010).

Co-occurring disorders are prevalent with food addictions. Clients with an eating disorder and a substance abuse disorder have more severe forms of disordered eating (Killeen et al., 2011). Research has found that bulimics are 4.6 times more likely to have a substance abuse disorder as compared to non-bulimics. Clients with other types of eating disorders were two to three times more likely to have a substance abuse disorder as compared to those without eating disorders. Additionally, women with bulimia nervosa and substance use disorders have been shown to have higher rates of other co-occurring psychiatric disorders, including depression, anxiety, PTSD, and personality disorders (Killeen et al., 2011).

Anorexia

Anorexia nervosa is the relentless pursuit of thinness. The average age of onset for anorexia is usually in adolescence or young adulthood (APA, 2013). Most anorexics grow up in families with high demands and are White, middle-, or upper-class adolescents. According to the Australian and New Zealand Clinical Practice Guidelines for the treatment of anorexia, 70% of patients with anorexia regain weight within 6 months of starting treatment but 15% to 25% of them will relapse within 2 years (2004). Most patients with anorexia report remission of symptoms within 5 years of their initial diagnosis (APA, 2013). About 50% of individuals with anorexia will require hospitalization at some point in their treatment and mortality rates for this disorder are about 5% per decade (APA, 2013).

Anorexics are 18 times more likely to die as compared to others of their age (National Institute of Mental Health [NIMH], 2011). Goals of treatment for this disorder include restoring the person to a healthy weight, treating underlying psychological issues, and eliminating the thought processes that lead to restrictions of caloric intake (NIMH, 2011). There is some research to suggest that antidepressants, antipsychotics, or mood stabilizers can be helpful to anorexic later in treatment (van Wormer & Davis, 2013). Family therapy is often important in addressing dynamics that may be contributing to the client's anorexia. The Maudsley method is a specific approach to eating disorders treatment that involves the family. Families learn to eat together as part of the recovery process for the individual (Rhodes, 2003).

Bulimia Nervosa

Those affected by bulimia nervosa binge on high-calorie foods and then find some compensatory strategy, such as vomiting, laxatives, or excessive exercise, to purge the calories they have consumed. Bulimia occurs in about 1.5% of women and 0.5% of men in the United States (Hudson et al., 2007). Mortality rates for bulimia are about 2% per decade with death occurring due to esophageal damage or electrolyte imbalances (APA, 2013).

Treatment goals are to eliminate unhealthy eating patterns (i.e., bingeing/purging) and help clients change the unhealthy thought patterns that are triggering symptoms (NIMH, 2011). Fluoxetine (Prozac) remains the only approved medication for the treatment of bulimia (NIMH, 2011). Clients with bulimia often respond well to treatment in the short term but relapse is common and bulimia can become a chronic disorder leading to periods of relapse of binge/purge behaviors over many years (Quadflieg & Fichter, 2003).

Binge Eating Disorder

Binge eating disorder involves episodes of binge eating similar to bulimia but without compensatory strategies to make up for the extremes of caloric intake. Some people can identify triggers for binge eating (such as depression or anxiety) but others cannot determine these factors. Estimates indicate that about 30% of clients in weight-control programs have this disorder (Karim & Chaudhri, 2012).

Trauma

Childhood trauma has been shown to be a major factor in the development of eating disorders with some samples finding rates of trauma as high as 90% in patients in eating disorder programs (Kong & Bernstein, 2009). Patients with eating disorders are more likely than those without these disorders to have a history of trauma and individuals with trauma histories are more likely to experience problematic eating patterns (Briere & Scott, 2007). The most common eating disorder symptom related to a trauma history is bulimic behaviors (Brewerton, 2007; Briere & Scott, 2007).

Poor outcomes of eating disorder treatment are most often seen in individuals who were sexually abused or who were exposed to violence at a very young age (Kong & Bernstein, 2009). Therapists working with trauma and eating disorders need to proceed with caution. Often they may underestimate the need for a focus on nutrition and proceed too quickly into trauma processing (Brewerton, 2007). As with other addictions, those with food addictions need to be taught effective coping skills to reduce anxiety so that they will not resort to old coping patterns (Brewerton, 2007).

Sex Addiction

Sex addiction involves compulsive sexual activities (such as masturbation, use of pornography, sexual behavior with other consenting adults, or cybersex) with great frequency such that the person focuses his or her life on achieving orgasms. If a sex addict is sexual with a partner, the identity of the person may not be important. The most important element of life for a sex addict is the pursuit of an orgasm that provides a mood-altering experience that has been likened to substance dependence (Carnes, 1989; Plant & Plant, 2003).

Clinicians must consider many factors when treating sexual issues. Cultural values, societal values, as well as ethnic and religious beliefs can influence the ways that individuals view sexuality. This can make it difficult to define what is normative sexual behavior. In addition, one cannot simply use high frequency sexual behavior to define addiction, as high frequency of sex with a stable partner has been shown to contribute to better psychological functioning (Långström & Hanson, 2006).

There is controversy around this disorder. Critics argue that excessive sexual behavior should be viewed as a symptom of another diagnosis or an underlying general medical disorder or simply an excuse for bad behavior (Karim & Chaudhri, 2012).

Estimates of the rates of sex addiction vary in part due to the lack of agreement about most appropriate diagnostic criteria. Coleman (1992) indicated that 5% of the U.S. population has compulsive sexual behavior, whereas Carnes (1991) estimated the number to be between 3% and 6%. The Internet has provided a new opportunity for those with a proclivity for sex addiction. Cooper (2000) surveyed a sample of those who used the Internet for sexual purposes and found that 17% of those scored in the problematic range for sexual compulsivity.

Sex addiction is much more commonly diagnosed in men but is being increasingly recognized in women and may have been underdiagnosed (Cyndi, 2004; van Wormer & Davis, 2013). It is a disorder that manifests in early adulthood. Goodman (1997) noted that hypersexual behavior peaks most commonly in men between the age of 20 and 30 years.

Those with sex addiction frequently have other co-occurring disorders. Carnes (1991) found that 42% of sex addicts had chemical dependency, 26% had impulsive spending problems, and 5% were compulsive gamblers.

Recovery from sex addiction has been conceptualized as a 5-year process (Carnes, 1991). The second 6 months of the first year of recovery is the time that sex addicts are most likely to relapse (Carnes, 1991). The client learns to establish healthy boundaries around sexuality, including whether pornography or cybersex will be considered infidelity and "out of bounds" (Carnes, Delmonico, & Griffin, 2007).

Individuals with sex addiction often have histories of trauma. Carnes (1991) reported that 97% of men and women in a sample of those being treated for sex addiction had histories of childhood emotional abuse and 72% had a history of childhood physical abuse. Additionally, 81% had a history of sexual abuse. Other researchers have found rates of childhood sexual abuse to be as high as 95% (Guigliamo, 2007). Evidence exists that combat trauma may be related to the later development of sex addiction (Howard, 2007). EMDR therapy has been successful in treating the effects of past and present trauma in those with sex addiction (Cox & Howard, 2007).

Internet Addiction

The true prevalence of Internet addiction in the United States is unknown. Young (1998) estimated that between 5% and 10% of all online users are addicted, which translates to approximately two to five million Internet addicts in the United States. Other estimates vary from as low as 3% (Whang, Lee, & Chang, 2003) to 50% of online game players (Kuss, 2013).

Research on Internet addiction is still limited. It is difficult to draw definitive conclusions about who is at most risk. Soule, Shell, and Kleen (2003) concluded that younger age is the only unifying demographic for Internet addicts. It appears that those who develop problems with addiction do so regardless of the amount of time they have been using the Internet in their lifetime (Leung, 2004).

Whang et al. (2003) examined a cohort of people who "overused" the Internet in Korea. They found that Internet addicts had significant problems with social behavior and used the Internet as an escape and to provide a source of intimacy. They were more likely to feel close to strangers and to be vulnerable to interpersonal dangers. Those who overuse the Internet were also more likely to access the Internet when stressed out by work or when depressed. In addition, they reported the highest degree of loneliness, depressed mood, and compulsivity.

Internet addicts who seek treatment may benefit from self-monitoring and behavior management strategies. Medications may be a useful adjunct to treatment for Internet addicts as some limited evidence suggests that they may support the client's efforts to reduce Internet use (Grant et al., 2013). However, there are no FDA-approved medications for the treatment of Internet addiction and this area of research is in its infancy (Karim & Chaudhri, 2012).

Internet gaming disorder has been included in the *DSM-5* as a "Condition for Further Study." This exploratory diagnosis includes gaming that occurs on the Internet as well as computerized games that are played offline. It is reportedly most often found in males aged 12 to 20 years (APA, 2013). Excessive game playing may lead to school problems, job loss, and marital conflicts as well as a neglect of physical health (APA, 2013).

Trauma

Individuals may use technology as a way to dissociate from traumatic memories related to childhood abuse or neglect (Schimmenti & Caretti, 2010). Internet addicts often present to treatment initially with a chief complaint of depression, bipolar disorder, or anxiety (Young, 2011) and clinicians should be mindful of assessing for trauma histories in these clients. EMDR therapy has been demonstrated to be helpful in treating Internet addiction (Bae & Kim, 2012).

SUMMARY

In this chapter, we have explored concepts related to addiction. There are many different ways to define addiction and various models that can be used to describe it. The authors utilize a biopsychosocial approach and augment this by integrating other perspectives.

There is a significant connection between trauma and addiction. Many clients will present with both of these disorders and the clinician's job is to provide effective and integrated treatment. Clients with both addiction and trauma will have greater difficulty healing from trauma and maintaining sobriety.

There are both substance and process addictions. In this chapter, the authors have described different categories of drugs including withdrawal syndrome. We also reviewed current literature on gambling, food addiction, sex addiction, and Internet/gaming addiction. The trauma connection was noted.

LEARNING POINTS

1. Chemical and behavioral addictions affect the individual, the family, and society.

2. There is no one right way to think about addiction. Rather, there are many models that are used to describe addiction; these were discussed. The authors view the Biopsychosocial Model as the most comprehensive view of addiction.
3. Many clients have comorbid addiction and trauma. Clinicians need to be prepared to work with both disorders simultaneously.
4. Common drugs of abuse were discussed, including depressants (alcohol, barbiturates, tranquilizers, opiates), stimulants (amphetamines, cocaine, caffeine, nicotine), hallucinogens (LSD, DMT, mushrooms, mescaline), prescriptions drugs, marijuana, club drugs, and inhalants.
5. Current research on behavioral addictions (food addiction, gambling, sex addiction, and Internet/gaming addiction) was reviewed.

CHAPTER 3

THE STAGES OF CHANGE

Each person comes for treatment with his or her own ideas, goals, values, and beliefs about life. All of these areas are important to consider in developing a treatment plan with that person. Clients also bring with them a level of motivation to change. It is important to carefully assess this on an individual basis.

Prochaska and DiClemente (1982, 1992) were the first to research and document what many clinicians likely already knew anecdotally: Clients presenting for treatment of addiction bring with them different levels of motivation to change. In this chapter, the authors will review the Transtheoretical Model (Prochaska & DiClemente, 1982, 1992) by describing its development, the important components of the model, and the research that has validated the application of the theory about the Stages of Change for addictions and other behaviors.

HISTORICAL DEVELOPMENT

Numerous models have been developed over the years to describe the process of change that occurs in psychotherapy (Horn, 1976; Rosen & Shipley, 1983). Models of behavior change also apply to life in general when someone decides to adopt a new behavior (e.g., increased exercise or starting to smoke), modify a habitual behavior pattern (e.g., eating less sugar), or stop a behavior pattern that is causing problems (DiClemente, 2003). The Stages of Change Model developed by Prochaska and DiClemente (1982, 1992) is the model that has generated the most research and it is also the one most often used to describe what individuals experience as they try to alter substance use (Connors, Donovan, & DiClemente, 2001; Connors, DiClemente, Velasquez, & Donovan, 2013). Extant research supports the validity of this model in identifying people's motivation to change in both clinical and nonclinical populations (DiClemente & Prochaska, 1998).

OVERVIEW OF THE THEORY

The Transtheoretical Model was described initially in the early 1980s (Prochaska & DiClemente, 1982) as a depiction of the change processes that clients experienced while in psychotherapy, regardless of the theoretical approach of the clinician. Research to that point had demonstrated that psychotherapy can help people change but *how* people changed remained unclear (Prochaska & DiClemente, 2005; Prochaska, DiClemente, & Norcross, 1992). Prochaska and DiClemente studied smokers who were in the process of trying to quit; this model was developed by examining the experience of these smokers who were at different points of the change process. A similar pattern of change was found in individuals who altered their smoking behavior without formal psychological support (DiClemente, Story, & Murray, 2000; Prochaska & DiClemente, 1982, 1992). The model incorporated three key elements: stages of change, processes of change, and levels of change. All three of these constructs are important in understanding where a person is in the change process and how psychotherapists can most effectively intervene.

Stages of Change

Prochaska and DiClemente (1982) initially described four specific stages that occur when people are attempting to change behavior: Precontemplation, Contemplation, Action, and Maintenance. The Preparation stage was later added after the stage of Contemplation as data analyses demonstrated that individuals spent time actively organizing themselves to change before they took steps to do so (Prochaska et al., 1992).

Relapse and Recycling is not a formal stage of the model but is an important clinical component of the process of creating new behavior patterns. Individuals often fall back to old behaviors as they attempt to change (DiClemente, 2003). Following relapse, clients reenter the change process at any point, including a return to Precontemplation (Connors et al., 2001). Most people who relapse return to the point of Contemplation or Preparation (Prochaska & DiClemente, 1984).

Following are the Stages of Change currently used in this model (Figure 3.1):

a. Precontemplation
b. Contemplation
c. Preparation
d. Action
e. Maintenance
f. Termination

The goal of treatment is to help clients move from one stage to the next in the process of change. Clients may move back and forth or become stuck at a stage but the clinician needs to be aware that the goal is to move the client forward in the change process.

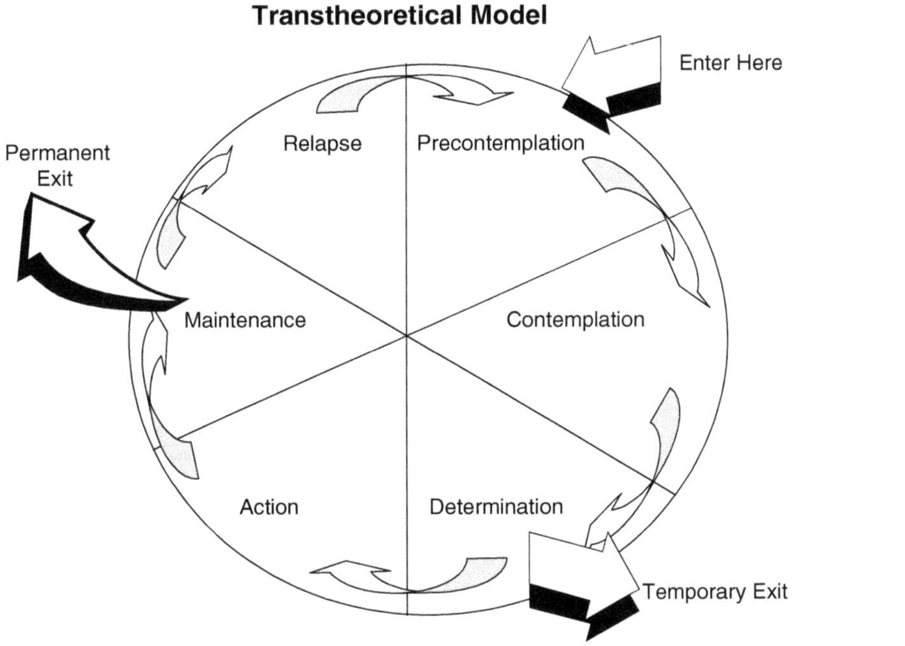

Precontemplation Stage
1. Assessment of readiness to change
2. Framing messages
3. Offering incentives
4. Building up one's referent power

Contemplation Stage
1. Using one's referent power to motivate change
2. Eliciting commitment to change

Determination or Preparation Stage
1. A decision is made to change. Start a game plan

Action Stage
1. Enhancing self-efficacy beliefs
2. Contracting for behavior/rewards
3. Teaching/coaching
4. Providing selective reinforcement

Maintenance Stage
1. Providing and promoting active social support
2. Fading out contact
3. Preventing relapse

Relapse Stage
1. Compassion
2. Assess what was learned, what's different
3. Many start new cycle

FIGURE 3.1 Graphic of Stages of Change.
Source: Prochaska and DiClemente (1982).

These stages will be discussed further and readers are also referred to Part II: Clinical Implications and Practical Interventions. Relapse and Recycling, while not a stage, will be discussed in detail.

As clients progress through the Stages of Change, they become potentially more accepting of the fact that they have a problem and more active in the process of change. However, there is no specific timeline that every client will follow in the behavior change process. In addition, not every client will transition through all of the stages. Some may never get beyond Precontemplation. Some clients may move back and forth among the stages. The process of change is as unique as the individual.

Processes of Change

The Transtheoretical Model was based on research that explored specific processes of change that smokers or those trying to lose weight were using (Prochaska, DiClemente, & Norcross, 1992). As clients became more active in the change process and further along the stages, they were using more of these change strategies (Prochaska, Velicer, DiClemente, & Fava 1988). These change processes included the following:

a. Consciousness raising: increasing one's awareness of the problem behavior
b. Dramatic relief: experiencing and expressing emotions about one's problem behavior and how to resolve it
c. Environmental reevaluation: learning about how one's problem affects others
d. Self-reevaluation: understanding feelings related to the problem behavior
e. Self-liberation: making a conscious choice to change oneself
f. Reinforcement management: building rewards into one's life
g. Helping relationships: receiving support from caring others
h. Counterconditioning: replacing problem behaviors with more adaptive behaviors when dealing with situational triggers
i. Stimulus control: changing one's environment to manage triggers of problem behavior

Table 3.1 provides a more comprehensive description of these change processes.

Levels of Change

Human beings lead lives that are complex and complicated. People often have a variety of issues that may be contributing to problems and/or that they might consider changing. Prochaska and DiClemente (1984) identified the following levels of change that are possible in someone's life and that are potential foci of psychotherapy:

a. Symptom/situation: Is the client presenting with depression or anxiety? What are the major symptoms that bring the person to treatment? What life situations are impacting these symptoms?
b. Maladaptive cognitions: How is the person engaged in problematic thought processes that are interfering with his or her life?
c. Current interpersonal conflicts: Is the person coming to treatment because of a conflict with friends or work colleagues?
d. Family–systems conflicts: Does the client come to sessions with conflicts that are related to the nuclear or extended family?
e. Intrapersonal conflicts: What conflicts exist within the person? For example, is the person struggling to come out as a lesbian/gay person or with other identity issues?

These levels of change are seen as hierarchical (a–e), each building upon and integrated with the previous level of change. As the source of problems progresses to higher levels of change (e.g., to the family–systems or intrapersonal level), the individual's treatment will be more complicated by involving more levels of change. Prochaska and DiClemente (2005) noted that higher levels of

TABLE 3.1 Titles, Definitions, and Representative Interventions of the Processes of Change

Process	Definitions: Interventions
Consciousness raising	Increasing information about self and problem: observations, confrontations, interpretations, bibliotherapy
Self-reevaluation	Assessing how one feels and thinks about oneself with respect to a problem: value clarification, imagery, corrective emotional experience
Self-liberation	Choosing and committing to an act or belief in ability to change: decision-making therapy, New Year's resolutions, logotherapy techniques, commitment enhancing techniques
Counterconditioning	Substituting alternatives for problem behaviors: relaxation, desensitization, assertion, positive self-statements
Stimulus control	Avoiding or countering stimuli that elicit problem behaviors: restructuring one's environment (e.g., removing alcohol or fattening foods), avoiding high risk cues, fading techniques
Reinforcement management	Rewarding one's self or being rewarded by others for making changes: contingency contracts, overt and covert reinforcement, self-reward
Helping relationships	Being open and trusting about problems with someone who cares: therapeutic alliance, social support, self-help groups
Dramatic relief	Experiencing and expressing feelings about one's problems and solutions: psychodrama, grieving losses, role playing
Environmental reevaluation	Assessing how one's problem affects physical environment: empathy training, documentaries
Social liberation	Increasing alternatives for nonproblem behaviors available in society: advocating for rights of repressed, empowering, policy interventions

Source: Prochaska, DiClemente, and Norcross (1992).

conflicts make it more difficult to determine what historical and current factors are creating the problem.

Psychotherapy has traditionally focused on only one or two of these levels of change based upon the theoretical orientation of the therapist and the assessment of the level on which the problem behavior can be found (Prochaska & DiClemente, 2005). In addition, higher levels of change will result in a more complicated and longer treatment process. Clients and their therapists need to be in agreement about the level(s) that are viewed as the source of the problems and the targets of change in order to make certain that treatment is focused on the client's wishes (Prochaska & DiClemente, 2002).

Applications

The Transtheoretical Model has been applied to a wider and wider range of behavioral processes. It has been shown to be relevant for smoking (DiClemente et al., 1991), alcohol abuse (Heather & McCambridge, 2013), gambling (Wohl & Sztainert, 2011), sex addiction (Reid, 2007), eating disorders (Bardone-Cone, 2012), Internet/gaming addiction (Park, Park, Lee, Kwon, & Kim, 2012), and bereavement (Calderwood, 2011) as well as other health-related behaviors such as exercise (Hirvonen, Huotari, Niemela, & Korpelainen, 2012), diabetic treatment adherence (Plotnikoff, Lippke, Johnson, & Courneya, 2010), human papillomavirus (HPV) vaccine use (Patel et al., 2013), and fruit–vegetable consumption (Horwath, Schembre, Motl, Dishman, & Nigg, 2013). Despite its greater application to a wide variety of presenting concerns, the Transtheoretical Model continues to be primarily focused on the process of change that occurs in initiating and stopping addictions for both clinical and nonclinical populations (DiClemente & Prochaska, 1998; Morales, Pascual, & Carmona, 2010).

Part II of this book focuses on the clinical applications and interventions utilized when clinicians work with a wide variety of addictive behaviors. The following is a detailed review of each Stage of Change that will lay the groundwork for that discussion. In Part II the clinical interventions appropriate for each stage will be described.

EXPLORATION OF THE STAGES OF CHANGE

Precontemplation

Individuals who are in the stage of Precontemplation often do not think that they have a problem or may have limited awareness of the extent of their problems. They may see issues but have no desire to change at this point. If one asks a client "Do you see yourself changing this behavior in the next 6 months?" and the answer is "No," the client is said to be in Precontemplation. Precontemplators may be unaware of the dangers of their substance use or behavioral patterns and the negative effects that these are having on them or those around them. Some people in this stage may know on some level that their use is causing difficulties but they choose not to see the problems associated with their use or behaviors.

Precontemplators present to psychotherapy for many different reasons, including work, relationship, or mental health issues; these concerns may or may not be understood as related to addiction. They may wish to change in some way. When they experience pressure to change from others, they may do so. However, once they no longer experience this pressure to change, they will often go back to their old behaviors.

Clients in Precontemplation can be quite defensive in treatment and are often described as resistant to interventions. They may actively refuse to see the maladaptive elements related to their problem behavior or they may simply be quite passive in treatment. Clients in this stage will often avoid implementing change strategies that are suggested to them, preferring to stick with their old ways of coping. However, clients in this stage may not always be unreachable. While there may be a small group within this stage that is fully committed to *not* changing, a larger percentage of individuals may remain open to interventions that would move them to the next stage (Balmford, Borland, & Burney 2008).

DiClemente et al. (1991) studied smokers who had volunteered for a smoking cessation program. The group studied included individuals in the Precontemplation Stage. As compared to participants in other stages, clients in Precontemplation had fewer previous episodes of quitting, fewer concerns about quitting, less confidence about quitting, and made fewer attempts at quitting during the smoking cessation program. Other authors have found similar effects for smokers, including a higher level of tolerant attitudes toward smoking in Precontemplators as compared to those in other stages (Morales et al., 2010). Similar patterns in Precontemplators have been seen in research examining those in treatment for alcohol use problems (Schulz, Kremers, & de Vries, 2012).

CASE VIGNETTE

Jeff was a 56-year-old White male who presented to a partial hospital program for assessment. Jeff's case manager drove him to the intake meeting and indicated that Jeff wanted to attend the dual diagnosis day program. The case manager stated that Jeff wanted help maintaining sobriety and stabilizing his depressed mood.

Jeff had a long history of alcohol use, beginning at the age of 10 years. He started to drink any alcohol that he could find in the house at this young age in order to deal with the stress of family violence and abuse that he endured. Soon he found peers in the neighborhood with whom he could drink and was a regular alcohol user by the time he entered high school.

Jeff had been in numerous treatment programs through the years. He reported that he usually entered treatment due to some health crisis or conflict with a spouse (he was married and divorced twice). After discharge, he would eventually resume his alcohol use, usually within a few days or weeks. At intake, he noted that he was drinking a fifth of whiskey per day prior to hospitalization. "I just like how I feel when I drink."

When Jeff was asked about his desire to change, he noted, "Oh, I have no intention of stopping. Once I get out, I'm gonna drink again." The clinician explained the dangers of resuming alcohol use at the level that Jeff intended. In addition, the therapist explained that the partial hospital's policy was to accept only clients who had some motivation to change. "That ain't me," he replied. Jeff and the clinician determined that the program was not appropriate for him at that time, much to the disappointment of his case manager.

The Stage of Contemplation

People in the stage of Contemplation are aware that they have a problem behavior and are beginning to consider the idea of change. Potential behavior changes for those in Contemplation may include abstinence or reducing addictive behavior. Individuals in this stage are engaged in an examination of problem behavior and often feel distressed about their use, behaviors, and/or its effects.

However, these individuals are making no commitment to change and may remain stuck in this stage indefinitely. Prochaska and DiClemente (1984) followed 200 smokers who were in the Contemplation stage during a 2-year project. The majority of study participants who were in Contemplation at the start of the project remained in this stage at the end. Despite the fact that these individuals were wrestling with the impact of their behavior, they did not make any significant steps to change it. Contemplators may not be ready to make a commitment to themselves or others that they will change; they may never be ready.

In this stage of Contemplation, individuals consider the pros and cons of the problem behavior as well as the pros and cons of change. They conduct a cost–benefit analysis about potentially changing their behavior. Contemplators often remain stuck in considering the positive ideas about their substance use (or behavior) as well as the effort, energy, and loss that would be involved in making a change (Prochaska et al., 1992). Thoughts like these serve as a potential barrier to behavior change.

Most of the smokers studied by DiClemente et al. (1991) were classified as Contemplators because they indicated that they were considering an attempt to quit smoking within the next 6 months. In comparison to those in Precontemplation, Contemplators had more previous attempts at quitting smoking, indicated greater concern about quitting, had greater confidence in their ability to quit, and saw fewer advantages and more disadvantages in regard to their smoking. At 1-month and 6-month follow-up, a significantly greater number of Contemplators had attempted to quit or had quit smoking as compared to those classified in the study as Precontemplators.

Carney and Kivlahan (1995) as well as DiClemente and Hughes (1990) studied polysubstance abusers and alcohol abusers, respectively. They utilized a measure of an individual's position on the Stages of Change scale and found that those in this stage endorsed items related to thinking about change. However, the authors also found that these individuals scored low on items related to action although they were currently in treatment to address their behavior. Although someone may realize the problems associated with his or her behavior and be entertaining the need to change, he or she may never get beyond this point.

CASE VIGNETTE

Arthur was a 45-year-old gay man who presented to outpatient psychotherapy upon referral from his psychiatrist. He had a history of previous treatment with other therapists and indicated that he "really liked what therapy can do." Arthur's primary diagnoses were major depressive disorder (chronic and severe) and alcohol dependence. Arthur acknowledged at intake that he was HIV positive and was a long-term survivor of the disease. He had been diagnosed with AIDS in the past but his viral load and T-cell count were both in a much healthier range.

Arthur reported that he had a long history of alcohol and drug use. "It was the 70s and 80s; who didn't!" He came out just after being discharged from the military and had been active in the bar scene and sex clubs in Los Angeles and San Francisco. Arthur had worked in the restaurant industry and noted that substance use was "just a part of the job. We all did it to get through the long shifts." He talked animatedly about his love of good wine. At intake, Arthur was not working but received Social Security disability benefits as income.

Arthur reported that he had quit all of his drug use "except alcohol." He noted that he was still drinking wine "only with good food and on special occasions" but Arthur reported that he cooked "good food" for himself every night. He admitted that his substance use had likely contributed to contracting HIV and was an unhealthy response to stress. That was the reason that he gave up all substances except alcohol. "I'm not sure. I think that alcohol is different, it is the one that I can control." The therapist helped Arthur begin to make the connection between his alcohol use and other problems in his life. Arthur agreed to think about this and agreed to consider moderation management as a way to explore the issue. He entered into a period of Contemplation.

The Stage of Preparation

The stage of Preparation was initially called Decision Making in the original formulation of the Transtheoretical Model. However, data analyses used to validate the model supported only four unique stages and Decision Making was eliminated. Further examination of the data utilizing cluster analysis highlighted Preparation as its own unique stage and it was reinstated in the model (Prochaska et al., 1992).

Preparation incorporates elements of behavior change and intention (Prochaska et al., 1992). Clients in the Preparation stage are intending to change their behavior within the next month and have often made some small steps in that direction, such as smoking fewer cigarettes or delaying their first cigarette of the day (Norcross, Krebs, & Prochaska, 2011). However, they have not made any substantial behavioral changes in the past year. They have not committed to fully changing their behavior but they seem to be on the cusp of doing so.

In Preparation, clients begin to explore the changes that will need to be made when they alter the addictive behaviors. They develop an action plan for change and work to develop the motivation to commit to this plan. This plan may include an exploration of treatment options in the area (inpatient detox, day treatment, intensive outpatient) as well as a consideration of the available additional supports that they might need in order to change, such as support groups or the use of medications to promote abstinence or behavior change. If clients have previously attempted to change and experienced relapse, they may consider what led them to relapse and how to deal differently with the events/emotions/relationships that triggered them. In short, they explore available resources and supports and put into place whatever may be helpful in order to promote change.

Clients in Preparation are considering more adaptive coping responses to triggers of use (counterconditioning) as well as ways to avoid or reduce exposure to these triggers (stimulus control). In addition, clients are considering how they will reward themselves and/or be rewarded by others by altering their behavior. Although they are not fully committed to change in the moment, their motivation is growing (Norcross et al., 2011).

In DiClemente's study of smokers (1991), individuals in Preparation had made more attempts to quit in their lifetimes as compared to those in Precontemplation or Contemplation. In addition, those in Preparation had greater confidence in their ability to quit and to maintain behavior change as compared to peers in earlier stages. On 1-month and 6-month follow-up, individuals in Preparation had made more attempts to quit and were currently not smoking as compared to those in previous stages.

CASE VIGNETTE

Anna was a 30-year-old married White female who sought psychotherapy for depression and alcohol use. Anna had been married to her husband for 8 years. She indicated at intake that she was concerned about her alcohol use. Her husband drank alcohol daily and became intoxicated every night. He expected her to drink with him and became critical of her if she did not. "I have been drinking more and more to placate him and keep my marriage together."

Anna indicated that she wanted to try reducing her alcohol use. She was not ready to completely eliminate alcohol from her life but wanted to see if she could develop a healthier relationship with it. She was ready at intake to do so but wanted support in determining how she could do it. Anna and her therapist talked about a referral to a psychiatrist for a medication evaluation as a first step and discussed ways that she could consider reducing her use. "I'm not quite ready to do that. Soon, though." Within a few weeks, Anna was implementing strategies to reduce her alcohol use and was having success doing so. She discovered ways that she could limit her drinking, despite her husband's continued heavy use. She found an exercise class to attend after work, delaying her arrival home when she would normally begin to drink wine. Anna called to set up an appointment with a psychiatrist to determine if medication would help to improve her depressed mood.

Anna is an example of a client who came to treatment in Preparation. She was motivated to change her alcohol use but wanted help in figuring out how to accomplish it. Once she had the support of therapy, she entered the Action stage and quickly altered her relationship with alcohol.

The Stage of Action

This is the shortest of all the stages; it lasts up to about 6 months. Clients who are in the stage of Action live up to its name: they are ready to make changes in their lives. It should be noted that some clients, even those who have done a good job in the Preparation Stage, never make it to Action. Individuals in this stage are changing or have changed their behavior, experiences, or their environment in order to overcome their problems (Prochaska et al., 1992). Clients in Action devote significant time and energy to changing and exhibit visible behavior changes that are readily noticed by others (Norcross et al., 2011).

At the heart of this stage is a successful alteration of an addictive behavior. People give up their addiction and make the behavioral changes that they have been planning. This may include stopping the behavior completely or cutting back on behavior to reach a predetermined goal. Significant behavior change and observable efforts to support the change process are the primary indicators of this stage (Norcross et al., 2011).

There continues to be a debate about what is an appropriate alteration of an addictive behavior. For some, abstinence is the only appropriate indicator of positive behavior change. For others, a harm reduction approach that allows the client to determine the goal of treatment (e.g., successful reduction of use) would be acceptable. Practitioners who utilize harm reduction strategies focus on reducing the negative effects of a behavior (e.g., heavy alcohol consumption, use of dirty needles by intravenous [IV] drug users) with the goal of improving the quality of life of the individual (van Wormer & Davis, 2013).

Those who support a harm reduction approach would be more open to reduction in use as a criterion of change, provided that a specific guideline for use is preestablished and is followed. For example, a person who drives while intoxicated is charged with operating under the influence (OUI). As a result, he or she may decide to reduce use of alcohol to the weekend only, commit to reducing consumption of alcohol, or commit to never drinking and driving. This person may or may not be an addict. The target behavior for the change could be part of a long pattern of abuse or a one-time lapse in judgment. Either way, steps have been taken to prevent this behavior from recurring. Harm reduction advocates would say that if this person adheres to this new alcohol use guideline, he or she has successfully changed his or her behavior.

Individuals in this stage usually have high levels of willpower and have confidence that they can change their behavior (Prochaska & DiClemente, 2005). Clients in Action utilize behavioral change strategies that they developed in the Preparation stage to avoid relapse. They may stay clear of certain environments (people/places/situations) that might jeopardize their behavior change. If they must be exposed to a situation that could bring up urges to use, they learn to implement skills to deal with the environmental stresses in order to avoid relapse. Due to the stress that comes from trying to change behavior, individuals in action often rely on social support that can come from helping relationships (Prochaska et al., 1992).

Behavior change does not occur in a vacuum. Rather, individuals must convince themselves or be convinced by others that a change is necessary and determine that the adverse consequences of continuing the behavior outweigh whatever benefits the behavior offered them. Additionally, individuals must prepare themselves to make the change and then work to maintain these changes once they are initiated (Prochaska et al., 1992).

CASE VIGNETTE

Edward was a 38-year-old married White male who presented to outpatient treatment upon referral from his wife's therapist. Edward's alcohol use had become a significant issue in their marriage; his wife was insisting that Edward get treatment.

Edward was able to acknowledge that alcohol was a problem for him. He had a long history of alcohol use and had numerous attempts at sobriety in various treatment centers. Edward had been involved sporadically in Alcoholics Anonymous (AA) and was beginning to attend meetings at the time of intake. He reported, "I just can't stop drinking but I don't know why."

Edward talked about a long-standing history of depression that was unremitting. He had never been on an antidepressant and stated that he had wanted to improve his mood "naturally." Edward also acknowledged a history of emotional and physical abuse by his mother, beginning at the age of 5 years.

Edward had never made the connection between his depressive and trauma-related symptoms and his difficulties maintaining sobriety. He was relieved to learn that there might be other important elements to change in his life that would help him abstain from alcohol. He noted that he wanted to save his marriage and immediately committed to attend AA daily and accepted a referral to a psychiatrist. Edward wanted to take action immediately to improve his mood and to achieve long-term sobriety.

Maintenance

The stage of Maintenance begins after about 6 months of Action. In this phase, individuals continue the behavior change begun in the previous stages. The individual learns to stabilize his or her life with the incorporation of new patterns that replace the unwanted behavior. For most, Maintenance will be a lifelong process. Others may consider themselves out of the Maintenance phase when they have no urges to return to their old behavior and are completely confident that they will never return to these patterns.

There are two major tasks that encompass the Maintenance stage. First, a person is working to solidify the behavioral changes made during the Action stage in regard to the problem behavior. In short, he or she maintains abstinence or a specific reduction in the problem behavior. Second, the individual is working to avoid relapse by engaging in actions that replace or avoid the old behavior (Norcross et al., 2011). This includes dealing with and managing any urges or craving to return to old behaviors that arise.

Many of the change processes that are present in the stage of Action may also be found in the stage of Maintenance (Connors et al., 2001). For example, clients in Maintenance will continue to use behavioral strategies to cope differently with things that cue old behavior (counterconditioning) and determine how they can change their environment to avoid these cues whenever possible (stimulus control). Individuals will also use the willpower (self-liberation) that they developed in the Action stage to reinforce their beliefs that they can sustain the changes made and further solidify the idea that they are committed to this new way of living (Prochaska & DiClemente, 1983). They will continue to look for ways to reward themselves for staying with their plan of behavior change (Prochaska et al., 1992).

A person needs to have successfully altered his or her behavior for at least 6 months prior to starting this phase. Most relapses to old behavior are likely to occur before 6 months' time (Connors et al., 2001). Individuals often recycle through the Stages of Change before they are able to successfully change their behavior (Prochaska & DiClement, 2005).

Although clients are in Maintenance, they are still at risk of possible relapse. If a client relapses to old behavior patterns, he or she will recycle into the Stages of Change at some point. Most often, clients will return to Contemplation, Preparation, or Action in order to reengage with his or her behavior change. However, some clients may be so discouraged or so immediately caught up in their addiction that they sink back into Precontemplation (Connors et al., 2001).

CASE VIGNETTE

Ted was a 39-year-old married White male who presented to treatment with symptoms of depression and anxiety that he had struggled with for many years. Ted reported in the initial session that he had experienced emotional, physical, and sexual abuse by his parents while growing up. He felt that he was finally ready to address this trauma history.

Ted also had a long history of alcohol use from the time that he was 12 years old. His drinking accelerated through his teenage years and he developed alcoholism in his early 20s. Despite marrying and becoming a father, Ted continued to drink for many years as a way to manage his underlying psychiatric symptoms.

At the age of 34 years, he decided to change this behavior and entered a treatment center. He reported that he found the inpatient and day treatment programs helpful and that AA was the most important component of his recovery. Ted had been sober for nearly 5 years when he presented to treatment. He had a solid network in AA, was connected to a sponsor, and regularly attended meetings. Ted had successfully mastered the stage of Maintenance.

Termination

The stage of Termination marks the end of the change process for an individual. Clients in Termination are 100% confident that they will be able to maintain behavior change across all situations and environments. Individuals in Termination report no urges ever to return to the original problem behavior. In short, these people do not consider themselves "in recovery" but rather "recovered" (Prochaska & DiClemente, 2005). People are classified as being in Termination if they have been able to successfully maintain behavior change for at least 5 years (Prochaska & DiClemente, 2005). Snow, Prochaska, and Rossi (1992) studied former smokers and alcoholics in Maintenance, reporting that 17% of the previous smokers and 16% of the previous drinkers were more appropriately identified as in Termination.

CASE VIGNETTE

Mary was a 39-year-old, widowed White female who entered outpatient therapy upon referral from the local substance abuse treatment facility. She had been in all levels of care in their program, beginning with a stay in the detox, partial hospital, and intensive outpatient therapy.

Mary had developed a significant alcohol addiction after her husband of 10 years died. Mary's husband was always in excellent health and known for being quite athletic. However, he suddenly began to have intense headaches of unknown origin that were later linked to a large brain tumor. He went through surgery and chemotherapy and radiation treatments but he died about a year after diagnosis. Mary had always been a social drinker but she began to use alcohol quite heavily to deal with the stress of her husband's illness and the toll that it was taking on them both emotionally.

Mary utilized psychotherapy very effectively to process her grief about her husband's death and made a decision to quit drinking. She attended AA meetings, worked her way through the 12 steps with a sponsor, and slowly became reconnected with her life beyond alcohol. She reported, "I just feel like I'm coming to life again after being in a pit with no way out."

After 2 years of weekly treatment, Mary slowly weaned herself from psychotherapy. She transitioned to biweekly sessions for about 1 year and then to monthly "check ins" for the next 3 years. Mary reported, "I don't even think about drinking. It is just not even in my mind anymore." She noted that she had no urges to drink and never reacted to any triggers to use. After 5 years of sobriety, Mary was in Termination.

Relapse and Recycling

Relapse is defined as "increased use of substances either after a period of abstinence or a period of lower substance use" (Nordfjærn, 2011, p. 313). This could also apply to a return to old behaviors. It is important to distinguish a relapse from a "lapse." A lapse is a slip back to old behavior that occurs on one or two occasions (Connors et al., 2013; DiClemente, 2003). A relapse is a sustained pattern of behavior. Just because a client has "lapsed" does not necessarily mean that the client will fall into a relapse (Connors et al., 2001). The outcome of a lapse will likely be affected by the responses of the client and the therapist to this challenge to the change process. If the therapist can help the client to learn from the experience, the lapse may not turn into a full relapse.

Relapse and Recycling is not officially considered to be a Stage of Change. However, it is a very important component of the change process and should be included as an important part of the model. Many clients relapse as part of this process and it is not uncommon that clients will fall back to old behaviors several times before they are able to sustain the new behavior pattern (Connors et al., 2013). After relapse, clients reenter the change process at some point. The clinician's task in working with a client who has relapsed (and who continues in treatment) is to help stabilize the client. The client examines his or her current status in the Stages of Change Model with respect to the target behavior (Connors et al., 2013).

A number of client variables have been associated with relapse. Xie, McHugo, Fox, and Drake (2005) identified the following client characteristics as indicative of a greater risk of relapse: male gender, lower level of education, living independently, and lack of participation in substance abuse treatment. Other factors that were found to be somewhat related to relapse were older age, lack of employment, and longer time to first episode of remission of the addiction. Researchers are also beginning to examine the neurobiological mechanisms that may predispose some clients to relapse (Lasseter, Xie, Ramirez, & Fuchs, 2010) and how environmental factors can interact with neurobiology to trigger relapse (Fuchs, Lasseter, Ramirez, & Xie, 2008).

Ramo and Brown (2008) compared relapse patterns in adolescents and adults who had been treated for drug/alcohol problems. Participants reported what led them to use substances within 18 months of their involvement in treatment. Differing patterns emerged for the adults and adolescents regarding what factors led to relapse. Approximately two thirds of the adults relapsed (67%) due to social situations that led to temptations and triggers, while one third (33%) relapsed due to negative emotional states. Adolescents relapsed primarily in social situations in an effort to increase their positive emotional states (69%) and a smaller proportion relapsed due to interpersonal conflicts and social pressure.

CASE VIGNETTE

Mark was a 45-year-old gay man in psychotherapy to deal with an unrelenting depression that had plagued him for years. He had been sober from alcohol addiction for 10 years, was active in AA, and reported that he had no cravings to return to alcohol use. He then decided that he no longer needed to attend AA and quit going to meetings. Despite his therapist's warnings, Mark indicated that he was not at risk of relapse and that he wanted to focus more fully on recovery from depression.

In a therapy session 6 months later, Mark casually mentioned that he "met friends for drinks" on the previous weekend. When questioned by his therapist, Mark acknowledged that he was drinking again. He maintained that it was "not a problem" and that he "could handle it much better since I've had 10 years away from it." Mark had recycled to Precontemplation. He would eventually drop out of treatment as his addiction took over his life. Fortunately, Mark did return to treatment 1 year later and reengaged with his therapist.

Patterns of Change

Prochaska and DiClemente (1982) originally conceptualized behavior change as a linear progression along the continuum from Precontemplation to Maintenance (Prochaska & DiClemente, 1992). Linear change of behavior is possible and rapid behavior change does sometimes occur. However, a more in-depth examination of the experiences of clients indicated that behavior change was a much more complicated process. For example, Schachter (1982) found that those who quit smoking on their own make an average of three to four attempts to quit before they are actually able to maintain this behavior change. Many people cycle through the Stages of Change several times before actually making a permanent change; some people cycle through some or all of the stages and never permanently change. The Stage of Change in which a person presents says a great deal about motivation and what interventions are necessary and appropriate. As noted above, relapse is often a part of the behavior change process related to addictions (Prochaska & DiClemente, 1992). Ideally, these relapse experiences teach clients about what factors led them to old behaviors and help them to know how to prepare themselves more effectively for future efforts at quitting.

Another graphic illustration of the Transtheoretical Model (see Figure 3.2) depicts the pattern of change as a spiral. Because relapse is most often a part

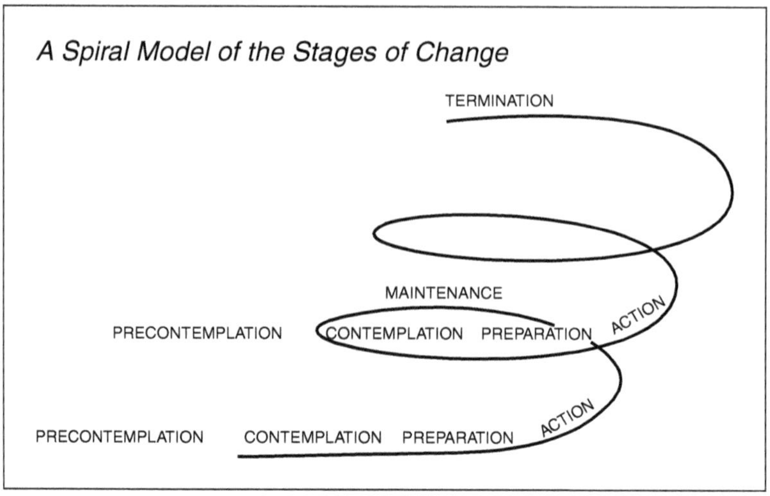

FIGURE 3.2 A spiral model of the Stages of Change.

of the process of change (especially with addiction), individuals cycle through the various stages and can return to any of the previous stages. Most individuals will return to a stage in which they once again consider changing the target behavior, armed with what they have learned from previous change efforts. In that way, clients are not simply going in circles but can progress in the approach to the behavior.

Implications for Treatment

It is very important for therapists working in the field of addiction treatment to consider the Transtheoretical Model of the Stages of Change in working with clients. Many clients come to treatment centers or to individual therapy with presenting concerns related to addiction. Some clinicians might assume that this automatically means that the client is fully ready to change behavior. This is not necessarily true. Of smokers who were engaged in some form of a smoking cessation program, 30% to 40% entered the program in Contemplation while 50% to 60% were in Precontemplation (Prochaska & DiClemente, 1992). Of clients presenting to treatment centers, 40% are in Precontemplation, 40% are in Contemplation, and only 20% are in Action (Norcross et al., 2011). If a therapist develops an action-oriented program that targets only those ready to change, he or she is missing the majority of the treatment-seeking population. It is very important to carefully assess client motivation for change and intervene appropriately (see Part II: Clinical Implications and Practical Interventions). Effective treatment for addictions matches interventions with client readiness. Treatment needs to be individualized and unique, as each client is unique. Psychotherapists need to consider what is motivating clients initially to enter treatment and to help empower them to explore their own goals.

Retention of clients in treatment is another consideration (DiClemente & Prochaska, 1998). Clients who drop out of treatment have been viewed historically as resistant and difficult. The Transtheoretical Model allows for a different view of clients who are not successful in treatment, namely, that there was likely a mismatch between the structure of treatment and the client's wishes (Norcross et al., 2011). In fact, a client's Stage of Change was a more powerful predictor of who would drop out of treatment as opposed to other variables, such as the severity of the problems, level of education and socioeconomic status (DiClemente & Prochaska, 1998). This research highlights the importance of assessing client motivation and willingness to change when initiating treatment.

Client Progress

Client progress during and after treatment may be understood from the perspective of the Stages of Change Model. Clients who come to treatment in Precontemplation are likely to make the least progress in changing behavior as compared to those in Contemplation or Preparation (Prochaska et al., 1992). An individual's Stage of Change or readiness for change upon entering treatment may be predictive of progress toward a goal of abstinence at the end of treatment (DiClemente & Prochaska, 1998; Prochaska, 1991). A client is more likely to be abstinent at the end of treatment if he or she entered treatment further along in the change process. Said differently, clients who start treatment in Preparation are more likely to be abstinent at the end of treatment than those in Contemplation, and those who start treatment in Contemplation are more likely abstinent at the end of treatment than those in Precontemplation. If clients move at least one stage in 1 month, the client's chances of taking action within 6 months doubles. If the client moves two stages, the client's chances of making change within 6 months is three to four times greater (Prochaska, Velicer, Fava, Rossi, & Tsoh, 2001).

Reframing Denial and Resistance

When clients in treatment for addiction are not successful in achieving abstinence, they have historically been labeled as "in denial" or "resistant." This view puts the responsibility for lack of treatment response solely on the client and sees motivation for change as a trait that certain clients lack. However, it has not been substantiated that client traits are the root of treatment responsiveness or lack thereof (Miller, 1985).

Client behaviors that might be viewed pejoratively as client characteristics that are barriers to treatment progress are reframed using this model. Instead of seeing clients as in denial, clients are seen as lacking information or awareness of a problem. Therapists can help to educate clients about their problems and their impact without needing to view them as disconnected from reality. Resistance is not seen as a specific trait that clients possess but rather as an issue with client motivation. Therapists may then more easily explore factors that are impeding client willingness to change from a nonjudgmental perspective. Reframing client behaviors in this way is useful to both client and therapist as it removes unhelpful judgment from the therapy room.

SUMMARY

The Transtheoretical Model of the Stages of Change is the most widely researched conceptualization of the change process for people working at recovery from addiction. Assessing client motivation for change is an essential component of effective treatment. A client's current Stage of Change will inform treatment decisions to help make them more relevant and useful for the individual. Therapists need to continue to explore how to best meet the needs of clients in various stages of change by designing different kinds of interventions.

In this chapter, the authors discussed the Transtheoretical Model in detail. We have reviewed the Stages of Change, the levels of change, and the processes of change. Research was presented to substantiate the utility of this model for a variety of presenting concerns. Finally, we discussed how the Stages of Change Model provides a useful perspective to guide interventions with clients.

LEARNING POINTS

1. The Stages of Change Model developed by Prochaska and DiClemente is one of many models of behavior change in the field of psychotherapy. However, this model is the one that has received the most attention in research and is most often used to describe the experience of behavior change for those with addictions.
2. The model was originally developed with four stages: Precontemplation, Contemplation, Action, and Maintenance. Preparation was added later. These stages were each described in detail.
3. Clients enter Relapse and Recycling following a return to old behaviors. They must then make a decision whether or not to reengage in the process of changing. Although Relapse is not a formal stage in the model, it is critical to understand how it impacts clients.
4. There are 10 change processes that clients use more frequently as they progress further in treatment.
5. Five levels of change are described; clients can change in various ways. Therapists need to ensure that they are working on the same level of change as the client.
6. Treatments need to be matched to client motivation if they are to be effective. Many interventions only target clients who are in Action. The majority of clients with addictions who enter treatment are not in this stage.

CHAPTER 4

TRAUMA

In this chapter, the authors review basic definitions and concepts related to trauma and posttraumatic stress disorder (PTSD). Clinicians must be aware of the differences between trauma and diagnoses in the *Diagnostic and Statistical Manual of Mental Disorders,* 5th edition (*DSM-5*) related to the effects of trauma. Many people experience traumatic events in their lives without developing long-term symptoms or diagnoses. After reviewing potentially traumatic events (PTEs), the authors describe the physiological and psychological effects of trauma and current evidence-based treatments. The chapter closes with an exploration of the connection between trauma and addiction.

DEFINITIONS OF TRAUMA

Trauma has been defined in various ways. It can be viewed as a general assault on the body connected to

1. "An agent, force, or mechanism that causes harm" (Merriam-Webster Dictionary, 2013b); or
2. "A serious injury or shock to the body" (Free Dictionary by Farlex, 2013).

Psychological trauma connotes a more specific reference to an event that can cause psychological problems. The Free Dictionary (Free Dictionary by Farlex, 2013) includes these in its definitions of trauma:

1. "An emotional wound or shock that creates substantial, lasting damage to the psychological development of a person."
2. "An event or situation that causes great distress and disruption."

Experts in the field of Eye Movement Desensitization and Reprocessing (EMDR) treatment make the distinction between "Big T" and "small t" traumas. "Big T" traumas are those that are typically considered very traumatic, such as combat, sexual assault, and natural disasters. "Small t" traumas are events that are linked more uniquely to an individual's history. These events are more everyday experiences (such as being criticized by a teacher in front of a class) that cause the individual distress at the time and may play an active part of an individual's negative self-concept. Usually "small t" traumas are a series of events that make up a larger picture of distress for the individual. Both "Big T" and "small t" traumas may have lasting impact on an individual. Although "small t" traumas can cause symptoms of PTSD, "Big T" traumas are required in order to meet formal diagnostic criteria for PTSD (Shapiro, 2007a, 2012).

Traumatic Events That Can Lead to PTSD

Houston, Shevlin, Adamson, and Murphy (2011) reported that an estimated 50% to 70% of people in the United States experience at least one traumatic event in their lifetime. One tenth of those who endure a life-threatening PTE will develop either PTSD or another psychiatric disorder (Kessler, Sonnega, Bromet, Hughes, & Nelson, 1995; Kessler et al., 2005). In the National Comorbidity Study, 7.8% of the U.S. population met criteria for PTSD (Kessler et al., 1995). Rates of PTSD vary based on numerous factors such as the type of PTE that is experienced as well as characteristics of the individual.

Listed below are a variety of PTEs that may cause a person to develop PTSD.

1. Interpersonal violence: violence of one person against another, whether mass violence (Briere & Scott, 2006; Cerdá et al., 2012) or individual assault (Lauritsen & Heimer, 2008)
2. Natural disasters: an environmental event that impacts a large number of people and causes harm (Briere & Elliott, 2000; Briere & Scott, 2006; Nygaard & Heir, 2012)
3. Domestic violence or intimate partner violence: physical, sexual, and psychological maltreatment of one partner against another in both gay and straight relationships (Barber, 2008; Begun et al., 2003; Douglas & Hines, 2011; Scott & Babcock, 2010; Tesch, Bekerian, English, & Harrington, 2010; Tsui, Cheung, & Leung, 2010)
4. Child abuse/neglect: Mistreatment of children can take many forms, including physical, emotional, and sexual abuse and can have long-lasting effects (Baz & Wang, 2012; Boden, Horwood, & Fergusson, 2007; Briere & Scott, 2006; Felitti & Anda, 2010; Finkelhor, 2009).
5. Transportation accidents: accidents that occur during travel and include large-scale accidents such as airplane or train accidents (Handley, Salkovskis, Hackmann, & Ehlers, 2009) and motor vehicle accidents (Beck & Coffrey, 2007; Buckley, 2007; Kupchik et al., 2007)
6. War: traumatic events that occur during national or international conflicts, including combat (Andreasan, 2010; Ben-Ezra, 2011; Eagan Chamberlin, 2012; Howard, 2007; Phillips et al., 2010), torture (Hardi & Kroo, 2011), and being a refugee (Ter Heide, Mooren, Kleijn, de Jongh, & Kleber, 2011)
7. Work as a first responder: police, firefighters, or emergency medical personnel (Chopko & Schwartz, 2009; Marmar et al., 2006)
8. Heart attacks/stroke: experiencing an acute health crisis (Edmondson et al., 2012, 2013)

Survivor Variables That Affect the Development of PTSD

Characteristics of the person who experiences the trauma influence his or her response. Some of the factors include:

1. Gender: Although men experience more PTEs, women have higher rates of PTSD (Ditlevsen & Elklit, 2012; Tolin & Foa, 2008).
2. Age: Due to the effects of the aging process that create physical and cognitive vulnerability, children, adolescents, and older adults are at greater risk for PTSD (Hiskey, Luckie, Davies, & Brewin, 2008; ; Koenen, 2006; Koenen et al., 2008; Koenen, 2006; Pervanidou, 2008; Taylor & Weems, 2009; van Veen et al., 2013).
3. Intelligence: Individuals of lower intelligence are more likely to develop PTSD as they have fewer coping resources (Breslau, Chen, & Lou, 2013; Macklin et al., 1998).
4. Socioeconomic status (SES): Individuals of lower SES have fewer resources and experience more criminal activity in their neighborhoods, making them more vulnerable to PTSD (Ben-Porat, Boaz Yablon, & Itzhaky, 2013).
5. Previous psychiatric disorders: Those with a preexisting psychiatric disorder are more at risk for PTSD as coping ability may be compromised by premorbid symptoms (Breslau, 2002, Hapke, Schumann, Rumpf, John, & Meyer, 2006).
6. Previous trauma exposure: Those who have experienced trauma previously are more at risk for developing PTSD in a current trauma even if the past event did not result in PTSD (Breslau, Chilcoat, Kessler, & Davis, 1999; Neuner et al., 2004; Weber et al., 2008).
6. Subjective distress during the trauma: Those who react with greater distress while the trauma is happening are more likely to develop PTSD afterward (O'Hare, Sherrer, & Shen, 2006).
7. Having a more reactive premorbid physiology: If someone is more easily physiologically aroused before a trauma, he or she will likely react more intensely to a traumatic situation, creating greater subjective distress (Jovanovic & Ressler, 2010; Linehan, 1993a; Tyagi et al., 2013).

These variables contribute to a higher or lower chance of developing PTSD.

Characteristics of the Traumatic Situation

There are also factors related to the traumatic situation itself that will influence the likelihood that someone will develop PTSD. Some of these situational features include:

1. Interpersonal violence: This type of trauma contributes to higher rates of PTSD as it is a personal attack on someone by another individual (Briere & Scott, 2006; Harding & Helweg-Larsen, 2009; Iverson et al., 2011).
2. Experiencing physical injury during the trauma: Physical injury during the trauma may make an individual more vulnerable to PTSD, depending on how the injury is managed (Holbrook, Galarneau, Dye, Quinn, & Dougherty, 2010).
3. The extent of combat exposure: Those individuals who have greater amounts of combat exposure are more likely to develop PTSD (Osório et al., 2013).

4. Witnessing death or fearing one's own death: Situations in which an individual sees someone else die or fears his or her own death are more likely to lead to PTSD (Hughes et al., 2011).
5. Death of a loved one or friend during the trauma: Witnessing the death of someone known personally contributes to the development of PTSD at higher rates (Hughes et al., 2011).
6. Sexual victimization: Sexual victimization (i.e., sexual abuse in childhood or sexual assault) has been identified as a stressor that more likely leads to PTSD as compared to other types of violence (Cortina & Kubiak, 2006; Tolin & Foa, 2008).

These situational characteristics contribute to higher rates of PTSD and should be considered in evaluating a survivor of a traumatic event.

Effects of Trauma

The effects of trauma are multiple. It is important to consider how people are affected physiologically and psychologically as well as how long lasting these effects might be. Below is a brief exploration of these issues.

Brain

Understanding the relationship between upper and lower brain systems is critical when considering the effects of trauma. Reactions to the traumatic event start in subcortical areas where the amygdala (a component of the limbic system) activates the autonomic nervous system and the fight/flight response (Steenkamp, van der Walt, Schoeman-Steenkamp, & Strydom, 2012). As stress increases, the cerebral cortex becomes increasingly overwhelmed and higher order thought processes are less and less available to the person. The individual's capacity to think abstractly and to organize behavior becomes compromised (Ogden, Minton, & Pain, 2006). In the height of a traumatic situation, the functioning of the cerebral cortex, hippocampus (memory storage), and the thalamus (connecting sensory information to the upper regions of the brain) become extremely compromised, as the individual is more in "survival mode" due to heightened activation of the amygdala (Bergmann, 2012; Kimble, 2007; Olszweksi & Varrassee, 2005; van der Kolk, 1996).

Trauma may result in changes in brain structure and function with specific emphasis on areas in the limbic system, including the hippocampus and amygdala (Kimble, 2007; van der Kolk, 1994). The amygdala, the part of the brain that automatically perceives threat, can be changed through trauma, either activating a warning when no danger is present or failing to adequately give warning in dangerous situations (Bergmann, 2012; van der Kolk, 1996). The hippocampus, wherein our memories are stored, has been found to be smaller in those with PTSD (Lindauer, Olff, van Meijel, Carlier, & Gersons, 2006). The thalamus, usually responsible for passing sensory information to upper brain structures, may be dysregulated and contribute to dissociative responses to any events that trigger memories of the trauma (Kimble, 2007).

Body

The body's other major communication system is the endocrine or hormonal system, also known as the hypothalamic–pituitary–adrenal (HPA) axis and the adrenergic system. Hormones are primarily regulated by the hypothalamus in the brain. This system releases chemicals that affect tissues in different parts of the body (Martin, 2013). Although this system is slower and less precise, it can still exert a powerful effect on the individual (Bergmann, 2012). When a traumatic situation occurs, the hypothalamus activates hormones (Mehta & Binder, 2012).

Adrenaline (aka epinephrine) contributes to the arousal of the sympathetic nervous system, increasing heart rate, breathing rate, and activating other body systems so that there is a surge of energy to deal with the situation (Martin, 2013). If the situation is over quickly, the body slowly returns to baseline. However, if the situation continues for a long time, this flow of adrenaline can lead to a person being in hyperarousal. When people experience PTSD, triggers of their trauma can activate this system, leading the person to be frequently in that state and to experience other symptoms of heightened physiological activation such as nightmares, dissociation, and aggression (Briere & Scott, 2006). There may be some benefit in treating nightmares and other symptoms of hyperarousal with Prazosin, a blood pressure medication (Raskind et al., 2013).

Noradrenaline (norepinephrine) is the hormonal system that balances out adrenaline and attempts to calm the body after activation. After a stressor, this hormone will work to decrease the heart and breathing rates as well as other bodily systems to help decrease activation. However, if too much of this hormone is released, it can lead to feelings of fear and helplessness. In the extreme situations, this oversupply of norepinephrine can lead to dissociation (Boriskin, 2004).

Cortisol is a hormone that is also activated by stress or trauma. This hormone supports the functioning of the immune system and the body's ability to respond to stress (Briere & Scott, 2006). During a trauma, higher cortisol levels impair the functioning of the hippocampus and access to memory (Kimble, 2007). Yehuda et al. (1990) found that trauma survivors have lower levels of this hormone, contrary to the prevailing belief that they would have higher levels. It is postulated that chronic trauma wears the body down. Cortisol dysregulation may contribute to chronic health problems such as high blood pressure, weight gain, and a reduced ability to fight infection (Bergmann, 2012; Briere & Scott, 2006).

The stomach is another area that is affected by stress. When danger is sensed, the stomach will produce extra serotonin. This can be experienced as queasiness or "butterflies in the stomach." When someone faces a trigger of trauma, the stomach can react in this way and give them false messages of danger (Boriskin, 2004).

Psychological

Many therapists believe that if someone has been through a trauma, he or she has PTSD but that is not necessarily the case. People can experience psychological trauma and not develop long-lasting effects. In addition, individuals may also have lasting effects of a trauma but not meet full criteria for PTSD. Clients can also experience other psychiatric diagnoses as a result of trauma, such as generalized anxiety disorder, panic disorder, or major depression (Briere &

Scott, 2006). Clinicians need to be considerate of client symptoms to determine the most accurate diagnosis. Accurate diagnosis drives appropriate treatment.

Some protective factors may help prevent individuals who have been traumatized from experiencing major life disruption or developing PTSD. Certain variables, such as balanced psychological functioning, higher intelligence, and fewer life stressors may serve to buffer the individual from developing PTSD (King et al., 2012). There are certain qualities that an individual possesses that effect his or her reactions during or after a traumatic event that make them less likely to develop PTSD. These include a problem-solving coping response to the event, increased belief in one's ability to deal with stress (self-efficacy), positive social support, and viewing symptoms or the traumatic event as less disruptive to one's life (King et al., 2012).

Resilience has been studied as a factor in how people can manage major stresses and respond in ways that promote growth in themselves and their relationships. Posttraumatic growth (PTG) connotes positive changes that occur in someone's psychological makeup as a result of a traumatic event (Moran, Schmidt, & Burker, 2013). Some of the possible positive changes include a greater appreciation for life and an openness to new possibilities, an increase in spirituality, and a greater sense of personal strength (Calhoun & Tedeschi, 2004; Tedeschi & Calhoun, 1995). People who experience PTG have been found to possess the following five character traits (Peterson, Park, Pole, D'Andrea, & Seligman, 2008):

1. Interpersonal skills (such as humor, kindness, and social intelligence)
2. Cognitive skills (creativity, curiosity, and willingness to learn)
3. Fortitude (bravery, honesty, and the ability to have perspective)
4. Temperance (fairness, forgiveness, and prudence)
5. Transcendence (gratitude, hope, and religiousness)

In short, a clinician cannot assume that trauma equals PTSD or significant distress in someone's life. Some people will have preexisting elements of their personality that will buffer them from the effects of the trauma. Others have personality characteristics that will allow them to experience PTG. The clinician should listen carefully not only to the history of trauma but also the individual's response.

THE *DIAGNOSTIC AND STATISTICAL MANUAL OF MENTAL DISORDERS, 5TH* EDITION (*DSM-5*)

The *DSM*-5 defines PTSD as resulting from a person experiencing, witnessing, or learning about actual or threatened death, serious injury, or sexual violence. As a result of the trauma, the person then experiences the following in order to receive the diagnosis:

1. At least one intrusion into awareness of trauma-related material. This could include distressing memories, dreams, or intense reactions to events or stimuli that remind the person of the trauma
2. At least one manifestation of avoidance of memories/feelings/thoughts or external situations that are reminders of the trauma

3. At least two changes in thoughts or mood including lack of memories of the events, a shutting down of emotions or feelings of being connected to others, and/or negative beliefs about self
4. At least two changes in reactivity including difficulties with sleep, concentration, increased hypervigilance, and/or an exaggerated startle response

For a full review of the diagnosis, the reader is directed to the *DSM-5* (American Psychiatric Association [APA], 2013).

In the first few days after an individual experiences a traumatic event, he or she may find that life is disrupted in many ways, including thinking repetitively about the event, experiencing intense emotions, or having difficulty concentrating. No diagnosis is given to an individual during the first few days after trauma as most people will have some symptoms. The following are the diagnostic categories that are given based on the amount of time since the traumatic event:

1. Acute stress disorder (ASD): Symptoms are similar to PTSD but the duration is 3 to 30 days after the traumatic event
2. Acute PTSD: Symptoms last up to 3 months after the trauma
3. Chronic PTSD: Symptoms last more than 3 months after the trauma. This also includes "with delayed expression," meaning that someone does not have any or all symptoms until at least 6 months after the event (APA, 2013).

As previously noted, not everyone who experiences a trauma will develop PTSD. It is important to understand a similar relationship between PTSD and ASD. Some people who develop ASD will no longer be symptomatic after 30 days. About 80% of clients who meet the criteria for ASD will have PTSD 6 months later and approximately 70% will still have PTSD 2 years after the original traumatic event (Bryant & Harvey, 2000). Additionally, there can be people who do not initially have symptoms (and do not meet criteria for ASD) but who eventually meet criteria for PTSD.

People who are exposed to one trauma are more likely to experience multiple traumas (Kessler, 2000). People who experience multiple forms of trauma at a young age (such as sexual abuse in childhood) or sustained episodes of trauma (such as torture or genocide) may be said to have "complex trauma" that may develop into complex PTSD (Cloitre et al., 2011; Herman, 1992; van der Kolk et al., 2005). Complex PTSD or disorders of extreme stress not otherwise specified (DESNOS) are specific manifestations of PTSD and complicate individuals' constellation of symptoms as well as their healing process.

Dissociation

One of the possible results of trauma is the rupture of an individual's identity; the end result may be dissociation. Dissociation has been defined as "a disruption or discontinuity in the normal integration of consciousness, memory, identity, emotion, perception, body representation, motor control and behavior" (APA, 2013, p. 291). In other words, traumatic events can be pushed completely out of conscious awareness as the person tries to deal with the intense pain of the experience. Anxiety, avoidance of reminders of the trauma, and even conversion reactions, where the stress associated with the trauma is transformed into physical symptoms (such as seizures or paralysis), may occur (Forgash & Knipe, 2008). Manifestations of dissociation may affect an individual's behavior, affect, sensation, or knowledge, leading to memory loss or the individual feeling disconnected from his or her environment (Braun, 1989).

One may think of dissociation as a protective mechanism that keeps the person from being overwhelmed by the situation (Steinberg & Schnall, 2001). For example, when an individual is abused as a child, he or she may feel anger about what is happening and want to run away. However, because running away is not an option for most children, the child may use the only mechanism available to keep from being overwhelmed by emotions and push these feelings and memories out of awareness by dissociating (Forgash & Knipe, 2008).

People who are dissociating may lose awareness of the world around them for brief or lengthy periods of time (Steinberg & Schnall, 2001). This can cause significant problems in that the person may not be able to remember people, places, or experiences. Others may think that the person is lying or just being difficult. One of the goals of treatment for clients who dissociate is to help them to identify what is triggering a dissociative reaction and to teach skills to regulate emotions in order to avoid the need to "blank out" (Forgash & Knipe, 2008; Steinberg & Schnall, 2001).

van der Hart, Nijenhuis, and Steele (2006) developed a theory of structural dissociation. These authors identified various levels of dissociative experiences that can affect the functioning of the individual. The individual experiences a split in conscious awareness as a result of the trauma. In order to cope, the person develops an "emotional part" of self (EP) that hold the effects of trauma and an "apparently normal part of self" (ANP) that helps the individual function in everyday life. In primary dissociation, the person has one EP and one ANP. In secondary dissociation (also known as DESNOS), the individual possesses more than one EP and one ANP. In tertiary dissociation, the individual has two or more ANPs and two or more EPs, resulting in dissociative identity disorder. As individuals are classified on this continuum from primary to tertiary dissociation, their symptoms become more severe and are more disruptive in their lives as their level of dissociation increases.

If not effectively understood and treated, dissociation can be an impediment. If a client does not have good emotion regulation skills, he or she may reflexively utilize dissociation to deal with painful feelings and topics (Steele & van der Hart, 2009). If a person has secondary or tertiary dissociation, other parts of the personality may not like the focus of treatment and may block the efforts of the therapist (Forgash, 2008; Forgash & Knipe, 2008). In addition, some parts of self may hold awareness of aspects of a trauma that go unprocessed if these parts are not included in the reprocessing of trauma, making treatment incomplete (van der Hart, Groenendijk, Gonzalez, Mosquera, & Solomon, 2013).

Evidence-Based Treatments for PTSD

In recent years, there has been significant emphasis on the use of "evidence-based" treatment although confusion about the meaning of this term continues to exist. Many clinicians believe that evidence-based treatment means following a rigid and structured approach (i.e., a manual). In reality, evidence-based treatment is "the integration of the best available research with clinical expertise in the context of patient characteristics, culture, and preferences" (APA, 2005, p. 1). Some of the evidence-based treatments for PTSD include prolonged exposure (Foa, Hembree, & Rothbaum, 2007); cognitive processing therapy (Resick & Schnicke, 1996); EMDR (Foa, Keane, Friedman, & Cohen, 2009); and Acceptance and Commitment Therapy (ACT; Hayes, Strosahl, & Wilson, 2012).

All of these clinical approaches have been shown to be effective in treating clients with trauma. However, the authors choose to use EMDR as a primary form of treatment for two reasons. First, we have found that clients are able to move through the reexperiencing of trauma more rapidly and with less distress when using EMDR as compared to other methods. Second, EMDR can be applied to treating both trauma and addiction. Most other forms of trauma treatment are applicable only for the traumatic event with ACT being the only other method that can address both disorders.

The Trauma/Addiction Connection

There is a high incidence of trauma in individuals with substance use disorders who seek treatment (Peirce, Kindbom, Waesche, Yuscavage, & Brooner, 2008). About 22% to 43% of people living with PTSD will at some point in their lifetime have a substance use disorder; rates as high as 75% have been found in veterans (Jacobsen, Southwick, & Kosten, 2001). More than two thirds of people seeking treatment for a substance use disorder report one or more traumatic life events (Back et al., 2000; Clark, Masson, Delucchi, Hall, & Sees, 2001; Wasserman, Havassy, & Boles, 1997). People who actively use substances are two to three times more likely to have witnessed a serious injury or deaths of others as compared to the general population (Cottler, Nishith, & Compton, 2001; Kessler et al., 1995). More than two thirds of people who seek treatment for substance use disorders report experiencing one or more traumatic life events (Back et al., 2000; Clark et al., 2001; Wasserman et al., 1997).

Trauma is also at the root of many behavioral addictions such as gambling (Petry & Steinberg, 2005), sex addiction (Carnes, 1991), food addictions (Kong & Bernstein, 2009), and Internet/gaming addiction (Schimmenti & Caretti, 2010). Individuals with these addictions often have histories of untreated trauma from childhood or other more recent life experiences (Miller, 2012).

Therapists must consider how trauma is contributing to an individual's symptoms because trauma and addiction are often connected. Clients with untreated trauma may have greater difficulty maintaining sobriety as well as greater difficulty in healing from trauma (Ford, Hawke, Alessi, Ledgerwood, & Petry, 2007; Peirce et al., 2008; Schumacher, Coffey, & Stasiewicz, 2006). The challenge is to determine when and how to address each of these disorders. These important questions are addressed later in the book (see Chapter 12, Treating Comorbid Trauma and Addiction with EMDR Therapy).

SUMMARY

In this chapter, we have explored the definitions of trauma and PTSD as well as life experiences that may be potentially traumatic for individuals who experience them. Most individuals who endure a trauma will not develop PTSD. They will process the trauma utilizing the natural process of healing. Although we will not often see these clients in our offices, it is important to not jump to the conclusion that a survivor of a traumatic event is traumatized by it.

We also reviewed individual and situational variables that can make it more or less likely that an individual will develop PTSD. Most of these factors are outside of the control of the individual and yet they can have powerful influence on his or her susceptibility to PTSD. Clinicians should consider these factors in working with clients. Evidence-based treatments were reviewed to guide clinicians in current research-based interventions.

Finally, we explored the biological and psychological effects of trauma and the link between trauma and addiction. Clinicians who work with trauma survivors should have some familiarity with these variables.

LEARNING POINTS

1. Trauma and PTSD are not the same. Many people experience traumatic events and never develop PTSD.
2. Some individuals will develop ASD after a traumatic event but do not then meet criteria for PTSD (after 30 days). In addition, there will be individuals who do not meet criteria for ASD who will later manifest symptoms of PTSD (sometimes years later).
3. Certain characteristics of the potentially traumatic event as well as individual characteristics may make it more likely that an individual will develop PTSD.
4. Even though someone does not meet the criteria for ASD or PTSD, he or she still may be affected by a traumatic experience in an ongoing way.
5. Trauma and addiction are intimately connected. Clinicians who work with addictions must assess clients for their trauma history if they want to provide treatment that is comprehensive and successful.
6. Types of dissociation and symptoms of dissociation were discussed. Clients may come to treatment with a long pattern of dissociating in stressful situations. Clinicians need to be mindful of examining clients for this symptom as it can serve to block effective treatment and recovery.
7. The effects of trauma on the body were delineated. This review demonstrated how trauma can change the body in ways that affect the survivor's behavior.
8. Evidence-based treatments for trauma were reviewed. The authors outlined why EMDR is currently their preferred mode of intervention.

CHAPTER 5

ASSESSMENT OF ADDICTIONS AND TRAUMA

Comprehensive assessment is an important foundation for any treatment. This evaluation is critical to providing an understanding of the client's current issues and guiding the clinician in the development of a treatment plan. In addition, clinicians need to focus on assessment of both trauma and addiction. This chapter provides a brief overview of the assessment process with particular emphasis on the assessment of trauma and addiction. Screening tools that the authors have found to be helpful are recommended.

WHAT IS ASSESSMENT?

Assessment is the evaluation of a client's presenting concerns as well as the contextual factors for those concerns. In this chapter, we focus on the evaluation of trauma and/or addiction. We believe that clinicians need to think about assessment as an ongoing process that occurs throughout treatment as clients and their clinicians continue to collaborate.

ESTABLISHMENT OF RAPPORT (RELATIONSHIP BUILDING)

The clinician's first goal with a client is to establish good rapport. A client needs to experience the clinician as an ally who is willing to walk through the process of change with the client. Trust is an essential component of the developing relationship between client and therapist; clients who feel empowered by their clinicians tend to do better in treatment (Fisher & Oransky, 2008; Manso & Rauktis, 2011).

The therapeutic alliance is seen as critically important in addiction and trauma treatment (Nordfjærn, Rundmo, & Hole, 2010; Ruglass et al., 2012) although some researchers contend that it has less of an impact on substance abuse treatment outcomes (Carroll, 2005). When clients perceive that the therapist is authoritarian or not really listening to their concerns, they may experience more negative treatment outcomes (Moyers & Miller, 2013).

ISSUES PERTINENT TO THE ASSESSMENT PROCESS

There are a number of important issues that should be considered for all clients during the assessment process. With any client it is important to complete a psychosocial assessment that considers the following issues.

Referral

It is important to consider the way that a client has been referred to you. If you know the referral source, you may have greater confidence that the person referring the client has a good understanding of your practice and skills. Clients who are coming voluntarily are much more likely to be internally motivated, open to forming a relationship, and motivated to change (Martin et al., 2003; Moore, Tambling, & Anderson, 2013; O'Hare, 1996).

Presenting Problems and Symptoms

What does the client indicate as the chief reason for coming to treatment? It is important to assess the client's major symptoms as well as reasons for coming for help.

Mental Status

It is critical to conduct some form of a mental status examination for clients coming to treatment. Components of a mental status examination include general appearance, speech, orientation to person/place/date/time, mood, affect, thought process, judgment, and memory. Clients are assessed for hallucinations as well as suicidal and homicidal ideation (Mason, Worsley, & Coyle, 2010; NIDA, 2010b; Pallentino & Lang, 2012). It is important to be sure that the client is alert, aware, and can effectively participate in the assessment.

Client Motivation and Goals

Clients come to treatment for a variety of reasons. Initially, the clinician needs to understand the client's motivation for engaging in the treatment process and his or her desire or willingness to change (Brandon et al., 2004; Cullen-Drill & Schilling, 2008; Harrison & Scarpitti, 2002). This is, of course, a key foundation of this book and the work of Prochaska and DiClemente (1982, 1992).

Prior Treatment

The assessment should include a discussion of any previous treatment that the client has experienced, including the client's assessment of this experience.

Developmental History

Clients should be asked about developmental history. These questions will help the clinician to understand if there were any problems that occurred early in life that may be identified as the foundations for current concerns.

Family Systems Issues

The clinician should assess the client's family history, including family of origin, current nuclear family, and extended family. It is important to understand the role of family in relation to the client's addiction and consider involving them in treatment (Baird, 2011; Davis, 2004; Juhnke & Hagedorn, 2006; Platter & Kelley, 2012; Rotunda & Doman, 2001; Rowe, 2012). A family diagram or genogram can provide a useful way to gather and organize information about family issues (Butler, 2008).

Client Characteristic and Qualities

No two clients are the same. There are many different variables to consider when assessing a client for treatment in general and specifically for treatment of trauma and/or addiction. The following are some of the elements that are most important to consider.

Medical Issues

The clinician should explore the client's physical health status. The *Diagnostic and Statistical Manual of Mental Disorders,* 5th edition (*DSM-5*) diagnostic guidelines for many psychiatric diagnoses recommends that the clinician rule out underlying medical conditions as a source of symptoms (Adrian & Barry, 2003; American Psychiatric Association [APA], 2013). If a client has been primarily involved in an addictive process, he or she probably has not been attentive to healthy living and physical well-being and may require treatment of illnesses such as HIV or hepatitis B or C (Muga et al., 2012).

Culture/Language

Culture can impact the way that a problem is viewed and/or what is seen as an appropriate response to mental health problems or substance abuse (Dias, 2008). Language is also important. It is likely most effective for treatment to be done in the client's native language, as differences exist in how clients relate stories in their native tongue versus other languages (Katsavdakis, Sayed, Bram, & Bartlett, 2001).

Religion/Spirituality

Assessments should also contain information about a client's religious/spiritual background and practice. Clients may struggle with situations that are impacted by their worldview about the meaning of life (Pruett, Nishimura, & Priest, 2007). In particular, it is very helpful for clients in recovery from addictions to have some spiritual foundation for support in this process (Breslin & Lewis, 2008; Priester et al., 2009).

Gender/Sexuality

Sexuality is a very important part of any individual's life. Clinicians need to assess a client's sexual life and encourage discussion of concerns. There are some particular concerns in trauma and addiction treatment that are relevant for those in the lesbian/gay/bisexual/transgender (LGBT) community, as prejudice and stigma contribute to higher rates of mental health problems in this population (Bockting, Miner, Swinburne Romine, Hamilton, & Coleman, 2013; Hepp et al., 2005; Matthews, Lorah, & Fenton, 2006; Meyer, 2003; Morin & Rothblum, 1991; Myers, 2013; Nuttbrock et al., 2010; Roberts, Austin, Corliss, Vandermorris, & Koenen, 2010; Scrimshaw et al., 2013).

Differently Abled Individuals

Individuals with disabilities are at higher risk for substance abuse problems compared to those in the general population (Smedema & Ebener, 2010; U.S. Department of Health and Human Services, Office on Disability, 2010; VanDerNagel, Kiewik, Buitelaar, & DeJong, 2011). It is important to assess the issues around being "differently abled" in this culture.

Veteran Status

Trauma and addiction are major issues for many veterans, especially those who were in combat or were injured during military service (Baker et al., 2009). *Unfortunate Hero* by Evans (2010), a combat veteran herself, may be a useful resource for veteran clients with these issues.

Socioeconomic Status

Socioeconomic status (SES) has a significant impact on health, including mortality rates (Doubeni et al., 2012; Warren & Hernandez, 2007). SES may impact access to care, capacity for self-care, stress level, and a variety of other prognosticators of health.

Defense Mechanisms

Defense mechanisms are automatic unconscious processes that occur in an individual in response to a thought, feeling, or situation in the environment that is seen as threatening (Evren et al., 2012). A comprehensive assessment includes an analysis of these defenses. Certain defense mechanisms play a critical role in maintaining addictions (Connors et al., 2013). Clinicians should listen for denial, rationalization, minimization, repression, regression, and distortion in client verbalizations, as these are common defenses seen in these individuals.

Dissociation Versus Blackouts

A distinction should be made between dissociation and blackouts because sometimes the symptoms look similar. Both involve memory loss and escape from emotional discomfort in the client (Klanecky, Harrington, & McChargue, 2008; Steinberg, 2000).

Blackouts occur when an individual is intoxicated by substance use. When a significant amount of a substance has been consumed, an individual may not remember events that occurred while using. This is a chemically induced period of amnesia (Moak & Anton, 1999).

Please refer to Chapter 4, Trauma, for a discussion of dissociation. Clients may seem to "drift off" in session. They may stare off into the corner of the room or at the ceiling or appear deep in thought. At times, they may simply be reflecting on the topic at hand. However, this behavior may also represent dissociation, losing contact with some aspect of current reality. It is important to understand what the client is experiencing and inquire about it. Utilizing the Dissociative Experiences Scale (DES) may be helpful in understanding a client's perspective.

ALCOHOL AND OTHER DRUG ASSESSMENT

It is critical to understand each person's relationship to alcohol and other drugs, including nicotine. It is also important to understand that each person is unique and that this is an issue that can be quite complicated. If this issue is beyond the scope of your specialization and you have serious concerns, it can be extremely helpful to suggest that the client consider having a complete evaluation by a trained specialist.

Nonuse to Addiction Continuum

It can be helpful to think about alcohol and other drug abuse (AODA) on a continuum.

————————————————————I——————————

Nonuse Social Use Abuse Addiction

During the assessment process, the clinician asks questions in order to develop a picture of the individual and the person's pattern of use. The clinician develops a hypothesis about where the client falls on the continuum of nonuse to addiction. Following the assessment, the clinician may give the client feedback about this. It is also useful to ask the client where he or she feels that he or she falls along this continuum. It may be surprising how accurate a client's self-assessment can be!

Definitions

There are no universal definitions of abuse and addiction used by all clinicians. Please refer to Chapter 2 for further discussion of this issue.

The authors think about these issues in the following way:
There are certain people who never use or use very occasionally. They never get into trouble with their use and can be described as nonusers or purely social or occasional users.

Abusers are individuals who either get into trouble with drugs and/or alcohol or have the potential for getting into trouble. They do something to hurt themselves or someone else. Some examples of abuse might be a person who drinks to the point of blackout and has no memory of using, a person who is irresponsible at home or at work as a result of use, or a person who becomes abusive or angry under the influence of drugs or alcohol.

When a person is an addict, he or she has crossed an invisible line into addiction. He or she has developed a compulsion to use. The use becomes the driving force in life. As one 18-year-old female client stated, "I spent my day trying to figure out how to get alcohol, how to pay for it and how I could use it."

Sometimes there is an overlap of symptoms and it becomes difficult and confusing to determine whether someone is an addict or an abuser. For example, if someone is arrested for operating under the influence (OUI) of alcohol, is he or she an addict or an abuser? This could be a person who had a bad night and a (very bad) lapse of judgment, or this could be a person who has a serious addiction and uses daily.

People can work their way across this continuum and cross the line into addiction. How long this takes depends on the person. In general, the younger the person is when he or she starts to use, the faster the addiction process progresses (Wittchen et al., 2008). There is no way to predict who will cross this line into addiction and no warning signs when it is about to happen.

It is important to note that some drugs cause physical dependency. This means that when the person stops using he or she will go into what is called withdrawal syndrome and will have a physical reaction to not having the drug in his or her system. Many of the symptoms can be quite serious and some withdrawals can be life threatening. For example, heroin can cause a physical dependency and the withdrawal is extremely difficult but usually not life threatening. Alcohol, a legal drug, has a severe withdrawal syndrome that can lead to death (see Chapter 2, Addictions).

Biopsychosocial Disorder

In order to appropriately assess abuse or addiction, one must look at the whole person and the biological, psychological, and social issues that impact his or her use. Each person is unique and will therefore have a unique relationship with alcohol and other drugs.

Biological

What chemical has the person chosen to use? What are its properties? How would it affect most people? Is there a chance of physical dependency? If the person stops the drug, is there a chance of withdrawal syndrome? Is there the possibility of a genetic predisposition or cause?

Psychological

Is the person using to minimize pain? Is the person abusing? Addicted (using compulsively)? What is the person's basic psychological makeup? Is there a mental disorder as well?

Behavioral

What is reinforcing the use?

Social

What is the environment? Is there a family problem or difficulty? Is there peer pressure?

Screening Tools

A formal assessment of addiction is customarily provided by a clinician with specialized training. These assessments may be required for court proceedings, for child custody evaluations, or for work-related issues. However, clinicians without specialized training can supplement their diagnostic acumen in regard to addiction by utilizing screening instruments such as the CAGE Questionnaire, the Michigan Alcohol Screening Test (MAST), and the Drug Abuse Screening Test (DAST).

CAGE Questionnaire

The CAGE Questionnaire was originally developed to screen for alcohol dependence. It has now been adapted to include screening for drug use problems (CAGE-AID). The following four questions comprise this measure:

1. Have you felt you ought to **C**ut down on your drinking or drug use?
2. Have people **A**nnoyed you by criticizing your drinking or drug use?
3. Have you felt bad or **G**uilty about your drinking or drug use?
4. Have you ever had a drink or used drugs first thing in the morning to steady your nerves or to get rid of a hangover (**E**ye-opener)?

An individual's score is totaled up. If someone endorses two or more of these items with a "yes" response, this is considered a "Positive CAGE," warranting further in-depth assessment (Appendix A1).

Michigan Alcohol Screening Test

The Michigan Alcohol Screening Test (MAST) is a 22-item screening instrument that was developed in 1971 to assess for alcohol problems in the general population. It is one of the oldest and most accurate alcohol screening tests available, reportedly identifying dependent drinkers with up to 98% accuracy (Selzer, 1971). Questions on the MAST assess for an individual's perspective on social, vocational, and family problems that are associated with heavy drinking. An individual receives 2 points for a negative answer to numbers 1, 4, 6, and 8; 2 points are received for a positive answer to the rest of the questions, except numbers 3, 5, 10, and 17, which receive 1 point and numbers 9, 20, and 21, which receive 5 points. Number 7 is not scored. Points are added up and the test is interpreted as follows:

0 to 3 = not having a problem
3 to 4 = maybe having a problem
5 and above = probably having a problem

Despite its reported accuracy, the MAST has two major drawbacks. First, it asks the patient for problems over the course of his or her lifetime. In this way, it does not do an effective job in assessing current severity of alcohol problems. It is also much longer than screening instruments such as the CAGE and may not be easily used in some environments such as a medical office (see Appendix A2).

Drug Abuse Screening Test

The Drug Abuse Screening Test (DAST) was developed in 1982 to screen for drug problems other than those related to alcohol (Skinner, 1982). It is a 20-item self-report screen that was modeled on the MAST. The DAST has been found to have good psychometric properties and can be another important component of an assessment of substances.

It is important to be careful if you use these tools. They are very general and sometimes not very accurate. For example, Question No. 9 on the MAST is asking whether the person has ever attended an Alcoholics Anonymous meeting and the individual receives 5 points if the answer is positive. Five points puts the individual in the category of someone who probably has a problem. There is no place to discuss why you attended the meeting, for example, whether you attended with a spouse for support. Unless, explored, a support person could end up assessed as someone with a problem (Appendix A3)!

Comprehensive AODA Assessment

Objective scales may be a very time-efficient way to gather information about a client's drug and alcohol abuse. When the time is available, however, it is helpful to ask a series of more open-ended questions in order to gain a comprehensive assessment of a client's relationship with chemicals. This kind of assessment allows one to obtain a clear picture of the biopsychosocial issues pertaining to a client.

The following is a series of questions first developed at Day One (Drug Rehabilitation, Inc.) in Portland, Maine, an agency for adolescent drug users and their families, when one of the authors was employed there. The questionnaire has been revised by the author. Asking these questions and looking at signs and symptoms of addiction should give you a good idea of what your client needs.

It is important to establish rapport with your client if possible. The better your relationship, the more open the client is likely to be in answering these very personal questions. Initially, you may want to ask questions about more neutral areas of the client's life to establish this rapport.

1. What are you using currently?

   Ask about all the drugs. Keep a list with you, so you won't skip any drug categories. Be careful about your own biases. Do not assume a certain kind of person would not use a certain drug. Refer to Chapter 2, Addictions, for an overview of these drugs

2. What have you used?

   Get a good history of what the client has used in the past.

3. How long have you used?

   Age of first use for each drug is important. In general, the earlier that a person starts to use, the more likely it is that the person will develop an addiction.

4. How did you feel when you had your first drink or drug?

   Observe carefully when the client answers this question. Watch his or her face. Addicts often describe this experience as if it were the start of a love affair (which for some of them, it is).

5. What is the extent of your current use?

   Assume heavy use. Addicts often minimize the extent of drug or alcohol use. If you act like you expect to hear about heavy use, you are more likely to get an accurate picture. For example, ask if the client uses daily or in the morning. If they do not, clients may scoff at you a bit but if they do, they are more likely to tell you.

6. Do your friends use?

   "Birds of a feather flock together," especially when dealing with kids. If you get a picture of a person's social group, it can give some clues about the person's use.

7. Are you close to someone who has a chemical problem?

   This may give you a hint about the environment in which the person exists. Heavy users tend to hang out with heavy users. The individual may also be affected by someone else's use.

8. Have you ever borrowed money or done without to get drugs?

   For a teen, the honest answer to this is "yes." For others it is a sign of a problem.

9. Have you ever received negative feedback about your drug use? From whom?

   Many users go years without receiving or taking in negative feedback. If this is happening it can be a sign of a problem.

10. What time of day do you use?

    Again, assume heavy use. Ask if the client uses in the morning. This can be a sign of addiction, heavy use, or physical dependency because the person may be in withdrawal and seeking to alleviate symptoms.

11. Do you sneak using? Why?

    All kids have to sneak. Many adults, particularly women, sneak as well, and it is a sign of a problem. After all, if it was not a problem, you would not have to sneak.

12. Do you hide stuff?

    All kids hide their use, at least from some people. Some adults hide their use as well and this can indicate a problem.

13. Do you have rules for using? What are they?

    This is a sign of addiction. People who do not have a problem do not make rules.

14. Have you broken them?

    People who have drug and/or alcohol problems generally cannot follow their own rules, particularly over a long period of time.

15. Do you use alone?

    Not everyone who uses alone (for example, drinking a glass of wine when dining alone) is an addict, but a pattern of using alone is a symptom of addiction. Using alone means it is no longer a social event.

16. Have you ever tried to quit? Why? What happened?

    This is the opportunity to assess for turning points, pain connected with use, and the client's motivation to change.

17. Have you ever thought of suicide? Tried it?

    There is a high correlation between addiction, depression, and suicide. This also allows you to assess for depression.

18. How do you feel when you get high? When you are straight?

    If the person is not getting high any more it speaks to tolerance, which is a sign of addiction. Also, if it is painful to be straight it is a sign. Assess for cravings.

19. Have you shifted from one chemical to another?

    If one drug does not work any more due to tolerance, an addict will often add another chemical in an attempt to get high

20. Do you avoid people who do not use?

    Heavy users often feel uncomfortable around those who do not use.

21. Do you know what blackouts are? Have you had any? Memory losses?

    Blackouts are an overdose of alcohol or drugs; this causes memory loss (amnesia). This is a sign of addiction if it is a pattern.

22. Have you done things you were ashamed of when you were using?

    Pretty much any addict has.

23. Who is the most important person in your life?

    This helps determine the kind of connections and relationships the person has; addicts tend to isolate.

24. Do you sometimes use because it makes you more comfortable around people?

    Addicts and abusers alike often use to feel more comfortable in social situations.

25. Do you sometimes use to forget your problems?

    Use of chemicals to manage feelings or to cope can be a sign of addiction or a serious problem.

26. Do you sometimes use to change your mood?

    This is a trick question and helps assess how honest the client is being. "Everyone" who uses drugs does it to change his or her mood.

27. Have your ever felt guilty or bummed out after drinking or taking drugs?

    Those with addiction issues often do or say things that they later feel ashamed about. They do things they would not do if they were not using.

28. Have you noticed you are able to handle more drugs or alcohol than you could when you first started using?

    As addiction progresses, tolerance develops. The individual uses more and more to try to obtain the original effect.

29. Have you ever tried to control your use?

    People who do not have problems do not try to control their use. Conversely, those who do have problems may be able to control their use for a short period of time. This is usually short-lived if a problem exists.

30. Are you having an increasing number of financial/work/school problems?

    Many people are able to hold their lives together even as addiction progresses. If the person is experiencing difficulties in these areas, it is often a sign of addiction or a developing problem.

31. Do you sometimes have the "shakes" or feel anxious in the morning and find that it helps to have a drink or use drugs?

    This can be a sign of physical withdrawal.

32. Do you have a family history of alcohol/drug abuse?

    There can be a genetic link to addiction. In addition, it can be a learned behavior influenced by the environment.

33. What are your interests/goals?

    Probe for changes in these areas and increased isolation. Addicts do not have many interests or goals aside from using. Addicts become increasingly isolated as use progresses.

34. Do you think you have a problem with drugs or alcohol?

    This will give you some sense of how self-aware the person is, how much denial there is present, and what is his or her motivation for change. A surprising number of clients know whether they are abusing or addicted, if they are being completely honest.

35. How honest have you been in this assessment? Somewhat honest? Completely honest?

    It is surprising how many clients will admit they were not completely honest. This gives the clinician some sense of whether the assessment is accurate. You can probably assume that you do not have the full picture no matter how many questions you ask!

It is important to note that the answer to one or two of these questions will not give you a clear picture of the person's use. However, taken as a group, the answers will give you an idea of the person's relationship to chemicals and will help you explore all aspects of the client's life.

As a clinician, if you are open, you will probably have an intuitive sense about whether your client has an addiction issue or a problem with alcohol or drugs in addition to the factual information you gather in this brief assessment. Listen to this. When possible, do a complete assessment.

ASSESSMENT OF OTHER ADDICTIVE DISORDERS

In addition to AODA, it is important to assess for other addictive disorders. These disorders include eating, gambling, sex addiction, and Internet/gaming addiction. Addictions of all kinds have similar elements. However, each of the behavioral or "process" addictions has unique qualities.

Food Addiction

There are three disorders related to eating that are sometimes categorized as food addiction: anorexia, bulimia, and binge-eating disorder (see Chapter 2, Addictions). Treatment of food addictions may require a referral to an eating disorders specialist, especially if the disorder is life threatening. Clinicians are encouraged to be mindful of this in the assessment process.

Food addictions are one of the behavioral addictions for which "abstinence" is not a goal to be considered. Would we tell someone that they can "never eat" again? Of course not! Moderation management or harm reduction is the appropriate goal for these disorders. However, some clients may benefit from abstaining from certain "trigger" foods, such as sugar and white flour.

Cotton, Ball, and Robinson (2003) identified four questions that serve as a useful screen for a possible eating disorder. If a client responds positively to any of these questions, the clinician should plan to further assess eating patterns.

1. Do you worry that you have lost control over how much you eat?
2. Do you make yourself sick when you feel uncomfortably full?
3. Do you currently suffer with or have you ever suffered in the past with an eating disorder?
4. Do you ever eat in secret?

In addition, if there are time limitations, these authors identified a positive response to either of these two questions as most effective in identifying a possible eating disorder:

1. Does your weight affect the way you feel about yourself?
2. Are you satisfied with your eating patterns? (See Appendix A4.)

Gambling

Gambling has many forms. These include casinos, race tracks, underground betting on sporting events through a "bookie," scratch tickets, the lottery, bingo, or Internet gambling. It is important to be aware of the many ways people can gamble.

Men are more likely to have a gambling disorder than are women (Petry, Stinson, & Grant, 2005). There is a growing population of people who are engaging in Internet gambling. It is not known whether access to gambling at home may increase the incidence of gambling problems in women.

Finance issues must be assessed in those with gambling problems. Problem gamblers spend on average $400 per month on gambling, whereas those with pathological gambling spend $2,000 or more per month (Petry, Weinstock, Ledgerwood, & Morasco, 2008). Financial devastation and the concomitant relationship stress is often the impetus for a gambler to seek treatment.

A suicide assessment is very important when dealing with problem gamblers. Gamblers are the most likely of all addicts to consider suicide (17%–80%) and to attempt it (4%–23%; Maccallum & Blaszczynski, 2003); clinicians should monitor the self-destructive urges in gamblers and assess regularly for suicidal ideation.

The Short Gambling Quiz consists of nine questions (see Appendix A5). These are a subset of items from the Problem Gambling Severity Index. If a person endorses two of the items, he or she may be developing a gambling problem. A score of three or greater indicates that the person has a current gambling problem and would warrant a more comprehensive assessment.

Sex Addiction

Like gambling, sex addiction is more commonly found in men than women. The male to female ratio of sex addiction is reported as somewhere in the range of 3:1 to 4:1 (Carnes, 1991, 1998). However, sex addiction is now identified in women more frequently and may have been underdiagnosed in the past. Clinicians need to be cautious to not allow gender bias to cloud the assessment.

Screening for sex addiction can be done with the Sex Addiction Screening Test (SAST; Carnes, 1998). The test consists of 45 items that explore sexual history and practices. Six or more "yes" responses to items 1 to 20 indicate a potential problem with sex addiction. The test also includes subscales of items on the Internet, men, women, and gay men. Addictive dimensions of preoccupation, loss of control, relationship disturbance, and affect disturbance are also identified (see Appendix A6).

Internet/Gaming Addiction

Although it is not an official *DSM-5* diagnostic category, Internet gaming disorder is listed under conditions for further study (APA, 2013). These addicts may devote 8 to 10 hours per day to gaming, leading to the neglect of other activities. As with other addictions, Internet addicts may underestimate the amount of time that they have lost in online activities. Self-monitoring (tracking) of the number of hours per day spent online may be a useful first step in raising the client's awareness of the impact of the time spent on the Internet (Young, 2011).

Internet gaming disorder has also been described as Internet use disorder, Internet addiction, or gaming addiction (APA, 2013). However, excessive use of the Internet for other purposes (such as social media) should not be considered for this diagnosis and research is needed to further examine these other uses of the Internet. Wölfling, Beutel, and Müller (2012) identified the need for a standardized assessment of both Internet addiction and gaming addiction.

The assessment of Internet addiction (Widyanto & McMurran, 2004) consists of 20 items that measure the amount of time that the individual spends online. Each item is scored on a scale ranging from 0 (*not at all*) to 5 (*all the time*). Points are then added, leading to a rating of no problem or possible mild, moderate, or severe Internet addiction (see Appendix A7).

ASSESSMENT OF TRAUMA

Individuals may experience trauma and not develop posttraumatic stress disorder (PTSD). In fact, many people who experience a trauma do not end up with PTSD symptoms (Breslau, Chen, & Luo, 2013). The body's natural process of healing often occurs and, over time, people are able to put the incident in perspective. Some will actually experience posttraumatic growth and be permanently changed for the better by the incident (Moran, Schmidt, & Burker, 2013).

For the purposes of this chapter, the authors will focus on screening for the distress that a client experiences about an incident. We do not often see people in our offices who experience the benefits of posttraumatic growth when they first come in although it is important to be mindful of this possibility and to help clients celebrate when this is the case. It is also important to help clients make meaning of the experience as part of the therapeutic process when that is possible and to foster the movement toward this kind of healing. Initially, our task is to help clients identify how current symptoms are connected to a traumatic incident (or incidents). In this light, we suggest the following assessment tools.

Life Events Checklist

The Life Events Checklist (Blake et al., 1995) is a 17-item checklist that screens for traumatic incidents in the respondent's life. Sixteen items cover situations that are known to be potentially traumatic events and that commonly may result in PTSD (e.g., accidents, abuse). One item asks the respondent to identify any incident other than those listed that may be potentially traumatic.

The checklist does not establish that someone has PTSD or has experienced distress as a result of the different experiences. Hence, it is not a diagnostic measure. However, its value is in identifying incidents that may have affected a client. The clinician's job is then to explore the meaning and potential ongoing impact of the incidents. The Life Events Checklist can be used in conjunction with other measures, such as the PTSD checklist (PCL), to explore the further meaning of the incidents (see Appendix A8).

PTSD Checklist

The PCL (Weathers, Litz, Herman, Huska, & Keane, 1993) is a 17-item self-report checklist for symptoms of the *DSM-IV* symptoms of PTSD. It is described as a measure that may be used to both screen for and diagnose PTSD. It is also often used to monitor response to treatment. There are three versions of the checklist: civilian (measures stressful experiences in general), military (measures stressful military experiences), and specific (measures response to a specific incident). Each symptom is rated as to how bothersome it has been in the last month on a 5-point scale from 1 = *not at all bothersome* to 5 = *extremely bothersome*.

The PCL is scored by adding up the numbers of items endorsed as well as the intensity of the impact (1–5). Total scores will range from 17 to 85 with higher scores indicating greater distress. In order to correlate with diagnostic criteria in the *DSM-IV*, a person must endorse at least one item in Questions 1 to 5 (reexperiencing), three items in Questions 6 to 12 (avoidance), and 2 items in Questions 13 to 17 (arousal) and rate these items as a 3 (moderately) or higher (see Appendix A9). Please note that this checklist is based on the *DSM-IV*. Clinicians will need to adapt its use to *DSM-5* criteria for PTSD.

Dissociative Experiences Scale-II (DES-II)

As we have noted in previous chapters, dissociation (the blocking from awareness of certain information in the present day) is a common symptom of trauma survivors. Dissociation is a process that often occurs reflexively for clients as a method of self-protection, often unconsciously. A client may or may not be aware of dissociation. He or she may even dissociate in sessions when trauma material is discussed or elements of the traumatic experience are triggered.

Clinicians need to be aware of indications that the client is dissociating. Are there major changes in eye contact that suddenly occur? Does the client suddenly stare off into space, begin to stare blankly at the therapist, or seem to look right through you? Do the client's eyes become red? Does the client's voice or posture change when discussing certain topics? If a client does have awareness of the dissociative process or its effects, a self-report tool can be a useful source of information for both the client and the therapist (Bernstein & Putnam, 1986).

The DES-II is a 28-item questionnaire that was originally developed by Carlson and Putnam (1993) to screen for dissociative identity disorder (DID). The client rates each of the 28 items on the percentage of time that it occurs (from 0% to 100%). All of the scores are then averaged to give a total score. Scores of 20 or greater are indicative of some kind of trauma-related disorder with scores of 30 or more suggestive of DID. However, a positive finding on the DES needs to be followed up with a more extensive assessment of dissociation such as the Structured Clinical Interview Diagnostic (SCID; First, Gibbon, Spitzer, Williams, & Benjamin, 1997). (See Appendix A10.)

SUMMARY

In this chapter, the authors summarized many issues pertinent to the assessment process. It is important to obtain a clear picture of all aspects of the client's life and concerns.

Understanding the nonuse to addiction continuum of use of substances is helpful. Some people will be able to use in moderation, some will have developing problems, and others will have crossed into addiction. The clinician's job is to gather information to identify where the client falls on the continuum.

The authors utilize the model of biopsychosocial disorder when assessing a client's substance use. Although there are many models of addiction, this one provides the most comprehensive overview of a client's relationship to chemicals. All aspects of the person's life are explored.

In addition to specific tools for assessment of substance use disorders, other process addictions were explored, including food, gambling, Internet addiction, and sex addiction.

Clinicians also need to assess for the presence of a trauma history. Some clients may not have made the connection between their traumatic experiences and their symptoms. The clinician's job is to determine if they are affected and in what ways.

Comprehensive assessment is critical to the treatment of both addiction and trauma. Clinicians need to be attentive to a variety of variables that are important in understanding clients' experience. By engaging in effective assessment, clinicians can then provide the most effective treatment.

LEARNING POINTS

1. It is important to build rapport with clients and establish a strong therapeutic alliance.
2. A comprehensive assessment needs to include developing a picture of the client's life and symptoms.
3. Although formal addiction assessment requires specialized training, any clinician can screen for addiction. The chapter has outlined ways to screen for addiction and addiction-related concerns.
4. Clinicians should always consider trauma as one possible underlying concern for any client and screen for this regularly.

PART II

CLINICAL IMPLICATIONS AND PRACTICAL INTERVENTIONS

INTRODUCTION

Part II of this book focuses on the practical applications of the theoretical material presented in Part I. A chapter on each of the Stages of Change will be presented where both Eye Movement Desensitization and Reprocessing (EMDR) and non-EMDR interventions will be discussed. Initially, however, some clinical issues relevant to working with clients with addictions will be explored.

THE SCOPE OF THE ISSUE

Approximately 17.5% of all clients 18 years and older who have been diagnosed with mental illness also have substance abuse disorder (Substance Abuse and Mental Health Services Administration [SAMHSA], 2013). About 50% of people in treatment for alcohol and other drug abuse also have mental health disorders (Fletcher, 2013). There is a high co-occurrence of anxiety and depression issues. About 55% of women who seek alcohol and/or drug treatment have trauma and/or posttraumatic stress disorder (Fletcher, 2013).

Often, they do not identify addiction as a chief complaint. They come in presenting with a wide variety of other issues, including mental health concerns such as anxiety or depression, and environmental or adjustment issues, such as job or relationship difficulties. They do not connect that these concerns may be related to or caused by using alcohol, drugs, or other addictive behaviors. In order for the clinician to develop a clear diagnostic picture, addiction needs to be explored and assessed in treatment.

There is both tremendous stigma about addiction in our culture and tremendous denial about the negative consequences of this behavior. There continues to be a moralized outlook toward those with addictions; this leads to labeling and those with addictions being seen as not socially desirable

(Buchman & Reiner, 2009). Many health care providers do not ask about addiction issues and many clients are not forthcoming about the truth of these behaviors. This presents a huge dilemma. In particular, many mental health issues are exacerbated by addiction, and addictions can underlie many physical and psychological issues or make them worse.

Dual diagnosis or comorbidity is "when two disorders occur in the same person, simultaneously or sequentially.... Comorbidity also implies interactions between illnesses that affect the course and prognosis of each" (NIDA, 2010b, p. 1). Individuals with mood, anxiety, antisocial, or conduct disorders are two times more likely to have problems with alcohol or other drug abuse (NIDA, 2009b). In addition, those with drug disorders are two times as likely to have mood or anxiety disorders (NIDA, 2009b). Approximately 6 out of 10 substance abusers have a concurrent mental illness (Volkow, 2007). The most commonly used substances by people with serious mental disorders are alcohol, marijuana, and cocaine in that order (Mueser et al., 2003). Very few people present to a practitioner's office with addiction as a chief complaint. Instead, people present with a myriad of other complaints, including mental health symptoms, stress, difficulty sleeping, and physical complaints.

These clients often understand that they have problems other than their psychiatric diagnosis. They may not make the connection that other behaviors, particularly the use of chemicals, are increasing or exacerbating their symptoms. About 17.5% of all clients presenting with a mental health diagnosis have a concurrent substance abuse disorder (SAMHSA, 2012). The authors believe that in order to deal with the problem effectively, their mental health concerns and their addiction issues need to be dealt with concurrently.

THERAPIST AVOIDANCE

It comes as no surprise that therapists do not like dealing with addictions. They will avoid asking about these issues for a myriad of reasons. Often clients complain about symptoms but do not connect them to addictions. Many do not self-identify as having an addiction problem until the symptoms are very serious. It is easy for a therapist to overlook them.

So why do providers avoid this population? Thoughts and/or feelings that come from the therapist's own historical background or unresolved issues may interfere with being totally objective with clients (also known as countertransference; Weiss, 1994). According to Weiss, a therapist may be concerned about a lack of knowledge about the issues, have unconscious anxiety about his or her own issues, may be avoiding looking at his or her own addictions or addictions in family or friends, or have anxiety about being unable to control the client's behavior.

Stereotypes about addiction are prevalent. Many people believe that certain people cannot be addicted or be substance abusers based on class, gender, profession, or age. It is still widely believed that an addict is a "skid row" drunk, although those diagnosed with severe alcohol problems make up only about 1% of the population (Fletcher, 2013). In reality, there is no stereotypical addict but rather addiction is present in a wide variety of people.

One's own views about who may or may not be an addict may interfere with adequate assessment. For example, a trainer was doing substance abuse education at a large community mental health agency. The audience was full of experienced clinicians who worked with dual diagnosis clients (comorbid addiction and mental health issues) but for the most part they knew very little about addictions. One of the most experienced social workers presented the case of a 30-year-old woman who presented with depression; the clinician was concerned about the possibility of alcoholism. While trying to make an accurate assessment of the client, the trainer asked if the client had ever used any drugs other than alcohol. The therapist was quick to deny this, citing that the client was well educated, smart, and professional. This clinician had never asked about any other drug use. This is an example of how one's own stereotypes can interfere with working with clients. As a clinician, one never knows what a client has used until the questions are asked; even then, clients may deny, lie, or minimize, but one is more likely to obtain an accurate picture if one is thorough in the assessment.

Providers may be overwhelmed by clients who present with addiction issues, particularly if the clients' lives are filled with chaos and unpredictability. These individuals are often devalued and perceived as "second class" citizens. Sometimes this feeling shifts to the provider, who may feel less prestige when working with this population (Weiss, 1994).

These clients may refuse help. This can lead to anger and frustration on the part of the provider and to what has been called "transference hate and rage." In turn, this may lead to more confrontation on the part of the provider, followed by power struggles. The therapist may blame the client for an inability to succeed. Many providers discharge clients when this happens (Shaffer, 1994).

In addition, many therapists may feel personally disappointed if the client is not ready for recovery. If the client reports that using drugs and/or alcohol is a positive experience, the therapist may have a difficult time accepting this (Shaffer, 1994).

Treatment failures follow when countertransference interferes (Shaffer, 1994). Najavits et al. (1995) studied 52 therapists working with 140 cocaine-dependent outpatient clients using a scale they called Ratings of Emotional Attitudes to Clients by Treaters (REACT). They found that many of the therapists had the following emotional reactions when dealing with these clients: anxiety about performance; conflict with clients (including power struggles and manipulation); meeting their own personal needs (such as financial, sexual, and intellectual gratification); and that therapist empathy, tolerance, and affection toward the clients appeared to be moderate but not strong. This study suggests that therapists have stronger negative feelings about these clients than 12-step counselors do and that negative feelings toward substance abusers were common and increased over time. However, overall, most of the feelings reported by therapists toward these clients were positive and included empathy and caring.

WHAT KIND OF THERAPIST WORKS WELL WITH ADDICTION?

Most of the literature about what kind of individual works best with addiction issues involves drugs and alcohol and is about psychotherapists and counselors.

According to Jonker, De Jong, de Weert-van Oene, and Gijs (2000), the therapeutic relationship plays a role in the outcome of treatment. They analyzed 93 patients at four Dutch centers, using an "Interpersonal Checklist." Results showed that the ideal therapist was either a "managerial autocrat" or a "sociable extrovert." The ideal therapist was seen to be female, older, or the same age as the client, with no personal history of drug and alcohol abuse. About 58% of clients said that gender played an important role in treatment. These results are in contrast with the view that the therapist should be warm, understanding, and emotional, and suggest that for some clients at least a confrontational approach may be helpful.

Qualities of the therapist have been found to predict treatment outcome. The therapist's ability to be empathic has been found to be of primary importance. Increased dropout rates and increased relapse rates have both been found to correlate with therapists who have reported to have low empathy (Moyers & Miller, 2013). The therapist's ability to show "intrinsic interest" has been found to be more important than the therapist's "position, technical knowledge or orientation" (Cramer, 2002).

Nordfjaern et al. (2010) studied seven patients and six treatment "dropouts" in Norway to determine positive and negative perceptions of treatment. The authors concluded that both the therapeutic alliance and good social relationships made a difference in terms of successful treatment. The therapeutic alliance was seen as more important than any specific interventions utilized (Nordfaern et al., 2010).

Miller and Rollnick (1991) discuss the importance of a good collaborative relationship between the client and the provider. Important elements include empathy, acceptance, genuineness, and egalitarianism on the part of the provider. Strong therapeutic alliance is described as shared goals and predicts a better outcome. The therapist should be affirming, understanding, and empathic. These qualities have been linked with the strength of the alliance and are seen as part of the healing experience (Moyers, Miller, & Hendrickson, 2005).

Moyers et al. (2005) studied clients who were seen by therapists using motivational interviewing techniques. They found some clients responded well to techniques that did not fit this model of empathy and nonconfrontation. Therapists were able to use confrontation, warnings, and directing the client if the therapist was seen by the client as having good interpersonal skills.

In summary, there is a long-held belief that therapists who are in recovery are better suited to doing substance abuse counseling. This does not appear to be the case. In addition, it appears that some clients do not respond well to a more confrontational approach, whereas others, when there is a strong therapeutic alliance, may tolerate and even welcome this approach. A strong therapeutic alliance may be a key to promoting change in the treatment process.

CONFRONTATION—THE OLD APPROACH

Confrontation is defined as "the process by which the therapist provides direct, reality-oriented feedback to the client regarding the client's own thoughts, feelings, or behavior." This feedback may be given because the therapist is concerned, worried, exasperated, or at a loss as to what else to do (White & Miller, 2007, p. 2).

In the past, there was a widespread belief that it was necessary to confront clients when dealing with addiction. Harsh confrontation emerged in the 1950s and 1960s as the norm in addiction treatment. Synanon was established in 1958 as the first treatment community administered by recovering addicts, and, by the mid-1970s, over 500 programs were modeled on its approach (White & Miller, 2007). The standard approach learned by providers was a hard-line attack on the problem. Providers routinely asked individuals who did not believe there was a problem, due to denial, to give up the thing in life they most valued, something that had provided a positive experience (until it did not any more), and that had been enjoyable. Addiction served its purpose by providing comfort, peace of mind, decreased anxiety, or whatever else its function had been in the user's life. Clients were understandably resistant.

Some clients benefit by a direct approach but it needs to be tempered by compassion and a good relationship with the provider. When the therapist has a good connection to the client, the client may be more open to feedback.

A NEWER APPROACH—OFFERING THE CLIENT A CHOICE

The old models of treatment, although effective for certain clients, were a detriment to many. Most people want self-determination, and newer ways of dealing with addiction offer people a choice about what to do with their lives. This means a provider must come to terms with the fact that some clients may continue addictive behaviors and life-endangering habits despite interventions. The Transtheoretical Model of the Stages of Change developed by Prochaska and DiClemente is the focus of this book and is an example of this kind of process.

A NOTE ABOUT FAMILY INVOLVEMENT

It can be very helpful to involve family, friends, or significant others in this process. Other people may have a clear and accurate view of the issues and the extent of the abuse than the abuser does. Listening to family members' concerns may help the client break down some of the denial that is so much a part of addiction. In addition, family members often unconsciously support the client's behavior, thus enabling the behavior to continue. Becoming aware of this behavior and changing it may hasten the client's progress through the Stages of Change.

A NOTE ABOUT HARM REDUCTION

Most addiction providers support and promote abstinence as a treatment goal. Clients are often ambivalent about this and resist this change. Although abstinence may be ultimately the best course of action, harm reduction is a viable alternative. Harm reduction is described as alternative behaviors developed to minimize the harmful consequences of drug and alcohol use (Marlatt, 1998). Strategies include clean-needle programs for IV drug users to prevent the spread of HIV and other diseases, education about how to use safely (i.e., do not drink and drive), and moderation management programs (Levy, 2007) that help individuals cut back alcohol and other drug use if individuals are not ready to quit. Providers may find it helpful to use some of these strategies with clients.

SUMMARY

We have presented issues about the scope of the problem, therapist avoidance, and what kind of therapist works well with addiction. In addition, we have discussed the older, confrontational approach of working with clients versus the newer approach of offering clients a choice. We have noted the importance of family involvement and harm reduction.

LEARNING POINTS

In this introduction to Part II, we have discussed the following:

1. A large number of clients come to treatment with addiction issues but do not connect them to difficulties in their lives.
2. There is a high percentage of comorbidity of mental health and substance abuse disorders.
3. Many therapists prefer not to work with addiction but it is important to address this issue.
4. Some clients respond to confrontation when there is strong therapeutic alliance but many clients prefer to be offered a choice about when to change their addictive behaviors.
5. Clients do better in treatment when there is a strong therapeutic alliance with the therapist, regardless of the therapist's orientation.
6. Family involvement in addiction treatment may be helpful.
7. Harm reduction is a viable treatment strategy that may be considered, especially early in treatment.

CHAPTER 6

THE STAGE OF PRECONTEMPLATION

I swallowed
Some of the Beloved's sweet
Wine,
And now I am ill.
My body aches,
My fever is high.
They called in the Doctor and
He said,
Drink this tea!
Ok, time to drink this tea.
Take this pill!
Ok, time to take these pills.
The Doctor said,
Get rid of this sweet wine of his
Lips.
Ok, time to get rid of the
Doctor.

Rumi

Rumi was a Persian mystic and poet who lived in the 1200s. Although this is considered one of his "joke" poems, one may note that as far as many centuries back, providers gave advice to their patients that was sometimes not welcome and that patients resisted following, even to the point of leaving treatment. This remains true today. It is particularly important when one deals with addicted clients to pay attention to the therapeutic relationship and how one gives feedback.

This chapter explores the therapeutic issues involved in the stage of Precontemplation. Specific Eye Movement Desensitization and Reprocessing (EMDR) therapy and traditional treatment intervention that are useful in this stage are discussed.

THE WORK OF THIS STAGE OF PRECONTEMPLATION

Very simply put, in this stage of Precontemplation, clients have not yet begun to think about changing and giving up addictive or problematic behavior (Prochaska & DiClemente, 1982). The client may have had some negative consequences as a result of the addiction but the idea of change is not imminent. He or she may have even thought about giving up the behavior but has not thought about it in a serious way. If the clinician asks the client "Are you thinking about changing your behavior in the next 6 months?" and the answer is "no," the client would be in this stage (see Chapter 3, The Stages of Change). The treatment goal in this stage of Precontemplation is to help the client to move to the next stage of Contemplation. Behavioral change is not the focus. Instead, treatment centers around exploration and increased awareness. This is often not an easy task. The Precontemplation Stage may be a long one and some clients may never move to Contemplation.

TRADITIONAL INTERVENTIONS AT THIS STAGE

The goal in the stage of Precontemplation is for the therapist to help clients begin to think about making a change. Interventions at this stage include inviting the client to engage in the process of contemplating his or her use and/or behaviors. Education about the effects of abuse and addiction may be helpful, if the client is open. The therapist asks the client if he or she is open to talk and think about the issue. The therapist must also carefully assess the client's motivation to change. Open-ended questions will reveal more information than questions that can be answered by a simple yes or no.

Motivational Interviewing

Utilizing motivational interviewing techniques may be helpful in working with clients with addictions. Readers are referred to the classic text *Motivational Interviewing* by Miller and Rollnick (1991) as it is beyond the scope of this book to describe this model in great detail. In order to desire change, clients generally need to feel some pain. Most of us resist change and will not do so unless the pain of staying the same is greater than the pain of changing. Although not based on confrontation, these techniques are directive and the therapist works to create some discomfort in the client, which may promote change and increased motivation. The work is based on five basic principles.

Express Empathy

Miller and Rollnick (1991) believe that acceptance of the client leads to change being promoted. It is important to listen carefully and reflectively as well as to understand that clients will naturally be resistant. How many of us want to be told what to do?

Develop Discrepancy

The therapist may point out the differences between what is seen as the client's long-term goals and plans and the present behaviors. The therapist helps the client to connect this to addictions that are preventing the realization of the goals and helps clients to see the consequences of actions.

Avoid Argumentation

This speaks for itself. Do not get into arguments or power struggles with clients. The therapist should let the client decide for him- or herself what the goals are.

Roll With Resistance

Be careful not to push clients to change before they are ready. The therapist must recognize that ambivalence about changing is a normal part of the process and work to help clients shift perceptions about belief systems and behaviors. This is a difficult issue for clients to discuss. The therapist must recognize that the addictive and abusive behaviors have in some ways provided a sense of comfort and/or protection to the client.

Support Self-Efficacy

The client ultimately has the decision about how and when to change. These clients often feel shame and hopelessness. The therapist should always maintain a belief and a hope that the client can change.

Some of the basic techniques recommended by Miller and Rollnick (1991) include:

1. Active listening: This involves carefully listening to what the client is saying and wanting. The therapist may repeat back to the client what he or she has said, paraphrasing the content in order to make sure that what the client has said matches what the therapist has heard.
2. Reflection: The therapist reflects back to the client what has been heard and asks for clarification if necessary.
3. Summarizing: After the client has spoken, the therapist recapitulates what has been said.
4. Tap into the reservoir of doubt: It is important to help clients connect any negative experience to the use of alcohol or other drugs or to addictive behaviors if

possible. Clients often do not make this connection themselves. The therapist needs to pay attention when clients question their behaviors or use patterns or begin to talk about looking for options.

5. Ask before giving advice. Obtain the client's permission to do this.

Educate clients whenever it is possible. Look for "teachable moments" when you can teach about the effects of addictive behaviors. The most important thing you can do is help your clients make the connection between alcohol and other drug abuse or addictive behaviors and the difficulties the client may be having in life. Offer alternatives when appropriate.

WHAT IF THE CLIENT SAYS "NO"?

If the client refuses to discuss the issues, then there is little the therapist can do unless one wishes to engage in a power struggle. The work for the therapist is to relinquish control of the outcome and place the issue and the decisions around it squarely back in the hands of the client.

As treatment progresses, the therapist may help the client raise consciousness around the addiction issues. For example, if the client has difficulty, the therapist may ask, "Do you think that would have happened if there was no alcohol involved?" or "Do you think your drug use played a part in that?" or "Do you think that your gambling contributed to your financial problems this month?" This invites the client to explore the issues more completely.

Some therapists may decide to not work with a client who refuses to acknowledge his or her addiction or life-threatening behaviors. It may not be useful to engage with a client who is physically dependent on drugs or alcohol; hospital detoxification may be a more appropriate referral. Clients who come to sessions intoxicated present a special challenge. Most therapists will refuse to see a client in this state because it is not a productive use of time. It is helpful to talk to clients upfront about this and make it a condition of treatment to come in free of drugs and alcohol.

If the client is making no progress working on other issues or appears really stuck or on a plateau, the therapist may decide to end treatment if the client refuses to consider the idea that addiction or abuse could be part of the problem. As therapists, we need to be careful not to enable our clients by completely avoiding and ignoring the issue. It requires careful, thoughtful skill to decide when to confront and when not to. Avoiding the issue altogether may allow the client to continue with serious and life-threatening behaviors.

EMDR THERAPY INTERVENTIONS

It is probably more conducive to use EMDR therapy in the later Stages of Change, when the client is more motivated to make changes. However, there may be some protocols that would be useful to support the client's process and readiness to engage in contemplation.

Affect Tolerance

This protocol may be useful to help the client learn how to identify and manage feelings that lift up in treatment around other issues. If the client decides to enter into Action, this will be extremely helpful in the future treatment. Addiction has been called a disorder of affect (Khantzian & Albanese, 2008). Many clients struggle with identifying and modulating strong feelings. They often need help to develop skills to tolerate their feelings.

Resource Development Installation

Resource Development Installation (RDI) is an EMDR tool that is used to help clients build ego strength. This can be extremely helpful for any client, whether or not the trauma protocol will be utilized in the future.

Robin Shapiro's Two-Handed Interweave

This is a technique that is useful when a client is expressing ambivalence about an issue. Because ambivalence is so prevalent among addicted clients, this can be particularly helpful (see Chapter 1, Eye Movement Desensitization and Reprocessing Therapy, for more information about how to use these protocols).

CASE VIGNETTES

The following case vignettes give examples of clients in the Precontemplation Stage.

CASE VIGNETTE 1

The Case of the Naïve Therapist

In the interest of full self-disclosure, this author (Abel) admits to having been the therapist for this family. Often we learn as much from our clients as they learn from us and that certainly was the case in this instance. As a therapist new to the field of addictions, it is easy to want to control a situation, particularly one that is seen as dangerous. In addition, many therapists are still trained in the older confrontation model. When I first began to work in this field in the 1980s, that is the model I was taught. It would be years before the Stages of Change and motivation would emerge in the literature and years after that before it became in vogue as a way to practice.

I saw this family over 25 years ago when I was new to dealing with drugs and alcohol, more than a bit naïve and undereducated about addictions. The family consisted of an adolescent boy who was the identified patient, brought to a drug and alcohol agency by his parents' due concerns about his drug abuse and acting out. The family was intact, both parents were still married, and there was a latency-age sister. The agency philosophy was to include all members of the family and to do a drug and alcohol assessment of each member of the family during a family therapy session.

During the assessment of the father, he revealed that he had used heroin in the past. The therapist, believing at the time that all heroin users must be addicts and feeling more than a little anxious, responded by telling him he could not use heroin or any other drugs or alcohol because he was an addict. The session ended and another appointment was scheduled. Needless to say, the family never returned to the clinic.

In truth, not all heroin users become addicts (Zinberg, 1984). In addition, clients do not usually respond well to being told what to do, particularly in the first session when the identified problem is the child, not the parent, and when no therapeutic alliance has developed.

The therapist learned from this situation and realized that engaging the client in a process of decision making may have been much more helpful. She learned to be more careful about meeting the client where he or she was at and to walk through a process of helping the client make his or her own decisions about addictions. Her work became more thoughtful and more helpful to the clients.

CASE VIGNETTE 2

The Case of the Bamboozled Client

Sherry, a 30-year-old single woman, was accompanied to her first session by her father, who reported that he had concerns about her drinking. Sherry was visibly upset that her father was at the session with her and wanted to talk without him. The therapist asked him to leave the session, which upset him a great deal, but he went to sit in the waiting room.

During the course of the initial assessment, the therapist asked the client if she was willing to discuss her alcohol use and she agreed, thus moving her from the stage of Precontemplation to the stage of Contemplation. She had already begun to feel some negative consequences of her alcohol use: negative feedback from her family, difficulty at work after nights of drunken binges. She had no intention of quitting drinking. She felt like she was "bamboozled" by her father into coming to therapy and was not ready to discuss the issue seriously or make significant changes. However, she was willing to talk about it.

CASE VIGNETTE 3

The Case of a Young Adult Marijuana Addict

Henry was brought to treatment by his parents, who were very concerned about his marijuana use. He had experienced some trouble with the law and had a very serious drug-related car accident. Henry identified his issues as lack of motivation, lack of career direction, and his homelessness; he had been staying on friends' couches because his parents refused to enable him by letting him stay in their home. Henry entered treatment in Precontemplation. Despite his difficulties, he did not connect his life difficulties with his drug use. Therapy focused on helping him to do that. When he talked about his problems the therapist asked him questions that helped him see the connection. He quickly moved to the stage of Contemplation and began to think about changing.

These case studies illustrate different outcomes for clients who entered therapy in Precontemplation. If the therapist is careful about how questions are asked and leaves the decision about changing to the client, the client is more likely to change. The client moves to the stage of Contemplation, which is discussed in the next chapter. In addition, the client is less likely to "leave the doctor," and to engage in a process with the therapist that is beneficial.

SUMMARY

In this chapter, we discussed the stage of Precontemplation. Clients in this stage are not ready to think about making a change. The therapist's job is to help the client to begin to consider that he or she may have an abuse or addiction problem. Once the client is ready to think about changing, he or she moves to the next stage of Contemplation. The issue of client resistance and ambivalence was discussed. In addition, motivational interviewing techniques were discussed as well as some pre-EMDR interventions that can be helpful.

LEARNING POINTS

1. The stage of Precontemplation was defined. Precontemplation is the initial stage of the Stages of Change. Clients in this stage have no awareness that their substance use/behavior is a problem and they have no intention of changing.
2. Motivational interviewing techniques were highlighted, including the principles and the basic skills that therapists can use.
3. EMDR techniques useful at this stage were listed.
4. There was a discussion of how to deal with client resistance.
5. Three different case examples were presented.

CHAPTER 7

THE STAGE OF CONTEMPLATION

When a client has moved from the stage of Precontemplation to the stage of Contemplation, this means that he or she is willing to engage, at least temporarily, in a period of thinking about quitting or changing addictive behaviors. In this chapter, we look at some of the pertinent issues of this stage as well as traditional and Eye Movement Desensitization and Reprocessing (EMDR) therapy interventions with clients.

THE WORK IN THIS STAGE

A client in the stage of Contemplation is actually thinking about changing. He or she is not yet ready to make the change but has gotten to the point of mulling over the issues. Why is he or she in treatment? The client has probably begun to experience some pain around his or her addictive or problem behaviors, such as receiving negative feedback from others, physical problems, and/or embarrassment about behaviors (see Chapter 3, The Stages of Change).

Individuals who develop problem behaviors or addictions often do so because it is a positive experience, at least in the beginning. People like the benefits, which may include a sense of peace, relaxation, social disinhibition, or increased energy. As time passes, the person starts to have negative experiences. It is only then that the person starts to question his or her use and behaviors. Howard Shaffer and Stephanie Jones (1989) call these moments when the pain outweighs the pleasure "turning points." They add up to an experience of difficulty rather than pleasure. Often there is one major turning point when the person makes the choice to change. In the addiction field, this is also known as "hitting bottom." After the individual realizes that he or she has a problem and wants to change, it can be days, weeks, months, or even years before the change occurs. In some cases, the person may never make the change.

AMBIVALENCE

This stage of Contemplation is marked by ambivalence. Ambivalence is defined as:

1. "Simultaneous and contradictory attitudes or feelings (as attraction and repulsion) toward an object, person, or action"
2. a. "Continuous fluctuation (as between one thing and its opposite)"
   b. "Uncertainty as to which approach to follow" (Merriam-Webster, 2013a; www.Merriam-Webster.com)

Dealing with ambivalence is a very important part of treatment for addictions and problem behaviors (Miller & Rollnick, 1991). It is a key focus of the Contemplation stage.

Individuals in the throes of ambivalence may look like individuals who have no intention of changing. Even if a client says that he or she is 100% ready to change, there is likely still a part of him or her that remains ambivalent about the change and that part needs to be acknowledged (Shaffer & Simoneau, 2001). Shaffer (1994) postulates that when the individual begins to experience the negative consequences of what was previously a positive experience it sets up a conflict inside the individual. The defense mechanism of denial is developed as a means to manage these conflicting feelings. Shaffer and Simoneau (2001) suggest that a key factor in treatment is not only recognizing the client's ambivalence around change but also directly focusing on it. The clinician raises the opposite of what the client presents as the means to deal with what is seen as ever-present ambivalence. For example, if the client talks about the dangers of overeating, the clinician may help the client look at the positive parts of the behavior, that is, the pleasure experienced. The therapist never takes a stand, never offers an opinion, but allows the client to engage in the struggle. Unlike motivational interviewing where the therapist helps move the client toward what is seen as positive change, here the therapist remains completely neutral (Miller & Rollnick, 1991).

The Stage of Painful Awareness

Often clients are painfully and sorely aware of negative behaviors and the difficulties caused by them. Contrary to what many of us learned in our graduate school programs, insight does not always produce change. A client may clearly be aware of the negative behaviors experienced and yet be unable to change them. This client needs to stay in Contemplation and figure out what the blocks are to making the change. We call this the "stage of painful awareness." This painful awareness needs to be honored as a normal part of the process and clients need support and encouragement that "this too shall pass" and change is possible.

THE GOAL OF THIS STAGE

According to Prochaska and DiClemente (1982, 2005), the goal at this stage of Contemplation is to help clients get ready to move to the next stage, which is Preparation/Determination, when clients begin to prepare for the change. Part of the process is to deal with the ambivalence inherent in all clients. In addition, providers need to continue to educate about the effects of the addictive behavior and the impact it can have on work, relationships, health, and so forth. This allows clients to have the information necessary to make a decision about change.

TRADITIONAL INTERVENTIONS

Interventions at this stage, and all the stages, must be tailored to individual need, as each client is unique. In this stage, individuals are evaluating the pros and cons of changing. Essentially, the client is doing a cost–benefit analysis. Change is extremely difficult for people and the pain of change needs to be less than the pain of staying the same for clients to want to go through the pain of changing. As part of the decision-making process, these clients may also be seeking information. These are people who may be able to make some connection between their use and the pain they experience but are often still very ambivalent about giving up something that has served them well in the past.

Therapists continue to educate about the effects of alcohol and other drug abuse, eating, gambling, or whatever problem behavior the client is experiencing, and the impact this has on the client's life. The therapist merely provides information and does not try to sway the client; the information itself is what allows the client to know enough to make a choice.

Therapists may continue to use motivational interviewing techniques; they need to avoid being controlling and continue to roll with the resistance that is so prevalent in this stage. The decision to change (or not) rests completely with the client.

Imagine what it would be like to be asked to give up something that was extremely important to you, that was the focus of your life and that, until recently, only gave you pleasure. Imagine being confronted by a therapist who was full of facts and rationales for why you should do this. Imagine how you would feel if you just weren't ready to do this yet, even if you could see some good reasons why you should be. Imagine what this would be like and allow yourself as a clinician to be gentle with your clients and be present with their ambivalence.

Cost–Benefit Analysis

This is a very important part of this stage (Connors, Donovan, & DiClemente, 2001). This can be done as a discussion in therapy sessions or it can be given as a written assignment to be completed as homework. It may take some time to complete this process.

Here is an example of a cost–benefit analysis:

Reasons to Continue Drinking	Reasons to Quit Drinking
Easier to socialize	Health problems: stomach
Less inhibited	Negative feedback from wife
Feel more normal as a drinker	Expensive
	Starting to drink in the mornings
	Blackouts
	Missing work, too many sick days
	Less successful at work

Here is another example of a cost–benefit analysis. This one uses a format based on the work of Marsha Linehan (Dimeff & Linehan, 2006):

Stop Drinking	Do Not Stop Drinking
Pro: feel healthy	Pro: party!
Pro: save money	Pro: independence!
Con: uncomfortable	Con: health issues
Con: lose friends?	Con: chaotic life

Dialectical Behavioral Therapy

Dialectical behavioral therapy (DBT) is a treatment originally developed by Marsha Linehan for clients with borderline personality disorder (BPD; Linehan, 1993a). This comprehensive treatment incorporates individual therapy, a psychoeducational skills group, and additional resources (i.e., medication management, skills coaching) to help the client learn self-management and self-regulation skills. The goal is symptom reduction as well as to help clients to build meaningful lives (Linehan, 1993a).

Although originally developed for clients with BPD, there is now a specific DBT treatment for clients with comorbid substance abuse and BPD (Dimeff & Linehan, 2008). Randomized control trials have demonstrated the efficacy of this treatment for this population (Linehan et al., 1999, 2002). Although there is no research for clients who do not have BPD, Dimeff and Linehan (2008) encourage clinicians to consider using this treatment focus for substance abusers who have not been successful with other treatments or who present with chronic suicide ideation (Dimeff & Linehan, 2008).

Some of the components of DBT skills training useful in working with clients in the stage of Contemplation include developing distress tolerance skills. Linehan's (1993a) Wise Mind ACCEPT Skills are a part of her program that could be very affective for those still actively engaged in addictive behaviors.

Wise Mind ACCEPT Skills

Some clients may not believe that they can manage stressors without the addiction. Before beginning to work toward changing behaviors, they need to see that there are alternative coping mechanisms available, which could provide the same benefits. The ACCEPT skills include:

1. *A*ctivities: Clients learn to develop a wide variety of activities, which are used to distract from negative thoughts and change emotions.
2. *C*ontributing: Clients learn to focus on others, rather than self.
3. *C*omparisons: By discovering that others may have it worse, clients learn to develop a different perspective about their own problems. In addition, clients may be taught to compare current distress to a time in the past when they were not managing their emotions as effectively. This helps clients to gain perspective about progress that has been made.
4. Opposite *E*motions: One way to learn to cope with emotions is by replacing the current emotion with one that is less negative. Clients are encouraged to engage in activities that create the opposite or different emotion from the one that they are experiencing.
5. *P*ushing away: Clients learn to push away experiences by leaving physically or by pushing it away in one's mind.
6. *T*houghts: Clients learn to substitute one thought for another, less painful one.
7. *S*ensations: It can help to focus on other sensations as a distraction; for example, holding ice cubes when upset.

These techniques are used to distract from stressors that are causing distress. Clients can benefit from practicing these skills as an alternative to their addictive behavior.

Exploration of the Issues

The stage of Contemplation is largely an exploration for the client. There are many ways to accomplish this exploration, including the techniques listed above. In addition, the following are some ways that may help facilitate this process:

1. Ask the client to measure the glass he or she drinks from, count the cookies, and so forth. This is a reality check that may bring home exactly what he or she is doing and minimize denial.
2. Experiment with a period of time when the client will abstain from the addictive or problem behavior. The clinician may ask for a period of time longer than he or she thinks the client can be abstinent or the client may choose the amount of time. Be sure to let the client know no judgment is involved but that this is a way to learn something in the process. Both the clinician and the client will learn more about the client's relationship to the addictive behavior.
3. Ask the client to spend some time and add up how much money has been or will be spent on the addiction for a certain period of time. This brings home another "cost" of the addictive behavior.
4. The clinician can help the client make the connection between problems he or she is experiencing and the addiction; for example, ask "Do you think that would have happened if you were not drinking?" or "Do you think your gambling had anything to do with that?"

All of the information gathered may be processed as part of the stage of Contemplation.

EMDR THERAPY

Many EMDR interventions are extremely helpful at this stage. The following protocols are useful for almost any client, even if the client has not yet determined to change. In addition, Robin Shapiro's Two-Handed Interweave is particularly helpful at the stage of Contemplation (see Chapter 1, Eye Movement Desensitization and Reprocessing Therapy). All of these techniques would be considered "pre-EMDR" because they all help prepare for work with the standard trauma protocol.

SAFE/CALM PLACE

This protocol helps clients to relax and develop coping skills under stressful situations. The client visualizes a place where he or she feels calm or safe and bilateral stimulation is utilized to reinforce the relaxed state. In addition, clients are taught to use the image and a cue word to help learn to self-soothe and manage anxiety (see Chapter 1, EMDR Therapy, and Appendix B1).

RESOURCE DEVELOPMENT INSTALLATION

This protocol is helpful for almost any client as well. Development of ego-strength and a sense of self-efficacy is an important precursor to successful change. The increased self-esteem, strength, patience, perseverance, or whatever qualities that are installed using this protocol serve to help a client feel more clear and more resolved about making change in his or her life (see Chapter 1, Eye Movement Desensitization and Reprocessing Therapy, and Appendix B2).

AFFECT TOLERANCE

Clients who have addictions or addictive behaviors have difficulty with affect. They have problems identifying and managing feelings (Khantzian & Albanese, 2008). The Affect Tolerance protocol (York & Leeds, 2001) is one technique that can be used to help clients become more able to manage these feelings. Clients develop an image of the affect, a negative cognition, positive cognition, Validity of Cognition, Subjective Unit of Disturbance, identify emotions, and locate the feeling in the body. The goal is not elimination of the affect but learning how to manage it (see Chapter 1, EMDR Therapy, for this protocol and information about how to use it).

TWO-HANDED INTERWEAVE

Robin Shapiro's Two-Handed Interweave (Shapiro, 2005) is an extremely helpful way to deal with the cost–benefit analysis and the ambivalence that is a hallmark of this stage of Contemplation. The client metaphorically puts all of the positive reasons for change in one hand and the negative in the other. The client opens and closes each hand and studies what is in that hand. Bilateral stimulation may be used. The client merely observes the process and notices what is in each hand. At the end, the client discusses what has been learned and what may be the next steps. Please see the examples of Michael and Clarissa at the end of this chapter.

DESENSITIZATION OF TRIGGERS AND URGE REPROCESSING PROTOCOL POSITIVE TREATMENT GOAL

If the client is open to exploring what life would be like if he or she did not use or abuse, then this protocol could be used (Popky, 2005). The client develops a vision of life without the problem behavior; bilateral stimulation is used to reinforce this vision. Most likely, the client would have to be fairly open to the idea of change before this would be of benefit (see Chapter 1, EMDR Therapy, and Appendix B5).

A NOTE ABOUT COUNTERTRANSFERENCE

Clients at this stage may act out their ambivalence in ways that may affect the therapist. For example, clients may cancel sessions, cancel sessions at the last minute, arrive late, miss appointments without calling, end therapy without notification, or "forget" to pay the therapist. This is all "grist for the therapeutic mill" and these are all issues that need to be discussed.

However, these are all things that may be irritating to the therapist. We all know it is not fun to sit and wait for a client who does not show up. Even those of us who are very understanding about the issues may find it difficult when our work or our personal lives are impacted by these clients. It is very important to process these feelings with a peer, peer group, in supervision, or with a consultant. This will help prevent one's own issues from interfering with the work in therapy.

In addition, it is very important to remain patient with such clients. Sometimes these clients have a very slow process. The therapist must keep in mind at all times that the client has self-determination and free will about all decisions. It is also important to remain mindful of the fact that some clients in the stage of Contemplation may never move to the stage of Preparation/Determination and that is their choice.

CASE VIGNETTE 1

The Case of Parker: The Ambivalent Drinker

Parker, aged 51 years, came to therapy because he was beginning to believe that drinking was causing him difficulties and was concerned about his health. In addition, he was receiving negative feedback from his wife of 25 years about the amount he was drinking. He reported that he drank four to five beers daily, followed by a bottle of wine. He experimented with marijuana when he was younger, but he had not used other drugs in the past or now. He did all his drinking at home, never was at risk of getting into trouble at a bar or in the community because he was alone when he drank, and for the same reason, he never received negative feedback from friends. On the surface, it looked like he entered treatment in the stage of Action, but upon further exploration in actuality he was in Contemplation. He wanted to make a change but he was more interested in cutting back his drinking than quitting. He tried to cut back but had a very difficult time, was successful some days, and some days he drank more than he wanted. The therapist explained that sometimes it is harder to cut back than quit. The therapist believed that he was an alcoholic and when she asked what he thought, he said he was alcoholic. The work of Contemplation helped him to decide whether to quit or continue to try to cut back. He engaged in a cost–benefit analysis. His reasons for quitting included concerns about his health, the impact his drinking was having on his marriage, and his relationship with his grandson.

When it came time to list the reasons for continuing to drink, he looked at his therapist and said, "Honestly, there are no good reasons to continue drinking." In that moment, he moved to the next phase of Preparation and began to make for plans for how to quit.

CASE VIGNETTE 2

The Case of Michael: Using the Two-Handed Interweave

Michael came to treatment with the goal of quitting his drinking and initially he was able to do that. He was 54 years old, married for 12 years, and with two young children. He attended Alcoholics Anonymous regularly and used his sessions to deal with relapse prevention. If he had cravings, he utilized EMDR in his sessions by using the Hase/Cravex protocol (see Chapter 1, EMDR Therapy, and Appendix B4). He was able to list and avoid triggering situations, except one. The neon lights on the liquor store were a major trigger for him. He felt like they were calling him, enticing him to come inside to buy alcohol, and one night he did just that. He drank the alcohol in his car, went home, ate dinner, and no one was the wiser. He moved from Action/Relapse Prevention to Relapse/Recycling and then back to Contemplation that night. He wondered if he could actually begin to drink again.

The therapist utilized Robin Shapiro's Two-Handed Interweave with the client. In one hand, the client placed all the reasons he wanted to drink. In the other, he placed all the reasons he should quit. As he opened one hand and then the other, the client looked at all aspects of the issue. He saw himself as having an angel on one shoulder that promoted health and abstinence; the other shoulder had a devil that tempted him to continue drinking. As the processing continued, he shifted to looking more at the angel image (sobriety) and saw the devil image (continued drinking) backing away. At the end of the processing, he decided he wanted to ally with the angel and continue to be abstinent. He moved once again into the stage of Action.

CASE VIGNETTE 3

The Case of Clarissa: Binge Eating

Clarissa, aged 32 years, came to treatment to work on issues connected to her binge eating. Initially, Clarissa appeared to be in the stage of Action but following a long discussion in one therapy session, it became clear that in fact she was very ambivalent and actually in Contemplation about what changes she wanted to make in her life to support eating in a healthy way. She noted, "A big part of me does not want to give up my bingeing." The therapist utilized Robin Shapiro's Two-Handed Interweave to deal with her ambivalence. In her right hand, she placed "I want to eat healthily." In her left hand, she placed "I don't want to eat healthily." As the client processed these issues by opening and closing each hand and contemplating the position in it, she noted, "I feel weaker if I don't eat well. I want to stay longer in the right hand." She was able to move to the stage of Preparation.

SUMMARY

In this chapter, we have reviewed the issues that are salient to the stage of Contemplation. Many clients (and many of us!) do not want to make a choice; we want it all. There comes a time in the life of an addict when consciously or unconsciously a choice must be made...continue the addictive behaviors or move toward health. In this stage of Contemplation the work of the clinician is to help the client grapple with that decision and allow the client to make a choice for him- or herself. The client may or may not move to Preparation at that time.

LEARNING POINTS

1. In this stage of Contemplation the client is thinking about making a change.
2. This stage is marked by ambivalence.
3. It is important to remember that the pain of changing must outweigh the pain of staying the same before a client will change. The moments when a client begins to feel this pain are called "turning points."
4. The therapist remains neutral about change but points out issues that connect the client's behavior and the addiction.
5. The therapist helps the client make a decision about change by helping the client to do a cost–benefit analysis.
6. The therapist continues to educate about addiction and problem behaviors.
7. The therapist helps clients learn to manage affect and deal with stress by offering a variety of techniques in the therapy, including EMDR therapy techniques.
8. When, and if, the client is ready the therapist helps the client move to the stage of Preparation.

CHAPTER 8

THE STAGE OF PREPARATION/ DETERMINATION

By the time a client reaches the stage of Preparation/Determination, he or she is ready to actively explore treatment options. This is a very important stage. What happens in this stage lays a foundation for the stage of Action that follows. It is important to note that a client in this stage may never move to Action. In fact, at any time he or she may move back to Contemplation or even Precontemplation.

This is an active stage. The work in this stage requires the therapist to lay out options and help the client choose from them. The client considers the best options given his or her circumstances and personality.

The authors believe, as stated previously, that there is no one cookie-cutter approach to treatment and recovery. In fact, it may be more helpful to think about a road map: There are many choices about which road to travel and which turn to take. What is chosen depends on one's timetable and needs. The choices may vary widely from person to person. It makes sense that if a client is matched with appropriate services, recovery will improve and rates of recovery may be higher. No one wants to be pushed onto a recovery path that does not feel right or is inappropriate or more suitable for someone else.

THE WORK AT THIS STAGE OF PREPARATION

In this stage of Preparation, clients have made some commitment to change. The work is to set goals and priorities and develop a change plan.

Clients may continue to experience ambivalence. It is not unusual for clients to waffle back and forth between stages. Clients may need to return to the stage of Contemplation.

The therapist should look at the client's previous attempts at change in order to predict outcome. This can be an important part of the learning process for both therapist and client. What worked? What did not work? What could be tried that is different? For example, the authors (Abel & O'Brien, 2010) wrote previously about a woman who had comorbid alcoholism and posttraumatic stress disorder (PTSD). She had made several attempts at sobriety but was unsuccessful. The therapist knew that something different needed to be tried in order for her to be successful. In that case, the client was able to use the Eye Movement Desensitization and Reprocessing (EMDR) standard protocol for trauma to resolve issues around her husband's suicide. Once her trauma was resolved, she went on to a healthy recovery from alcoholism and was able to maintain sobriety.

It may take weeks, months, or even years to move to Action. As stated previously, some clients never get to the point of Action and making the changes necessary to let go of addictions and addictive behaviors.

Clients need to look at what would be necessary to make appropriate lifestyle changes to support recovery. Like Contemplation, this stage of Preparation is one of exploration, but now the client must explore the many and varied resources available and make a decision about which ones to pursue.

The following is a summary of what options are available for clients. There may be other, local options that could be explored in the therapist's community. If a client has previously utilized certain services in the local area and not been successful, it may become necessary to search out more specialized options or treatment centers in a broader geographical range.

TREATMENT OPTIONS AND CONSIDERATIONS

Traditional Interventions

Medication

Appropriate medication supports recovery. This can be appropriate psychiatric medications or medications to deal with cravings. If a client has been diagnosed with a co-occurring disorder (i.e., a mental illness, such as schizophrenia, bipolar disorder, or depression), psychiatric medication may be an important part of the client becoming stabilized enough to get into recovery. A psychiatric evaluation by a physician familiar with addictions and co-occurring disorders would be important. Therapists are cautioned about recommending the use of benzodiazepines and other tranquilizers; while they may provide short-term relief, they are highly addictive drugs. Used in combination with alcohol, they can be life threatening.

There are a number of medications that are available for the treatment of addictions. Historically, professionals in addiction treatment programs have shunned the use of medications as they see total abstinence from all medication to be the only indication of being truly "clean and sober" (LaPaglia, 2011). The vast majority of clients in specialty addiction treatment do not receive the option of medication-assisted recovery (Fitzgerald & McCarty, 2009).

Medications have been demonstrated to provide a helpful addition to addiction treatment (Fitzgerald & McCarty, 2009; Sturgess, George, Kennedy,

Heinz, & Müller, 2011). Three possible results occur when clients utilize these medications:

a. The continued use of a substance becomes a negative experience; or
b. The continued use of a substance no longer creates a euphoric effect; or
c. Cravings for the substance are reduced (Kampman, 2009).

Below is a list of some current medications presently being used in addiction treatment (Fitzgerald & McCarty, 2009; Kampman, 2009):

Alcohol Addiction

Antabuse (Disulfiram)
This interferes with the metabolism of alcohol in the body, leading to a buildup of acetaldehyde. When the person uses alcohol, he or she turns red in the face, becomes nauseous, and/or vomits. Antabuse needs to be taken daily in order to have this effect, so many clients may simply avoid taking it when they plan to drink. Supervising the client in taking Antabuse can increase adherence.

Campral (Acamprosate Calcium)
This drug provides some relief from the physical discomfort (e.g., sweating, anxiety, and sleep disturbance) and resulting emotional distress that people can feel when they are first abstinent from alcohol.

Revia (Naltrexone)
This drug blocks the intoxicated feeling from alcohol and can reduce cravings. It can be taken in an oral form or in a long-acting injectable form that provides therapeutic benefit for up to a month.

Opioid Addiction

Methadone
This is a synthetic opioid that decreases withdrawal symptoms and cravings. It is prescribed in specific dosage levels based on the amount needed to decrease cravings in the client and to block the high associated with the use of heroin or other opioids if it is consumed. It is normally administered at a methadone clinic and requires daily visits (at least initially) for administration. The mortality rate for untreated heroin addicts is approximately 5%, whereas mortality rates for clients on methadone maintenance reduce to about 1.4% (Kampman, 2009).

Subutex (Buprenorphine)
This blocks the effects of opioids. In addition, it can be prescribed from a physician's office and does not require attendance at a special clinic (Orman & Keating, 2009).

Suboxone (Buprenorphine and Naloxone)
This drug is the same as Subutex with naloxone added. The addition of naloxone causes the reversal of the effects of all narcotics in the individual's system. It is sublingually administered.

Revia (Naltrexone)
This drug provides relief from cravings and blocks the high.

Nicotine Addiction

Nicotine Replacement (Gum, Lozenges, Patch, Inhaler)
These medications administer nicotine in a different way than smoking, which reduces the discomfort associated with immediate withdrawal from nicotine. These medications are used in combination with behavioral strategies and have been shown to increase the chances of quitting.

Chantix (Varenicline)
This is a prescription medication that blocks the pleasurable feeling of smoking. It is usually used for 12 to 24 weeks; clients begin taking the medication before their official quit date. There is some evidence of increased depression and suicidal thoughts in those taking Chantix (Keating & Lyseng-Williamson, 2010). Clients and their clinicians should monitor the clients' mood and self-destructive thinking, especially those with a history of these symptoms.

Other Addictions

There are currently no other medications formally approved for the treatment of addictions. However, research is ongoing in this area. Clinicians need to stay current with the latest developments as medications may eventually provide an important component of treatment for any addiction.

Detoxification
Some alcohol and other drug abuse clients may need medical detoxification in a hospital setting or in a monitored outpatient setting. This may be crucial, depending on what drug the client is using. If the client is physically dependent, some withdrawals may be life threatening or extremely uncomfortable. This usually involves a short hospital stay, about 3 to 7 days, although some withdrawals may take longer, depending on the drug. Medications may be used to ease the withdrawals.

In certain circumstances, clients may be able to work with their physicians to complete a medically supervised detoxification on an outpatient basis.

Therapists are not expected to be experts: It is important to consult with medical personnel and to have clients evaluated medically about the possible need for detoxification. This is especially true if clients talk about stopping "cold turkey" or give up drugs or alcohol and start having symptoms. When in doubt, get a second opinion. It is very important to have a signed release of information and be able to communicate with the client's primary care physician around these matters (see Chapter 2, Addictions, for more information on each drug category).

Inpatient or Residential Treatment, Halfway Houses, Group Homes, and Sober Living

Inpatient treatment is less available at this point in history largely because medical insurance is less likely to cover this level of care. Clients may ideally benefit from longer term stays in the hospital, but insurance may cover a few days, a week, or a couple of weeks. As a result of this, clients who are well off financially have more access to these programs.

It can be very beneficial for a client to be in a residential treatment program. These programs offer a safe, drug-free environment where the client may participate in group therapy, individual therapy, and education about addiction. Many programs have family components that include the client's significant others in the healing process. This kind of intense treatment with a safe environment may be particularly beneficial for those with histories of relapse or serious trauma. In addition, group homes and halfway houses provide sober environments for clients who need longer periods of time in a structured, safe environment. In some communities, there are sober houses where individuals rent apartments and live with others who are committed to a sober lifestyle.

Intensive Outpatient Treatment

Intensive outpatient programs (IOP) provide the client with many hours of treatment per week but allow the client to remain in his or her environment. Usually, the client attends for about 4 or 5 hours a day or in the evening. Clients attend group and individual sessions and have aftercare to support ongoing recovery. Attendance at self-help groups may also be required.

Aftercare may also be part of the program. Clients may attend group therapy to support recovery and/or receive individual support.

Self-Help Groups

Self-help groups are groups of peers that come together for the common purpose of recovery. They are not connected to professionals or agencies. There is usually no mental health professional who facilitates the group. Clients benefit a great deal from the peer support and camaraderie they provide. Many individuals feel a great deal of stigma about addiction. This provides a safe, accepting environment where one can socialize with others who have chosen not to use alcohol, drugs, or participate in certain behaviors.

There are many different kinds of self-help groups. Some are not available in all parts of the United States. In addition, some communities may have developed specific types of self-help meetings only available in that area.

Many support groups also now offer electronic meetings. Members may go online for groups, support, and information. This is particularly helpful for those who are too timid to go to meetings or who are infirm or otherwise unable to attend a meeting in the community. Often dual-diagnosis clients, those with two co-occurring disorders, feel uncomfortable at meetings; online support may be particularly helpful for these individuals.

Twelve-Step Groups

All 12-step groups are based on the model first developed for Alcoholics Anonymous (AA), with some variations depending on the issue to be worked on.

Alcoholics Anonymous. AA is a worldwide organization that currently has more than two million members. AA was started by Bill Wilson and Dr. Bob in May of 1935, following a meeting in an Akron hotel. Bill was struggling to stay sober and following this get-together, realized that two "drunks" meeting together could help each other (Robertson, 2000). The goal of this fellowship is for members to share their "experience, strength, and hope" in order to maintain sobriety. There are no fees, only voluntary donations. It is a nondenominational group; however, there is talk about and reliance upon a Higher Power concept, which some clients may find difficult. The structure of the group involves utilizing 12 steps and 12 traditions toward recovery. There are different types of meetings: open, closed, gender specific, and others for specific populations (i.e., gays and lesbians; www.aa.org).

Al-Anon/Alateen. There is a group for family members called Al-Anon that was developed by Lois, Bill Wilson's wife, in 1951. It is also based on the 12 steps and 12 traditions and offers support for those affected by alcoholism. There are presently over 24,000 Al-Anon groups in 130 countries. Alateen is part of Al-Anon family groups; these are meetings specially organized for teenagers affected by alcoholism (www.al-anon.org).

Narcotics Anonymous. This group is based on the 12 steps and 12 traditions of AA but is for those dealing with drug abuse. It was started in 1953, and in 1983, following the publication of its basic text, attendance increased dramatically. Meetings are now available in 129 countries.

This group does not focus on one particular drug but, rather, all of them (www.NA.org).

Overeaters Anonymous and Food Addicts Anonymous. These groups are for those dealing with eating addictions or difficulties. Overeaters Anonymous (OA) is based on helping members develop "physical, emotional, and spiritual wellbeing." The program does not promote any one particular diet and is not focused on weight loss, weight gain, or maintenance but rather helps members to stop eating compulsively.

Food Addicts Anonymous (FA) is a more structured program that offers a specific eating plan. Members abstain from eating sugar and flour, weigh and measure food, avoid snacking, and avoid individual binge foods. There are no phone or Internet meetings because the belief is that attending meetings helps break the isolation that is often part of overeating (www.oa.org; www.foodaddictsanonymous.org; www.foodaddicts.org).

Gamblers Anonymous. This group is for gamblers and those with a gambling problem or addiction. It started in 1957 following a chance meeting of two gamblers. Members profess a desire to stop gambling (www.gamblersanonymous.org).

Gam-Anon. This is a family group for those affected by gambling (www.gam-anon.org).

Sex and Love Addicts Anonymous. This group is for individuals who either compulsively seek out or compulsively avoid relationships, sex, or attachments (www.slaafws.org).

Other 12-Step Groups. There are literally dozens of meetings that have developed based on the 12-step model. They are available in communities in varying degrees. Online support is usually possible. These include Cocaine Anonymous (CA), Clutterers Anonymous (CLA), Codependents Anonymous (CoDA), Debtors Anonymous (DA), Marijuana Anonymous (MA), Smokers Anonymous (SA), and Workaholics Anonymous (WA; Wikipedia, 2013).

SMART Recovery

SMART Recovery was started to help people with all kinds of addictions, including alcohol, drugs, gambling, and problem activities or behaviors. The goal is abstinence from the behavior, but those who are undecided about changing are welcome. SMART stands for Self-Management and Recovery Training. SMART Recovery is based on a 4-point program: (a) building and maintaining motivation; (b) coping with urges; (c) managing thoughts, feelings, and behavior; and (d) living a balanced life. The program is not spiritually based although members are welcome to believe whatever they want. There is no support for the disease model or belief in a higher power as part of the program. SMART Recovery was started in 1994. It is described as a collaborative effort among professionals, some of whom are in recovery, and nonprofessionals. There is no fee for services although donations are welcomed (www.smartrecovery.org).

Celebrate Recovery

Celebrate Recovery is a national program developed for individuals recovering from any issue, including addiction or alcohol and/or drugs, codependency, gambling, sex addiction, or eating. It has been described as a Christ-centered ministry. It uses the beatitudes of Jesus as well as the 12 steps to support the recovery process (www.celebraterecovery.com).

Women for Sobriety

This is the first national self-help group that was started for women alcoholics. The goal of the program is to help women achieve sobriety and maintain ongoing recovery. It was started in 1976 by Dr. Jean Kirkpatrick and is described as the result of one woman's search for recovery. It is based on 13 statements, which are affirmations that are positive and that encourage emotional and spiritual growth. The groups are facilitated by certified moderators; in addition, there is an online forum, where members meet to send messages and chat (www.womenforsobriety.org).

LifeRing

LifeRing was started in 2001. It is a network of support groups that provide social reinforcement for recovery. Each individual develops his or her own personal program. It is based on these three principles: sobriety, secularity, and self-direction (lifering.org).

Secular Organization for Sobriety

Also known as Save Our Selves, this group was started over 28 years ago as an alternative to 12-step groups. It is seen as a nonreligious alternative to those meetings. Individuals, rather than a Higher Power, are credited for entering into and maintaining sobriety (cfiwest.org/SOS/index.htm).

Moderation Management

This is a self-help group for individuals who want to learn how to use alcohol in moderation rather than being abstinent. The program is specifically geared toward problem drinkers; behavioral change is the key (www.moderation.org).

Psychotherapy

Individual

Outpatient therapy may be extremely useful as a support in recovery. This is particularly helpful for those individuals who are hesitant to discuss their issues in a group setting. Individuals work on relapse prevention and developing the long-term lifestyle changes that are necessary in order to maintain sobriety or behavior change. In addition, clients may resolve underlying issues that have either supported habits or interfered with recovery in the past. EMDR can be a very helpful part of this process.

Group

In group therapy, clients get the support from both therapist and peers that is necessary for recovery. Clients may benefit from the honest feedback about their interactions with others and ways that they may be sabotaging or supporting their own recoveries. Groups vary; psychoeducational groups, aftercare groups, early recovery groups, psychodynamic, cognitive–behavioral, and long- or short-term groups are available in many communities.

Family

Involving the family may also be very helpful. In family therapy, members are able to analyze their relationships and roles as well as look at how the family has learned to organize itself around the addictive behaviors. Family members are able to discuss ways to interact differently and make changes. All members may benefit from exploring how they have supported (enabled) the addiction process and what may be done differently in the future to change these patterns and support recovery for all.

Preparing for Life Changes

Clients needs to be aware that life will be very different when the addictive substance or behavior is no a longer available. Entering into long-term recovery may be one of the most difficult endeavors in life.

Addiction serves a purpose in each person's life. What purpose it serves varies from individual to individual. Although the addiction now causes pain, enough pain to create the desire to change, the original purpose that it served must be explored. Clients must develop alternative coping mechanisms and ways to deal with feelings. While preparing to change, it is helpful for clients to begin this exploration and to problem solve about what might be important to support the process. What does each client need? The answer is really different for each person and will continue to evolve and change as the client enters the next stage of Action.

EGO SYSTEMS WORK

According to Carol Forgash, an ego system is understood as "an organized system of behaviors and experiences that have various boundaries, or as syndromes of behavior and experience that are clustered around some common principle. The states may be organized to enhance adaptability in coping with events or problems" (Forgash, 2008, p. 15). For example, a client may have an ego system that includes a child part, parent part, and addict part, among others. The parts may be organized around certain roles or skills necessary to adapt in the world. They may also be organized developmentally, around certain ages or functions.

All clients have different "parts of self" or parts of the ego system. Clients who have experienced trauma and subsequently developed dissociative defense mechanisms or dissociative disorders may have very clearly delineated parts; seriously dissociated clients may even have separate and distinct personalities (see Chapter 4, Trauma). Different parts may have different motivation around the need or desire to recover from addictions. It may be very helpful to explore the different parts of self that are part of an individual's personality and engage those parts in the recovery work.

For example, one part may actively try to sabotage the recovery work. Another part may be very strong and, despite ambivalence, actively endeavor to stay in recovery. A clinician may ask "What part of you wants to stay in recovery?" or "Is there a healthy part of you that wants to change?" It is important to help clients know and explore the "darker" parts, the parts that are in pain and may be traumatized. It is perhaps even more important to help clients identify and understand the parts that are resourceful, strong, and open to change. In this way, clients begin to integrate all parts of self.

It is helpful to have clients explore their parts in the therapy process. This can be done in a variety of ways. The clinician and the client may work together to list the different parts. Clients may do maps, inner landscapes, drawings, or pie charts to illustrate the parts of self (Forgash, 2008). Figure 8.1 is an example of one client's drawings. As part of her preparation and exploration, she drew these pictures and looked at the qualities contained in each part and the developmental stage of the part. This helped her to explore her ambivalence about change and her conflicts about entering into abstinence. Ultimately she was able to become sober.

In addition, clients may want to read about parts. One helpful book is *Why Did I Do That? How You Make Sense and Why There Is Hope* by Dorie Cameron (2009). This very simply written book is an introduction to looking at ego systems from an Internal Family Systems perspective. Clients will learn about the impact of trauma on the ego and the development of parts, such as the Firefighter, that are in service to the ego.

FIGURE 8.1 Parts of self.

Once these parts of self have been determined, the dialogue about parts of self may continue throughout Preparation and into the Action phase. In Part III, the case of Joanne is an example of a client who successfully utilized parts work as part of her recovery.

EMDR THERAPY

Please see Chapter 1, Eye Movement Desensitization and Reprocessing Therapy, for detailed descriptions of these protocols. (See also Appendix B1.)

Safe/Calm Place

Visualizing a calm or safe place and utilizing bilateral stimulation to reinforce this image is a very helpful resource for an individual preparing to change. This technique will be a useful adjunct to any work done in the stages to come and may be utilized frequently.

Desensitization of Triggers and Urge Reprocessing Positive Treatment Goal

This protocol is extremely helpful at this stage. This is only part of the Desensitization of Triggers and Urge Reprocessing (DeTur) model. The client visualizes the treatment goal he or she has established. For example, the client sees what life would ideally be like without the substance or addiction of choice. Bilateral stimulation is utilized to reinforce the treatment goal.

Resource Development Installation

Using the Resource Development Installation (RDI) protocol is also extremely helpful in this stage. Clients identify qualities that they need in order to maintain treatment goals. These qualities are explored and installed by using bilateral stimulation. With these qualities "front loaded" before the client makes changes, the client may feel more of a sense of confidence when entering recovery.

A book that may be very helpful for clients is *Tapping In* by Laurel Parnell (2008). This is a book that clients may use themselves to work on developing different resources. Clients learn how to tap their own knees to install various qualities. If a client is in crisis it may be useful to have this coping mechanism available. The clinician may guide the client in "tapping in" while on the phone in a crisis (Parnell, 2008).

Affect Tolerance

These clients have particular difficulty managing affect. This protocol can be helpful in Preparation and in ongoing treatment. Clients identify and work with emotions that feel overwhelming or out of control. Bilateral stimulation is used to desensitize the feelings and help clients learn how to manage them.

Standard Protocol

One of the biggest clinical decisions to be made is whether to use the standard protocol for trauma before the client enters into recovery. Some clients have traumas that are driving their addictions. They are unable to enter into recovery without first dealing with the trauma. Some clients are unable to work on the trauma without an initial period of recovery. It is a very tricky and complex clinical decision to be made. As stated previously, it is important to treat each client individually when making a determination about when to use the standard protocol. The issue will be discussed in detail in Chapter 12, Treating Trauma and Addiction with EMDR Therapy.

Some inpatient programs offer EMDR as part of treatment. The EMDR may be concentrated, that is, the sessions occur more than once a week for an hour or longer. The clients are given a safe, structured environment to do the work, with much support, and no opportunities for relapse. This may be extremely helpful for some clients.

CASE VIGNETTE 1

The Case of Multiple Relapses: Jody

Jody, aged 38 years, had a long history of periods of sobriety followed by relapses. He had unmanaged depression as well. This contributed to his difficulty controlling his urges to drink. As Jody entered the stage of Preparation once more, it was determined that a course of antidepressant medication would be of benefit. The antidepressants helped to stabilize his moderately severe depression so he could get ready for the next stage of Action. In addition, he chose to use Antabuse to help prevent relapse.

CASE VIGNETTE 2

The Client Who Needed Inpatient Treatment: Carrie

Carrie was aged 50 years when she was referred to a substance abuse clinician. She had a history of depression and was on antidepressant medications. She was motivated to stop drinking but had a very difficult time and had multiple relapses. She entered treatment in the stage of Preparation. She explored several options with her therapist and together they determined that she could benefit from inpatient treatment. She had the resources and the insurance to pursue this. She contacted several programs and made the decision to attend a 30-day program in the Southwest. This program also provided EMDR treatment. Because she was a trauma survivor, this was important to her.

CASE VIGNETTE 3

The Client Who Was Flooded With Affect: Marguerite

Marguerite was a 32-year-old depressed woman who was on medication and was having difficulty maintaining sobriety. It was determined that Marguerite could benefit from the standard protocol for trauma to support her recovery from addiction. One issue central to her struggle was the sudden death of her father when she was an adolescent; the unresolved trauma fueled her need to drink.

After the first trauma session, she had a very difficult time and returned to the second session flooded with feelings. She reported that this was interfering with her ability to do more EMDR work. The Affect Tolerance protocol was used to help her manage her feelings.

The client worked on her feeling of sadness. She developed an image of a dark, hot, solid round object located in her gut.

Negative cognition (NC): I can't handle it;
Positive cognition (PC): I can deal with my feelings;
Validity of Cognition (VoC): 1;
Emotions: overwhelmed, sad;
Subjective Unit of Disturbance (SUDS): 10;
Body: chest, gut.

Seven sets of eye movements were completed. At that point the client reported that the image had changed to a swirling, moving, light-colored globe. The SUDS was 2. The VoC was 7. The client reported that she felt much lighter and was able to proceed with the trauma work.

These case studies illustrate the issues involved in the stage of Preparation for three different clients with three different needs. When each client is considered individually, the treatment plan for each is unique and developed to meet the specific needs of that client. What works for one client will not necessarily work for another. The therapist must be very thoughtful and judicious and work with the client to develop the appropriate plan.

SUMMARY

The stage of Preparation is a very important part of the process of change. In this stage, the client, with the help of the clinician, explores the options and possibilities for support during recovery. As noted before, this is likened to a road map that provides the client with various avenues to choose from and paths to take on the journey toward recovery. The client selects the supports that are ultimately perceived as most helpful and prepares to use those options.

Because each individual is unique, what works for one client may not work for another. Each client must seek out the resources that are ultimately in his or her best interests and that promote his or her recovery from the many available options. There are many traditional resources available. We have discussed medications, detoxification, hospital and residential care, self-help groups, and other treatment programs, such as individual, group, and family therapy.

The importance of preparing clients for the lifestyle changes to come was noted. In addition, EMDR techniques are available that enhance and support recovery. For many clients who have relapsed in the past, it may be extremely helpful to utilize some of these different techniques.

LEARNING POINTS

1. The stage of Preparation is a stage of exploration and planning for action steps.
2. There are many options available for clients, including self-help groups and intensive outpatient, inpatient, and outpatient therapy.
3. Medication should be considered if the client needs it to support recovery.
4. EMDR treatment is a viable option; the trauma protocol may be necessary for some clients in order to promote recovery.
5. Each client is unique and needs an individualized treatment plan.

CHAPTER 9

THE STAGE OF ACTION

Ready, set, go! At this point your client has contemplated making a change and, presumably, has set up a viable action plan. This is the point when the client begins to actively change. Although the authors are describing it in a fairly linear way, the process is a fluid one. Clients often move back and forth from stage to stage. A client may appear ready to be in the stage of Action and begin to make changes and then, for whatever reason, moves back to Preparation or even to Contemplation before possibly returning to Action. This is the shortest stage, lasting up to about 6 months (Prochaska & DiClemente, 1982, 1992). It is the point when the client actually says, "This is the time to change."

THE WORK AT THIS STAGE OF ACTION

At this point, the client makes the changes and begins the necessary adjustments by implementing the plans that were made during the stage of Preparation. These changes may include developing and maintaining a drug- or alcohol- or addiction-free environment, keeping things that would trigger a return back to the old behaviors out of the environment, changing the way he or she socializes, developing new coping mechanisms and skills, and modifying problem behaviors. Some people may choose not to give up addictions completely but may develop strategies to cut back on certain behaviors and uses of substances. Clinicians help the clients to utilize the resources to begin this process of change. The two key elements of this stage are: (a) a clear decision and a commitment to change and (b) the appearance of the new behavior, which is evidence of this change (Connors, Donovan, & DiClemente, 2001).

It is very important to start working on relapse prevention in this stage. Clients need to begin to plan their lives to try to avoid a return to old behaviors.

WHAT IS RELAPSE PREVENTION?

According to Marlatt and Gordon (1985), relapse prevention "refers to a wide range of strategies designed to prevent relapse in the area of addictive behavior change" (p. xii). Clinicians help clients develop ways to prevent lapses and also to prevent lapses from turning into full-blown relapses.

There are two different ways to think about relapse. One is that any time an individual returns to old, addictive behaviors this is seen as a move out of recovery and into relapse. The client must "start over" and begin the recovery process again. Alcoholics Anonymous (AA) and other 12-step programs are proponents of this way of thinking. If an individual uses or returns to the old behaviors, even for 1 day, the recovery process is ended and the person is a seen as being out of recovery (Marlatt & Gordon, 1985).

Another way to think about relapse is that it is part of the process of recovery. If the individual has one short period of return to old behaviors, this is called a lapse. Individuals may learn lessons from a lapse; this could be viewed as positive because the lessons learned are beneficial and support future recovery efforts. An ongoing, continuing pattern of return to the old behaviors is defined as a relapse. Either way, progress that has been made and the lessons learned are all of part of the recovery process (Marlatt& Gordon, 1985). The authors of this book proscribe to this second way to thinking. Relapse is an important part of the process of change for many clients; learning from relapse and developing alternative coping skills is a primary lesson in recovery that begins in this stage of Action (see also Chapter 12, Treating Trauma and Addiction With EMDR Therapy, and Chapter 3, The Stages of Change).

Clients identify potential triggers for relapse in this stage and begin to problem solve about how to manage these triggers. An important assignment may be for clients to make lists of triggers. This is an ongoing process, as triggers may change and new triggers may come into awareness as time goes on. *Anything* can be a trigger. Life may be a trigger. Once the triggers are identified, clients take steps to learn ways to avoid them and/or to cope differently with them.

TRADITIONAL INTERVENTIONS

Some interventions that are not part of EMDR therapy that may be helpful to clients in this stage of Action are:

1. Developing healthy coping mechanisms to deal with the stress of change

Change may be difficult for any individual, especially if there is ambivalence about it. Ambivalence, a hallmark of addiction, continues to manifest in this stage. Even if there is a well-developed plan, clients may be faced with many different kinds of life stressors. Clients need to explore these stressors and develop healthy ways to handle them. These may be different for different people; they can be as varied as the clients themselves and may include big life events such as weddings, funerals, divorces, and the like, but may also include daily stressors such as job and family conflicts. Sometimes, what appear to be very small and minor events, such as having to get groceries or flying in an airplane, may be very stressful for a client in early recovery.

2. Exercise

Research has demonstrated that there are benefits of regular aerobic exercise (Ross & Thomas, 2010). Exercise has been shown to reduce the effects of aging, provide relief from stress, and help to balance mood (Lutz et al., 2008). Clients who are dealing with the physiological and psychological stress of making the changes in the Action phase will likely benefit from exercise of some kind.

3. Relaxation and fun

Individuals who have process or substance addictions often depend on these unhealthy behaviors as a way to relax or to have fun. In the Action phase, clients are learning to live life without these dependencies. They need to relearn how to have fun. The clinician helps the client identify and utilize alternative strategies for relaxation and enjoyment. Individuals in this stage often find there is more time available now that time is not filled up with addictive behaviors and may become bored. It can be helpful to develop a hobby, take a class, or take up a sport or other activity to fill this time.

4. Identifying triggers

Just about anything may be a trigger. In response to a question about triggers, a client responded, "You need to understand everything is a trigger! Life is a trigger!" As much as possible, clients need to try to identify triggers and develop alternative coping mechanisms for when these occur. That said, sometimes triggers seemingly appear out of nowhere; sometimes lapses (a onetime slip or return to old behaviors) or relapses (a pattern of behavior) occur on impulse, without any identifiable precipitants (see "Apparently Irrelevant Behaviors" below). Clients may make lists of triggers and plan alternative behaviors for dealing with the responses to these triggers when they occur. It is very helpful, in terms of prevention, to plan ahead and look at alternative coping strategies before the triggers occur.

5. Control of the environment

It is important that clients learn the effects that the environment may have on choices about behavior. Providing clients with information about the power of social influence may be critical to recovery. Many clients believe, often falsely, that they can resist the influence of peers. Clients may need to change friends, develop new places to socialize (i.e., stay out of bars and away from groups or activities that will trigger the addiction), and develop different lifestyle choices.

6. "Apparently irrelevant behaviors"

These are behaviors that one may not immediately connect to the addiction or to a risk for relapse. However, when examining the triggers that lead to relapse, these behaviors may emerge as critical (Shafer, Telch, & Chen, 2009).

For example, a client returned to gambling behavior and had no idea how it occurred. Upon exploration of the events that led up to this relapse, the client reported that he had taken a different exit off the highway because he had to wait too long in the traffic at his normal exit. This was the exit that he took whenever he had the urge to gamble on the way home. After a discussion, the client realized that this seemingly unimportant decision made a significant contribution to his relapse.

7. Urge surfing

This is a technique where one learns to ride out an urge rather than act on it; that is, one notices the urge and sits with it until it passes (Ostafin & Marlatt, 2008). These urges have a natural life of their own and, if not acted upon, will naturally subside. Bowen and Marlatt (2009) demonstrated the effectiveness of utilizing this mindfulness-based intervention for assisting college-age smokers who were trying to quit. Clients need to learn not to "feed" their cravings. Cravings and urges need to be noticed, acknowledged, and allowed to pass (Brewer, Elwafi, & Davis, 2013).

8. Journaling

Keeping a daily log or journal may be a very helpful tool for clients in this stage of recovery. Clients can use this as a way to monitor triggers; write about ways of coping with urges and cravings; become more aware of the purpose alcohol, drugs, or addictive behaviors have in his or her life; and to identify and deal with feelings. Because so many people with addictive behaviors have difficulty with being aware of and managing affect, the journal is a very helpful tool.

9. Workbooks and other structured activities

Some clients benefit from doing "homework" in this stage. There are a number of recovery workbooks available for client use. Some of them are listed in the Resources section of this book.

EMDR THERAPY

Several EMDR therapy techniques and interventions are particularly useful at this stage.

1. Hase protocol/CRAVEX (see Chapter 1, EMDR Therapy, and Appendix B4)

The Hase protocol is very helpful in helping clients deal with any cravings or urges that appear in this stage. The specific urges or cravings are targeted and desensitized using bilateral stimulation. Theoretically, the desensitizing leads from the memory or feeling of the urge back through channels in the brain to the origins of the addiction. This process may help the client decrease the sensation of the craving. It may lead to clients exploring underlying issues and may help them avoid using or returning to old behaviors. The therapist may then explore these issues with the client and reinforce or develop new skills as needed. The authors have found this to be an extremely helpful intervention.

2. Popky/DeTUR protocol (see Chapter 1, EMDR Therapy, and Appendix B5)

The DeTUR protocol is used to help clients manage urges to return to old behaviors. Clients identify triggers and then these triggers are desensitized utilizing bilateral stimulation. A client's previous anxious association in the face of certain triggers may then be replaced with a relaxed physiological state. According to Popky, the client must be committed to working with *all* the triggers to the addiction for this to be effective.

3. Resource Development Installation (RDI; see Chapter 1, EMDR Therapy, and Appendix B2)

In this stage of Action, clients may continue to benefit from the development of resources to build up ego strengths. Clients may find that they need even more resources to handle the stresses of this process of change. RDI (Korn & Leeds, 2002) may be implemented to develop these new strategies. It can be helpful to use bilateral stimulation to reinforce even what may seem like small changes or gains. The client focuses on the feeling, locates it in the body, and then short sets of bilateral stimulation are used. In addition, the client may also visualize the future; using the "future template," this is reinforced with bilateral stimulation while the client visualizes a "habit free" future.

4. Affect Tolerance (see Chapter 1, EMDR Therapy)
In this stage of Action, clients may find that they are flooded with feelings. If a client has utilized the addiction or addictive behaviors to manage affect, then they may become overwhelmed when the addiction is no longer available as a coping mechanism. The Affect Tolerance protocol may be very useful as clients learn to manage these feelings. With help from the therapist, the client identifies the target feeling, develops an image of it, identifies both a negative cognition (NC) and a positive cognition (PC), identifies emotions about the feeling, and locates it in the body. The target feeling is desensitized by using bilateral stimulation. The client is also helped to develop other affect management techniques.

5. Standard Protocol (see Appendix B3)
The beginning of early recovery may not be an ideal time to do trauma work. The client may be feeling vulnerable about the myriad lifestyle changes that are occurring and the resultant fragility around making so many changes. It is probably best to wait until recovery is more stabilized. However, if the underlying trauma a client has experienced is interfering with progress in this stage, trauma work may be considered (see Chapter 12, Treating Trauma and Addiction with EMDR Therapy).

6. Safe/Calm Place (see Chapter 1, EMDR Therapy, and Appendix B1)
This is almost always helpful for clients to manage stress and anxiety. Clients visualize a place where they feel calm or safe and this is reinforced with bilateral stimulation.

CASE VIGNETTES

The following case vignettes illustrate clients who are the stage of Action.

CASE VIGNETTE 1

Edmund: The Anxious Drinker

Edmund came to therapy to deal with issues related to his anxiety. During the assessment, it came to light that Edmund was drinking alcohol nearly every day to help him relax and unwind. At times his use would be heavy (more than five drinks a day). His therapist provided information about the connection between alcohol use and anxiety. Edmund began to track his use of alcohol and focused on reducing it. When he began to actively reduce his alcohol use, he entered the stage of Action. As a result, he experienced a significant reduction in his anxiety. Eventually, Edmund reduced his alcohol intake to social use on special occasions.

CASE VIGNETTE 2

Kiki: The Depressed Polysubstance Abuser

Kiki was 20 years old when she went to therapy to deal with her polysubstance use: She had a history of using alcohol and marijuana on a daily basis for the last 3 years. She also experimented with cocaine, benzodiazepines, and hallucinogens. An only child of two professional parents, she had a long history of depression. It became clear to her therapist that she had used drugs to self-medicate.

Kiki came to therapy in Action. She had been abstinent for 42 days and was attending AA, where she was working with a sponsor. She was concerned because she was experiencing an increase in urges and cravings. The therapist utilized the Hase/CRAVEX protocol to help her desensitize these urges.

The target was Kiki's last craving. She was sitting in her room alone and bored. The level of urge (LoU) was 5. The NC was "I can't handle my own thoughts." The PC was "I am better without using alcohol and drugs." After nine sets of bilateral stimulation, the LoU reduced to zero and the PC was installed. It was interesting to note the way that the client processed the memory of the urge. She appeared to developmentally review her substance use, from her first use, which was a very positive experience, through the more difficult and painful times, to the decision to quit using and enter recovery.

CASE VIGNETTE 3

Stephanie: The Client Who Lapsed and Returned to Action

Stephanie was 46 years old when she first initiated treatment. She was concerned about her alcohol use, which was interfering with her ability to concentrate and be successful on the job. She also suffered from major depression. She entered into a period of recovery that lasted 7 years. During that time, she worked on her traumas with EMDR, including the devastating accidental death of her best friend when she was a child. She made significant progress and terminated therapy.

She returned to therapy about 3 years later because she was concerned about her relationship with her husband and trying to decide whether to divorce him. Shortly after her return, she went on a business trip overnight. While she was away, she drank one glass of wine. This was an impulsive move; a waiter walked by her with a tray, she took a glass and drank the alcohol. She felt devastated and shamed. Because she was active in AA, she contacted her sponsor, went to a meeting, and picked up a white chip, signifying her willingness to continue the process of change, reenter the Action phase, and be sober.

Her therapist talked to her about the difference between a lapse and a relapse. Stephanie appreciated that she would not have to discount the previous progress that she had made. She discussed possible reasons for the lapse: being alone, away from home, stress about the marriage, and her unresolved need to rebel. She found a way to integrate the AA way of thinking about relapse and her belief that her first 7 years of recovery were not wasted. When asked how much sober time she had, she said "7 years plus" whatever new amount of time she accumulated. Thus, she was able to honor all the time she spent in recovery.

These studies illustrate different ways that clients enter into and cope with the stage of Action.

SUMMARY

In this chapter, the authors discussed the stage of Action, the shortest of all Stages of Change, lasting 3 to 6 months. Although many clients never reach this stage, when they do, it is a stage of activity and behavior change. They implement the changes that were planned in the stage of Preparation. Clients are committed and motivated at this point to give up old behaviors. Relapse prevention was discussed. Action steps include exercising, learning to have fun and relax in new ways, identifying and managing triggers for use, learning to manage cravings and urges, developing new coping mechanisms, and altering one's environment to support these changes when possible. Several EMDR techniques may be very useful: Safe/Calm Place, Popky/DeTUR, Hase/CRAVEX, RDI, and Affect Tolerance. The standard protocol for trauma may be carefully utilized if underlying trauma is interfering with recovery.

LEARNING POINTS

1. The stage of Action is the shortest stage; it lasts 3 to 6 months.
2. In this stage, clients implement the changes developed during the stage of Preparation.
3. The commitment to change is obvious; clients make the changes in behavior.
4. Clients develop relapse prevention strategies in this stage
5. Clients work on developing new coping mechanisms, exercising, learning to have fun and relax in a different way, changing the environment when possible, identifying and managing triggers, and "urge surfing."
6. Several EMDR protocols may be useful: Popky/DeTUR, Hase/CRAVEX, Affect Tolerance, and RDI. The Safe/Calm Place protocol is always potentially helpful.
7. The standard protocol may be useful but should be used judiciously.

CHAPTER 10

THE STAGE OF MAINTENANCE AND RELAPSE PREVENTION

This stage of Maintenance is all about preventing relapse. Clients learn to consolidate and maintain the changes that have taken place in the Action stage and develop a long-term method of staying sober. This stage begins after 3 to 6 months in Action and usually continues throughout the client's life. Some clients may consider themselves completely healed from addictive behaviors and move into Termination (see Chapter 3, The Stages of Change). However, this is not the norm and it helps to think of this process as ongoing.

THE WORK AT THIS STAGE OF MAINTENANCE/RELAPSE PREVENTION

The client must be cognizant of the work of relapse prevention for the rest of his or her life. It helps to think of recovery as a lifetime process. Just as each client needs an individualized approach to preparing for and entering into recovery, each client needs a unique approach to maintaining this recovery. The client's needs may change over time and the recovery plan may need to be adjusted. Think of recovery as a cafeteria: There are many choices about what to have as part of this process. Each client will need and choose different things.

Clients must be aware of any long-term behavioral changes that need to occur to support this process (Prochaska & DiClemente, 1982, 1992). This can involve some difficult choices. Each client must continue to identify and work with any triggers that are in his or her life. For example, if visiting family is a trigger, the client will need to make some difficult decisions about how to set boundaries and implement self-care skills around the family. If certain friends are triggers, some friendships may need to end or be reorganized. If certain environments are triggers, the client may need to stay away. This can create grief for the client, as life is changed and reorganized (Dayton, 2005; Fletcher, 2001). There is also ongoing grief about not being able to revert to one's former coping mechanisms.

During this stage, clients may resolve any long-term conflict that may have either supported the addiction or prevented the client from having long-term mental health. Any unresolved family of origin issues may be looked at and resolved at this point (Connors, Donovan, & DiClemente, 2001).

Shaffer and Jones (1989) studied cocaine addicts who recovered without any outside intervention. These individuals identified four areas that were seen as really important in terms of looking at ongoing recovery. These areas are as follows.

Friends

Clients need to determine whether to let go of old friends who may be triggers for using. Changing one's environment, that is, not "hanging out" with one's user friends, staying away from bars or party houses, and so forth, may be very important.

Exercise

Exercise supports recovery. It is one way for clients to release endorphins that make the individual feel good. It is one of the most helpful things an individual may do.

Eating

Addicts and others who have addictive patterns do not usually have good eating habits. Developing strong nutritional supports was seen as one way to support recovery.

Spirituality

Developing a sense of spirituality is also very important. This may or may not include a religious belief system or practice but includes creating some sense of purpose or reason for being. It is important to encourage clients to explore these resources and develop a sense of spirituality.

These four areas have been identified by Shaffer and Jones (1989) as primary in terms of recovery.

Fletcher (2001) studied individuals who had been labeled as problem drinkers and either gave up alcohol or moderated alcohol consumption. She calls these individuals the "masters." Most had 5 or more years of sobriety. In her group of participants, 97 recovered by using Alcoholics Anonymous (AA). A larger group, 125 people, either received no help or used other resources, such as SMART recovery, Women in Sobriety, religion, or some kind of treatment or counseling. Fletcher concludes from these individuals that there is no one solution to being in recovery. Each person finds his or her own way.

There are lessons to be learned from these masters. One is that giving up alcohol may be a painful process; the client must be allowed to grieve. In addition, the masters reported that eventually most did not battle with urges to drink, did not miss drinking, and felt the process became easier with time. Most masters came to what they needed by trial and error but were able to find a program or solution that worked.

INTERVENTIONS IN THIS STAGE

Traditional Interventions

There is an almost endless list of options that could be utilized by clients in the stage of Maintenance. Some of the things to be considered are as follows.

Psychiatric Medications as Necessary
Appropriate psychiatric medications help a client to manage mental health symptoms, which in turn makes it easier for a client to maintain sobriety. There is some controversy about this in some self-help recovery programs that teach total abstinence, so a client may need help and support to process the decision to utilize this resource.

Self-Help Groups
Ongoing attendance at self-help group meetings is extremely important for some individuals. Others may balk at this or attend for a period of time, then either decrease or stop attendance. Each individual should look carefully at what works best.

Ongoing Counseling
Clients in this stage of Maintenance may be ready to engage in counseling to work through the issues inherent in this stage of recovery and to help develop the ongoing life adjustments necessary to maintain the changes that have occurred. There are many approaches—that is, cognitive–behavioral, psychodynamic, Eye Movement Desensitization and Reprocessing (EMDR)—and clients will need to explore and decide upon the best choice.

Relapse Prevention
This is an ongoing process. Clients need to continue to identify and monitor triggers and develop ongoing strategies for managing any urges and cravings that occur.

EMDR THERAPY

A number of EMDR therapy interventions may be particularly helpful at this stage.

Safe/Calm Place

There is always benefit in using this protocol to promote relaxation and calm as the individual deals with the changes inherent in this stage of change (see Chapter 1, EMDR Therapy, and Appendix B1).

Hase/CRAVEX Protocol

This protocol is very beneficial in terms of working through and desensitizing any urges or cravings that manifest in this stage. Clients identify the urge or craving, rate the level of urge on a scale of 0 to 10, identify a negative cognition (NC), a positive cognition (PC), feelings about the craving, and location in the body. Bilateral stimulation (BS) is utilized to decrease the urge (see Chapter 1, EMDR Therapy, and Appendix B4).

Desensitization of Triggers and Urge Reprocessing Protocol

The Desensitization of Triggers and Urge Reprocessing (DeTUR) protocol is also good for helping clients manage and deal with triggers. Each trigger is listed and BS is used to decrease the urges (see Chapter 1, Eye Movement Desensitization and Reprocessing Therapy, and Appendix B5 for complete instructions).

Resource Development Installation

Clients may benefit from the ongoing development of resources as they struggle to resolve the issues of this stage. Resource Development Installation (RDI) is an excellent tool for helping clients develop the ego strength needed to maintain recovery (see Chapter 1, EMDR Therapy, and Appendix B2).

Affect Tolerance Protocol

Individuals with addiction issues often have difficulty managing emotions. The addictive behavior itself was once a coping mechanism for dealing with the intensity of feelings and an alternative coping mechanism must be developed. This protocol may be extremely helpful (see Chapter 1, EMDR Therapy).

Standard Protocol for Dealing With Trauma

If the client is motivated, has good coping mechanisms, good inner and outer resources, and has developed affect tolerance, then this could be the perfect time to use the standard protocol for trauma resolution. Working through past trauma issues will be a support for a lifetime of recovery. Clients must be prepared for the potential intensity of this kind of therapy and be helped to develop the necessary supports to do the work (see Chapter 1, EMDR Therapy, and Chapter 12, Treating Trauma and Addiction with EMDR Therapy).

CASE VIGNETTES

Following are three examples of clients in the stage of Maintenance/Relapse Prevention who utilized EMDR therapy in a variety of ways.

CASE VIGNETTE 1

Letting Go of the "Longings": Daisy

Daisy was 36 years old when she first entered therapy. She had a significant trauma history, including physical abuse by her father when she was a child and abandonment by her mother. She also had a history of alcoholism and was actively drinking when she came into treatment.

Her alcohol issues were dealt with first. She quit drinking and about a year and a half later began to do trauma work using EMDR. After a particularly intense EMDR session, she began to have intense feelings of "love" and "longing" for alcohol; this made her very uncomfortable. She also had many memories or flashbacks to early childhood incidents. Alcohol had been her way of coping with distress. When she no longer had alcohol as a coping mechanism, it became difficult for her to visualize how to proceed without it.

Daisy and her therapist made the decision to put the trauma processing on hold for one session and to utilize the Hase/CRAVEX protocol to desensitize these cravings. The following is a transcript of the session.

"Longing"
Image: sitting in her chair at home in the living room.
Level of urge (LoU): 8 out of 10.
NC: I am flawed.
PC: I am learning to believe I am normal.
Emotions: shame.
Body: chest.

Bilateral Stimulation (BS)
Set No. 1: Why can't I be like everyone else?
BS
No. 2: Why can't I go to my wedding and have champagne?
BS

No. 3: Why did I have to ruin it? Why couldn't I enjoy it and have it not be a problem?
BS
No. 4: I am acting like it was a choice. It wasn't a choice. I couldn't choose my parents.
BS
No. 5: It still sucks.
BS
No. 6: I don't want to be an alcoholic. I want to be normal.
BS
No. 7: Weird; the two sides of myself are talking—this is not fair versus really, what is the big deal?
BS
No. 8: Part of me, the alcoholic part, thinks it is ridiculous that I can't safely have a glass of wine.
BS
No. 9: I feel stuck; I think I could pull it off.
BS
No. 10: How long before my drinking increases, before I started sneaking drinks?
BS
No. 11: Is it inevitable?
BS
No. 12: That is what always happens.
BS
No. 13: I am flawed and I am not normal.
BS
No. 14: It is crazy how much this still hurts; it's been over a year and a half.
BS
No. 15: Will it ever get easier?
BS
No. 16. It can't get harder; it's bad when I drink, right?
BS
No. 17: Yeah, it is really bad when I drink.
BS
No. 18: Yeah.
BS
No. 19: I get it.
LoU: 0.
PC: I am learning to believe I am normal.
VoC: 7.
Body: clear.

As evidenced by this transcript of the session, the client was able to clear her "longings" to drink and was able to return to doing the trauma work. Although drinking clearly caused difficulties, she needed to grieve the loss of the coping mechanism it had provided for her, come to the realization that it was not in her best interests to continue using alcohol, and develop healthier coping mechanisms as she proceeded through the stage of Maintenance/Relapse Prevention.

CASE VIGNETTE 2

Gavin: Recovery From Cocaine Addiction

Gavin was in recovery from cocaine dependence for several months when he reported an increase in his urges to use. He was triggered when he was driving home from work on Fridays, which was when he used to be preparing to use. The Hase Memory of Addiction protocol/CRAVEX was utilized to desensitize these urges; the urges decreased and he was able to maintain his recovery.

CASE VIGNETTE 3

Soledad: A Crisis in Recovery

Soledad was brought up in the Western Caribbean and moved to the United States when she was a teenager. Her childhood was marked by serious neglect and abuse; both parents completely abandoned her when she was in her early adolescence. Soledad entered into recovery from alcohol dependence and after about 3.5 years of recovery did some serious EMDR trauma work with the standard protocol used to resolve her early childhood trauma. She was in a long-term relationship with a man who helped her through her early recovery. As she got healthier, she began to have more demands and needs for intimacy. His response to this was to initiate an affair. Soledad was traumatized when she learned about this and flooded with panic. Her only coping mechanism in the past had been to drink when faced with a crisis like this. She had begun to think about the fact that she had no other way to manage feelings. In therapy, it was decided that she could benefit from utilizing the Affect Tolerance protocol. The following is a transcript of that session.

Affect Tolerance Protocol—Panic

Image of the panic: chaos, shattered glass, all colors, hot, restless, located in her heart.

NC: I am shattered.

PC: I am strong and will get through it.

Emotions: sad, angry, hate.

Subjective Unit of Disturbance (SUDS): 10.

Body: heart.

Bilateral Stimulation (BS)

Set No. 1: Hate, so much for naught, feeling emotional: vulnerable, this is exactly why I didn't want to feel anything.

BS

No. 2: Anger, hate.

BS

No. 3: Pain, unfairness, easier not to feel.

BS

No. 4: This is the exact age my mother was when my father left her; what if I am on the same path, what if I have a breakdown? I am afraid I will turn into someone who cannot care for her daughter; this is the driving force behind my decisions; I can't trust myself and I am afraid I will end up in the state hospital.

BS

No. 5: I hate emotions, I don't want any, I only want to feel in control, pulling strings, dictating outcomes, and then I am comfortable.

BS

No. 6: I never want to feel like this again, to love someone so much it hurts; I finally put myself out there and took walls down and this is what happens.

BS

No. 7: I'd rather be numb; love turned to hate and anger; I don't want to feel this; I want to shove love away so when it goes bad I don't have to feel homicidal thoughts about that person.

BS

No. 8: I want to wrap myself in a bubble and stay numb.

BS

No. 9: I am tired of rebuilding shattered pieces; there are a bunch of shattered pieces encased in a maraca.

At this point, the therapist checked the SUDS, which was a four and asked the client to check in on the original image. The image changed to the shattered pieces encased in a maraca. The time was up for the session, so the therapist asked the client to develop a most PC for the day's work. The client chose "Someone figured out how to make beautiful music out of this; I think of it that way." The client did not get the SUDS down to zero. That is par for the course with this protocol. The goal is to decrease the intensity of the affect and to help the client to manage it better. This was accomplished. The client reported later that she felt better and more able to deal with her feelings.

Following this session, Soledad was able to feel more in control of her panic/anxiety. She was able to begin to think more logically about her options and to recommit to her sobriety as the priority in her life.

SUMMARY

In this chapter, the stage of Maintenance/Relapse Prevention was discussed. This is a stage that begins 3 to 6 months after the client enters the stage of Action and usually continues for the rest of life. In this stage, the client continues to develop coping strategies for maintaining the changes made in the earlier stages and begins to work on the resolution of long-term issues and conflicts. Appropriate non-EMDR and EMDR interventions were outlined. It is very important to be careful about when to do the EMDR trauma protocol, but this is a stage when this could be optimal.

LEARNING POINTS

1. This stage begins about 3 to 6 months after Action.
2. In this stage, clients continue to work on developing supports for long-term recovery. They continue to work with triggers and affect tolerance.
3. Clients work on the resolution of long-term conflicts and issues.
4. There is no one way to be in Maintenance; each client develops an individual approach to long-term recovery.
5. Several EMDR and pre-EMDR protocols may be extremely helpful in this stage: Affect Tolerance, RDI, Safe/Calm Place, Hase/CRAVEX, and DeTUR.
6. This is a stage where it may be optimal to work on resolving traumas through the use of EMDR.

CHAPTER 11

RELAPSE AND RECYCLING

Relapse and Recycling is not a stage, according to Prochaska and DiClimente (1982, 1992). It is best described as an event or a series of events that remove the client from the change process and lead to a recurrence of old behaviors. Clients who have not been able to sustain the changes made in the previous stages may be seen as in this phase.

In the best of all worlds, your client will move through the stage of Maintenance and work on preventing relapse for the rest of his or her life. In reality, the relapse rate is very high. It is difficult to obtain accurate figures about relapse rates due to the fact that many people are self-quitters and because self-help groups are anonymous (Marlatt & Gordon, 1985). It is estimated that up to 90% of people who enter drug and alcohol treatment will relapse and about 40% will experience periods of treatment, then relapse, and then move toward recovery (Gracer, 2007; Moore et al., 2013; Scott, Foss, & Dennis, 2005). The relapse rate is higher during the first 90 days of recovery and tapers off after that (Marlatt & Gordon, 1985; Nordfjærn, 2011). Therefore, this experience can be expected for the majority of our clients. They need to be prepared for the fact that it is part of the process of recovery; at the same time, we must take care not to invite them to relapse or make it seem like it is inevitable. When clients do relapse, it is important to help them to learn from this process.

The distinction must be made between a "lapse" and a "relapse." A lapse is a one-time event; the client then returns to recovery. A relapse is a series of events where the client reverts to old behaviors (Marlatt & Gordon, 1985; Wileyto et al., 2004).

Relapse may seem to "come out of nowhere" for some clients; they seem to be doing everything appropriate in terms of good recovery and then they lapse or relapse. For other clients, it may come after a period of declining self-care and lack of attention to maintenance issues (Marlatt & Gordon, 1985; Moore et al., 2013). Relapse can be seen as a teacher; if clients learn about the whys and wherefores of relapse, they will be less likely to do it again (Clarke & Myers, 2012; Marlatt & Gordon, 1985). In this chapter, we will discuss how to manage relapse with a client.

THE WORK IN THIS PHASE OF RELAPSE AND RECYCLING

Client stabilization is the first order of business (Prochaska & DiClemente, 1982, 1992). Some clients who relapse put themselves into life-threatening situations. For example, clients who use copious amounts of drugs or alcohol may be in physical danger; dealing with this medically becomes the first order of business.

If the client relapses and old behaviors recur, he or she leaves this process of change and the movement toward letting go of addictions/negative behaviors. He or she must reevaluate his or her motivation for change from the point of view of this lapse or relapse. Some clients may move back to Precontemplation, and some may be further along in the process and jump back into Action or Preparation. At this point, the therapist must help the client determine again what Stage of Change he or she is in and develop a plan based on the client's motivation for change at this point. After determining the stage that your client is now in, utilize the interventions for that Stage of Change.

Traditional Interventions

The clinician helps the client determine whether this is a one-time lapse or a more serious relapse, that is, a return to the former patterns (Marlatt & Gordon, 1985; Wileyto et al., 2004). One may help the client see the lapse or relapse as a part of a learning process that will teach something necessary and important about the reasons the client uses as well as what is now needed to continue recovery in a new way. The triggers for the relapse are analyzed. It can be helpful to do a behavioral chain analysis, to look at the events that lead to the lapse or relapse, and determine what alternative behaviors may have been utilized (Landes, 2013; Linehan et al., 2002). The clinician helps the client move toward a renewed commitment to change, again potentially traveling through the process of change.

EMDR Therapy

This may be the time to introduce EMDR therapy, if it has not been tried previously. The EMDR protocols used at this point are the ones that are appropriate to the stage to which the client has returned.

There is some anecdotal evidence that clients benefit from EMDR therapy both during and after entering recovery (Abel & O'Brien, 2010; Marich, 2009). It is the authors' experience that the use of EMDR therapy enhances and supports engagement in recovery from addiction.

A WORD ABOUT THERAPIST ISSUES

This stage may be a difficult one for both client and therapist. Clients may feel shame about the relapse. They may also feel a sense of hopelessness; for clients with a long history of relapse, this can be very discouraging. Clients may miss appointments or drop out of treatment at this point.

It can also be discouraging for the therapist. Countertransference issues may emerge at this point. If as a therapist you have any need to control your clients, you will need to be careful to hold it carefully in check. Clients continue to have self-determination and may or may not be willing to reenter recovery at this point. It is not the clinician's decision although it is your job to point out the issues and offer choices. As a clinician, you need to walk with clients through this process. You may decide you cannot continue to work with someone who is too resistant or not benefiting from treatment; this is a clinical decision not to be made lightly. It is possible you may feel that you are enabling your client by allowing him or her a certain safety or support that prevents him or her from "hitting bottom" or experiencing turning points. You may also decide that your client needs services you cannot provide and make a referral. At all times it is important to hold hope for the client. This can be a stage that is not for the faint of heart. Hang in there.

CASE VIGNETTES

The following are three case vignettes that illustrate the relapse process as part of treatment.

CASE VIGNETTE 1

Beatrice: The Client Who Relapsed After Inpatient Treatment

Beatrice, aged 60 years, returned from 30 days at an inpatient facility where she was treated for alcoholism and she immediately relapsed. She also dropped out of outpatient treatment. She returned to therapy with her individual therapist about a year later, finally motivated to begin again. The therapist initially used the DeTUR protocol positive treatment goal to help her get refocused on her goal of abstinence. This protocol was followed by the use of Resource Development Installation (RDI) to help develop ego strengths. The Hase/CRAVEX protocol was used to target her most recent urges and relapses. Involvement with Alcoholics Anonymous (AA) also followed. Beatrice was able to begin a period of long-term sobriety.

CASE VIGNETTE 2

Maureen: The Client Who Drank Vanilla

Maureen, aged 49 years, had five solid years of good recovery when she went to visit her dying father-in-law, a man who had triggered her drinking in the past. Although the visit was discussed in advance and Maureen had many recovery tools, she came back feeling very shaky. She got up very early the day after she got home and decided to make a cake. After assembling all of the ingredients on the counter, she impulsively downed an entire bottle of vanilla.

She immediately felt both nauseous and intoxicated and went back to bed for several hours. When she got up, she was mortified about what had happened. She contacted her sponsor, went to AA, and picked up a white chip, indicating her desire to reengage in recovery. She saw her therapist that week; the Hase protocol was utilized to process the lapse. She returned to the stage of Action following her lapse and took healthy steps toward change immediately. She was able to maintain ongoing sobriety.

CASE VIGNETTE 3

Penelope: The Client Who Returned to the Stage of Precontemplation

Penelope, aged 28 years, a single working class woman, went to therapy to deal with her anxiety and depression. She denied drug use or abuse when questioned initially. After 2 years of therapy, when she was making little progress, she "confessed" to her therapist that she was smoking marijuana daily; she felt that she was an addict and wanted to be abstinent. She went through the stages of Contemplation and Preparation on her own, without discussing her issues in therapy. She entered the stage of Action and stopped smoking marijuana immediately after her announcement. She had an extremely difficult time: Her anxiety and depression increased and she took a medical leave of absence from her job for 2 months to deal with her issues. She attended Narcotics Anonymous (NA) regularly. After about 4 months of recovery, she met a man in NA. He had just entered the program and was also trying not to use marijuana. She refused to engage in a discussion with her therapist about the pros and cons of entering into a relationship at this early stage of recovery and got involved with him sexually. Together, they both started to smoke marijuana. Penelope went from the stage of Maintenance/Relapse Prevention to Relapse/Recycling. She then returned to the stage of Precontemplation and refused to discuss the issues, choosing the relationship and the drug over her own health. The therapist felt it would not be productive to continue in therapy unless she was at least willing to discuss the pros and cons of using marijuana. When Penelope refused to do this, the therapist made the decision to discontinue therapy. The therapist felt she would be enabling the use of marijuana if these issues were ignored. No EMDR techniques were utilized due to the nature of the client's resistance and denial.

These examples show the wide variety of the types of relapse seen in clients.

SUMMARY

Relapse and Recycling is not a stage but rather an event that occurs for many clients. It is a very common experience; up to 90% of people lapse or relapse. Stabilization after relapse is key. Then the therapist helps the client reevaluate the experience and determine what stage in the process of change the client is now in and what interventions are now appropriate. Relapse is seen as a "teacher"; much may be learned from the experience that will promote future growth. Therapists should be aware of countertransference issues that emerge at this point.

LEARNING POINTS

1. Up to 90% of clients who engage in trying to change behaviors have a lapse or a relapse.
2. There is a difference between a lapse and a relapse. A lapse is a one-time event; a relapse is a longer-term change in behavior.
3. The work of this stage is to help clients make a decision about what to do following a relapse.
4. Clients reenter the process of change at different stages. The therapist helps the client determine what stage the client is in following a relapse. The interventions appropriate to that new stage are then utilized.
5. Therapists must be patient and aware of any countertransference issues that lift up.

CHAPTER 12

TREATING COMORBID TRAUMA AND ADDICTION WITH EMDR THERAPY

In this chapter, we review the overlap between trauma/posttraumatic stress disorder (PTSD) and specific types of addictions. We discuss the controversy about whether a client with a substance use disorder needs to be abstinent prior to doing trauma work. We also review what clients need in order to do Eye Movement Desensitization and Reprocessing (EMDR) standard protocol and what clients should not be included in this process. The application of EMDR therapy for clients with these disorders, including how to decide if the clinician should consider intervening when a client does not have stable sobriety, is discussed.

TRAUMA AND ADDICTION

PTSD was first established as a formal diagnosis in 1980 when the third edition of the *Diagnostic and Statistical Manual of Mental Disorders* (*DSM-III*) was released (American Psychiatric Association [APA], 1980). Since that time, there has been a dramatic increase in research about trauma and its effects. In the last 20 years, researchers have examined the overlap between trauma and PTSD with substance use disorders, including how the type of trauma and substance of choice influence these relationships (Bailey & Stewart, 2013).

It is estimated that between 50% and 70% of people in the United States have experienced at least one traumatic event in their lifetime (Houston, Shevlin, Adamson, & Murphy, 2011; Kilpatrick et al., 2000), with some researchers reporting rates as high as 89% (Breslau, 2002). This is consistent with research about other cultures (Frans, Rimmö, Aberg, & Fredrikson, 2005).

Approximately 1 out of 10 people who experience a potentially traumatic event will develop PTSD or another mental health disorder (Kessler, Sonnega, Bromet, Hughes, & Nelson, 1995; Kessler et al., 2005). About 7.8% of the U.S. population met criteria for PTSD in the National Comorbidity Study (Kessler et al., 1995). Although men are much more likely to experience a potentially traumatic event, women develop PTSD at rates twice that of men (Tolin & Foa, 2008). Rates of PTSD range from 16% to 70%, depending on the type of traumatic event experienced (Kessler et al., 1995). However, the effects of trauma and resultant PTSD often go undiagnosed (Grinage, 2003).

THE CONTROVERSY

There is disagreement in the psychotherapy field as to when EMDR therapy using the standard protocol for trauma should be used with clients who have addiction issues. This is of particular concern when the client's addictive process involves life-threatening drug or alcohol abuse. Some people believe that the individual should be sober or abstinent before the trauma work occurs (Hase, 2010). Others believe that if the trauma is "fueling" the addiction, the trauma work should take place (Abel & O'Brien, 2010; O'Brien & Abel, 2011; Shapiro, Vogelmann-Sine, & Sine, 1994; Zweben, Clark, & Smith, 1994). Then and only then will the recovery begin. There is very little in the literature to support either position. There is also little noted about the impact of process addictions and how that affects trauma processing. Leeds (2009), in particular, cautions about utilization of the trauma protocol when a client is actively using substances.

It is very difficult to avoid trauma issues when a client wants to discuss them and it is clear that the trauma is interfering with the client's ability to stay sober or abstinent. The authors wrote about this issue (Abel & O'Brien, 2010; O'Brien & Abel, 2011) and have found that it may be very helpful to proceed with caution and utilize the standard protocol for trauma with certain clients who are continuing to use substances in order to promote entry into recovery. Margo and Dana, who are discussed in the case studies section of this book, are both examples of clients who, despite their best efforts, were not able to be in recovery without working on trauma first. Trauma issues may interfere with recovery and progress being made in the recovery (Zweben et al., 1994). According to Shapiro, Vogelmann-Sine, and Sine (1994), trauma issues that are not processed appropriately may play a part in maintaining addiction.

We believe that this is not a decision to enter into lightly. It requires thoughtful and careful assessment of a client to determine if this is appropriate. However, we do believe that some clients will never get into recovery if the trauma is not resolved. The issues involved in making the decision about this will be discussed in the following. It is clear that there needs to be more research.

WHAT DO CLIENTS NEED BEFORE UTILIZING THE EMDR STANDARD PROTOCOL

All clients need certain skills and abilities before the EMDR standard protocol could be utilized. It goes without saying that people are very different and unique. Some clients who use chemicals will not be ready to do trauma work with the EMDR standard protocol until they stop using. Some abstinent clients will not be ready until they develop other skills. Client stabilization is the first order of business. Trauma work will be more successful when the client has a degree of stability (Herman, 1992; Najavits, 2002).

Clients make new connections between the "dysfunctional memory network and the memory networks that hold more adaptive information" with the use of the EMDR standard protocol (Shapiro, 2006, handout). In order to be able to do this processing, the client must be able to tap into memories without excess fear and there must be positive networks available to the client. The past experiences of the client alone do not predict whether these positive networks exist (Shapiro, 2006). If access to these networks is not strong or does not exist, work must be done to help the client increase them. This includes using EMDR protocols such as Resource Development Installation (RDI; Korn & Leeds, 2002). In difficult cases such as complex PTSD, there is potential for a "volcano" of emotion to erupt. This will likely interfere with the processing of trauma. These clients also need much preparatory work in order to do the standard protocol effectively (F. Shapiro, personal communication, November 27, 2013).

Clients need to have two things before they are ready to do the trauma protocol: One is affect tolerance, the other is internal/external resources (Korn & Leeds, 2002; York & Leeds, 2001). Clients need to be able to identify and tolerate feelings as well as the destabilization that may occur during and sometimes after the processing. They need to have a certain mount of ego strength as well as certain qualities, such as strength and perseverance, to do what may be a very difficult process. In addition, they should have some external supports, that is, friends, family, a church, or self-help group.

For many, EMDR trauma work is a scary and/or unusual process for them to consider undertaking. Clients need to feel safe and protected. This is where the relationship with the therapist comes into play. If the therapeutic alliance is a solid one, the client is more likely to have that sense of safety and be able to proceed with the processing work.

Getting Past Your Past, by Francine Shapiro (2012), is a helpful text for both clinicians and clients. Clients who read this book have access to information that will help them prepare to do the EMDR processing and will learn much that will help them prepare for EMDR therapy.

WHEN NOT TO USE THE STANDARD PROTOCOL

Clinicians need to assess a client's readiness for utilizing the EMDR standard protocol prior to initiating this treatment. Even if the client has requested this therapy or a referral source has indicated that the client is appropriate for it, clinicians must take responsibility for evaluating whether a client is truly ready for what can be a very destabilizing process. It is the clinician's responsibility to ensure that the client is not harmed by engaging in this process prematurely (Leeds, 2009; Shapiro, 2001). Some of the major factors that may preclude a client from utilizing this protocol are as follows.

Poor Affect Tolerance

If a client becomes easily flooded by emotions and overwhelmed, then treatment should first assist the client with the development of skills to manage feelings (Korn & Leeds, 2002).

Psychosis

Clients with symptoms of a psychotic disorder should be assessed for their level of stability. The EMDR standard protocol has been successfully used with clients with psychosis with adaptations (van der Berg & van der Gaag, 2012), but this type of treatment requires clinical expertise and specialized knowledge. In general, clinicians should not jump into trauma processing with a client who has psychosis.

Suicidal Ideation or Attempts

Clients with suicidal ideation and past suicide attempts should be carefully evaluated. Suicidal thinking is generally a contraindication for trauma processing (Shapiro, 2001) although it may be used. Clinicians should use good clinical judgment and consider consultation before proceeding.

Substance Use

As we have previously noted, clients who are actively using substances may not be good candidates to initiate trauma processing. This is discussed in detail in the following.

Dissociation

Clients who have more intense levels of dissociation, especially complex PTSD and dissociative identity disorder (DID), should be treated with specialized protocols prior to processing trauma (Forgash & Knipe, 2012; Korn, 2009). Very experienced clinicians should do this work.

Health Status

Clients who are in fragile health may not be good candidates for EMDR standard protocol. Some examples of health conditions that would warrant caution include cardiovascular problems, seizure disorders, or head injuries (Leeds, 2009). In cases with complicating medical issues, clinicians should seek a release of information for the primary care physician and/or specialist to determine whether a client is appropriate for trauma processing. Ideally, physicians should give the client medical clearance before proceeding.

HOW TO DECIDE TO USE THE STANDARD PROTOCOL

The authors (Abel & O'Brien, 2010; O'Brien & Abel, 2011) wrote previously about the decision-making process involved in determining whether or not a client with addiction issues and trauma is ready to do the standard protocol and when to initiate that process. This is an expansion of those ideas.

This is a complex clinical decision. Each client should be considered individually and carefully. It is probably better to err on the side of caution. At the same time, our clients should not suffer needlessly. If unresolved trauma is helping to maintain an addiction, the standard protocol should definitely be an option.

These are the questions that should be considered. There is no magic answer in terms of using the protocol or not. The collective answers will give you a picture of your client and will lead to the information you need to make a decision. The amount of experience and the degree of confidence that a clinician has will influence this decision. It is also important to discuss this with the client and make this a joint collaboration, with informed consent.

1. What is the client's Stage of Change? What is the client's motivation?

   How motivated is your client? Obviously, a client in the stage of Preparation or Action is more ready to do the work involved than a client in Precontemplation or Contemplation. Does the client want to do the work? This is important. If the clinician, not the client, is more interested or motivated, it is not time to engage in trauma work.

2. The person's addiction history: Did the trauma trigger the use?

   Complete a thorough history of the person's use and use patterns and behaviors. Also look at the trauma history. Is there a clear connection between the use/behaviors and the trauma? If there is, it may be a good indication that the standard protocol is appropriate.

3. The client's history of trying to quit: What happened?

   Has the client tried to quit in the past? Was this successful, even for a short time? Why did the person try to quit? Are the negative consequences of using outweighing the positive ones at this point? Is there any evidence of withdrawal symptoms? Did the person have support to quit in the past? If not, what support would be needed now?

4. What external/internal resources does the person have?

   Does the person have ego strength? Does the person have an internal strength or stamina? How does the person feel about himself or herself deep down? Are there external supports, such as friends, family, spouse, or partnership? Church? Groups?

5. Does the client have a single or complex trauma history?

   Explore the trauma history in detail. A single or simple trauma will probably resolve more quickly. A client who has multiple traumas or complex PTSD will need more resources and will take longer to process the trauma.

6. What is the client's functional level?

   Is the person able to participate in life? Activities of daily living? Work? Will he or she need time off from work to do the processing or be able to take time if it becomes too painful or if he or she gets destabilized? How independent is the person? Is this a strength or a weakness?

7. What is the client's current stress level?

   If the stress level is high, it may be better to postpone doing the standard protocol.

8. Does the client have affect tolerance?

   As noted above, clients need to be able to tolerate affect in order to do this kind of trauma work. It was also noted that clients with addictions have poor ability to tolerate affect. However, clients are all different. Some addicted individuals have better affect tolerance than others. Clients who do the standard protocol should have some skills in this area and plans about what will happen if he or she becomes destabilized in the process.

9. Does the client need detoxification?

   If a client is physically dependent on a substance, he or she may go into withdrawal syndrome when not using. If this is the case, the standard protocol would not be appropriate. A medical evaluation would be the first order of business. Although it may be appropriate to use this protocol with a client who is not currently able to be abstinent, it is important that the client *not* use drugs and alcohol during the time of processing. The authors ask clients to abstain from drugs before, during, and after the use of the standard protocol in order to promote optimal treatment. Drugs and alcohol should not be used to medicate dysphoria that occurs during the processing.

10. What is the quality of the therapeutic relationship?

    This is a key factor. It may be the most important factor to consider. If the therapeutic alliance is a good one, the client is likely to feel safe and protected during the process. Many trauma survivors have a very difficult time trusting others. Building trust in the relationship is a two-way street. The clinician needs to trust that the client is being honest about addictive behaviors before the trauma work can proceed. The client needs to know that the clinician is available should difficulties arise, both during and after the session.

This is not an easy decision for the client or for the therapist. After assessing the answers to the above questions, the therapist develops a hypothesis about the best way to proceed: abstinence or no abstinence from addiction before the trauma work begins. Although one should probably err on the side of caution, it is possible to be too cautious and lose the opportunity to resolve the issues in a timely fashion that would lead to optimal healing.

So what if you begin the trauma work and difficulties arise? What if the client begins to use during the process? This may be anxiety provoking; after all, we all want the work to proceed without flaw. Remember, individuals with comorbid addiction and trauma diagnoses may be difficult and complicated clients. In this case, you rely on yourself, your experience, and your therapeutic skills. The clinician will need to regroup; so will the client. If the client has relapsed, the individual's motivation for change must be reassessed. At this point, one takes a step back and utilizes other resources to provide safety and to develop stabilization. Use all your therapy skills to determine how to proceed. The Affect Tolerance protocol, Safe/Calm Place, RDI, DeTUR protocol, and CRAVEX/Memory of Addiction protocol may all be helpful during this process of reevaluating the work. You may refer back to previous chapters on the Stages of Change and utilize the resources there after reassessing the client's motivation.

Despite the pain involved in being traumatized and addicted, clients are often remarkably resilient. If you have a good therapeutic alliance, use that to let your client know you are available to maintain safety and to continue with the work. Remember that it is the client's choice about how far to proceed with this work and whether to continue in the healing process.

SUMMARY

In this chapter, the authors reviewed the trauma/addiction connection. We discussed the controversy about when to use the standard protocol for trauma with clients with addictions: Some believe that clients should be abstinent before proceeding, others believe that utilizing the standard protocol helps to promote recovery. We discussed what clients need before utilizing the standard protocol is appropriate. We also discussed which clients should not use the standard protocol. Finally, we outlined factors to consider about when to use the standard protocol with clients.

LEARNING POINTS

1. There is a significant overlap between a history of trauma and the development of chemical and process addictions.
2. Some clinicians believe that a client should be free of addictions and addictive behaviors before trauma work is initiated. Others believe that this work is essential if the addiction is the result of trauma. This involves a complex clinical decision that should not be undertaken lightly.
3. The skills that clients need before undertaking EMDR trauma work were discussed.
4. The factors that would suggest that EMDR is contraindicated were reviewed: poor affect tolerance, psychosis, suicidal thinking, substance abuse, dissociation, and complicating medical issues.
5. The authors reviewed 10 factors to consider regarding the processing of trauma in those with ongoing addiction and addictive behaviors.

AFTERWORD

When they choose recovery, our clients choose a challenging path. They give up the only coping mechanisms they know—addictive behaviors—and opt for a life of health. It is not an easy road to travel. Recovery is a lifelong process and it is not an easy one. But when the recovery is a good one, it brings much joy, old patterns are changed, and life can become beautiful and fulfilling again.

Therapists who work with addiction and trauma are also choosing a challenging path. This can be a very tough group of clients, with many challenges ahead for both the client and the therapist. Many therapists would choose to work with clients who are healthier. In the days of managed care, these clients require more sessions and longer time in treatment to accomplish their goals. They are challenging, but they also have much to teach us about change and recovery. A therapist who chooses to work with this population will never be bored. Self-care will be paramount.

PART III

CASE STUDIES

INTRODUCTION

In this section of the book, several case examples are discussed in detail. These cases represent Eye Movement Desensitization and Reprocessing (EMDR) treatment with individuals who have difficulties with addictions. They are not meant to be prototypes but are examples of how the therapists used individualized approaches to assess, develop treatment plans, and work through issues with clients using EMDR therapy. When each client is treated as unique, the chances of success appear to increase. In addition, this is when a clinician may feel most creative in the work.

All identifying information has been changed to protect the confidentiality of the clients.

CASE STUDY 1

DANA: CONSECUTIVE DAY EMDR

Francine Shapiro (2001) initially developed Eye Movement Desensitization and Reprocessing (EMDR) as a treatment for posttraumatic stress disorder (PTSD). More recently, EMDR has been used more broadly: for anxiety, depression, and substance abuse, among other disorders. While the EMDR protocols are structured, there is also room for creativity in this treatment. Consecutive day EMDR (CDEMDR) is an example of how a clinician may be innovative with the use of EMDR.

CDEMDR is a relatively new way to think about treating trauma and addictions using EMDR. It may be used in inpatient or outpatient settings. It could also be used as an alternative for inpatient treatment.

For the purpose of this book, CDEMDR treatment will be defined as EMDR sessions occurring on consecutive days. It includes sessions occurring two or more times during a week.

REFERRAL

Dana, a White male, was 50 years old when he first came for treatment. He was referred by another local therapist who did not have experience with addictions and felt Dana would be better served by a clinician who had that expertise. Dana had a history of alcohol dependence and was using cocaine weekly at the time of the intake.

PRESENTING PROBLEMS

Dana came to therapy because he wanted to stop using cocaine. He had a history of serious childhood trauma. If he stopped using cocaine for longer than a week he would be triggered by these memories and use cocaine to squelch them. About 10 years earlier, he worked with a male therapist for about 3 to 4 years. This therapist was leaning backward in his chair while Dana was discussing his history of trauma. When Dana told him about the most serious event, about which he had the most shame, the therapist fell over backward in the chair. This put an end to Dana's ability to trust him and he felt that no therapist would be able to handle his degree of trauma.

When he came to treatment, Dana had serious issues with trust. He trusted no one. In particular, he had trust issues with women, which he revealed during the initial phone call. This therapist, a woman, discussed with him how working with a female could possibly help him resolve some of these issues and Dana decided to explore this opportunity further.

Dana came to therapy to work on the following issues:

1. Lack of trust
2. Anger; he described himself as extremely short tempered
3. Depression; he was not suicidal and was not on any medication
4. Cocaine addiction
5. Serious childhood trauma, including sexual abuse by father and physical and emotional abuse by mother
6. Loneliness
7. Fear of holding his grandchildren

SOCIAL HISTORY

Dana came from a Maine family with a long line of fishermen. He grew up in a "shack" near the beach (although beach property in Maine is now extremely valuable, in the past certain areas were considered "trashy") and eventually became a fisherman himself. He also worked several other blue-collar jobs that paid well. Dana presented as extremely intelligent. He was, however, very uneducated and did not finish high school. He was funny, energetic, a bit "rough around the edges," with a strong presence, and swore frequently. He was a very hard worker and work meant a great deal to him. He was the middle child among five children, with two older brothers and two younger sisters. Three of the siblings were described as having addiction problems. All the siblings still live in the general vicinity of the parents.

Both parents were alive and lived together in the family home. The father had Alzheimer's disease and the mother was very ill. Both were described as extremely abusive, both physically and verbally. Dana was sexually abused by his father and watched his father abuse one of his sisters. His father's mother died when the father was 2 years old and he lived with seven different families growing up; Dana felt that he was probably sexually abused himself. Mother abused Dana physically and emotionally, beat him, gave him enemas, and stuck him with diaper pins, among other events. She came from a family of 14 children. The boys in her family all left as teens and went to the woods to live. Mother was raped when she was a young teenager. Dana still had regular contact with his parents and had become a caretaker to them, despite their ongoing abusive behaviors.

Dana left home when he was a teenager and lived on his own. He met his future wife when he was in his late teens and she was aged 15 years. They immediately moved in together, were married when she became pregnant, and lived together until they were divorced 15 years ago. Dana and his wife had four children, two boys and two girls, all of whom are now grown. Dana was particularly concerned because he had avoided being affectionate with his children when he was bringing them up due to his own abuse and fears that he might hurt them; he was now avoiding being affectionate with his young grandchildren.

There is a long history of alcoholism in the family. Dana began to drink when he was 15 years old. He went to rehab in 1990 and had no alcohol since that time. However, he began to use cocaine at that point. He estimated that he had used over a million dollars worth of drugs. He lost his job, his wife, and family, and went bankrupt as a result of his cocaine use. Before he came to treatment, he had tapered his cocaine use to approximately once a week.

COURSE OF TREATMENT

Dana came to two therapy sessions in April 2009. During those two sessions, the therapist did an assessment and began to discuss the possibility of EMDR with Dana. Despite his fears, he was able to tell her about the worst of the abuse that he had experienced. After an assessment, the therapist diagnosed Dana with cocaine dependence and PTSD. The therapist began to discuss EMDR with Dana because it became immediately clear that the underlying trauma was driving his addiction. She (and he) felt that he would not be able to be abstinent until the underlying trauma was processed. The client seemed amenable to the idea and the therapist began to work on a treatment plan.

One session occurred in May 2009. Dana was trying to quit cocaine again by himself but found it extremely difficult. The therapist worked with Safe Place and the Desensitization of Triggers and Urge Reprocessing (DeTUR) positive treatment goal, both as an entry to the EMDR work and to see how he responded. He did extremely well with both protocols. The therapist recommended that he read *Quitting Cocaine* by Schaffer and Jones (1989) but that was out of print and difficult to locate.

In June 2009, Dana canceled his next session at the last minute. He knew this meant that he had to pay his fee and later in the week he did that, minus $10. He did not set up another appointment.

What followed was a series of checking-in phone calls and it quickly became apparent that he was testing the therapist. He admitted that he paid $10 less than he was supposed to because he wanted to keep the lines of communication open but he was not ready to commit to doing the work. He came in and paid the money. The therapist said she would get him a copy of the Schaffer and Jones book to read and then forgot to do it. This was successfully dealt with over the phone and trust was discussed. This ultimately helped to deepen the relationship.

In January 2010, Dana decided that he finally needed to do something about his cocaine use. He was extremely discouraged. The therapist recommended that he go to inpatient treatment due to the severity of his addiction and trauma history. He began to explore that option and agreed to come to a therapy session to discuss it. During that session, he told the therapist that he did not want to go to inpatient treatment; he wanted the therapist to consider doing the work with him. He would take a week off from work and wanted to do an intensive piece of therapy. After much discussion, the therapist agreed to do this and a contract was developed. The decision and the structure of the work arose organically from the needs of the client and the therapist's willingness to organize and do the work.

What follows is a discussion of the structure of treatment that was developed.

THE STRUCTURE OF OUTPATIENT CDEMDR

It is important to carefully structure outpatient CDEMDR. EMDR may be quite destabilizing for some clients, particularly those with dual diagnoses or complex PTSD.

In the case presented here, the client was an active cocaine addict with a serious history of complex PTSD. It was important to the therapist that the client be safe during the process. She set up the structure of a day treatment or partial hospital program without the support of a larger staff. Seeing the client every day allowed the therapist to check on the client frequently and intervene if necessary.

The following is the outline of the structure:

1. The client received five 90-minute EMDR sessions, one a day for 5 days. A follow-up session was scheduled 3 days later.
2. No use of alcohol or drugs during treatment; despite his frequent use, the client was able to do this.
3. Daily journaling.
4. Daily exercise.
5. Daily phone call to the therapist a few hours after the session to report on reactions to the session.
6. Eat well/do not skip meals.
7. Twelve-step meeting daily.
8. Do something to take mind off trauma issues, that is, movie, television, "junk book," and so forth.
9. No canceling appointments for any reason.
10. Mutual trust; the therapist would be available for the client. In return, she expected commitment and honesty.

This contract was reviewed as part of preparing for the treatment. It was developed mutually with the client and he was able to largely follow it. Due to the rural setting in which he lived, 12-step meetings were not available as often as would be ideal. He was not able to attend a meeting every day. However, he was compliant with the rest of the contract.

Dana arranged for the week off from work. He had meetings with his children to tell them what he was about to do. Despite past ruptures in their relationships due to Dana's behaviors, they were all supportive of him. He also connected with some other old friends, including a past Alcoholics Anonymous (AA) sponsor to ask for support.

The therapist and the client agreed to start with the trauma protocol because the abuse was underlying the addiction. The therapist and client both carefully monitored the client's cravings and planned to switch to the Hase/CRAVEX protocol when necessary to deal with them. In addition, Resource Development Installation (RDI) would be used if appropriate. Flexibility during the treatment was a key factor.

THE INTENSIVE CONSECUTIVE DAY TREATMENT

Treatment occurred during the last week of January 2010.

Day 1

Treatment began with the standard protocol, with the focus on the past sexual abuse by his father.

Image: all black, lying next to his father while father masturbated, trying to roll away.
Negative cognition (NC): I am not safe.
Positive cognition (PC): I can be loving and relax.
Validity of Cognition (VoC): 1.
Emotions: flood of horror, anger.
Subjective Units of Disturbance (SUDS): 6.
Body: chest.

During the processing, Dana had many images of abuse by his father. In addition, issues around his mother began to emerge. After 26 sets of bilateral stimulation using the Tak/AudioScan, the SUDS was 0 and the VoC was 7, with a clear body scan.

Day 2

Initially, we reviewed the session from the previous day; the SUDS remained 0.

Dana came into the session reporting that he was having cravings for cocaine and requested that we work on them. The Hase/CRAVEX protocol was used to desensitize the cravings.

Image: in his truck, driving.
Level of Urge (LoU): 8.
NC: I am worthless.
PC: I have value.
VoC: 4.
Emotions: sad.
Body: chest.

After three sets of bilateral stimulation, the LoU was 0 and the VoC was 7.

Some RDI was utilized to build a "firewall" around the urges.

Day 3

This was the middle of the week and Dana wanted to tackle what he considered his most painful issue, the severe abuse by his mother.

Image: mother smearing his face with his feces.
NC: I am worthless and empty.
PC: I am normal.
VoC: 4.
Emotions: anger, sadness.
SUDS: 10.
Body: waist, lip, legs.

Dana processed this memory very quickly. After 15 sets of bilateral stimulation, the SUDS was 0 and the VoC was 7. The body scan was clear. During the processing, Dana experienced his sadness, horror about the event, remembered what happened, and moved to a place of forgiveness, "She did the best she could." He began to recognize that some of his strengths were because he survived all of this.

We continued to work on the cravings and urges he felt, using the Hase/CRAVEX protocol.

Image: by himself driving, the night before.
LoU: 5.
NC: I am weak.
PC: I have the strength to move past this.
VoC: 5.
Emotions: pain, sadness, loss.
Body: all over.

After five sets of bilateral stimulation, the LoU was 0 and the VoC was 7. Dana imaged being drug free in the future while bilateral stimulation was used to reinforce this state.

Day 4

We reviewed the treatment to date and continued to work on abuse by mother.

Image: watching mother prepare vitamin B_{12} shots.
NC: I am not safe.
PC: I have strength to resist.
VoC: 7.
Emotions: anger, fear, urge to fight.
SUDS: 4.
Body: shoulders, back, arms.

Dana processed this extremely quickly. There appeared to have been some generalizing effect from previous processing. After two sets of bilateral stimulation, the SUDS was 0 and the VoC was 7. Dana had a small craving that morning (LoU: 1). He used the image developed in his RDI work and "threw up a firewall" around the craving.

Day 5

During this session, an aftercare plan was developed. This included sessions once a month to check in with this therapist, phone calls to the therapist to give updates, Narcotics Anonymous (NA) meetings, going to the doctor for an exam and to the dentist, and future plans for a family session with his children. We processed and evaluated the accomplishments made during the week.

A follow-up session occurred 3 days later. In that session, we continued to discuss the process of the treatment and Dana's feelings about it. Dana felt great at that point. He described himself as improving every day; colors looked different to him, smells were different. He felt much more calm and relaxed. His cravings were short-lived and he was able to talk himself through them. He was beginning to work on his aftercare plan.

He was very excited about how much better he was feeling. During the past week, he connected with old friends, asked for and received support, began to clean up his apartment, bought new clothes, and began to make appointments to get his teeth fixed and to have a physical exam. These self-care skills had disappeared while he was using drugs. There appeared to have been some generalizing effect around past traumas and Dana felt that for the time being his trauma was resolved. He presented as very happy with his new life. His biggest issue was feeling that he did not deserve all this good feeling, based on his past behavior.

Dana is not someone who wanted to be in ongoing psychotherapy. Despite his intelligence and insight, he did not want to spend time talking about old issues. EMDR was the perfect therapy for him and he responded to it extremely well. He was able to process all the pertinent issues and responded positively to all of the protocols used. In addition, he was able to give feedback about what protocol would be helpful to him on what day.

At 3-year follow-up, Dana remained abstinent. He reported that he felt happier than he ever had in his life. He now felt that he deserves this happiness and was making plans for the future.

DISCUSSION

Based on this anecdotal evidence, it would appear that CDEMDR treatment is a viable treatment option. In addition, it may be seen as an alternative to inpatient treatment for certain clients. It allows for the structure and follow-up necessary when working with clients who have very serious diagnoses and who are likely to become quickly destabilized.

The client discussed herein had very serious issues with trust and before he was able to engage in any kind of treatment, he tested the therapist and made sure she was available to him. The relationship was a key factor. The therapist was able to be honest and authentic; in turn, the client began to open up. The therapist was able to accept and not react negatively to the most severe traumas he presented. In addition, the client and the therapist developed an easy, bantering relationship that helped facilitate the process.

CDEMDR treatment is very intensive. The client and the therapist must be aware of this and prepared to manage it. It is, however, a viable alternative for inpatient therapy or for a client who has time constraints or needs therapy to occur quickly. It appears to be a very fast way of dealing with client issues.

SUMMARY

This author has presented a case where CDEMDR was used with much success. In fact, during the course of treatment, the results were seen as quite miraculous. There was a "perfect storm" of events, which allowed the treatment to occur: a client who

1. Was motivated to do the work and change
2. Was willing to take the risk to trust
3. Had the money to pay for treatment and could take a vacation
4. Had a therapist who was willing to take the extra time to do this treatment and willing to be innovative
5. Perhaps most important, the therapeutic relationship was a solid one, based on mutual understanding and an easy, bantering relationship laced with a good, appropriate amount of humor

Inside the structure of the process of EMDR, there is room for this kind of creativity. It can potentially be beneficial for some clients to experience CDEMDR.

CASE STUDY 2

JOANNE: A TRADITIONAL CASE INVOLVING TRAUMA AND ALCOHOLISM

This case involves a client who came to therapy following treatment at an intensive outpatient program (IOP). She had a significant trauma history that had likely interfered with her ability to maintain sobriety. Once her traumas were resolved through the use of Eye Movement Desensitization and Reprocessing (EMDR), she was able to enter a long-term, healthy recovery.

REFERRAL

Joanne was referred by a local hospital substance abuse program where she had completed detoxification as well as an IOP for 4 weeks; she was continuing in an aftercare psychotherapy group that met weekly. She was referred for relapse prevention and trauma work.

IDENTIFYING INFORMATION

Joanne was a 28-year-old single mother of a 6-year-old son when she first met with her therapist. She had been married for a short time to her son's father but was divorced for several years at the time of intake and had shared custody. She worked full-time at a local business and was an Army veteran. She lived with her boyfriend whom she described as supportive.

ADDICTION HISTORY

Joanne's substance of choice was alcohol. She described herself as alcoholic and had been diagnosed as such in the IOP. She had a long history of alcohol use, beginning in early adolescence, including a history of blackouts and serious, almost fatal overdoses. Although she experimented with other drugs, including marijuana and cocaine, alcohol was her preferred drug.

When she entered treatment, she was sober, in the stage of Maintenance/ Relapse prevention. Her sobriety was shaky at that point. Although she wanted to be sober, she had not yet developed coping mechanisms and had difficulty with affect tolerance. She was somewhat comfortable with angry feelings but did not know how to appropriately express these feelings. Other feelings were somewhat foreign to her and she could not identify or manage them.

SOCIAL HISTORY

Joanne was the oldest of three children born to a mother whom she described as "having a major mental illness." No diagnosis was available. She described her father as alcoholic. Her younger brother also had a diagnosis of bipolar disorder and marijuana abuse.

When she was a child, Joanne lived in poverty and she grew up with inadequate food and clothing. She often went to school in dirty clothes, hungry, and was teased by peers about her appearance. Her mother was unable to provide adequately for her emotionally or to manage her behavior, so she was sent to live with her maternal grandmother, following her parents' divorce, at the age of 5 years. Joanne noted that her grandmother was very strict but provided the only consistency that she had as a child. As a young adolescent, she began to act out by breaking rules and talking back to her grandmother and was sent to live with her father and his new wife in Florida. Her father also abused her physically and threatened her. While she was living with him, she experienced her first bout of depression and was hospitalized at the age of 13 years following a suicide attempt. When she was released from the hospital, she was immediately put on a bus to return to Maine alone.

Joanne enlisted in the Army at age 17 years; she was discharged honorably at the end of her period of duty, returned home, and got married shortly thereafter. She gave birth to her son, Matt, and was divorced from his father when Matt was 1 year old. At the time of intake, her son was 6 years old. She became involved with her present boyfriend about 4 years before she entered treatment.

SUMMARY OF TREATMENT

In the beginning of treatment, the process was inconsistent. Joanne had no ability to trust at that point and would not call when she was experiencing difficulty. She missed appointments, did not return phone calls, and appeared to have dropped out of treatment several times. Eventually, she would return. She had two serious relapses. Both times her blood alcohol level was extremely high and she almost died from alcohol poisoning. The second time this happened, the Department of Health and Human Services stepped in and her son was removed from the home, giving his father full custody. Joanne loved her son more than anything else in her life, so this event served as a turning point

(Schaeffer & Jones, 1989) for her. She became increasingly motivated to stay sober and hired an attorney to help her regain custody. She reengaged with her aftercare group at the hospital, went to Alcoholics Anonymous (AA), and began to regularly attend therapy sessions. She slowly began to trust her therapist.

Once Joanne got serious about being sober, she did not relapse again. She began to engage in a therapeutic relationship and worked on a number of issues, including her anxiety, anger, affect management, feelings of jealousy, lack of trust, feelings of isolation, abandonment, and her family of origin issues.

Relapse Prevention

Treatment focused on helping Joanne develop strategies for relapse prevention. A number of triggers were identified, including issues related to her mother, intense emotions, grocery shopping, nice weather, pain, feeling or being alone, her 30th birthday, being around alcohol, illness (her own or others), and negative thinking. She attended AA for a short time and found this helpful although she resisted continuing to attend. She was able to develop strategies for dealing with all of her triggers. She took Lexepro and Campral in the beginning of her recovery to help her manage depression and cravings.

In addition, some EMDR protocols were utilized in her therapy to support her sobriety and help her to manage her feelings, her triggers, and cravings.

Safe/Calm Place

Joanne visualized a field near where she lived with her grandmother. Her cue word was "lily." She was able to use this image to increase her sense of relaxation and sense of calm.

Positive Treatment Goal (Desensitization Triggers and Urge Reprocessing [DeTUR])

Joanne was able to visualize a sober life. This was reinforced with bilateral stimulation.

Resource Development

Strength was the quality she needed to have reinforced. She drew upon the feeling of strength she felt when she was in boot camp and visualized carrying that feeling into her present life to support her sobriety.

Hase/CRAVEX Protocol

This protocol was utilized to help Joanne deal with her cravings for alcohol. The following is an example.

Image: standing in her kitchen at 9 a.m.
Level of urge (LoU): 8 out of 10.
Negative cognition (NC): I am weak.
Positive cognition (PC): I am stronger than my worst craving.

Validity of Cognition (VoC): 4 to 5 out of 7.
Emotions: shame, anger, discouragement.
Body: tummy.

Bilateral stimulation commenced.

Set 1: a black hole, not filled.
Set 2: no friends, no one cares, alcohol used to be a friend, lack of trust, her friends burned her like alcohol did.
Set 3: emptiness, can I trust myself to start making friends?
Set 4: work, betrayal by friends in the past.
Set 5: friend dying of cancer, being the friend she would like to have?
LoU: 0.
VoC: 7.
Body: clear scan.

Following this session, Joanne reported that her cravings were reduced and were never again as intense as they had been prior to this session. She also realized that she needed to work to fill the "hole" by learning how to make more social connections and trust more.

Ego Systems Work

It was very helpful for Joanne to look at her "parts of self" (see Chapter 8, The Stage of Preparation/Determination). She was able to define three different parts: the healthy adult, the wounded child (who was quite young), and the addict. Initially, Joanne hated her addict part and wanted to ignore her. Over time she was able to see that it was not helpful to do this; when that part was ignored, Joanne was more at risk for relapse. She learned how to check in with that part on a daily basis, ask that part what she needed, and try to meet those needs. One evening in her aftercare group, another client was complaining about her addict part and how much she hated it. Joanne was able to speak up and teach the group how she had learned to love that part of herself!

In addition, Joanne learned to honor and listen to her "inner child." She was able to pay more attention to the pain of her childhood, her traumas, and develop alternate coping mechanisms.

She engaged her "adult part" to help her negotiate the world. Joanne had no good role models for problem solving or relationships, but she had some innate skills. She was able to allow her adult part to step forward and take charge when necessary.

Each night before she went to sleep, Joanne checked in with all these parts of herself and thus learned how to identify and begin to meet her own needs.

Trauma Treatment

This ego-systems work was a precursor for the EMDR work to follow and was an important part of her preparation for doing EMDR.

One aspect of the treatment plan for this client was coordination of care with the hospital personnel from the center that initially referred Joanne. She continued in the aftercare group at that facility for over a year and developed a good relationship with her group leader.

Joanne was seen as extremely fragile. Hospital personnel were very concerned about her relapses and the possibility that she would either end up in the hospital again or die. Although the underlying trauma issues appeared to be related to her relapses and her lack of sense of self, hospital personnel requested that the EMDR work be put on hold until Joanne was stronger. Joanne was able to do some of the Resource Development Installation (RDI) and affect tolerance work that is seen as an important foundation for the trauma work (Korn & Leeds, 2002).

Joanne has a number of serious childhood traumas that impacted her development as an adult. They included the following:

a. Age 5 years—being placed with a foster family and feeling abandoned
b. Neglect—dirty at school, hair falling out due to malnourishment
c. Age 6 years—stepmother threatened her with a knife
d. Verbal abuse by grandmother
e. Physical abuse by grandmother
f. Physical abuse by father
g. Sexual abuse by trailer park manager, older boy, friend's brother, and carnival worker
h. Age 15 years—car accident

It appeared that all of these traumas and her inability to process them was fueling her craving to use alcohol. The standard EMDR protocol was utilized once Joanne's sobriety was more solid, after about a year with no use.

The following is an example of use of the standard protocol. The issue is her stepmother threatening her with a knife. The event targeted was one of the first and most serious traumas identified by the client.

Image: stepmother holding the knife, in the kitchen, pointing it at Joanne and her brother.
NC: I am unlovable.
PC: I am lovable.
VoC: 1.
Emotions: anger, fear, empty.
Subjective Units of Disturbance (SUDS): 10.
Body: all over.

Bilateral stimulation began.

Set 1: jealousy: father chose another woman over her.
Set 2: father with other women: father, and stepmother eating steak and not allowing her brother or her to have any, dumping potpourri on the steak.
Set 3: feeling threatened by stepmother: alone, anger toward father.
Set 4: lots of memories: her teddy bear taken by father.
Set 5: a wall: brain trying not to remember.
Cognitive Interweave by Therapist: What would happen to you if you remembered?

That's what it is. I won't remember, I won't go back, I can deal with not knowing.
Set 6: the town, kissing a boy and getting into trouble.
Set 7: a door that needs to be open, fear, alone, weight on chest.
Set 8: that house represents so much pain, sick to her stomach.
Set 9: anger, why?
Set 10: true terror in that house.
Set 11: so many lies, so much terror.
Set 12: lies, terrorized.

The time for the session was up. The client reported that the SUDS was zero, VoC 7, body scan was clear.

The client utilized EMDR extremely effectively and efficiently. Although she was terrified about what she would experience in the session, she proceeded with the trauma work in this and subsequent sessions. She became increasingly strong and stable.

CASE DISCUSSION

This is an example of a client who came to treatment through a traditional route. She had been treated in detoxification and intensive outpatient treatment before presenting to individual therapy for relapse prevention and trauma work. She appeared to be in the stage of Relapse Prevention/Maintenance when she started therapy. However, it quickly became apparent that she was both ambivalent about her recovery and lacked appropriate skills to maintain sobriety. She was seriously traumatized, making it difficult for her to trust her therapist and engage in the therapeutic process. Over time, she was able to develop the trust that allowed her to proceed with therapy. Following a serious crisis when she lost custody of her son, she was able to develop the motivation to change, allowing her to engage more fully with therapy. She utilized both traditional coping skills for relapse prevention as well as EMDR. She was able to regain custody of her son and developed a healthy way of coparenting with his father.

At this writing, Joanne has 3 continuous years of sobriety.

SUMMARY

This is an example of a client who had severe alcoholism and who almost died. She was not trusting of the therapy process initially but eventually she developed a close working relationship with her therapist over time. Ultimately, she was able to recover. A flexible approach utilizing many different therapeutic techniques was both extremely helpful and highly necessary for working effectively with her in treatment.

CASE STUDY

3

TINA: THERAPY IN STAGES WITH A TRAUMATIZED ADOLESCENT MARIJUANA ADDICT

Psychotherapy with an adolescent can be a very fragile process. Adolescents are often brought into treatment by their parents and are not self-motivated. In addition, adolescent substance abusers are often unmotivated to change because experimenting and/or using substances is very often accepted in their peer group.

According to the National Institute of Drug Abuse's (NIDA) 2012 Monitoring the Future Study, 6.5% of 8th graders, 17.0% of 10th graders, and 22.9% of 12th graders used marijuana in the month before they were surveyed (NIDA, 2012b). Between the 1990s and 2007, marijuana use decreased. This trend may now be reversing. In 2012, 6.5% of 12th graders used marijuana daily as opposed to 5.1% in 2007 (NIDA, 2012c; see Chapter 5, Assessment of Addictions and Trauma).

REFERRAL

Tina's mother brought Tina, aged 18 years, to her own therapist because she was concerned about her daughter. She knew that Tina had been smoking marijuana. In addition, Tina was seriously traumatized when her best friend was killed in a car accident when Tina was 14. Her mother felt she had never resolved that loss. The therapist referred her for Eye Movement Desensitization and Reprocessing (EMDR).

IDENTIFYING INFORMATION

Tina was 18 years old when she first came to see her therapist. She was the youngest of three children; two older brothers were away at college. The mother and father lived together in a well-to-do suburban community. The father was employed at a local insurance company as an executive and the mother worked out of the home. Tina had started her freshman year of college in another state but failed her first semester and returned home to live with her parents.

PRESENTING PROBLEM

Tina described herself as depressed and seriously traumatized by her friend's sudden death. She described Molly as the closest person to her on the earth, and their two families were very close as well. Until she met Molly, she was shy and had few friends at school. She shared all her secrets with Molly and felt completely heard and understood. One Saturday afternoon, Molly came over to her house and asked Tina to go shopping with her and her older sister. Tina was very tired that day and chose not to go.

Several hours later, while napping in her room, she heard the phone ring and heard her mother's shocked responses to what was said on the line. She and her father took Tina into the living room where they told her that Molly had been killed in a car accident on the way home from the shopping trip; the sister had been driving. Tina was extremely upset and shocked by this. She felt responsible because she was asked to go on the shopping trip; she felt Molly would be alive if she had gone. She went through the motions of attending the funeral but also began to increase her marijuana smoking. Up to that point, her marijuana use had been experimental in nature but she began to smoke three to four times a day. She did not identify herself as having a problem with drugs but she was aware that she used marijuana to medicate her feelings about Molly's death.

DRUG AND ALCOHOL HISTORY

Tina first experimented with marijuana when she was 14 years old. She and Molly tried it together with Molly's older sister. They also experimented with alcohol at the same time. Tina never liked alcohol and never tried any other drugs. She began to use marijuana regularly, about once or twice a week. Her use increased after Molly's death and when she came to therapy she was using on a daily basis. She had no motivation to stop using but was motivated to have EMDR concerning the issue of Molly's death. She was in the stage of Precontemplation about her drug use but was willing to enter Contemplation. She agreed that she would stop using during the process of treatment and reportedly was able to do this.

Family History

There was a history of drug and alcohol abuse on her father's side of the family. In addition, there was a history of anxiety and depression on both sides of the family.

Only Tina's mother had received treatment. Tina had no prior psychotherapy.

THE PROCESS OF TREATMENT

Stage 1

Tina was extremely motivated to work on the issue of Molly's death. In addition, she was willing to stop using marijuana during the process. This was very important, as continued use of chemicals during EMDR work may block the processing or effect. The long-lasting impact of the trauma was also seen as contributing to her continuing marijuana use.

EMDR Treatment

Initially, Tina used the Safe/Calm Place exercise as a way to prepare for the work with the EMDR standard protocol. Her Safe (or what she called her "Happy Place") was skiing. She was able to use this image of skiing between sessions to relax.

Treatment with the standard protocol for trauma followed.

Target: Molly's death.
Image: the moment her parents told her about the death, in her family's living room.
Negative cognition (NC): it is my fault.
Positive cognition (PC): it is not my fault.
Emotions: sad.
Subjective Units of Disturbance (SUDS): 8.
Body: heart.

After 18 sets of bilateral stimulation, the SUDS went down to 3. Two more sessions were spent processing this issue. The SUDS went down to 2 and Tina felt that it was appropriate to end with a 2. This incident was so traumatic and so important, she felt it needed to stay at 2. That is when the processing was terminated. She reported feeling happier, more "fresh," and more engaged in life. EMDR processing triggered more feelings related to Molly's death, but she felt lucky that she was able to process these emotions and let some of them go. Dreams she had about Molly decreased. She no longer felt responsible for the death.

Stage 2

By all reports, Tina was doing much better following EMDR treatment. She reported that she was much less depressed and was more able to function in life. She had more acceptance of Molly's death and a greater spiritual perspective about the loss. Tina believed that the death had all happened for a reason, albeit one she did not understand. She indicated that she felt spiritually connected to Molly and imagined that she was like a guardian angel to her. She still grieved some for the loss but no longer held herself responsible for Molly's death.

She returned to school out of state where she had a successful first semester. However, during her second semester there, she was stopped by the police while driving and was arrested for operating under the influence. In addition, the police discovered drug paraphernalia in the car. Tina was sentenced by the court to drug counseling and told not to use drugs or alcohol. She returned to her therapist for treatment when she came home for the summer. This was 1 year after the end of her previous course of therapy. When she first came back, she was still using marijuana but she was motivated to explore this issue. She returned to therapy in the stage of Contemplation. It became clear that what was initially self-medication had now taken on a life of its own; her marijuana use had crossed the line to addiction.

Initially, treatment focused on education about addiction and helping her to do a cost–benefit analysis around her drug use. Tina then began to date a new man and the relationship became very serious very quickly. This man did not believe in using drugs and asked that Tina quit smoking marijuana. This became her primary motivation. She chose a "quit" date and stopped using. She did not report any withdrawal symptoms. She seemed to minimize how difficult the change was as well. However, she was able to maintain abstinence from marijuana. In addition, she set more goals for herself and her future, including the completion of her college degree. She understood that this new man was her motivation for quitting initially but she was able to develop her own motivation for herself: She felt better, more alive, and able to deal with her feelings as a result. Treatment focused on examining and coping with her triggers to use, developing more self-esteem and a sense of self, and affect management. She terminated therapy after 6 months of abstinence and returned to college.

DISCUSSION

Therapy sometimes happens in stages; clients often do not work on all their issues at once. This case is a clear example of this. Initially, Tina was willing to explore the issue of her marijuana use only superficially and only because she was motivated to work through the loss of her friend. Through the use of EMDR, she was able to resolve her friend's death and her symptoms of depression and grief decreased. She was, however, not able to change her marijuana use in any remarkable way.

A turning point for Tina was when she was arrested for operating under the influence and required by the court to engage in drug abuse therapy. Although she was not initially motivated to quit, she was motivated to explore the issue. Entering into a serious relationship with a man who was "anti" drug use was the final motivating force. She was able to be abstinent for 6 months. The relationship was ongoing at that point. If that relationship had ended, Tina may or may not have developed the self-motivation to continue to be drug free. A period of abstinence did allow her to experience the feeling of being more alive and more capable of dealing with her feelings. This alone could motivate her to continue to be drug free.

Would Tina have been able to become abstinent from drug use if she had not resolved her trauma issues? This is impossible to know for sure. It likely would have been very difficult for her to change her marijuana use, given the degree of trauma and unresolved affect that she experienced around the loss of her friend. She was not particularly motivated to quit marijuana initially and she used it to medicate the loss. It was easier to quit once she no longer needed to numb her feelings.

CASE STUDY 4

JACK: THE SEX ADDICT WHO WANTED TO QUIT SMOKING CIGARETTES AND MARIJUANA

This case illustrates the use of Eye Movement Desensitization and Reprocessing (EMDR) with a middle-aged man who wanted to quit smoking marijuana and cigarettes. Additionally, Jack was using porn to masturbate and wanted to eliminate this behavior. In the past, he had quit smoking; he came to treatment after a long period of relapse.

PRESENTING PROBLEM

Jack, a White male, aged 46 years, came to therapy because he wanted help quitting smoking marijuana and cigarettes and masturbating while he looked at porn on the Internet. In the past, Jack used these three things, marijuana, cigarettes, and porn, in combination, late at night while on his computer. He described himself as a sex addict. He worked hard to give up all of these addictive behaviors but found smoking cigarettes to be the most difficult habit to eliminate. He was able to be abstinent from all of these behaviors starting 3 years before he came to treatment, but relapsed and started to smoke about 6 months before he returned to therapy.

He first relapsed after an argument with his wife; his anger at her was the trigger. Then she went out of town and his fear of losing her, combined with the opportunity that her absence provided, allowed him to return to his old habits. He described continuing to have one episode a day when she returned. About a month before he returned to therapy, he went to Alcoholics Anonymous (AA) for support and began to take Prozac prescribed by his primary care physician.

IDENTIFYING INFORMATION

Jack was a very intelligent, well-educated professional man who was married to Maria for 20 years. They had three children. He was attractive, well spoken, and very sophisticated, both about therapy and the ways of the world. He had several courses of talk therapy in the past and was sporadically involved with AA at different times.

ALCOHOL AND OTHER DRUG ABUSE HISTORY

Jack began to use marijuana and alcohol when he was 14 years old. He stopped drinking when he was a teenager and attended AA but continued a pattern of regular marijuana use until he quit 3 years ago. As noted above, when he relapsed he used marijuana. For him, being sober equaled being boring. He craved the excitement that using drugs provided for him.

SUMMARY OF PROGRESS IN TREATMENT

Jack came to therapy in the Contemplation stage, ready to move into preparing for Action. He was very motivated to quit and change his habits.

The first step in treatment was to use the Safe Place exercise to help him learn to relax and modulate some of his feelings. He visualized a field of flowers and reported that this helped him feel calmer.

The Desensitization of Triggers and Urge Reprocessing (DeTUR) protocol, positive treatment goal, was utilized as the second step. Jack visualized a sober lifestyle, with no marijuana, cigarettes, or porn. Immediately following this session, he quit all three of these habits; he came into his next session and, to the surprise of his therapist, he announced that he had made changes in all these behaviors.

Resource Development Installation (RDI) was utilized to support his newfound sobriety. Jack worked with the resources of perspective, self-reliance, serenity, and tolerance. He learned to sit with his feelings, visualized himself feeling peaceful when he was abstinent, and visualized his wife going out of town and not using. He also used the resource of feeling calm and taking things in stride. All of the resource states that Jack was able to identify were reinforced with bilateral stimulation. In addition, he used prayer to support his recovery; these prayers were installed using bilateral stimulation. Jack would say his prayers at the same time eye movements were utilized to reinforce them.

The trauma protocol was used to deal with old traumas that occurred when he was a child, which appeared to be related to his anxiety. He was sober and completely abstinent before he worked on these traumas.

#1: The trauma was running away from a fight at the age of 9 years and other kids laughing at him;

Negative cognition (NC): I am weak.

#2: The trauma was moving to a new neighborhood at the age of 11 years;

NC: I am alone.

Bilateral stimulation was utilized to desensitize both these traumas.

Both NCs appeared to be connected to his difficulty with letting go of his addictions in the past. The resolution of these traumas supported his ability to stay abstinent.

DISCUSSION

Jack came into therapy motivated to make changes in his life. He had previous therapy and what had worked for him to manage his behaviors in the past no longer worked. He was haunted by old feelings of being abandoned, which were played out in his relationship with this wife. Until these issues were resolved, he was unable to have a relapse-free recovery. He is an example of a client who had experienced a significant amount of talk therapy. He knew how to quit; he just didn't know how to do it this time.

The challenge for a therapist in this position is "What can I do differently?" If talk therapy and AA helped in the past but these were no longer seen as useful, what different and unique approach would be available? EMDR provided an answer to that question and allowed a more innovative approach to his therapy. The total treatment lasted 10 sessions. Jack left feeling successful and strong about his new-found recovery

In addition, it should be noted that his use of Prozac may have contributed to and supported his ability to give up smoking and porn. Selective serotonin reuptake inhibitors (SSRIs) often have the side effect of reducing sex drive. Although this side effect is problematic for many clients, it can be of benefit to clients like Jack who are dealing with sex addiction.

CASE STUDY

5

AIDAN: THE CASE OF ADDICTION AND COMPLEX PTSD

Clients who are referred for Eye Movement Desensitization and Reprocessing (EMDR) therapy and/or addiction treatment often have complicated presentations. They may delay getting into treatment and when they finally do, the therapist is challenged to figure out where to start. Other clients, like Aidan, have been in previous treatment but issues central to their healing were not addressed. This case will illustrate the use of EMDR therapy with a client with significant childhood trauma, alcoholism, nicotine dependence, and sexual orientation issues. It illustrates the complexity of some cases and the need to move slowly with patients with significant dissociation.

REFERRAL

Aidan was encouraged to seek counseling by the employee assistance program (EAP) coordinator at his place of employment. He had indicated to her that he had some significant stressors in his life and needed support dealing with them.

IDENTIFYING INFORMATION

Aidan was a 29-year-old single, gay, White male who was a member of the computer services team at the home office of a large business. He had been employed with this organization since high school graduation and reported that he liked the work that he did.

He lived on his own in a rented apartment in the downtown area of the city.

PRESENTING PROBLEM

Aidan's chief complaint was, "I don't like my life. I hope that there is more out there for me." He presented with significant symptoms of depression that were consistent with a diagnosis of a major depressive episode, moderate. He reported suicidal ideation at the time of intake but he had no plan or intent and was able to contract for safety. He was taking Zoloft, 25 mg prescribed by his primary care physician to treat his depression.

He also acknowledged a history of emotional, physical, and sexual abuse, perpetrated by parents and friends of his parents. He met criteria for posttraumatic stress disorder (PTSD). He noted upfront that he had difficulty being alone with men, that it made him highly anxious. Because his therapist was a male, it was important to process whether or not this would effect his treatment; Aidan expressed a desire to continue.

Aidan also reported that he was drinking "regularly" and smoking a pack of cigarettes a day. When asked if he believed that he had a substance abuse problem, he said, "Yah, I think that I do."

Aidan had come out to himself as a gay man several years earlier but he did not share that with any family member or friends. He had grown up in a working class family and he believed that they could not accept his identity as a gay man so he chose to remain closeted.

DRUG AND ALCOHOL HISTORY

Aidan reported that he had not used drugs and alcohol during high school because he had seen the damage it had done to others in his family. Once he graduated from high school, Aidan moved out on his own and began to use alcohol and cigarettes regularly to deal with stress. He drank up to a six-pack of beer most days and smoked about a pack of cigarettes. He never went a day without alcohol or cigarettes; he noted that he liked the feelings and the fact that substances helped him function throughout the day. He also noted that he loved coffee. He had never tried other drugs as he had seen how use of LSD, mescaline, and opiates affected his older siblings and reported that he did not want to be out of control.

FAMILY HISTORY

Aidan was born the youngest child in a family with seven children, four brothers and two sisters. He had a difficult relationship with the rest of his siblings who were all described as alcoholics and drug addicts. Many of his siblings were on state assistance or lived in poverty. Aidan reported that they often came to him to borrow money with promises that they would pay him back when they got their checks; he was never repaid. He described himself as "the lost child" (Wegscheider Cruse, 1989) while growing up, making every effort to stay out of the chaos in the house by staying in his room for hours. However, he was now the family "hero" (Wegscheider Cruse, 1989), the successful one to whom everyone came for advice or money. He resented this role but had great difficulty setting boundaries.

He reported that he had a good relationship with his mother and felt her love for him. However, he hated his father and had intense anger internally whenever he had contact. His parents were still married and living together out of state. However, even from a distance, he was their primary caregiver responsible for their financial well-being. He would speak to them on the phone at least once a week and he remain "stirred up" with intense anger for several hours after that.

ABUSE HISTORY

Aidan and his siblings were emotionally and physically abused by their father. His father would frequently beat their mother in front of them after both parents had been drinking. He was accustomed to waking up in the middle of the night to the sounds of fighting in the house. He and his siblings endured beatings by their father under the guise of discipline but Aidan said, "they'd happen when dad was drunk no matter what we'd done." They were often criticized by their father. His father had a nickname for Aidan that was a girl's name. When he was young, Aidan remembers crying and begging his father to stop. This made his father all the more likely to continue using the nickname and laugh at Aidan's distress.

Aidan was sexually abused by two different men, both friends of his father, around the age of 11 to 12 years. He was told by his father to go with these men to help them at their houses. Once there, these men sexually abused him. He reported that he learned to just "go away" and to not trust men.

EDUCATIONAL HISTORY

Aidan reported that he did well in school and no learning problems were identified. He successfully completed high school and took as many computer classes as he could. However, he had few friends and remained socially isolated.

WORK HISTORY

Aidan worked outside the home since the age of 15 years. He earned a reputation as a hard worker and employers liked him. He took any opportunity to escape the violence and chaos at home. Initially, he worked as a janitor for several businesses. Eventually, he worked part-time in the computer services department for a local business. This led to his full-time job.

Aidan noted that he had been employed at his current job for 7 years. His employer appreciated his work ethic and he received frequent compliments on his job performance. However, his nickname was "the hermit" as he stayed in his office and avoided contact with people whenever possible, due to his anxiety.

SOCIAL HISTORY

Aidan moved out of the house right after high school graduation and got his own small apartment. Soon after, he "came out" to himself, realizing that he was a gay man. His use of alcohol allowed him to socialize with other gay men in bars. However, he was not friendly with these men outside of the bar scene as others might suspect that he was gay. He only attempted to be sexual when he was intoxicated and felt that he was not successful in his attempts at connecting with others. He would sometimes have "blackouts" when drinking and therefore would not remember much of what happened. It later became clear that these "blackouts" were more likely episodes of dissociation, triggered by close contact with a man.

Aidan also noted that he felt anxious just being around men in general. He would feel terrified if a man was sitting next to him and would move as fast as he could to get away. He had significant trust issues with men and this made sense, given his abuse history.

PREVIOUS TREATMENT

Aidan was in outpatient therapy for about 2 years when he was 19 years old. He was just coming out and found treatment to be helpful. However, he also noted that his therapist talked to him a few times about his past history of abuse. He dissociated during those conversations.

TREATMENT PROCESS

Aidan's therapist was clear at intake that this was a highly complex case and that treatment would need to move slowly.

Aidan had many issues that would need to be prioritized. In addition to significant depression, Aidan was drinking and having episodes of dissociation. EMDR processing was discussed as a treatment option but, given his anxiety about being in close contact with a man and his trust issues and resistance to the idea of EMDR, a traditional treatment approach was utilized for the initial phases of treatment.

Phase 1

The first task was stabilization. He was referred to a psychiatrist for evaluation and his Zoloft was increased to 100 mg. He began to have a little more energy and some improvement in sleep. He learned about depression and substance abuse. He began exercising regularly and found that this helped with his anxiety. Coping skills were explored, including skills of emotion regulation, distress tolerance, interpersonal effectiveness, and mindfulness (Linehan, 1993b). Seeking Safety skills (Najavits, 2002) were also implemented to help with emotion regulation, PTSD education, and grounding skills.

When Aidan first presented to treatment, he was in Contemplation. He was aware that substances were likely a problem but he was unsure of whether he wanted to change. In treatment, he learned about the role that substances might be playing as the root cause of his mood problems and in exacerbating his symptoms of depression. He indicated a willingness to cut down on his use but he was not willing to commit to making major changes. Over the next few months, Aidan cut down on his caffeine intake and decided to quit smoking. He noted a marked improvement in how he felt physically. However, he continued to drink and noted that he thought that he had this "under control." Aidan believed that he could manage his alcohol use and his therapist utilized harm reduction strategies and motivational interviewing techniques to help him explore these issue.

After several months of unsuccessful efforts to control his alcohol use, he recognized that he had an addiction. He began to attend Alcoholics Anonymous (AA) and found this to be a helpful support. After some initial lapses and one relapse, he stopped drinking and began to apply the 12 steps to his life. He had urges to drink but resisted them by utilizing AA meetings and coping skills. He processed what he was learning about his triggers and he never drank again. He began to recognize the connection between his mood, trauma history, and alcohol use.

A major component of Phase 1 treatment with Aidan was his dissociation. Whenever issues related to his abuse were brought up, he would sometimes look dazed. He knew that he would "go away" when things got stressful but he had never understood dissociation. Once other issues were stabilized, dissociation was discussed. Aidan and his therapist learned how to recognize when he was dissociating and to prompt his use of coping skills. He learned Dialectical Behavior Therapy (DBT) skills to manage emotion dysregulation and Seeking Safety skills to help with grounding.

EMDR Therapy

As a result of developing coping skills, Aidan became more open to exploring EMDR therapy. He developed a Safe/Calm Place to comfort him during times of stress. He chose a meadow:

Challenging situation: having to visit my parents at their house.
Safe Place: a meadow.
Image: "I am in the meadow in the middle of a forest with a lake on one side and hill on the other. All is lush and green. I am sitting in the middle of this meadow with a down blanket wrapped around me."
Sounds: birds chirping.
Smells: fresh smells of nature.
Physical: I feel the grass beneath me.
Emotions: at peace.

Bilateral stimulation was used to install the resource, leading to an increase in the feeling of peace.

He applied this resource to talking with his parents in their living room and could report feeling peace, despite how stressful these conversations were for him.

Aidan began to use this resource with other challenging situations at work. He reported each time that it helped him to calm himself.

He also developed resources for "strength" and being "grounded." At times, he found his anger would emerge when dealing with his father or other family members. He and his therapist utilized the Affect Tolerance protocol (York & Leeds, 2001) to reinforce the use of coping skills to deal with anger and other intense emotions.

As a result of Phase 1 treatment, Aidan began setting boundaries with family members. He was able to say no to his siblings' requests for money. He set limits with his father and found that he could have interactions with him without feeling disempowered.

Treatment Complications

Aidan's therapy was complicated by many events. During early treatment, two of Aidan's siblings died of health conditions related to substance use. In addition, his parents announced that they were moving back to live in the same city as Aidan and they expected him to take care of them. As the only fully functioning child in his family, Aidan felt that it was his duty to take care of his parents. However, he experienced several emotional setbacks with increased contact with his parents.

In addition, Aidan's insurance company threatened to cut off sessions as their reviewer indicated, "This patient will not get any better. He has reached his maximum potential." Aidan was furious to read this statement from the reviewer and this decision was appealed Ultimately, Aidan had to change insurance plans in order to continue in treatment. Fortunately, he had this option.

Phase 2: Trauma Processing With EMDR Therapy

After 3 years of preparatory work, Aidan was ready and willing to process his trauma history. He was open to using the EMDR standard protocol to deal with this history, given his successes with Resource Development and Affect Tolerance. A memory map of prominent incidents of abuse was developed and he selected 10 memories as most representative. He needed to pace himself slowly with memory work and the processing.

Below are examples of two of the memories that were processed.

Memory: abusive discipline.
Incident: my father disciplined me in abusive ways by making me put on my sister's dress and walk around on Main Street.
Image: me standing in my room, my mother is putting my sister's dress on me, I'm begging her not do to it and I'm crying.
NC: I am a bad person.
PC: I am okay as I am.
VoC: 2.
Emotions: sad, ashamed, embarrassed, hurt.
SUDS: 9.

Body: chest and breathing.
22 sets of bilateral stimulation.
SUDS: 0.
VoC: 7.
Body: scan clear.

At the end of this session, Aidan reported that this memory no longer held power over him. Over the next few months, several other memories related to the abuse from father were targeted with similar results.

After several months, he felt ready to target memories of sexual abuse. One example is below:

Memory: sexual abuse.
Incident: being molested by a friend of the family.
Image: I'm a paralyzed little boy, lying motionless, afraid to move.
NC: I am worthless.
PC: I am worthwhile.
VoC: 1.
Emotions: sad, scared.
SUDS: 10.
Body: tightness in my chest.
20 sets of bilateral stimulation.
SUDS: 4.
Incomplete session. We utilized his "safe place" to close this session.

Aidan returned the next week to continue processing. On reevaluation, he was asked, "When you think of that incident what comes up now?"

"I feel some tension in my chest, like it's hard to breathe."

SUDS: 3.
Body: tension in chest.
10 sets of bilateral stimulation.
SUDS: 0.
VOC: 7.
Body: scan clear.

He noted that the processing was "easier than I thought." This was likely due to the preparation work that was completed to increase his affect tolerance and use of resources prior to processing these memories.

He completed work on the other memories of abuse. We utilized EMDR focused on current triggers and future templates to reinforce gains. He felt "like a weight has been lifted."

Although he still had contact with his family, these interactions did not affect him in the same way. He learned to set limits with family members and was not manipulated by them. Aidan became much more social, both at work and in his personal life. He developed a friendship network and began to do things with others. He still enjoyed quiet time alone but noted that he could also enjoy time with different people. He began dating and found that he could tolerate being in the company of men without feeling panic.

CURRENT STATUS

Aidan took a break in treatment for a few months but then returned for biweekly "check ins" to continue the application of skills learned to his life. He focused on improving health and managing stress associated with a challenging job. At this writing, he has been clean and sober for 6 years.

CASE DISCUSSION

This case illustrates one of the many challenges of clinical work. Aidan initially came to therapy for help with work issues. However, during the assessment many different issues were identified, including active substance abuse and trauma-related symptoms including dissociation. Aidan met criteria for PTSD and Major Depressive Disorder but also had other symptoms consistent with a complex trauma history.

Treatment goals were prioritized. Stabilization was the first order of business. Aidan needed significant education about the impact of complex trauma and the therapy was titrated based on the stress level that he could tolerate. A critical component of this work was that his therapist recognized when Aidan was starting to dissociate. He would be prompted to use skills in session to ground himself.

Aidan was initially ambivalent about changing. He was willing to enter into a period of Contemplation and ultimately took Action to become abstinent. He entered into a long period of sobriety, with no relapses. He worked hard on resolving his trauma issues and accepting his sexuality. He was brave and became willing to risk change.

In addition, it should be noted that Aidan was able to develop an excellent therapeutic alliance with his therapist. Despite his initial fear of men and his distrust, he was able to engage in a long-term relationship that likely helped to promote his healing and change process.

CASE STUDY 6

MARGO: THE CLIENT WITH COMORBID ALCOHOLISM AND PTSD

This case study illustrates the importance of addressing substance use and abuse in addition to the clinical dilemma faced by many clinicians as to when or whether to use the trauma protocol with an active substance abuser. The client presented initially with active alcoholism as well as the trauma of her husband's suicide. The authors will discuss the factors that were considered in making the clinical formulation and the treatment plan for use of Eye Movement Desensitization and Reprocessing (EMDR) in this case.

PRESENTING PROBLEM

Margo, a widowed, White, 45-year-old woman with three daughters, was referred to this therapist by another therapist in the community. He had been doing couples' treatment with Margo and her boyfriend when he discovered Margo's alcoholism and referred her for substance abuse treatment because he felt that this issue was of primary importance. Margo presented to her new therapist with concerns about her increasing use of alcohol. In the past, she had been to several therapists for substance abuse counseling without success. She also had been to intensive outpatient (IOP) treatment. She relapsed following each course of therapy. She presented as very frustrated as well as extremely motivated to change these patterns of use. She was a well-educated, professional woman of high intelligence who was employed full-time. She described herself as isolated and depressed but was not on medications. She experienced some anxiety, as well as some posttraumatic stress disorder (PTSD) symptoms, including a startle response. She reported that she "did not know who she was."

Excerpted from Abel, N. J. & O'Brien, J. M. (2010). EMDR treatment of comorbid PTSD and alcohol dependence: A case example. *Journal of EMDR Practice and Research, 4*(2), 2–11. Reprinted with permission

SOCIAL HISTORY

Margo is the oldest of three children who grew up on the west coast of the United States. Her father was described as an alcoholic who stopped drinking in college. He is a "dry drunk," that is, an untreated alcoholic who is abstinent from alcohol but who continues to exhibit negative behaviors associated with drinking. Margo reported that he is controlling, negative, and very intelligent. Mother is "nice." She is described as subservient to dad. Margo has a sister who is 4 years older and is reportedly an active alcoholic. Her brother, 2 years younger, gave up alcohol the year before Margo came to this therapist but continued to smoke marijuana regularly. There was minimal communication in her family of origin and no modeling for appropriate ways to deal with feelings. The family practices a conservative religion. Growing up in this conservative religious environment was a "horror" for her; she was taught that suffering is good. In high school, Margo spent 6 months living in a religious group home for being "incorrigible." She reported that she had nothing in common with the drug addicts and prostitutes she met there.

After high school, Margo went directly to college where she met her husband. She was married immediately after graduation. She has three daughters, aged 17, 15, and 12 years. Six years before she came to EMDR treatment her husband committed suicide. He had been depressed for some time but the suicide was completely unexpected. Margo came home and found him in the garage, dead from carbon monoxide poisoning. This was seriously traumatizing to her and she felt grief stricken as well as unable to cope with parenting her daughters. Because she had no healthy coping skills, she immediately increased her consumption of alcohol. What she described as heavy social drinking quickly became more regular, heavier, and more abusive. She developed a dependency on alcohol and became unable to stop despite several episodes of therapy and IOP treatment for alcoholism. Her drinking continued to increase and she wanted to die as she saw no way out of the despair and depression related to her husband's suicide.

COURSE OF TREATMENT

When Margo first began treatment with her therapist, it was decided to focus on the alcoholism because this was her presenting issue.

The safe place exercise was the first pre-EMDR intervention used (Shapiro, 2001). It was somewhat difficult for her to find a place where she felt safe and secure but she came up with an image of a nearby beach. Her cue word was "wave." Once she established this image, she worked well with it and felt more relaxed than in the past: She became able to use this to deal with her anxiety.

This was followed by implementing part of the Desensitization of Triggers and Urge Reprocessing (DeTUR) protocol: the positive treatment goal. Margo was very clear about wanting to stop drinking. She visualized being abstinent, going through her daily life without using alcohol. The therapist reinforced this visualization with short sets of bilateral stimulation, using the Audiotac and tappers.

Resource Development Installation (RDI; Korn & Leeds, 2002) was utilized to shore up her ability to maintain sobriety. The qualities that Margo chose to reinforce were "strength" and "willpower." She was able to find times earlier in her life when she experienced these qualities and the Audiotac was used for reinforcement. She again visualized an alcohol-free life.

In addition, recovery techniques not related to EMDR or pre-EMDR were utilized. Margo was encouraged to attend Alcoholics Anonymous (AA), to obtain a sponsor, to practice techniques for appropriate affect management, and to identify triggers for her use as well as techniques to learn how to manage her cravings.

Margo continued to relapse despite efforts to quit using alcohol. She was extremely upset and frustrated about this inability to stop drinking. After much discussion in treatment, she and her therapist determined that the suicide trauma was interfering with her ability to stay sober. She used alcohol as a way to cope with the feelings resulting from this trauma and her alcohol consumption increased considerably after the suicide. Her ability to tolerate affect had improved somewhat, as had her internal and external resources (Korn & Leeds, 2002), but she had not mastered these skills. Her therapist determined that she would not maintain sobriety without working through her husband's suicide. An important factor in this decision was that Margo had a strong therapeutic alliance with her therapist and was able to use that as a resource. Her sobriety was shaky but she was strongly motivated to change.

TRAUMA PROTOCOL

At the outset of the sixth therapy session, Margo and her therapist decided to begin to work with the trauma protocol. Later, Margo reported that we "jumped into" the trauma work and that she was glad that we did. It took three hour-long sessions to work through this event. It was clear that the organizing issue was Margo's sense of responsibility for her husband's suicide.

The target was her husband's suicide.

The image was seeing her husband's body in the car in the garage.

NC: it is my fault.
PC: it is not my fault.
VoC: 3.
Emotions: fear, panic, a need to escape.
Body: head to chest.
Subjective Units of Distress (SUDS): 10.

In the initial EMDR processing, Margo began by chronologically reviewing the events of the day of the suicide. She expressed considerable emotion. She also processed events that had occurred earlier in the week, including her husband's birthday and some regrets she had about not asking him about how he was doing. She began to see that she had been feeling trapped in the relationship and remembered that she had considered divorce. Her husband's depressive episodes became more obvious to her. With the help of a therapeutic interweave, she was able to see that she did not cause his death. By the close of the session, the SUDS was a 7 out of 10.

Upon reevaluation at the start of the second session, the SUDS had dropped to a 5. She reported that although she felt sad there was not the same "punch" to it. In this session, she continued to process events surrounding the suicide and dealing with the reactions of her children and family. Processing proceeded smoothly. The SUDS was 3 at the end of Session 2.

At the beginning of Session 3, Margo reported that the week had been a very emotional one. During the week, she felt lonely and wounded but also pleased about how hard she had worked doing the EMDR processing. She was able to stay sober all week. This was difficult but she attended AA, which she had previously resisted, walked a lot, called people, and let herself feel her feelings, which she described as a strange and new experience. The SUDS at the beginning of this session was a 2. During the processing, she described seeing herself coming out of a dark place as well as her fears about getting close to people. She began to see herself taking down walls. She came up with a dilemma: drinking versus taking the risk of changing and being healthy. The therapist utilized Robin Shapiro's Two-Handed Interweave (Shapiro, 2006). The client visualized the drinking in one hand and a different, riskier life in the other. Bilateral stimulation was utilized. The client began to laugh. She saw it as no contest. Drinking equals death, while not drinking means growing up and being accountable. The SUDS at the end of this session was 0 and the PC was installed.

Upon reevaluation in ongoing treatment, the SUDS has remained 0.

RELAPSE

Following this session, Margo seriously began to invest in her sobriety following these sessions. She attended AA regularly, used a sponsor appropriately, and began to work on the 12 steps. She maintained her sobriety until 6 months later when she went on vacation and visited her family. She was severely triggered by the interactions with her family. Upon her return home, she went to the grocery store, purchased mouthwash, and consumed it. At the next treatment session, the therapist utilized the protocol developed by Hase (2006) to process the memory of addiction. In this case, there was a specific relapse to process.

Incident: mouthwash relapse.
Image: being in the grocery store ready to pick up the mouthwash.
LoU: 10.
NC: I am stupid.
PC: I am making healthy choices.
VoC: 4.
Emotion: shame.
Body: core.

As processing began, Margo was flooded with feelings. Her abandonment issues surfaced. She felt extremely frightened about opening herself up and risking abandonment; she drank to manage these feelings. She attracted needy people, focused on them, and then could not care for herself appropriately. She grew up feeling negated by others and continued to negate herself.

After 11 sets of bilateral stimulation, the LoU was zero and the PC was installed.

That was the last time that Margo relapsed. In subsequent sessions, she did, however, report that she felt cravings and urges on occasion in her life. The Hase protocol was utilized four times to deal with these urges. The following is an example of one session after she was triggered by a conversation with her boyfriend.

Image: sitting outside after getting off the phone with her boyfriend.
LoU: 8.
NC: I am not lovable.
PC: I can love myself enough.
VoC: 2.
Emotions: disgust.
Body: all over.

Margo processed this urge to use alcohol for 12 sets of bilateral stimulation. Again, old losses and disappointments emerged as well as feelings of low self-worth. She saw that she habitually drank to manage these feelings. She also became aware of her ability to make choices and choose healthy responses. At the end of the session, the LoU was a zero and the VoC was installed.

CLINICAL FORMULATION

Margo presented to the therapist with concerns about her increasing alcohol consumption. She self-identified as an alcoholic. It was therefore very clear that dealing with her alcoholism would be of primary concern in the therapy.

The therapist considered which came first, the trauma or the addiction, and it was clear that the trauma was a trigger for increased substance use. The client was unable to quit using despite many efforts. She lacked internal and external resources; however, she was extremely motivated and had a strong therapeutic alliance with her therapist. She did not have a childhood history of complex trauma. Overall, she functioned at a high level in the world and was successful at her job. All these factors were considered when making the decision to proceed with the trauma protocol. Once the client did the trauma work, she was able to enter a period of abstinence.

This client was motivated and used the sessions well.

A FINAL NOTE ABOUT THE CLIENT

The client utilized the EMDR treatment very successfully and was satisfied with the outcome. She wrote a statement, which was read at a local EMDR International Association (EMDRIA) meeting where this material was presented. She has given the authors permission to include an excerpt here.

> After a few (EMDR) sessions I noticed a huge difference. It was like a door opened in the dark room I had locked myself into. For so long I had been unable to get out, afraid of the feelings that would inevitably find me and

> overwhelm me, driving me back. For the first time I was able to face them with someone else and see them for what they really were. And to have someone hold my hand [authors' note: not literally] so I didn't have to face them for the first time alone! It has made all the difference. It sounds melodramatic but before EMDR I would truly get caught up in a maze of terror that I was helpless to control or see coming. Like swimming along and getting caught in a riptide. I could not break the pattern of thought or even see it.
>
> Since I first started working with (my therapist) my life has changed completely. It has been a lot of hard work and there have been a lot of tears but I no longer wish to die and I have... continuous sobriety. I am able to have joy in my life again... I believe with all my heart that I would not have been able to do this without EMDR. If (my therapist) had waited for me to get sober before trying (this) therapy I do not believe I would be still alive today, I was in too much pain and I had failed for... years. EMDR saved my life.

Margo remained sober and the urges to drink alcohol diminished significantly. At this writing, she has been abstinent for over 2 years.

CONCLUSION

In this book, we have explored concepts related to the diagnosis and treatment of both trauma and addiction, with a particular emphasis on Eye Movement Desensitization and Reprocessing (EMDR) therapy and the Stages of Change.

Part I of this book discussed the research foundations and theory of EMDR therapy for trauma/posttraumatic stress disorder (PTSD) and various addictions. Research provides an important foundation for evidence-based treatment. We hope that our discussion of the science behind our work has helped you, the reader, think more deeply about these issues and has provided important knowledge about these topics.

In Part II, we examined the Stages of Change in detail. Our intent was to provide clinicians with practical and detailed possibilities in terms of treating clients at each of these stages. We hope that we have given you some clear approaches about how to treat these complex issues.

In Part III, we presented specific cases that illustrated EMDR therapy with addictions. We hope that these cases helped illustrate how to work with these disorders and inspired you to do this work with your own clients, in your own way.

We look forward to learning more about how EMDR therapy can be helpful to clients with trauma and addictions. More research is needed in this area. We need to learn more about the individuals who are likely to respond to the various protocols and about factors that facilitate recovery from addiction, particularly about when to use the Standard Protocol with clients who are still in addictive processes and the efficacy of the particular addiction protocols. We believe research in this area is a priority.

APPENDIX A

SCREENING TOOLS

APPENDIX A1

CAGE QUESTIONNAIRE

1. Have you ever felt you ought to cut down on your drinking or drug use?
2. Have people annoyed you by criticizing your drinking or drug use?
3. Have you ever felt bad or guilty about your drinking or drug use?
4. Have you ever had a drink or used drugs first thing in the morning to steady your nerves or to get rid of a hangover?

Each affirmative response earns 1 point. One point indicates a possible problem. Two points indicate a probable problem.

CAGE-AID QUESTIONNAIRE

1. In the last 3 months, have you felt you should cut down or stop drinking or using drugs?

   Yes/No

2. In the last 3 months, has anyone annoyed you or gotten on your nerves by telling you to cut down or stop drinking or using drugs?

   Yes/No

3. In the last 3 months, have you felt guilty or bad about how much you drink or use drugs?

   Yes/No

4. In the last 3 months, have you been waking up wanting to have an alcoholic drink or use drugs?

   Yes/No

Each affirmative response earns 1 point. One point indicates a possible problem. Two points indicate a probable problem.

APPENDIX A2

MICHIGAN ALCOHOL SCREENING TEST–REVISED

The Michigan Alcohol Screening Test (MAST) is a simple, self-scoring test that helps assess if you have a drinking problem. Please circle the answers to the following "yes" or "no" questions:

1. Do you feel you are a normal drinker? ("normal" = drink as much or less than most other people)

   Circle answer: Yes/No

2. Have you ever awakened the morning after some drinking the night before and found that you could not remember a part of the evening?

   Circle answer: Yes/No

3. Does any near relative or close friend ever worry or complain about your drinking?

   Circle answer: Yes/No

4. Can you stop drinking without difficulty after one or two drinks?

   Circle answer: Yes/No

5. Do you ever feel guilty about your drinking?

   Circle answer: Yes/No

6. Have you ever attended a meeting of Alcoholics Anonymous (AA)?

   Circle answer: Yes/No

7. Have you ever gotten into physical fights when drinking?

   Circle answer: Yes/No

Source: Selzer, M. L. (1971). The Michigan Alcoholism Screening Test (MAST): The quest for a new diagnostic instrument. *American Journal of Psychiatry, 127*, 1653–1658.

8. Has drinking ever created problems between you and a near relative or close friend?

   Circle answer: Yes/No

9. Has any family member or close friend gone to anyone for help about your drinking?

   Circle answer: Yes/No

10. Have you ever lost friends because of your drinking?

    Circle answer: Yes/No

11. Have you ever gotten into trouble at work because of drinking?

    Circle answer: Yes/No

12. Have you ever lost a job because of drinking?

    Circle answer: Yes/No

13. Have you ever neglected your obligations, your family, or your work for 2 or more days in a row because you were drinking?

    Circle answer: Yes/No

14. Do you drink before noon fairly often?

    Circle answer: Yes/No

15. Have you ever been told you have liver trouble such as cirrhosis?

    Circle answer: Yes/No

16. After heavy drinking, have you ever had delirium tremens (DTs), severe shaking, or visual or auditory (hearing) hallucinations?

    Circle answer: Yes/No

17. Have you ever gone to anyone for help about your drinking?

    Circle answer: Yes/No

18. Have you ever been hospitalized because of drinking?

    Circle answer: Yes/No

19. Has your drinking ever resulted in your being hospitalized in a psychiatric ward?

    Circle answer: Yes/No

20. Have you ever gone to any doctor, social worker, clergyman, or mental health clinic for help with any emotional problem in which drinking was part of the problem?

    Circle answer: Yes/No

21. Have you been arrested more than once for driving under the influence of alcohol?

    Circle answer: Yes/No

22. Have you ever been arrested, even for a few hours, because of other behavior while drinking?

    (If yes, how many times ________)

    Circle answer: Yes/No

SCORING FOR THE MAST TEST

Please score 1 point if you answered the following:

1. No
2. Yes
3. Yes
4. No
5. Yes
6. Yes
7. to 22. Yes

Add up the scores and compare with the following score card:

0 to 2 = No apparent problem
3 to 5 = Early or middle problem drinker
6 or more = Problem drinker

APPENDIX A3

DRUG ABUSE SCREENING TEST

Directions: The following questions concern information about your involvement with drugs. Drug abuse refers to (a) the use of prescribed or "over-the-counter" drugs in excess of the directions, and (b) any nonmedical use of drugs. Consider the past year (12 months) and carefully read each statement. Then decide whether your answer is Yes or No and check the appropriate space. Please be sure to answer every question.

	Yes/No
1. Have you used drugs other than those required for medical reasons?	______
2. Have you abused prescription drugs?	______
3. Do you abuse more than one drug at a time?	______
4. Can you get through the week without using drugs (other than those required for medical reasons)?	______
5. Are you always able to stop using drugs when you want to?	______
6. Do you abuse drugs on a continuous basis?	______
7. Do you try to limit your drug use to certain situations?	______
8. Have you had "blackouts" or "flashbacks" as a result of drug use?	______
9. Do you ever feel bad about your drug abuse?	______
10. Does your spouse (or parents) ever complain about your involvement with drugs?	______
11. Do your friends or relatives know or suspect you abuse drugs?	______
12. Has drug abuse ever created problems between you and your spouse?	______
13. Has any family member ever sought help for problems related to your drug use?	______
14. Have you ever lost friends because of your use of drugs?	______
15. Have you ever neglected your family or missed work because of your use of drugs?	______

Reprinted with permission from the Center for Addiction and Mental Health (CAMH), Toronto, Canada.

16. Have you ever been in trouble at work because of drug abuse? _____
17. Have you ever lost a job because of drug abuse? _____
18. Have you gotten into fights when under the influence of drugs? _____
19. Have you ever been arrested because of unusual behavior while under the influence of drugs? _____
20. Have you ever been arrested for driving while under the influence of drugs? _____
21. Have you engaged in illegal activities in order to obtain drugs? _____
22. Have you ever been arrested for possession of illegal drugs? _____
23. Have you ever experienced withdrawal symptoms as a result of heavy drug intake? _____
24. Have you had medical problems as a result of your drug use (e.g., memory loss, hepatitis, convulsions, bleeding, etc.)? _____
25. Have you ever gone to anyone for help for a drug problem? _____
26. Have you ever been in a hospital for medical problems related to your drug use? _____
27. Have you ever been involved in a treatment program specifically related to drug use? _____
28. Have you been treated as an outpatient for problems related to drug abuse? _____

Scoring and interpretation: A score of 1 is given for each "yes" response, except for Items 4, 5, and 7 for which a "no" response is given a score of 1. Based on data from a heterogeneous psychiatric patient population, cutoff scores of 6 to 11 are considered to be optimal for screening for substance use disorders. Using a cutoff score of 6 has been found to provide excellent sensitivity for identifying patients with substance use disorders as well as satisfactory specificity (i.e., identification of patients who do not have substance use disorders). Using a cutoff score of less than 11 somewhat reduces the sensitivity for identifying patients with substance use disorders but more accurately identifies the patients who do not have a substance use disorder. A cutoff score of greater than 12 is definitely a substance abuse problem. In a heterogeneous psychiatric patient population, most items have been shown to correlate at least moderately well with the total scale scores. The items that correlate poorly with the total scale scores appear to be Items 4, 7, 16, 20, and 22.

APPENDIX A4

FOOD ADDICTIONS

SCREENING FOR EATING DISORDERS IN GENERAL

A positive answer to any of these questions may reflect an underlying eating disorder and the clinician is encouraged to further assess the client's eating patterns.

1. Do you worry that you have lost control over how much you eat?
2. Do you make yourself sick when you feel uncomfortably full?
3. Do you currently suffer with or have you ever suffered in the past with an eating disorder?
4. Do you ever eat in secret?

In addition, if there are time limitations, these authors identified either of these two questions as the most effective in identifying a possible eating disorder:

1. Does your weight affect the way you feel about yourself?
2. Are you satisfied with your eating patterns? (Cotton, Ball, & Robinson, 2003)

Reprinted from *Journal of General Internal Medicine*, 18/1, Cotton M., Four simple questions can help screen for eating disorders, 2003, with permission from Springer Science+Business Media.

APPENDIX A5

THE SHORT GAMBLING QUIZ

In the past 12 months have you gambled more than you intended to?

__________yes__________ no

In the past 12 months have you claimed to be winning money when you were not?

__________yes__________ no

In the past 12 months have you felt guilty about the way you gamble or about what happens when you gamble?

__________yes__________ no

In the past 12 months have people criticized your gambling?

__________yes__________ no

In the past 12 months have you had money arguments centered on gambling?

__________yes__________ no

In the past 12 months did you feel you had to persist until you won?

__________yes__________ no

If you answered yes to two or more of these questions, how often has it happened?

__________once__________ only sometimes__________ often

SCORING

If a person answers no to all questions, you can be very confident that he or she does not have a gambling problem. A score of 2 may indicate that he or she

---

Used with permission from the Problem Gambling Institute, Center for Addiction and Mental Health (CAMH), Toronto, Ontario, Canada.

is developing a problem but currently does not have a problem. If the person scores 3 or more, you can be very confident that he or she does have a problem; more than 97% of people who do not have a problem score less than 2 on these items. A score of 2 is a judgment call; the majority of people who do not have a problem score less than 2, but the majority of people who do have a problem score more than 2. This score may indicate a person who is in transition. Question 7 is used to adjust a person's score. If a person scored 3 or above but responded once only to question 7, then he or she may be at risk or in transition but probably does not currently have a gambling problem.

APPENDIX A6

SEXUAL ADDICTION SCREENING TEST–REVISED (SAST-R)

The Sexual Addiction Screening Test (SAST) is designed to assist in the assessment of sexually compulsive behavior, which may indicate the presence of sex addiction. Developed in cooperation with hospitals, treatment programs, private therapists, and community groups, the SAST provides a profile of responses that help to discriminate between addictive and nonaddictive behavior. Before starting the assessment, we need basic information in order to build your profile.

Please indicate gender.	Male	☐
	Female	☐
Please indicate orientation.	Heterosexual	☐
	Bisexual	☐
	Homosexual	☐

Please check any of the following that apply:

I have no concerns about my sexual behavior, but I am curious how I would score.	☐
I have no concerns about my sexual behavior but others are concerned.	☐
I am having problems with my sexual behavior, but I do not consider myself a "sex addict."	☐
I know I am a sex addict.	☐
I have sought therapy because of my sexual problems.	☐

Reprinted with permission by IITAP.

To complete the test, answer each question by placing a check in the appropriate yes/no column:

	YES	NO
1. Were you sexually abused as a child or adolescent?	☐	☐
2. Did your parents have trouble with sexual behavior?	☐	☐
3. Do you often find yourself preoccupied with sexual thoughts?	☐	☐
4. Do you feel that your sexual behavior is not normal?	☐	☐
5. Do you ever feel bad about your sexual behavior?	☐	☐
6. Has your sexual behavior ever created problems for you and your family?	☐	☐
7. Have you ever sought help for sexual behavior you did not like?	☐	☐
8. Has anyone been hurt emotionally because of your sexual behavior?	☐	☐
9. Is any of your sexual activities against the law?	☐	☐
10. Have you made efforts to quit a type of sexual activity and failed?	☐	☐
11. Do you hide some of your sexual behaviors from others?	☐	☐
12. Have you attempted to stop some parts of your sexual activity?	☐	☐
13. Have you felt degraded by your sexual behaviors?	☐	☐
14. When you have sex, do you feel depressed afterward?	☐	☐
15. Do you feel controlled by your sexual desire?	☐	☐
16. Have important parts of your life (such as job, family, friends, leisure activities) been neglected because you were spending too much time on sex?	☐	☐
17. Do you ever think your sexual desire is stronger than you are?	☐	☐
18. Is sex almost all you think about?	☐	☐
19. Has sex (or romantic fantasies) been a way for you to escape your problems?	☐	☐
20. Has sex become the most important thing in your life?	☐	☐
21. Are you in crisis over sexual matters?	☐	☐
22. Has the Internet created sexual problems for you?	☐	☐
23. Do you spend too much time online for sexual purposes?	☐	☐
24. Have you purchased services online for erotic purposes (sites for dating, pornography, fantasy, and friend finder)?	☐	☐

	YES	NO
25. Have you used the Internet to make romantic or erotic connections with people online?	☐	☐
26. Have people in your life been upset about your sexual activities online?	☐	☐
27. Have you attempted to stop your online sexual behaviors?	☐	☐
28. Have you subscribed to or regularly purchased or rented sexually explicit materials (magazines, videos, books, or online pornography)?	☐	☐
29. Have you been sexual with minors?	☐	☐
30. Have you spent considerable time and money on strip clubs, adult bookstores, and movie houses?	☐	☐
31. Have you engaged prostitutes and escorts to satisfy your sexual needs?	☐	☐
32. Have you spent considerable time surfing pornography online?	☐	☐
33. Have you used magazines, videos, or online pornography even when there was considerable risk of being caught by family members who would be upset by your behavior?	☐	☐
34. Have you regularly purchased romantic novels or sexually explicit magazines?	☐	☐
35. Have you stayed in romantic relationships after they became emotionally or abusive?	☐	☐
36. Have you traded sex for money or gifts?	☐	☐
37. Have you maintained multiple romantic or sexual relationships at the same time?	☐	☐
38. After sexually acting out, do you sometimes refrain from all sex for a significant period?	☐	☐
39. Have you regularly engaged in sadomasochistic behavior?	☐	☐
40. Do you visit sexual bathhouses, sex clubs, or video/bookstores as part of your regular sexual activity?	☐	☐
41. Have you engaged in unsafe or "risky" sex even though you knew it could cause you harm?	☐	☐
42. Have you cruised public restrooms, rest areas, or parks looking for sex with strangers?	☐	☐
43. Do you believe casual or anonymous sex has kept you from having more long-term intimate relationships?	☐	☐
44. Has your sexual behavior put you at risk for arrest for lewd conduct or public indecency?	☐	☐
45. Have you been paid for sex?	☐	☐

You have just completed the SAST (version 3.1). This assessment tool has been used since 1983 to help determine if sex addiction is a problem. This version of the SAST is new. It was updated to reflect changes in sexual behavior since the 1980s and to be of assistance whatever your gender or sexual orientation might be. The database on which the assessment is made is composed of thousands of clinical patients, online assessments (such as this one), and nonclinical populations. Please remember that this is a new version, so scoring may be adjusted with more research. It also is a simple screening tool that helps you sort out whether you have a problem or not. If you do have a concern, it is very important to see a trained therapist who understands sex addiction.

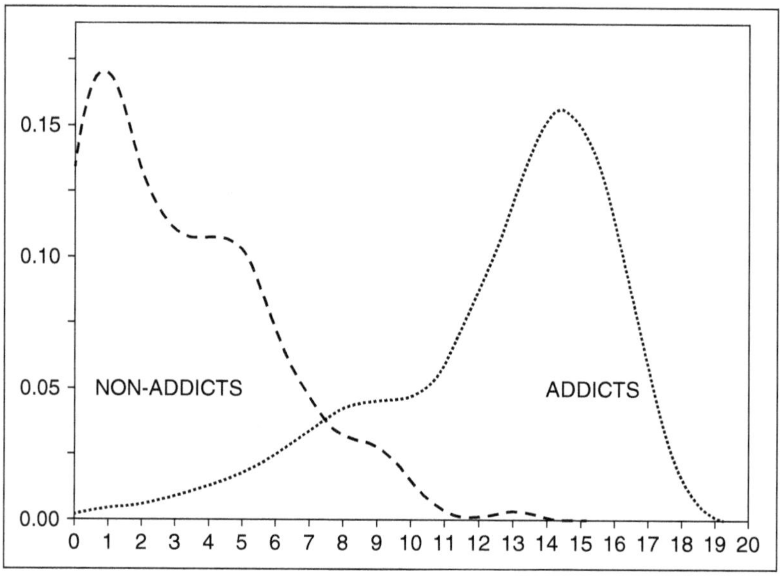

*Available on www.sexhelp.com

SAST-R SUBSCALES

Core-Item Scale	**Questions 1–20**	**(Over 6)**	________
Subscales			
Internet items	Questions 22–27	(3 or more)	________
Men's items	Questions 28–33	(2 or more)	________
Women's items	Questions 34–39	(2 or more)	________
Homosexual men	Questions 40–45	(3 or more)	________

Addictive Dimensions

Preoccupation Items 3, 18, 19, and 20	(2 or more)	________
Loss of control Items 10, 12, 15, and 17	(2 or more)	________
Relationship disturbance Items 6, 8, 16, and 26	(2 or more)	________
Affect disturbance Items 4, 5, 11, 13, and 14	(2 or more)	________

Associated features (not rated as a subscale)
Items 1, 2, 7, 9, and 21

APPENDIX A7

THE INTERNET ADDICTION TEST

Simply instruct the client to answer the 20-item questionnaire based upon the following 5-point Likert-type scale. Remember to inform clients to only consider the time spent online for nonacademic or nonjob (or recreational) purposes when answering.

To assess the level of addiction, answer the following questions using this scale:

0 = Not applicable
1 = Rarely
2 = Occasionally
3 = Frequently
4 = Often
5 = Always

1. How often do you find that you stay online longer than you intended?
2. How often do you neglect household chores to spend more time online?
3. How often do you prefer the excitement of the Internet to intimacy with your partner?
4. How often do you form new relationships with fellow online users?
5. How often do others in your life complain to you about the amount of time you spend online?
6. How often do your grades or school work suffer because of the amount of time you spend online?
7. How often do you check your e-mail before something else that you need to do?
8. How often does your job performance or productivity suffer because of the Internet?
9. How often do you become defensive or secretive when anyone asks you what you do online?

This test is used with permission by Dr. Kimberly Young, founder of the Center for Internet Addiction at Netaddiction.com.

10. How often do you block out disturbing thoughts about your life with soothing thoughts of the Internet?
11. How often do you find yourself anticipating when you will go online again?
12. How often do you fear that life without the Internet would be boring, empty, and joyless?
13. How often do you snap, yell, or act annoyed if someone bothers you while you are online?
14. How often do you lose sleep due to late-night log-ins?
15. How often do you feel preoccupied with the Internet when off-line, or fantasize about being online?
16. How often do you find yourself saying "just a few more minutes" when online?
17. How often do you try to cut down the amount of time you spend online and fail?
18. How often do you try to hide how long you have been online?
19. How often do you choose to spend more time online over going out with others?
20. How often do you feel depressed, moody, or nervous when you are offline, which goes away once you are back online?

SCORING

After all the questions have been answered, add the numbers for each response to obtain a final score. The higher the score range, the greater the level of addiction:

Normal range = 0 to 30 points
Mild = 31 to 49 points
Moderate = 50 to 79 points
Severe = 80 to 100 points

APPENDIX A8

LIFE EVENTS CHECKLIST

Listed below are a number of difficult or stressful things that sometimes happen to people. For each event, check one or more of the boxes to the right to indicate that (a) it *happened to you* personally, (b) you *witnessed it* happen to someone else, (c) you *learned about it* happening to someone close to you, (d) you are *not sure* if it fits, or (e) it *does not apply* to you.

Be sure to consider your *entire life* (growing up as well as adulthood) as you go through the list of events .

Event	Happened to Me	Witnessed It	Learned About It	Not Sure	Does Not Apply
1. Natural disaster (e.g., flood, hurricane, tornado, earthquake)					
2. Fire or explosion					
3. Transportation accident (e.g., car accident, boat accident, train wreck, plane crash)					
4. Serious accident at work, home, or during recreational activity					
5. Exposure to toxic substance (e.g., dangerous chemicals, radiation)					

(continued)

Source: Blake et al. (1995).

Event	Happened to Me	Witnessed It	Learned About It	Not Sure	Does Not Apply
6. Physical assault (e.g., being attacked, hit, slapped, kicked, beaten up)					
7. Assault with a weapon (e.g., being shot, stabbed, threatened with a knife, gun, bomb)					
8. Sexual assault (rape, attempted rape, made to perform any type of sexual act through force or threat of harm)					
9. Other unwanted or uncomfortable sexual experience					
10. Combat or exposure to a war-zone (in the military or as a civilian)					
11. Captivity (e.g., being kidnapped, abducted, held hostage, prisoner of war)					
12. Life-threatening illness or injury					
13. Severe human suffering					
14. Sudden, violent death (e.g., homicide, suicide)					
15. Sudden, unexpected death of someone close to you					
16. Serious injury, harm, or death you caused to someone else					
17. Any other very stressful event or experience					

APPENDIX A9

THE POSTTRAUMATIC STRESS DISORDER CHECKLIST

The posttraumatic stress disorder (PTSD) checklist (PCL; Weathers, Litz, Herman, Huska, & Keane, 1993) is an easily administered self-report rating scale for assessing the 17 symptoms of PTSD listed in the *Diagnostic and Statistical Manual of Mental Disorders*, fourth edition (*DSM-IV*). It has excellent test-retest reliability over a 2- to 3-day period. Internal consistency is very high for each of the three groups of items corresponding to the *DSM-IV* symptom clusters as well as for the full 17-item scale. The PCL correlates strongly with other measures of PTSD, such as the Mississippi Scale, the PK scale of the Minnesota Multiphasic Personality Inventory-2 (MMPI-2), and the Impact of Events Scale, and also correlates moderately with level of combat exposure.

Three versions of the PCL are available, although the differences are very small. The PCL-M is a military version and questions refer to "a stressful military experience." The PCL-S is a nonmilitary version that can be referenced to any specific traumatic event; the questions refer to "the stressful experience." The PCL-C is a general civilian version that is not linked to a specific event; the questions refer to "a stressful experience from the past." The scoring is the same for all three versions.

A total score is computed by adding the 17 items, so that possible scores range from 17 to 85. Used as a continuous measure, the PCL has good diagnostic utility. In Vietnam combat veterans, a cutoff of 50 on the PCL is a good predictor of a PTSD diagnosis based on the Structured Clinical Interview for *DSM-IV* (SCID) PTSD module. Principal components analysis revealed one large factor, consisting primarily of reexperiencing and hyperarousal items, and one much small factor, consisting primarily of emotional numbing items.

Source: Weathers, F. W., Huska, J. A., Keane, T. M. *PCL-C for DSM-IV*. Boston, MA: National Center for PTSD—Behavioral Science Division, 1991.

PTSD CHECKLIST–CIVILIAN VERSION (PCL-C)

Patient's Name: ______________________________

Instructions: Below is a list of problems and complaints that people sometimes have in response to stressful life experiences. Please read each one carefully and put an "X" in the box to indicate how much you have been bothered by that problem *in the past month.*

No.	Response:	Not at all (1)	A little bit (2)	Moderately (3)	Quite a bit (4)	Extremely (5)
1.	Repeated, disturbing *memories, thoughts*, or *images* of a stressful experience from the past?					
2.	Repeated, disturbing *dreams* of a stressful experience from the past?					
3.	Suddenly *acting* or *feeling* as if a stressful experience *were happening again* (as if you were reliving it)?					
4.	Feeling *very upset* when *something reminded* you of a stressful experience from the past?					

(continued)

No.	Response:	Not at all (1)	A little bit (2)	Moderately (3)	Quite a bit (4)	Extremely (5)
5.	Having *physical reactions* (e.g., heart pounding, trouble breathing, or sweating) when *something reminded* you of a stressful experience from the past?					
6.	Avoid *thinking about* or *talking about* a stressful experience from the past or avoid *having feelings* related to it?					
7.	Avoid *activities* or *situations* because *they remind you* of a stressful experience from the past?					
8.	Trouble *remembering important parts* of a stressful experience from the past?					
9.	Loss of interest in things that you used to enjoy?					
10.	Feeling *distant* or *cut off* from other people?					

(continued)

No.	Response:	Not at all (1)	A little bit (2)	Moderately (3)	Quite a bit (4)	Extremely (5)
11.	Feeling *emotionally numb* or being unable to have loving feelings for those close to you?					
12.	Feeling as if your *future* will somehow be *cut short*?					
13.	Trouble falling or staying asleep?					
14.	Feeling irritable or having angry outbursts?					
15.	Having difficulty concentrating?					
16.	Being *super alert* or watchful on guard?					
17.	Feeling *jumpy* or easily startled?					

PTSD CHECKLIST–CIVILIAN VERSION (PCL-S)

Patient's Name: ____

Instructions: Below is a list of problems and complaints that people sometimes have in response to stressful life experiences. Please read each one carefully and put an "X" in the box to indicate how much you have been bothered by that problem *in the past month.*
The event you experienced was _______________________ on _____________(date)

No.	Response:	Not at all (1)	A little bit (2)	Moderately (3)	Quite a bit (4)	Extremely (5)
1.	Repeated, disturbing *memories, thoughts*, or *images* of a stressful experience from the past?					
2.	Repeated, disturbing *dreams* of a stressful experience from the past?					
3.	Suddenly *acting* or *feeling* as if a stressful experience *were happening again* (as if you were reliving it)?					
4.	Feeling *very upset* when *something reminded* you of a stressful experience from the past?					

(continued)

No.	Response:	Not at all (1)	A little bit (2)	Moderately (3)	Quite a bit (4)	Extremely (5)
5.	Having *physical reactions* (e.g., heart pounding, trouble breathing, or sweating) when *something reminded* you of a stressful experience from the past?					
6.	Avoid *thinking about* or *talking about* a stressful experience from the past or avoid *having feelings* related to it?					
7.	Avoid *activities* or *situations* because *they remind you* of a stressful experience from the past?					
8.	Trouble *remembering important parts* of a stressful experience from the past?					
9.	Loss of interest in things that you used to enjoy?					
10.	Feeling *distant* or *cut off* from other people?					
11.	Feeling *emotionally numb* or being unable to have loving feelings for those close to you?					

(continued)

No.	Response:	Not at all (1)	A little bit (2)	Moderately (3)	Quite a bit (4)	Extremely (5)
12.	Feeling as if your *future* will somehow be *cut short*?					
13.	Trouble falling or staying asleep?					
14.	Feeling irritable or having angry outbursts?					
15.	Having difficulty concentrating?					
16.	Being *super alert* or watchful on guard?					
17.	Feeling *jumpy* or easily startled?					

PTSD CHECKLIST–MILITARY VERSION (PCL-M)

Patient's Name: ______________________________

Instructions: Below is a list of problems and complaints that people sometimes have in response to stressful military experiences. Please read each one carefully and put an "X" in the box to indicate how much you have been bothered by that problem *in the past month.*

No.	Response:	Not at all (1)	A little bit (2)	Moderately (3)	Quite a bit (4)	Extremely (5)
1.	Repeated, disturbing *memories*, *thoughts*, or *images* of a stressful experience from the past?					
2.	Repeated, disturbing *dreams* of a stressful experience from the past?					
3.	Suddenly *acting* or *feeling* as if a stressful experience *were happening again* (as if you were reliving it)?					
4.	Feeling *very upset* when *something reminded* you of a stressful experience from the past?					

(continued)

No.	Response:	Not at all (1)	A little bit (2)	Moderately (3)	Quite a bit (4)	Extremely (5)
5.	Having *physical reactions* (e.g., heart pounding, trouble breathing, or sweating) when *something reminded* you of a stressful experience from the past?					
6.	Avoid *thinking about* or *talking about* a stressful experience from the past or avoid *having feelings* related to it?					
7.	Avoid *activities* or *situations* because *they remind you* of a stressful experience from the past?					
8.	Trouble *remembering important parts* of a stressful experience from the past?					
9.	Loss of interest in things that you used to enjoy?					
10.	Feeling *distant* or *cut off* from other people?					

(continued)

No.	Response:	Not at all (1)	A little bit (2)	Moderately (3)	Quite a bit (4)	Extremely (5)
11.	Feeling *emotionally numb* or being unable to have loving feelings for those close to you?					
12.	Feeling as if your *future* will somehow be *cut short*?					
13.	Trouble falling or staying asleep?					
14.	Feeling irritable or having angry outbursts?					
15.	Having difficulty concentrating?					
16.	Being *super alert* or watchful on guard?					
17.	Feeling *jumpy* or easily startled?					

APPENDIX A10

DISSOCIATIVE EXPERIENCES SCALE-II

Directions: This questionnaire consists of 28 questions about experiences that you may have in your daily life. We are interested in how often you have these experiences. It is important, however, that your answers show how often these experiences happen to you when you are not under the influence of alcohol or drugs. To answer the questions, please determine to what degree the experience described in the question applies to you and circle the number to show what percentage of the time you have the experience.

For example:

0% 10% 20% 30% 40% 50% 60% 70% 80% 90% 100 %

(Never) (Always)

1. Some people have the experience of driving or riding in a car or bus or subway and suddenly realizing that they do not remember what has happened during all or part of the trip. Circle a number to show what percentage of the time this happens to you.

   0% 10% 20% 30% 40% 50% 60% 70% 80% 90% 100%

2. Some people find that sometimes they are listening to someone talk and they suddenly realize that they did not hear part or all of what was said. Circle the number to show what percentage of the time this happens to you.

   0% 10% 20% 30% 40% 50% 60% 70% 80% 90% 100%

3. Some people have the experience of finding themselves in a place and have no idea how they got there. Circle a number to show what percentage of the time this happens to you.

0% 10% 20% 30% 40% 50% 60% 70% 80% 90% 100%

4. Some people have the experience of finding themselves dressed in clothes that they do not remember putting on. Circle the number to show what percentage of the time this happens to you.

0% 10% 20% 30% 40% 50% 60% 70% 80% 90% 100%

5. Some people have the experience of finding new things among their belongings that they do not remember buying. Circle the number to show what percentage of the time this happens to you.

0% 10% 20% 30% 40% 50% 60% 70% 80% 90% 100%

6. Some people sometimes find that they are approached by people that they do not know, who call them by another name, or insist that they have met them before. Circle the number to show what percentage of the time this happens to you

0% 10% 20% 30% 40% 50% 60% 70% 80% 90% 100%

7. Some people sometimes have the experience of feeling as though they are standing next to themselves or watching themselves do something and they actually see themselves as if they were looking at another person. Circle the number to show what percentage of the time this happens to you.

0% 10% 20% 30% 40% 50% 60% 70% 80% 90% 100%

8. Some people are told that they sometimes do not recognize friends of family members. Circle the number to show what percentage of the time this happens to you.

0% 10% 20% 30% 40% 50% 60% 70% 80% 90% 100%

9. Some people find that they have no memory for some important events in their lives (e.g., a wedding or graduation). Circle the number to show what percentage of the time this happens to you.

0% 10% 20% 30% 40% 50% 60% 70% 80% 90% 100%

10. Some people have the experience of being accused of lying when they do not think that they have lied. Circle the number to show what percentage of the time this happens to you.

0% 10% 20% 30% 40% 50% 60% 70% 80% 90% 100%

11. Some people have the experience of looking in a mirror and not recognizing themselves. Circle the number to show what percentage of the time this happens to you.

    0% 10% 20% 30% 40% 50% 60% 70% 80% 90% 100%

12. Some people have the experience of feeling that other people, objects, and the world around them are not real. Circle the number to show what percentage of the time this happens to you.

    0% 10% 20% 30% 40% 50% 60% 70% 80% 90% 100%

13. Some people have the experience of feeling that their body does not seem to belong to them. Circle the number to show what percentage of the time this happens to you.

    0% 10% 20% 30% 40% 50% 60% 70% 80% 90% 100%

14. Some people have the experience of sometimes remembering a past event so vividly that they feel as if they were reliving that event. Circle the number to show what percentage of the time this happens to you.

    0% 10% 20% 30% 40% 50% 60% 70% 80% 90% 100%

15. Some people have the experience of not being sure whether things that they remember happening really did happen or whether they just dreamed them. Circle the number to show what percentage of the time this happens to you.

    0% 10% 20% 30% 40% 50% 60% 70% 80% 90% 100%

16. Some people have the experience of being in a familiar place but finding it strange and unfamiliar. Circle the number to show what percentage of the time this happens to you.

    0% 10% 20% 30% 40% 50% 60% 70% 80% 90% 100%

17. Some people find that when they are watching television or a movie they become so absorbed in the story that they are unaware of other events happening around them. Circle the number to show what percentage of the time this happens to you.

    0% 10% 20% 30% 40% 50% 60% 70% 80% 90% 100%

18. Some people find that they become so involved in a fantasy or daydream that it feels as though it were really happening to them. Circle the number to show what percentage of the time this happens to you.

    0% 10% 20% 30% 40% 50% 60% 70% 80% 90% 100%

19. Some people find that they sometimes are able to ignore pain. Circle the number to show what percentage of the time this happens to you.

0% 10% 20% 30% 40% 50% 60% 70% 80% 90% 100%

20. Some people find that they sometimes sit staring off into space, thinking of nothing, and are not aware of the passage of time. Circle the number to show what percentage of the time this happens to you.

0% 10% 20% 30% 40% 50% 60% 70% 80% 90% 100%

21. Some people sometimes find that when they are alone they talk out loud to themselves. Circle the number to show what percentage of the time this happens to you.

0% 10% 20% 30% 40% 50% 60% 70% 80% 90% 100%

22. Some people find that in one situation they may act so differently compared with another situation that they feel almost as if they were two different people. Circle the number to show what percentage of the time this happens to you.

0% 10% 20% 30% 40% 50% 60% 70% 80% 90% 100%

23. Some people sometimes find that in certain situations they are able to do things with amazing ease and spontaneity that would usually be difficult for them (e.g., sports, work, social situations, etc.). Circle the number to show what percentage of the time this happens to you.

0% 10% 20% 30% 40% 50% 60% 70% 80% 90% 100%

24. Some people sometimes find that they cannot remember whether they have done something or have just thought about doing that thing (e.g., not knowing whether they have just mailed a letter or have just thought about mailing it). Circle the number to show what percentage of the time this happens to you.

0% 10% 20% 30% 40% 50% 60% 70% 80% 90% 100%

25. Some people find evidence that they have done things that they do not remember doing. Circle the number to show what percentage of the time this happens to you.

0% 10% 20% 30% 40% 50% 60% 70% 80% 90% 100%

26. Some people sometimes find writings, drawings, or notes among their belongings that they must have done but cannot remember doing. Circle the number to show what percentage of the time this happens to you.

0% 10% 20% 30% 40% 50% 60% 70% 80% 90% 100%

27. Some people sometimes find that they hear voices inside their head that tell them to do things or comment on things that they are doing. Circle the number to show what percentage of the time this happens to you.

0% 10% 20% 30% 40% 50% 60% 70% 80% 90% 100%

28. Some people sometimes feel as if they are looking at the world through a fog, so that people and objects appear far away or unclear. Circle the number to show what percentage of the time this happens to you.

0% 10% 20% 30% 40% 50% 60% 70% 80% 90% 100%

DISSOCIATIVE EXPERIENCES SCALE–II

Description and Interpretation

Description

The Dissociative Experiences Scale–II (DES-II) is a copyright-free screening instrument. According to its authors Carlson and Putnam,

> it is a brief, self-report measure of the frequency of dissociative experiences. The scale was developed to provide a reliable, valid, and convenient way to quantify dissociative experiences. A response scale that allows subjects to quantify their experiences for each item was used so that scores could reflect a wider range of dissociative symptomatology than possible using a dichotomous (yes/no) format. (See Carlson & Putnam, 1993.)

Interpretation

The DES-II: When scoring, drop the zero on the percentage, for example, 30% = 3; 80% = 8 then add up single digits for client score.

Mean DES Scores Across Populations for Various Studies

General adult population	5.4
Anxiety disorders	7.0
Affective disorders	9.35
Eating disorders	15.8
Late adolescence	16.6
Schizophrenia	15.4
Borderline personality disorder	19.2
PTSD	31
Dissociative disorder (NOS)	36
Dissociative identity disorder (MPD)	48

DES, dissociative experiences scale; PTSD, posttraumatic stress disorder; NOS, not otherwise specified; MPD, multiple personality disorder.

Items From the DES for Each of the Three Main Factors of Dissociation

Amnesia Factor

This factor measures memory loss, that is, not knowing how you got somewhere; being dressed in clothes you do not remember putting on; finding new things among belongings you do not remember buying; not recognizing friends or family members; finding evidence of having done things you do not remember doing; finding writings, drawings, or notes you must have done but do not remember doing.

Items—3, 4, 5, 8, 25, 26.

Depersonalization/Derealization Factor

Depersonalization is characterized by the recurrent experience of feeling detached from one's self and mental processes or a sense of unreality of the self. Items relating to this factor include feeling that you are standing next to yourself or watching yourself do something and seeing yourself as if you were looking at another person, feeling your body does not belong to you, and looking in a mirror and not recognizing yourself. Derealization is the sense of a loss of reality of the immediate environment. These items include feeling that other people, objects, and the world around them are not real, hearing voices inside your head that tell you to do things or comment on things you are doing, and feeling like you are looking at the world through a fog, so that people and objects appear far away or unclear.

Items—7, 11, 12, 13, 27, 28.

Absorption Factor

This factor includes being so preoccupied or absorbed by something that you are distracted from what is going on around you. The absorption primarily has to do with one's traumatic experiences. Items of this factor include realizing that you did not hear part or all of what was said by another, remembering a past event so vividly that you feel as if you are reliving the event, not being sure whether things that you remember happening really did happen or whether you just dreamed them, becoming so absorbed in the story when you are watching television or a movie that you are unaware of other events happening around you, becoming so involved in a fantasy or daydream that it feels as though it were really happening to you, and sometimes sitting, staring off into space, thinking of nothing, and being unaware of the passage of time.

Items—2, 14, 15, 17, 18, 20.

APPENDIX B

PROTOCOLS

APPENDIX

B1

THE SAFE/CALM PLACE PROTOCOL

The idea of the *safe place* has been a staple in the practice of clinical hypnosis. The first known use of the Safe Place with Eye Movement Desensitization and Reprocessing (EMDR) was when Dr. Neal Daniels, an EMDR practitioner working at the Veterans Administration Hospital in Philadelphia, adopted this resource to assist the veterans with whom he worked to ground themselves and contain their affect before doing trauma work. Dr. Francine Shapiro saw the merit of this intervention and by 1995 included a formalized version into the first EMDR text.

THE SAFE/CALM PLACE PROTOCOL SCRIPT

Use another affect if more appropriate for the client (e.g., calm, control, courage).

Image

Say, *"I'd like you to think about some place you have been or imagine being that feels very safe or calm. Perhaps, being on the beach or sitting by a mountain stream."* (Pause)

Say, *"Where would you be?"*

____

____

Emotions and Sensations

Say, *"As you think of that safe* (or calm) *place, notice what you see, hear, and feel right now."* (Pause)
Say, *"What do you notice?"*

___

___

Enhancement

Say, *"Focus on your safe* (or calm) *place, its sights, sounds, smells, and body sensations. Tell me more about what you are noticing."*

___

___

Bilateral Stimulation (BLS)

Say, *"Bring up the image of that place. Concentrate on where you feel the pleasant sensations in your body and allow yourself to enjoy them. Now concentrate on those sensations and follow my fingers* (or whatever BLS you use)*."*

Use four to six sets.

Say, *"How do you feel now?"*

___

___

Repeat several times if the process has enhanced the client's positive feelings and sensations.
If positive, say, *"Focus on that."* Repeat BLS.
Say, *"What do you notice now?"*

___

___

Cue Word

Say, *"Is there a word or phrase that represents your safe* (or calm) *place?"*

___

___

Then say, *"Think of* __________ (cue word) *and notice the positive feelings you have when you think of that word. Now concentrate on those sensations and the cue word and follow* __________ (state BLS using)*."*

Use short sets (four to six) of BLS with any positive responses.

Say, *"How do you feel now?"*

Repeat several times. Enhance positive feelings with BLS several times.

Self-Cuing

Say, *"Now I'd like you to say that word* ________ (cue word) *and notice how you feel."*

Cuing With Disturbance

Say, *"Now imagine a minor annoyance and how it feels."* (Pause)
Say, *"Now bring up your safe* (or calm) *place and notice any shifts in your body."*

Do BLS.

Guide the client through the process until he is able to experience the positive emotions and sensations. Repeat as often as necessary.

Self-Cuing With Disturbance

Say, *"Now I'd like you to think of another mildly annoying incident and bring up your safe* (or calm) *place by yourself again, especially noticing any changes in your body when you have gone to your safe* (or calm) *place."*

Practice

Say, *"I'd like you to practice using your safe place, between now and our next session, at any time you feel a little annoyed. Keep track of how things go and we'll talk about it next time we meet. Do you have any questions before we stop?"*

APPENDIX B2

BASIC PROCEDURAL STEPS AND SCRIPT FOR RESOURCE DEVELOPMENT AND INSTALLATION

1. Describe an incident or stressful situation:

   How disturbing does it feel to you right now, from 0 to 10 where 0 is no disturbance or neutral and 10 is the highest disturbance you can imagine?

   Subjective Unit of Disturbance (SUD): 0 1 2 3 4 5 6 7 8 9 10

2. *Which positive resource, skill, or strength will help you to deal better with this stressful situation?* (Identify up to three of these if possible. It is fine to just identify one initially and go through Step 4. Then return to Step 2 to identify a second resource and later return to Step 2 to identify a third. Note: When possible, select resources that will assist both with the current stressful situation and with subsequent reprocessing of etiological experiences.)

   a. ____________________
   b. ____________________
   c. ____________________

   Describe a moment or situation in your life when you experienced that resource, skill, or strength.

   a. ____________________
   b. ____________________
   c. ____________________

3. *What image best represents this situation?*

   a. ____________________
   b. ____________________
   c. ____________________

   Where do you feel it in your body?

   a. ____________________
   b. ____________________
   c. ____________________

(continued)

Source: Leeds, A. (2009). *A guide to the standard EMDR protocols for clinicians, supervisors, and consultants.* New York: Springer Publishing Company. Reproduced with the permission of Springer Publishing Company, LLC.

4. *Now focus on the image and notice where you are feeling in your body. Then follow my fingers* (lights, taps, or tones). (Add one set of 6–12 movements.)
   What do you notice in your body now?
   a. ______
   b. ______
   c. ______

   (If the experience stays positive or gets stronger, do a second set of 6–12 movements.)
   Stay with that and follow again.
   What do you notice in your body now?
   a. ______
   b. ______
   c. ______

   Tell me a word or phrase that can help identify this resource.
   a. ______
   b. ______
   c. ______

   (Do a third set of 6–12 movements.)
   Focus on where you feel it in your body and repeat that word or phrase and follow again.

5. Repeat Steps 2 to 4 with two other resources. Then go on to Step 6.
6. *Focus on all the resources that we found during our session. Notice where you feel them in your body. Repeat the word or phrase for each one.*
   (Add one set of 6–12 movements.)
   Follow again.
   What do you notice in your body now? ______
   Now, notice these positive feelings as you think of the stressful situation you described at the beginning.
   (Add one set of 6–12 movements.)
   Follow again.
   What do you notice in your body now? ______
   Focus on the stressful situation you identified at the beginning. How disturbing does it feel to you right now, from 0 to 10 where 0 is no disturbance or neutral and 10 is the highest disturbance you can imagine?
   SUD: 0 1 2 3 4 5 6 7 8 9 10

7. At the next session, check on the patient's ability to cope with the identified stressful situation. Repeat Steps 2 to 6, as needed, on this or other target situations.

DETAILED PROCEDURAL STEPS AND SCRIPT FOR RDI

Select from the bold phrases listed in each step those appropriate for each client

Target situation

1(A). The clinician should select a target situation from a current situation that triggers maladaptive urges, overwhelming emotion (such as shame, fear, or anger), or depersonalization. This target situation is generally selected using a behavioral chain analysis. It can also be a reprocessed memory that is chronically incomplete.

Target situation:

Worst part

1(B). *As you think about* ____________ (the target situation), *what is the worst part of it now?*

Worst part:

Initial SUD or level of urge (LOU)
(Optional step)

1(C). *SUD: As you hold that situation in mind, how disturbing does it feel to you now on a scale from 0 to 10, where 0 represents neutral or no disturbance and 10 represents the most disturbing you can imagine.*

OR

1(D). *LOU: As you hold that situation in mind, how strong does that urge feel to you now on a scale from 0 to 10, where 0 represents neutral or no urge and 10 represents the strongest urge you can imagine.*

SUD or LOU level: 0 1 2 3 4 5 6 7 8 9 10

To identify a resource, select phrases from *either* 2(A), *or* 2(B) and 2(C), and 2(D).

Identifying a Resource (Abstract)	Identifying a Resource (Concrete)
2(A). *When you think about this situation, what qualities or strengths do you need?* Desired qualities or strengths:	2(B). *What would you like to be able to do in this situation?* Desired behavior: 2(C). *What would you like to believe about yourself in this situation?* Desired belief: 2(D). *What would you like to feel in this situation?* Desired emotion:

Select one resource from 2(E), 2(F), 2(G), *or* 2(H) at a time and continue to 4(F). Then return to the start of Step 2 for as many resources as needed until the patient achieves stability. When possible, select resources that will assist both with the current stressful situation and with subsequent reprocessing of etiological experiences.

Exploring Memories and Images of Resource Experiences

Mastery Experiences

2(E). *Think of a time when you were able to* ____________ (say client's desired behavior or quality).
Think of a time when you were able to believe ____________ (say client's desired belief).
Think of a time when you felt ____________ (say client's desired emotion).

Mastery Experience:

(continued)

Relational Resources—Models

2(F). *Think of people in your life who possess or embody this quality.*
Think of people in the world who can serve as a role model for you.
Think of people who made a difference in your life by showing you other choices.
Model:

Relational Resources—Supportive Figures

2(G). *Think of who you would want helping you, coaching you to do what is best for you, to think what is best for you, and helping you to feel* ____________ (say client's desired emotion).
Think of any friends, relatives, teachers, caregivers, animals, or pets who encouraged or sustained you?
Think of a spiritual guide, someone who gives you hope or strength.
Supportive Figure:

Metaphors and Symbolic Resources

2(H). *Close your eyes if you would like (or leave them open if you would prefer) and allow an image (or symbol) to come to you that would help you to be able to* _________ (say client's desired behavior or quality) *or help you to believe* __________ (say client's desired belief) *or help you to feel* (say client's desired emotion).
Symbol:

Resource Development—Accessing More Sensory and Affective Information
(Working with one resource memory or image at a time.)

3(A). *As you focus on* ________ (i.e., that experience, person, symbol, etc.), *what do you see? What do you hear? What do you smell? What sensations do you notice in your body? What emotions do you feel as you focus on this image or memory?*
Where do you notice these feelings in your body.
(Write *verbatim* client's words and phrases.)
Images:
Sounds:
Emotions and Sensations:
Location of Sensations:

Checking the Ecology and Validity of the Resource (VoR)

3(B). *As you focus on* _____________ (repeat words for resource image) *and notice the* ________ (repeat words for resource sounds, smells, sensations, feelings), *how do you feel now?*

Assess the VoR

3(C). *As you focus on the picture that represents the worst part of* ________ (the target situation), *how true or helpful do* ________ (repeat descriptions of the resource image and feelings) *feel to you now from 1, completely false or not helpful, to 7, completely true or helpful?* (Initial VoR of 1 is a caution.)
VoR: 1 2 3 4 5 6 7

Reflecting the Resource

3(D). *Close your eyes if you would like (or leave them open if you would prefer) and let yourself be aware of* ________ (repeat words for resource image) *and notice the*_________ (repeat description of resource feelings, sensations, smells, sounds).
(Repeat and vary the order of client's words for the image, sounds, emotions, and sensations.)

(continued)

Verify the resource has positive associations or affects

3(E). *What do you notice or feel now?*

When the client reports positive feelings and associations, continue to Step 4(A), Installation. If the client reports negative associations or affect, do *not* continue with this resource. Instead, start over with another resource.

Resource Installation

4(A). *Now, as you continue to focus on* ________ (say client's words for the resource image, emotions, and sensations), *follow my fingers* (or tones, lights, taps).

Do the first set of 6 to 12 movements. Then ask, *What are you feeling or noticing now?* ______________

Stop bilateral stimulation if client reports negative associations or affect. Neutralize and set these aside and start over with an alternate resource. With positive responses continue.

Do a second set of 6 to 12 movements. Then ask, *What are you feeling or noticing now?* ______________________________

Do a third set of 6 to 12 movements. Then ask, *What are you feeling or noticing now?* ______________________________

Linking verbal or sensory cues (occurs spontaneously sometimes).

Select one or more phrases from 4(B), 4(C), 4(D), or 4(E), then add two more sets of stimulation

---

(For mastery experiences)

4(B). *As you focus on that experience* (if needed repeat client's words of the image, emotions, and sensations), *think of the most positive words you can say about yourself now.*

(For models)

4(C). *Imagine seeing and hearing* _______ (name model person) *being as you would most like to be. If you would like to, imagine stepping right into* ___________*'s* (name model person) *body, so you can see through his or her eyes and feel how it is to be able to act, feel, and think like that.*

(For supportive figures)

4(D). *Imagine* ________ (supportive figure) *standing near you and offering you what you need. Imagine that he or she knows exactly what to say to you, exactly what you need to hear. Image a reassuring touch in just the way you need it.*

(For metaphoric or symbolic resources)

4(E). *Imagine seeing* ________ (name the symbol). *Imagine holding* ________ (name the symbol) *in your hands. Imagine being surrounded by* __________ (name the image or feeling). *Breathe in* __________ (name the feeling). *Notice where you feel the positive feelings in your body.*

4(F). Continue with two more sets of stimulation as long as processing appears helpful.

Do a fourth set of 6 to 12 movements. Then ask, *What are you feeling or noticing now?*

____

Do a fifth set of 6 to 12 movements. Then ask, *What are you feeling or noticing now?*

____

____

(continued)

Install additional resources for the same or additionally needed qualities or capacities

5. Repeat Steps 2(A) to 4(F) with as many additional resources for the same or other needed qualities or capacities until the patient can successfully complete the future template below.

Future Template

Select one or more phrases from 9(A), 9(B), 9(C), or 9(D), then add two more sets of stimulation.

6(A). *Think about* ________ (being able to act, think, or feel as in the resource experience or possessing this quality) *in the future as you next face* ________ (the target situation).

(For mastery experiences)

6(B). *Imagine being able to act with* ________ (name his or her mastery action) *as you remember doing in* ________ (say client's mastery memory). *Imagine thinking* ________ (say client's mastery belief). *Imagine feeling* ________ (say client's master emotion) *in the future as you next face* ________ (the target situation).

Select from the bold phrases listed in each step those appropriate for each client

(For models)

6(C). *Imagine seeing and hearing* (say client's model) *being as you would most like to be. Or, if you would like to, imagine stepping right into* ________ *'s body, so you can see through his or her eyes and feel how it is to be able to act, feel, and think like that in the future as you next face* ________ (the target situation).

(For supportive figures)

6(D). *Imagine feeling connected with* ________ (say client's supportive figure) *as you face this situation. Notice what that would be like for you. Hear* ________ (name supportive person) *saying exactly what you need to hear in the future as you next face* ________ (the target situation).

(For symbolic resources)

6(E). See and feel your symbol in just the way you need to. Be aware of this symbol in just the way you need to experience it in the future as you next face ________ (the target situation).

Continue with two more sets of stimulation as long as processing appears helpful.

Do the first set of 6 to 12 movements on the future template. Then ask, *What are you feeling or noticing now?*

Do a second set of 6 to 12 movements on the future template. Then ask, *What are you feeling or noticing now?*

Checking the Validity of the Resource (VoR)

6(F). *And now as you imagine being in* ________ (the target situation), *in the future, how true or helpful does* ________ (name the resource(s) and self-statement or say client's words for the image, sensation, feelings) *feel to you now from 1, completely false or not helpful, to 7, completely true or helpful?*

VoR: 1 2 3 4 5 6 7

(continued)

Repeat for each quality or resource

6(G). Repeat this process with additional resources until the VoR rises to a 6 and the SUD or LOU on the presenting target situation falls to a 5 or lower.

Reassess the target issue
SUD or LOU

6(H). *And now as you think of* ________ (name each of the installed resources) *and imagine being in* ________ (the target situation) *in the future, how disturbing does it feel to you now on a scale from 0 to 10, where 0 represents neutral or no disturbance and 10 represents the most disturbing you can imagine.*

OR

6(I). *And now as you think of* ________ (name each of the installed resources) *and imagine being in* ________ (the target situation) *in the future, how strong does that urge feel to you now on a scale from 0 to 10, where 0 represents neutral or no urge and 10 represents the strongest urge you can imagine.*

SUD or LOU level: 0 1 2 3 4 5 6 7 8 9 10

Verify stability in the target situation with feedback from patient log

7. Review the patient's log to verify the patient is now able to cope adequately with the target situation without giving in to maladaptive urges, overwhelming emotion, depersonalization, or is now able to successfully reprocess a previously, chronically, incompletely reprocessed memory.

APPENDIX B3

EMDR REPROCESSING PROCEDURAL STEPS SCRIPT

Target Selected From Master Treatment Plan List Targets

Phase 3: Assessment of the Target

Image

"What image represents the worst part of the incident?"

If the patient has no image, elicit another aspect of *sensory* memory: *"When you think of the incident, what part of the incident do you notice?"*

Negative Cognition (NC)

"What words go best with that image" (if there is no image, say —*"with that incident"*) *"that express your negative belief about yourself now?"*

Positive Cognition (PC)

"When you think of that image, what would you like to believe about yourself now?"

Validity of Cognition (VoC)

"When you think of that image" (if there is no image, say—*"with that incident"*), *"how true do those words"* (repeat the PC—as an "I" statement) *"feel to you now, on a scale of 1 to 7, where 1 means they feel completely false and 7 means they feel completely true?"*

0 1 2 3 4 5 6 7

Completely false Completely true

Emotions

"When you focus on that image," (if there is no image, say—*"on that incident"*) *"and think of those words ________________"* (repeat the negative cognition—as an "I" statement), *"what emotions do you feel now?"*

(continued)

Subjective Units of Disturbance Scale
"On a scale from 0 to 10, where 0 is no disturbance or neutral and 10 is the highest disturbance you can imagine, how disturbing does the incident feel to you now?"

0	1	2	3	4	5	6	7	8	9	10
(No disturbance–neutral)								(Highest disturbance)		

Location of Body Sensation
"Where do you feel it in your body?"

Orientation to reprocessing
"We'll start reprocessing now. As we do sets of eye movements (taps or tones), sometimes, things will change and sometimes they won't. You may notice other images, thoughts, emotions, or body sensations. Other memories may come up. Other times, you may not be aware of anything but the eye movements (taps or tones). Remember what we discussed with the metaphor of riding the train. There are no right or wrong responses. Just notice whatever happens. If you need to stop at any point, just show me the stop sign we rehearsed."

Phase 4: Desensitization
"I'd like you to focus on that image" (if no image—*"on that incident"*) *"and those negative words* (repeat the negative cognition—as an "I" statement). *"Notice where you are feeling it in your body, and follow my fingers"* (Or *"notice the lights," "the taps,"* or *"the sounds"*).
After a set of 24 to 30 complete movements
"Rest. Take a deeper breath. Let it go. What do you notice now?"

After patient reports, continue reprocessing
"Focus on that and notice what happens next."

Continue sets of eye movements down a channel of associations using the instructions above as long as patient reports indicate reprocessing is occurring. If the patient reports the same content without change after two sets of BLS, change the direction, height, speed, and/or width of the eye movements. If using auditory stimulation, change the speed or type of sound. If using kinesthetic stimulation, change the speed, intensity, or location of the stimulation.

Returning to target
Continue additional sets of bilateral stimulation until the patient reports no further disturbing material and reports only neutral or positive material. Also return to target if associations become so remote from the original target that clinical judgment suggests reprocessing of the selected target is no longer occurring. Then, to return to the target, say,
"When you bring your attention back to the original experience, what do you notice now?"

If the patient reports additional disturbing material
"Focus on that and notice what happens next."
When you return to target, if the patient reports ambiguous, or apparently neutral or positive associations on the target, check the SUD rating.

Check SUD scale
"Focus on the original experience. On a scale from 0 to 10, where 0 is no disturbance or neutral and 10 is the highest disturbance you can imagine, how disturbing does it feel to you now?"

(continued)

After checking the SUD scale
If the SUD rating is a 1 or higher, say,
*"What's the worst part of it now?"*_______________
Then say, *"Focus on that and notice what happens next."*
Or
*Where do you feel that in your body?*_______________
"Focus on that and notice what happens next."
If the SUD rating is 0, say,
"Focus on how the incident seems to you now and notice what happens next."
When the patient reports a SUD rating of 0 a second time, continue to the installation phase.

Phase 5: Installation
Check for a better PC
"Do the words" _______________ (repeat the positive cognition—as an "I" statement) *"still fit, or is there another positive statement that would be more suitable?"*

Check the VoC on the selected PC
"Think about the original experience and those words _______________*"* (repeat the selected positive cognition in the first person). *"On a scale from 1 to 7, where 1 means they feel completely false and 7 means they feel completely true, how true do those words feel to you now?"*

1	2	3	4	5	6	7
Completely false					Completely true	

Before each set of BLS in the installation phase, link the original experience and the PC
*"Focus on the original experience and those words*_______________*"* (repeat the selected positive cognition in the first person) *"and follow."*
Offer another set of BLS.

After each set of BLS in the installation phase, check the VoC again.

Check the VoC on the selected PC
"Think about the original experience and those words _______________*"* (repeat the selected positive cognition in the first person). *"On a scale from 1 to 7, where 1 means they feel completely false and 7 means they feel completely true, how true do those words feel to you now?"*

1	2	3	4	5	6	7
Completely false					Completely true	

When the VoC is rising
Continue the installation phase as long as the patient continues to report growing confidence in the selected positive cognition or other more positive material.

When the VoC does not rise to a 7
After several sets of BLS, if the reported material is not getting more positive and rising up to a VoC of 7, change the direction or type of BLS. If the patient continues to report a VoC of 6 or less—even after changing the direction or type of BLS—check for a blocking belief.
"What thought or concern keeps these words from feeling completely true?"

(continued)

This blocking belief can sometimes be directly targeted and resolved in a few more sets of BLS. Then, return to standard installation phase instructions above to complete the installation phase.

In other cases, starting from the patient's expressed blocking belief, you may need to use an affect bridge or somatic bridge to identify an associated memory and target that for reprocessing in this session or in the next session. This generally will mean the originally selected target will remain incomplete for this session until the source of the blocking belief can be reprocessed.

Completing the installation phase

When the patient reports a VoC of 7 and the material is no longer becoming more positive, go on to the body scan phase.

Phase 6: Body Scan

"Close your eyes. Hold in mind the original experience—as it seems to you now—and those words _______________*"* (repeat the selected positive cognition). *"Then bring your attention to all the different areas of your body, starting with your head and continuing down to your feet. Any place you feel any tension, tightness, or unusual sensations, tell me."*

For any reported negative sensations, offer additional sets of BLS until the patient reports only neutral or positive sensations. Then return to target again, and use the instructions above to do the body scan again to check for any new, residual sensations.

For reported positive sensations, continue BLS to enhance the positive sensations until they are no longer getting more positive. In the body scan phase, use the same standard directions between sets of BLS as in the desensitization phase.

*"Rest. Take a deeper breath. Let it go. What do you notice now?"*_______________

"Focus on that and notice what happens next."

Phase 7: Closure

Procedures for an incomplete session

An incomplete session is one where the SUD rating is above a 1; the VoC rating is less than a 6; or there are residual negative sensations reported in the body scan that were not reported before the session began and that appear to be linked to the targeted material.

Explain the need to stop. Offer encouragement for the patient's work in the session. When the desensitization phase is incomplete, skip the installation of positive cognition and the body scan. Explore the patient's somatic, emotional, and cognitive state. Assess the patient's need for structured containment or stabilization procedures.

"We are almost out of time and we will need to stop soon. You have done good work today. I appreciate the effort you have made. How are you feeling?"

If needed, offer one or more containment, calming, or sensory orienting exercises. When the patient is in a stable state, review the briefing statement below.

Closure procedures for a complete session

Offer acknowledgment for the patient's work in the session. If time remains, encourage the patient to discuss his or her observations about what occurred in the session. If appropriate, briefly mention any significant observed shifts or gains the patient does not mention.

"You have done good work today. How are you feeling?"

Brief the patient and request a log report

"The processing we have done today may continue after the session. You may or may not notice new insights, thoughts, memories, or dreams. You may notice changes in how you are functioning. To help us evaluate your responses to today's session, notice what you experience and make entries in your log. Remember to practice the _______________ *exercises we worked on to help you manage disturbances this week. We will review your log report and continue our work next time. If you have something urgent to report or need additional support before our next session, call me."*

APPENDIX B4

CRAVEX: AN EMDR APPROACH TO TREAT SUBSTANCE ABUSE AND ADDICTION

CRAVEX SCRIPT NOTES

The comorbidity of posttraumatic stress disorder (PTSD) and substance abuse gives sufficient reason to treat patients who are addicted with Eye Movement Desensitization and Reprocessing (EMDR). However, there are several pathways leading to addiction and PTSD is only one of them. Thirty years of addiction research have provided sufficient evidence for the crucial role of memory in drug dependency. The addiction memory (AM) serves as a useful concept for obsessive–compulsive craving to be seen in drug addicted patients (Boening, 2001). The concept of AM and its importance in relapse occurrence and maintenance of learned addictive behavior has gained growing acceptance in the field of addiction research and treatment. The characteristics of the AM are as follows:

- An *individual-acquired memory following drug consumption* in some individuals
- Based on *normal memory systems* and systems of neuronal information processing
- Can be *activated at any time* by relapse-endangering complex, internal, or external situations, thus experiencing cue-stimulated craving
- Becomes *part of the personality,* especially in the episodic memory (also known as the "one shot" learning mechanism)
- This neurobiological-based, imprinted, addictive behavior seems to *resist change* under normal circumstances

The implicit nature of the AM seems to qualify it as a target for EMDR treatment. There are two types of targets for EMDR concerning addiction memories:

- *Memories of drug consumption or relapse.* As an activated AM would initiate a chain of rather subconscious processes leading into drug consumption, these

---

Source: Luber, M. (2010). *Eye movement desensitization and reprocessing (EMDR) scripted protocols: Special populations.* New York: Springer Publishing Company. Reproduced with the permission of Springer Publishing Company, LLC.

memories of drug consumption—against willful intention—should qualify as targets for EMDR reprocessing.
- *Memories of intense cravings*. As craving seems to be the conscious representation of these processes, memories of intense craving should also qualify as targets for EMDR reprocessing.

The AM develops on the basis of experiencing drug use and drug effects. The AM includes a compulsive urge or craving for the drug and a loss of control in limiting or ceasing drug consumption and will more likely be an episodic type of memory. There are strong indicators that the AM consists of two components: a drug-independent memory of loss of control and a drug-specific memory of the addictive drug. Without adequate therapeutic interventions, it is hardly extinguishable (Wolffgramm & Heyne, 1995) as shown in the animal model where a remodeling of the AM facilitated by steroids extinguished craving in opiate-addicted rats (Wolff-gramm, Galli, Timm, & Heyene, 2000), and just to underline the findings—deleting the AM cured 100% of the animals of their addiction. Thus, altering or extinguishing the AM in human addicts could add an important component to well-established treatment modalities.

Reprocessing of the AM

The presumably episodic type of AM, its cue reactivity and power resembles the maladaptive traumatic memory forming the core of PTSD (van der Kolk, Burbridge, & Suzuki, 1997). There are two major hypotheses:

- Thus, the reprocessing of the AM with EMDR should lead to measurable changes of addiction symptoms, if the AM qualifies for maladaptive memory within the Adaptive Information Processing (AIP) Model.
- As the AM includes the urge to consume the drug of abuse, more aptly named craving, reprocessing of the AM should lead to a reduction in craving. Thus, in alcohol-dependent patients, the reprocessing of the AM should lead to a reduction of the craving measurable by the obsessive–compulsive drinking scale (OCDS), an instrument to measure alcohol-related craving (Mann & Ackermann, 2000).

Thirty-four patients with chronic alcohol dependency in an inpatient detoxification facility, were randomly assigned to one of two treatment conditions during a pilot study: treatment as usual (TAU) or TAU + EMDR. In the TAU + EMDR group, patients received two sessions of EMDR in order to activate and reprocess the addiction memory; they focused on the following targets:

- Memories of intense craving
- Memories of relapse

The craving for alcohol was measured by the OCDS pre, post, and 1 month after treatment. The TAU + EMDR group showed a significant reduction in craving posttreatment and 1 month after treatment, whereas TAU did not. The TAU + EMDR group showed less relapse at the 6-month follow-up. The results indicate that EMDR might be a useful approach for the treatment of AM and associated symptoms of craving (Hase, Schallmayer, & Sack, 2008).

CRAVING EXTINGUISHED (CRAVEX)—THE MANUAL

The name CRAVEX was given to this EMDR strategy because craving seemed to vanish during EMDR reprocessing of the AM in some of the patients. It is important when treating comorbid addicted and traumatized patients to take into account the severity of PTSD and the addiction simultaneously. Several strategies such as extensive stabilization—resource development and installation (Korn & Leeds, 2002) or the inverted standard protocol for unstable complex PTSD (Hofmann & Sack, 2006) address this problem.

Note: In comorbid clients, the addiction has to be treated first, as ongoing drug consumption is a clear no go for trauma therapy.

CRAVEX, as part of a treatment for comorbid addictive clients, focuses on reprocessing of the AM thus leading to stabilization in the addiction. The client should be able to stay sober for a sufficient period of time around a scheduled treatment session. Achieving even short-time sobriety has to be planned according to the drug of abuse. Chronic alcohol-addicted patients, for example, would need medical detoxification treatment in a specialized in- or outpatient unit to achieve sobriety without endangering their lives. Reduction of acute craving is reported for various drugs of abuse, such as nicotine, alcohol, and heroin.

During EMDR reprocessing, it is essential to monitor craving. Therefore, the Subjective Units of Disturbance Scale (SUDS) measure has been replaced by the level of urge (LoU), initiated by A. J. Popky in his DeTUR protocol for addictions (2005). This is an appropriate but small modification of the EMDR 8-phases procedure and with minimal modification in EMDR procedures the EMDR therapist can easily adapt to this approach. The standard EMDR protocol remains the guideline for treatment planning, thus addressing past, present, and future. Addressing the past means targeting memories of past cravings and relapse(s), thus leading to the reprocessing of the AM, or rather memories in the AM network. Focusing on the present means targeting current problems or triggers. Work in the future includes the future template to facilitate adaptive behavior in order to maintain abstinence.

CRAVEX SCRIPT: EMDR 8 PHASES

Phase 1: History Taking

During the history-taking phase, the standard history is taken. It is essential to use standard diagnostic procedures to screen for dissociative disorders and PTSD. Make sure to incorporate the rules of treatment planning for complex PTSD while working with this population. The therapist should take a history of the addictive behavior and a trauma history. The therapist should pay attention to the interaction of trauma and addictive behavior:

Say, *"When did you lose control over your addictive behavior?"*

___

___

___

Say, *"What was happening in your life when your drug consumption increased?"*

Also, the therapist should search for access to the memory of addiction, asking for recent relapse and intense craving as well as associated cues.

Say, *"When did you relapse recently?"*

Say, *"When did you experience intense craving for your drug, even if you just managed to stay sober?"*

Say, *"Is there anything you see, hear, smell, taste, or feel able to evoke craving?"*

The therapist should also ask for current stressors and about the fear of failing to sustain sobriety in order to elicit targets for the present part of the standard EMDR protocol and the future template.

Say, *"Are there any current problems that could disturb you and endanger your ability to stay sober?"*

Say, *"What are your fears about future dangers that may cause you to relapse?"*

For example, a client may discuss her spouse's ongoing skepticism to her sobriety as a current stressor and her fear of meeting old friends trying to persuade her to go drinking in the future. It is helpful to write down the traumatic material and addiction memories according to the 3-pronged protocol.

ADDICTION MEMORIES AND TRAUMATIC MATERIAL WORKSHEET

Addiction Memories

Past

Memories of relapse(s)

Most recent ______________________________

First ______________________________

Worst ______________________________

Memories of intense craving

Most recent ______________________________

First ______________________________

Worst ______________________________

Other memories related to addictive behaviors ______________

Present

Cues for craving

____

____

Current stressors resulting in addictive behaviors

____

____

Future

Future fears concerning addiction and addictive behaviors

____

____

Related Traumatic Material

Past traumas

____

____

Present trauma triggers

____

____

Future fears concerning trauma and addictive behaviors

____

____

Resources

___

___

Resources needed

___

___

The therapist assesses the areas in need of treatment and decides where to begin. In addition, the worksheet helps to address the question of past, present, and future targets for addiction or PTSD. The addiction is targeted first via reprocessing the AM. Memories of relapse or intense craving form the targets in the past, while cues for craving as well as current stressors are reprocessed in the present part of the standard EMDR protocol. The fears of the patient form the basis of building a future template and are reprocessed accordingly. This is standard EMDR therapy. Major traumas also can impact on addictive behaviors and are important to include in treatment planning.

Phase 2: Preparation

The basic preparation in Phase 2 is essential to work in this model. This includes establishing a Safe Place, introducing the basic mechanics of EMDR, and rationale and what to expect during the processing. It is helpful to prepare the client for the experience of drug effects.

Say, *"When we are working on a memory of craving or relapse, you may experience the need to take the drug. This is not a problem and will decrease as the therapy continues. You can seek appropriate support between sessions if you experience craving for the drug. In the session, you may experience a milder form of drug effect, like feeling relaxed or aroused according to the property of your drug of abuse."*

Prepare the client for the possibility of experiencing associated memories.

Say, *"Sometimes, though not very often, associated memories of some incident or problem may arise when we are working on a memory of craving. I'd like to suggest that we just continue with our work if that happens. These memories can be reprocessed in our work or we will address them in a separate session. We will just stay with the memory of relapse or craving with which we began."*

If a patient reports craving in the session, the modified absorption technique offers an approach to tackle acute craving. It can also be used when the patient seems unstable and may not be able to target a memory of craving or relapse. Therefore, it is appropriate to set up this resource before beginning reprocessing. When working with bilateral stimulation (BLS), make sure to work with care. Slow eye movements (EMs), for instance 3 to 12 EMs per set, and for tones, often 1/4 Hz and short sets seem effective to install a resource. The Butterfly Hug is helpful for severely traumatized patients.

CRAVEX RESOURCE FOR ACUTE CRAVING SCRIPT

The goal here is to reduce the craving (S. Franke, personal communication). Start with evaluating the LoU.

Level of Urge

Say, *"Please evaluate the intensity of your craving for* ________ *(state substance) on a scale of 0 to 10, where 0 is no craving or neutral and 10 is the most craving you can imagine, how strong does your craving feel now?"*

0 1 2 3 4 5 6 7 8 9 10

(No craving) (Most craving)

Say, *"How would you feel if you had taken your drug of abuse? Please describe up to three states of mind and body."*

1. ____
2. ____
3. ____

Often the answer will be relaxed, calm, and so forth.

Resources

Ask for any memory—except using a drug—containing at least parts of these states of mind and body as a resource, such as memories of exercising, success, good relationships, therapy, and so forth. Find one memory for Resources 1 through 3.

Say, *"Has there been a moment or situation in your life when you experienced a bit of this resource or quality?"*

____

____

Say, *"What was the moment or situation in your life when you experienced a bit of the body experience or state of mind of Experience 1?"*

____

____

Say, *"Good. Now, what was the moment or situation in your life when you experienced a bit of the body experience or state of mind of Experience 2?"*

____

____

Say, *"Okay, now what was the moment or situation in your life when you experienced a bit of the body experience or state of mind of Experience 3?"*

____

____

Installation

Assist the client in focusing on the resource memory (questions, vividness), using approximately 3 to 10 sets. Should the patient feel uncomfortable with the therapist-conducted stimulation, the therapist can instruct the client how to work with self-stimulation, such as the Butterfly Hug.

Say, *"The next step is to just focus on the memory, the image, and these pleasant sensations and then just follow my fingers. Does that feel comfortable for you?"*

If not, say the following:

Say, *"Cross your arms over your chest so that the tip of your fingers from each hand can touch the area that is located under the connection between the clavicle and the shoulder. Your eyes can be closed or partially closed looking toward the tip of your nose. Next, you alternate the movement of your hands, like the flapping wings of a butterfly. You breathe slowly and deeply (abdominal breathing), while you observe what is going through your mind and body such as thoughts, images, sounds, odors, feelings, and physical sensation without changing, pushing your thoughts away, or judging. You can pretend as though what you are observing are like clouds passing by. How is that for you?"*

Repeat the stimulation when the resource becomes stronger.

Say, *"What do you get now?"*

Say, *"Does it feel more positive?"*

Say, *"Just stay with that and follow my fingers!"* (or have the client use the Butterfly Hug).

Interrupt the client when any association into traumatic memory networks occurs.

Positive Cognition (PC)

Assist the client to find a PC. Connect the three resources and the PC and strengthen with BLS.

Say, "*When you bring up that picture or incident, what would you like to believe about yourself now?*"

____

____

Say, "*Think of your resources of* _______ (remind client of the three resource states) *and* ______ (state the PC). *Go with that.*"

____

____

Use 4 to 6 slow BLS, or the Butterfly Hug.

Say, "*What do you get now?*"

____

____

Cue Word

Say, "*Think of a word that represents your strength or skill and feel those positive feelings and sensations as you* ________ (state BLS)."

____

____

Reevaluation

Now take another look on the craving.

Say, "*Please evaluate the intensity of your craving for* _______ (state substance) *on a scale of 0 to 10 (LoU), where 0 is no craving or neutral and 10 is the most craving you can imagine, how strong does your craving feel now?*"

0 1 2 3 4 5 6 7 8 9 10

(No craving) (Maximum craving)

If the LoU has decreased and the client feels as if she can handle the remaining craving, continue with the assessment.

If the LoU has not decreased at all, check for a Touchstone Event concerning the issue, using the Float-Back Technique or Affect Scan (Shapiro, 2001); install resources appropriate to the issue, or reprocess the memory that may have been triggered before you continue with the assessment. Also, check further for complex PTSD or dissociative disorder not otherwise specified (DDNOS).

Phase 3: Assessment

An essential part of therapy is the reprocessing of memories in the AM network. The CRAVEX Worksheet provides instruction—according to the EMDR standard procedures—with just one slight modification: The nodes to target are memories of intense craving or relapse in abstinence-motivated clients.

Target Selection and Evaluation

Important guidelines for target selection, evaluation, and EMDR reprocessing:

1. *Relapse and intense craving.* Evaluate and reprocess two essential memories: a memory of relapse and a memory of intense craving.
2. *Recent first.* Target recent memories first, as these are easier to access and evaluate.
3. *First and worst.* The first and worst memory of each category should be targeted and at least evaluated in the course of therapy.
4. *LoU scale.* It is essential to monitor craving by using the LoU scale while reprocessing.
5. *LoU = 0.* Reprocessing should lead to maximum reduction of the LoU, preferably to zero, before switching to installation of a positive cognition.
6. *VoC and body scan.* A validity of cognition (VoC) of 6 to 7 is better—and a clear body scan indicates successful reprocessing.
7. *NC and PC.* Clinical observation indicates the necessity to elicit negative and positive cognitions. The experience of craving and relapse alter the patient's concept of self. The cognitions address this material and facilitate the generalization of treatment effects.

DIRECTIONS

Choose which memory to start with, either the memory of a relapse or an intense craving. Start the reprocessing with the most recent, then go to the first memory and then the worst memory. After these are completed, and if necessary, use the same script to work with the memory of relapse or intense craving that was not chosen at first and reprocess these memories.

Incident—Most Recent

Say, *"The memory that we will start with today is* __________ (select the memory of a relapse or an intense craving). *What was the most recent one that you remember?"*

____

____

____

____

Say, *"What happens when you think of the incident?"*

___

___

___

Picture

Say, *"What picture represents the entire incident?"*

___

___

___

If there are many choices or if the client becomes confused, the clinician assists by asking the following:

Say, *"What picture represents the most intense part of the incident?"*

___

___

___

When a picture is unavailable, the clinician merely invites the client to say the following:

Say, *"Think of the incident."*

___

___

___

Negative Cognition (NC)

Say, *"What words best go with the picture that expresses your negative belief about yourself now?"*

___

___

___

Positive Cognition (PC)

Say, *"When you bring up that picture or incident, what would you like to believe about yourself now?"*

___

___

___

Validity of Cognition (VoC)

Say, "*When you think of the incident (or picture) how true do those words* _______ (clinician repeats the positive cognition) *feel to you now on a scale of 1 to 7, where 1 feels completely false and 7 feels completely true?*"

1 2 3 4 5 6 7

(Completely false) (Completely true)

Emotions

Say, "*When you bring up the picture (or incident) and those words* _____ (clinician states the negative cognition), *what emotion do you feel now?*"

Level of Urge (LoU)

Say, "*Please evaluate the intensity of your craving for* ____ (state substance) *on a scale of 0 to 10, where 0 is no craving or neutral and 10 is the most craving you can imagine, how strong does your craving feel now?*"

0 1 2 3 4 5 6 7 8 9 10

(No craving) (Maximum craving)

Location of Body Sensation

Say, "*Where do you feel it* (the disturbance) *in your body?*"

___

___

Process this memory completely before moving to the next target.

Incident—First Memory (if Necessary)

Say, "*The memory that we will start with today is* __________ (select the memory of a relapse or an intense craving). *What was the first one that you remember?*"

___

___

___

___

Say, "*What happens when you think of the incident?*"

___

___

Picture

Say, *"What picture represents the entire incident?"*

___

___

If there are many choices or if the client becomes confused, the clinician assists by asking the following:

Say, *"What picture represents the most intense part of the incident?"*

___

___

When a picture is unavailable, the clinician merely invites the client to say the following:

Say, *"Think of the incident."*

Negative Cognition (NC)

Say, *"What words best go with the picture that express your negative belief about yourself now?"*

___

___

Positive Cognition (PC)

Say, *"When you bring up that picture or incident, what would you like to believe about yourself now?"*

___

___

Validity of Cognition (VoC)

Say, *"When you think of the incident* (or picture) *how true do those words* _______ (clinician repeats the positive cognition) *feel to you now on a scale of 1 to 7, where 1 feels completely false and 7 feels completely true?"*

1 2 3 4 5 6 7

(Completely false) (Completely true)

Emotions

Say, *"When you bring up the picture* (or incident) *and those words* _____ (clinician states the negative cognition), *what emotion do you feel now?"*

___

___

Level of Urge (LoU)

Say, *"Please evaluate the intensity of your craving for* _______ (state substance) *on a scale of 0 to 10, where 0 is no craving or neutral and 10 is the most craving you can imagine, how strong does your craving feel now?"*

0 1 2 3 4 5 6 7 8 9 10

(No craving) (Maximum craving)

Location of Body Sensation

Say, *"Where do you feel it* (the disturbance) *in your body?"*

___

___

Whichever the client chooses—either the relapse memory or memory of intense craving—be sure to process the other.

Incident—Worst Memory (if Necessary)

Say, *"The memory that we will start with today is* _________ (select the other memory—either of a relapse or an intense craving). *What was the worst memory that you remember related to that?"*

___

___

___

___

Say, *"What happens when you think of the incident?"*

___

___

Picture

Say, *"What picture represents the entire incident?"*

___

___

If there are many choices or if the client becomes confused, the clinician assists by asking the following:

Say, *"What picture represents the most intense part of the incident?"*

___

___

When a picture is unavailable, the clinician merely invites the client to say the following:

Say, "*Think of the incident.*"

___

___

Negative Cognition (PC)

Say, "*What words best go with the picture that expresses your negative belief about yourself now?*"

___

___

Positive Cognition (PC)

Say, "*When you bring up that picture or incident, what would you like to believe about yourself now?*"

___

___

Validity of Cognition (VoC)

Say, "*When you think of the incident* (or picture) *how true do those words* ____ (clinician repeats the positive cognition) *feel to you now on a scale of 1 to 7, where 1 feels completely false and 7 feels completely true?*"

1 2 3 4 5 6 7

(Completely false) (Completely true)

Emotions

Say, "*When you bring up the picture* (or incident) *and those words* _____ (clinician states the negative cognition), *what emotion do you feel now?*"

___

___

Level of Urge (LoU)

Say, "*Please evaluate the intensity of your craving for* ____ (state substance) *on a scale of 0 to 10, where 0 is no craving or neutral and 10 is the most craving you can imagine, how strong does your craving feel now?*"

0 1 2 3 4 5 6 7 8 9 10

(No craving) (Maximum craving)

Location of Body Sensation

Say, *"Where do you feel it* (the disturbance) *in your body?"*

___

___

Process this memory completely before moving on to the next target.

Now, go back and work with the type of memory that you did not choose first, for instance, if you started memories of relapse, now go back and use the script to work with memories of intense craving.

Make sure all memories of relapse or intense cravings are processed before moving forward to any of the traumatic material elicited or that came up while reprocessing. Check to see if they need to be reprocessed first. If so, use the script above.

Phase 4: Desensitization

The work in Phase 4 follows the standard EMDR protocol.

To begin, say the following:

Say, *"Now, remember, it is your own brain that is doing the healing and you are the one in control. I will ask you to mentally focus on the target and to* ________ (state BLS you are using). *Just let whatever happens, happen, and we will talk at the end of the set. Just tell me what comes up, and don't discard anything as unimportant. Any new information that comes to mind is connected in some way. If you want to stop, just raise your hand."*

Then say, *"Bring up the picture and the words* _____ (clinician repeats the NC) *and notice where you feel it in your body. Now follow* ______ (state BLS)."

___

___

This procedure is to be repeated until the SUDS = 0. Then the positive cognition is installed. Each traumatic event associated with the addictive problem that is not reprocessed during the normal course of the first target needs to be processed using the above protocol until the SUDS reaches an ecological 1 or 0 and the positive cognition is installed.

Note: According to experience from several sessions, feelings of well-being, happiness, and mild drowsiness, for example, surfacing early in Phase 4 indicate the processing of AM components (e.g., drug effects). This material should be kept in the process (say, "Stay with that") and does not indicate the end of a channel or of Phase 4. After the processing of this material, other components or negative affect may surface to be processed thus leading to complete solution.

Phase 5: Installation

Say, *"How does* _______ (repeat the PC) *sound?"*

___

___

Say, *"Do the words* _______ (repeat the PC) *still fit or is there another positive statement that feels better?"*

___

___

If the client accepts the original positive cognition, the clinician should ask for a VoC rating to see if it has improved.

Say, *"As you think of the incident, how do the words feel to you now on a scale of 1 to 7, where 1 feels completely false and 7 feels completely true?"*

1 2 3 4 5 6 7

(Completely false) (Completely true)

Say, *"Think of the event and hold it together with the words* ______ (repeat the PC)."

___

___

Do a long set of BLS to see if there is more processing to be done.

Phase 6: Body Scan

Say, *"Close your eyes and keep in mind the original memory and the positive cognition. Then bring your attention to the different parts of your body, starting with your head and working downward. Any place you find any tension, tightness, or unusual sensation, tell me."*

___

___

Phase 7: Closure

Say, *"Things may come up or they may not. If they do, great, write it down and it can be a target for next time. If you get any new memories, dreams, or situations that disturb you, just take a good snapshot. It isn't necessary to give a lot of detail. Just put down enough to remind you so we can target it next time. The same thing goes for any positive dreams or situations. If negative feelings do come up, try not to make them significant. Remember, it's still just the old stuff. Just write it down for next time. Then use the tape or the Safe Place exercise to let as much of the disturbance go as possible. Even if nothing comes up, make sure to use the tape every day and give me a call if you need to."*

___

___

Phase 8: Reevaluation

Follow the EMDR Standard 8 Phase procedure (Shapiro, 2001). Look at the treatment plan: further AM, cues, and so forth. After the processing of memories of relapse or intense craving, triggers for substance abuse and current problems (e.g., quarrelling with spouse) should be targeted and reprocessed.

PRESENT TRIGGERS

Say, *"We have some of the situations, events, and stimuli that trigger your addictive behaviors from when we first started. They were* ___________ (read the list from the worksheet). *Are they still issues for you? Are there any other ones that you have thought of since then or that you have noticed? Let's process these situations, events, or stimuli triggers one by one."*

___

___

If the client has a hard time coming up with the situations, events, or stimuli that are triggers, standard EMDR methods to elicit related memories such as the Float-Back Technique or Affect Scan may be used (Shapiro, 2001).

Situations, Events, or Stimuli Trigger List

T1:

___

___

T2:

___

___

T3:

___

___

T4:

____

____

Say, *"What situation, event, or stimulus that triggers you would you like to use as a target today?"*

____

____

Picture

Say, *"What picture represents the* ________ (state the situation, event, or stimulus) *that triggers you?"*

____

____

Negative Cognition (NC)

Say, *"What words best go with the picture that expresses your negative belief about yourself now?"*

____

____

Positive Cognition (PC)

Say, *"When you bring up that picture or* ________ (state the situation, event, or stimulus) *that triggers you, what would you like to believe about yourself now?"*

____

____

Validity of Cognition (VoC)

Say, *"When you think of the incident* ________ (state the situation, event, or stimulus) *that triggers you, how true do those words* ____ (clinician repeats the positive cognition) *feel to you now on a scale of 1 to 7, where 1 feels completely false and 7 feels completely true?"*

1 2 3 4 5 6 7

(Completely false) (Completely true)

Emotions

Say, "*When you bring up the picture or* ________ (state the situation, event, or stimulus) *that triggers you, and those words* _____ (clinician states the negative cognition), *what emotion do you feel now?*"

____

____

Level of Urge (LoU)

Say, "*On a scale of 0 to 10, where 0 is no urge to take the drug or neutral and 10 is the highest urge you can imagine, how do you feel it now?*"

0 1 2 3 4 5 6 7 8 9 10

(No urge) (Highest urge)

Location of Body Sensation

Say, "*Where do you feel it* (the disturbance) *in your body?*"

____

____

Work with each trigger until each one is fully processed.

FUTURE TEMPLATE

A future template as in standard EMDR protocols and procedures (e.g., difficulties in imagining saying no to a friend who wants to go out for a drink) is essential for stable treatment effects (Shapiro, 2006, pp. 51–53).

Image as Future Template

Say, "*I would like you to imagine yourself coping effectively with* ________ (state the goal) *in the future. With the positive belief* ________ (state the positive belief) *and your new sense of* ________ (state the quality, i.e., strength, clarity, confidence, calm), *imagine stepping into this scene.*"

____

____

Say, "*Notice what you see and how you are handling the situation. Notice what you are thinking, feeling, and experiencing in your body.*"

____

____

Say, *"Are there any blocks, anxieties, urges, or fears that arise as you think about this future scene?"*

If yes, say the following:

Say, *"Then focus on these issues or urge and follow my fingers* (or any other BLS)."

If the issues, especially the urge, do not resolve quickly, evaluate if the client needs any new information, resources, or skills to be able to comfortably visualize the future coping scene. Introduce needed information or skills.

Say, *"What would you need to feel confident in handling the situation?"*

Or say, *"What is missing from your handling of this situation?"*

If the block still does not resolve and the client is unable to visualize the future scene with confidence and clarity, use direct questions, the Affect Scan, or the Float-Back Technique to identify old targets related to blocks, anxieties, or fears. Use the standard EMDR protocol to address these targets before proceeding with the template.

If there are no apparent blocks and the client is able to visualize the future scene with confidence and clarity as in the following:

Say, *"Please focus on the image, the positive belief, and the sensations associated with this future scene and follow my fingers* (or any other BLS)."

Process and reinforce the positive associations with BLS. Do several sets until the future template is sufficiently strengthened.

Say, *"Go with that."*

Then say, *"Close your eyes and keep in mind the experience that you will have in the future. Then bring your attention to the different parts of your body, starting with your head and working downward. Any place you find any tension, tightness, or unusual sensation, tell me."*

___

___

If any sensation is reported, do BLS.

If it is a positive or comfortable sensation, do BLS to strengthen the positive feelings.

If a sensation of discomfort is reported, reprocess until the discomfort subsides. Check the VoC.

Say, *"When you think of the incident* (or picture) *how true do those words* ________ (clinician repeats the positive cognition) *feel to you now on a scale of 1 to 7, where 1 feels completely false and 7 feels completely true?"*

1 2 3 4 5 6 7
(Completely false) (Completely true)

Continue to use BLS until reaching the VoC = 7 or there is an ecological resolution. When the image as future template is clear and the PC true, move on to the movie as future template.

Movie as Future Template

During this next level of future template, clients are asked to move from imagining this one scene or snapshot to imagining a movie about coping in the future, with a beginning, middle, and end. Encourage clients to imagine themselves coping effectively in the face of specific challenges, triggers, or snafus. Therapists can make some suggestions of things in order to help inoculate them with future problems. It is helpful to use this type of future template after clients have received needed education concerning social skills and customs, assertiveness, and any other newly learned skills.

Say, *"This time, I'd like you to close your eyes and play a movie, imagining yourself coping effectively with* _____ (state where client will be) *in the future. With the new positive belief* ___ (state positive belief) *and your new sense of* ____ (strength, clarity, confidence, calm), *imagine stepping into the future. Imagine yourself coping with ANY challenges that come your way. Make sure that this movie has a beginning, middle, and end. Notice what you are seeing, thinking, feeling, and experiencing in your body. Let me know if you hit any blocks. If you do, just open your eyes and let me know. If you don't hit any blocks, let me know when you have viewed the whole movie."*

___

___

If the client hits blocks, address as above with BLS, interweaves, new skills, information or resources, direct questions, Affect Scan, or Float-Back, and so forth.

If the client is able to play the movie from start to finish with a sense of confidence and satisfaction, ask the client to play the movie one more time from beginning to end and introduce BLS. In a sense, you are installing this movie as a future template.

Say, *"Okay, play the movie one more time from beginning to end. Go with that."*

Use BLS.

Anecdotal reports from clinicians indicate an effect of the reprocessing of the AM in patients addicted to heroin or psychostimulants. According to research in the animal model, the same principles should apply. Clinical observation shows specific drug effects surfacing in the processing of the AM; therefore, with an amphetamine-addicted patient, arousal will show and should be held in processing the material. It could well be that the power of the drug in the central nervous system has implications on the dose of EMDR. A cocaine addict may need more sessions than a patient addicted to alcohol to reduce craving. Further research is absolutely necessary.

APPENDIX B5

THE DESENSITIZATION OF TRIGGERS AND URGE REPROCESSING PROTOCOL

DESENSITIZATION OF TRIGGERS AND URGE REPROCESSING SCRIPT NOTES

The DeTUR method is an urge reduction protocol used as the center of an overall methodology for the treatment of a wide range of chemical addictions and dysfunctional behaviors. This method was developed and refined by the author through client interaction and feedback from other Eye Movement Desensitization and Reprocessing (EMDR)-trained therapists using the same protocol. It was initially introduced as a stop smoking protocol at the first EMDR conference (Popky, 2010). This eclectic addiction treatment method is trauma based, combining client internal resources with external support including the 12-step model and other known and proven treatment methods such as cognitive behavioral therapy, solution-focused, Erickson, Thought Field Therapy, Satir, neurolinguistic programming, and so forth. The basis or foundation is the adaptive information processing (AIP) using bilateral stimulation (BLS) as outlined in EMDR to uncover and process the base trauma(s) or core issues as the underlying cause behind the addiction.

This protocol represents a small part of a complete treatment model that includes a treatment-team approach. Practitioners can fulfill these functions depending on their areas of expertise and personnel available:

- *Case manager*. To manage clients and their resources in the service of adaptive functioning and coping
- *Diagnostician*. To evaluate clients to assess for comorbidity with other disorders and subsequent referrals to psychiatrists for medication; appropriate medical personnel to check for any physiological or neurological difficulties; and mental health practitioners for individual, couples, or family therapy

---

Source: Luber, M. (2010). *Eye movement desensitization and reprocessing (EMDR) scripted protocols: Special populations.* New York: Springer Publishing Company. Reproduced with the permission of Springer Publishing Company, LLC.

- *Addiction expert.* To assess the severity of addiction(s) and the need for a detoxification program
- *Social worker.* To assess the need for other types of resources such as 12-step groups and other types of support networks, groups, or associations
- *Skills support.* To assess what skills clients need and either refer or provide clients with the learning needed

Note: Most clients presenting with addiction will need access to the wide range of services as frequently there are comorbidity issues, day-to-day stressors, and survival issues that need to be addressed along with other problems such as the need for food and shelter.

DETUR AND EMDR

This author has used the structure of the EMDR methodology to inform the creation of the DeTUR protocol. The similarities between EMDR and DeTUR are as follows:

- Require a thorough history taking, assessment, and diagnosis for ensuring client safety before starting treatment
- Use BLS
- Installation of the positive

The differences between EMDR and DeTUR are as follows:

- *Present versus past.* DeTUR targets the situations, events, or stimuli that bring up the uncomfortable feelings leading to the urges at the outset, then future issues, and works with the past as it opens up, while EMDR starts with past issues and then goes to present triggers and future issues. With the desensitization of each trigger and the installation of the positive treatment goal (PG), the client's ego strength seems to grow to a point where threads open leading back to core issues (if they arise) but only after sufficient ego strength is built. Once desensitized, triggers are no longer the stimuli for using. Instead, the triggers are connected to the new response, that of the treatment goal.
- *Sensation versus affect and cognitions.* DeTUR accesses positive experience through positive body states while the EMDR protocol addresses positive experience through affect and positive and negative cognitions.
- *LoU versus SUD and VoC.* DeTUR measures the level of urge (LoU) while EMDR measurements are the Subjective Units of Disturbance (SUD) and Validity of Cognition (VoC) scales.
- *Early processing versus later processing.* Initially, it was not considered advisable to use EMDR or any type of therapy on addicts early in recovery. Work on any traumatic issues was not done until they were stable and had a long period of abstinence. The concern was that an emerging traumatic event might be too overwhelming for the client to handle and cause the client to relapse, binge, or overindulge. However, using DeTUR, it is possible to work with addicts early in treatment.

Other important components of DeTUR:

- DeTUR protocol is flexible in order to be tailored to each individual client's needs, goals, and values.

- The therapeutic process is necessary in order to address client core traumatic events or issues underlying his or her psychological addiction.
- Therapeutic interweaves and interventions utilize the therapist's training and style, evolving continual client feedback, thus aiding clients in the processing of each step through completion of any or all core and causal issues.
- BLS in the AIP model is the catalyst and accelerator for uncovering and processing of core events or issues through to completion in order to prevent relapse.
- Client empowerment through resource accessing, identification, and installation of PGs; identification and desensitization of triggers; and techniques of relapse prevention.

It is also helpful to address the significant differences in this treatment approach versus the prevalent 12-step method advocated by Alcoholics Anonymous (AA), Narcotics Anonymous (NA), and the other treatment approaches for addictions.

- Client's attention is directed toward a positive, attractive, achievable, compelling goal of coping and functioning, *not* away from a negative behavior. The reason for this is that as soon as you are told not to think about something the result is to think of it.
- Abstinence, though highly recommended, is not required in the definition of the treatment goal; coping and functioning in a positive manner as described by the client is the treatment goal. It is his or her therapy.
- Relapse is reframed from failure to new targets of opportunity to be addressed in following sessions.
- Chemical withdrawal and anxiety appear to be addressed since the process seems to take place out of the client's conscious level of awareness, not requiring constant attention on the part of the client. Clients often report surprise that at the end of the day they had not engaged in the negative behavior, or that they had but not as often, or had noticed urges to engage and could put them aside.
- Targeting the individual triggers for desensitization allows this model to be used with clients early in recovery.

The purpose of the protocol is to uncover the core traumas and reprocess them through to completion. In achieving reprocessing, the triggers no longer stimulate the need to use or act out and the new response becomes the PG of coping and functioning successfully in life as determined by the client. Successful results have been reported by clinicians across the spectrum of addictions and dysfunctional behaviors: chemical substances (nicotine, marijuana, alcohol, methamphetamine, cocaine, crack, heroin, methadone, etc.), eating disorders such as compulsive overeating, anorexia, and bulimia, along with other behaviors such as sex, gambling, shoplifting, anger outbursts, and trichotillomania, and so forth. As new information becomes available, it is incorporated into the protocol.

THE STEPS OF DETUR

Step 1: Rapport

The basis of any good psychotherapy is gaining rapport with your client.

Step 2: History, Assessment, Diagnosis

Due to the long history of difficulties of addicted clients, it is mandatory to take a detailed history. Testing for dissociative disorders and or any other *Diagnostic and Statistical Manual of Mental Disorders*, fourth edition (*DSM-IV*) disorders ensures that the therapists know what problems might arise and have the necessary skills, competencies, or referral base to handle situations that might arise. This author has clients complete the dissociative experience scale (Carlson & Putnam, 1992), Beck depression inventory (Beck, Steer, & Brown, 1996), and the Lazarus multimodal forms (Lazarus & Lazarus, 1991) and review them before the history-taking session. The genogram is a useful visual reminder to detail information about family of origin, relationships issues, their present status, previous problems, previous therapeutic relationships, state of health, medications, and then their drug or addiction history. As in any therapeutic process, all standard client cautions and safety issues should be addressed. Most, if not all, of the clients in the addictive population have dual diagnoses.

It is important that clients be committed to complete the therapy. They should be made aware that rapid improvements, though satisfying, do not mean that the treatment is complete. These fast results sometimes lead clients to believe they have been cured and prematurely drop out of treatment. For treatment to be successful, triggers that bring up urges must be desensitized and core events or trauma reprocessed to completion. Consider the stories of individuals diagnosed with bipolar disorders, who, when feeling good, decide that they no longer need medication and discontinue using it, thus obstructing their progress.

Step 3: Support Resources

Clients need a safe environment to express their thoughts, feelings, fears, and so forth; a place where they can openly and freely speak their mind, be heard, and get feedback that is honest, supportive, nonjudgmental, and not critical. When things get tough, as before relapsing, they need someone to talk to or even to be able to hear themselves speak their thoughts out loud. Groups such as 12-step groups, Alcoholics Anonymous (AA), Narcotics Anonymous (NA), Cocaine Anonymous (CA), Rational Recovery (RR), Managed Moderation (MM), religious organizations, fraternal organizations, women's or men's groups, family, or friends should be supportive, nonjudgmental, and flexible to clients' needs, not just the group process.

Step 4: Accessing Internal Resource State

It is customary to ask clients about their problems when they come for treatment. Based on Robbie Dunton's work with children (R. Dunton, personal communication, 1990), this author began sessions using her question, "What do you like and do best?" followed by eye movements. This intervention allows clients to access positive internal states and sets a positive tone for the work to follow.

Step 5: Positive Treatment Goal (PG)

The PG is central to the client's treatment plan and should have the following attributes:

- Uses only positive language
- Occurs within the near future
- Achievable by the client
- Uses client's language about what it means to cope and function successfully
- It is attractive, magnetic, and compelling

It is important that the treatment goal be defined and owned by the client; it is his or her therapy, therefore his or her goal. Abstinence, though highly desirable, is not required as a necessity in the definition of the treatment goal; it will be implied.

Note: Although abstinence may be requested, it should not be part of the goal. It is very difficult concentrating on *not* doing something without focusing on the thing that you do not want to do.

Step 6: Associated Positive State

The next step is to have clients associate with their goal. Give them the experience of how it would feel to achieve their goal successfully and then using associative representation anchor the experience into their physiology. Physical anchoring or conditioned response are processes of being able to replicate the physiological experience associated with an emotion or state by linking it to a physical experience such as slight finger pressure on a part of the body. After obtaining permission, the idea is to exert slight pressure on, for example, a knuckle; this anchor becomes the concrete symbol of the experience. Often, this author chooses the knuckle of the little finger, since it seems to be the least intrusive.

Step 7: Identify Urge Triggers

This step is to figure out the situations, events, and stimuli such as emotions, smells, tastes, objects, or actions that trigger the urge to use. The idea is to help them recognize how they know when to use and to help them understand that they learned this behavior as a way to reduce the negative affect that was connected with early traumatic events. Using helped them cope with the symptoms of the trauma such as the negative feelings, sensations, and thoughts associated with the experiences.

Help clients create a list that specifies the details of the situations, events, and stimuli that trigger them and can be used as targets for processing. For example, if smoking clients report that they get the urge with morning coffee, after meals, and with drinks, mark them with $t_{\text{morning coffee}}$ t_{meals}, and t_{drinks}. For those with weight problems, the triggers can represent those times when they eat larger portions, wrong type of foods, unnecessary snacks, and so forth. After compiling the list of known triggers, prioritize them in the order of what seems to be important, weakest to strongest. Often, it is helpful to begin the desensitization with the weakest trigger while installing the positive state and then desensitize each of the following triggers until they end up with the most distressing trigger. This allows clients—at the same time—to build up their ego strength.

Step 8: Desensitize Triggers

It is during this desensitization process, where the therapists' individual style and skills are required; when clients get stuck, loops, abreacts, or other nodes open up. The cognitive or therapeutic interweave as taught in the EMDR Institute basic training is the therapist's best tool to aid clients during this desensitization or reprocessing phase. This author finds it to be more powerful when using it during processing.

Step 9: Install Positive State

As with the Installation Phase of EMDR, this step connects the positive state with the situation, event, or stimuli that triggered the urge. The idea is that whenever one of these triggering situations occurs, the using response is replaced with the positive state that the client has anchored. The effect is that after the reprocessing occurs, clients do not have to think about the process as it takes place outside their conscious experience and the new response begins to occur automatically. Ask the client to access the previous triggering event, apply pressure to the anchor, and then use BLS. Reinforce positive affect or thoughts with another set of BLS. When a negative response occurs, more dysfunctional material has been unearthed and can be addressed.

Step 10: Test and Future Check

This step tests the strength of the work by asking clients to bring up their triggers, asking for their LoU, and seeing if there is any remaining urge. If there is, go back to Step 8. If not, reinforce the client's success.

Step 11: Closure and Self-Work

End the session by reminding clients that the process may continue to move and teach them how to do self-soothing with BLS.

Step 12: Follow-Up Sessions

Follow-up sessions are for reinforcing the gains clients have made and targeting any new situations, events, or stimuli that have triggered them between sessions, or teaching new skills or information as needed.

DETUR PROTOCOL SCRIPT

Step 1: Rapport

The foundation for trust in any relationship is rapport. One of the most important characteristics of a therapist is the ability to gain the trust rapidly with the client and to maintain it throughout the therapeutic process. Rapport allows the therapist the right to ask questions and to elicit appropriate answers. This is crucial for the following steps in this model.

Step 2: History, Assessment, Diagnosis

Specific questions to delve into the addiction history are the following:

Say, "*What is the problem that you want to address?*"

____

____

____

____

Say, "*How long have you been using each substance?*"

____

____

Say, "*When did you start?*"

____

____

Say, "*Why did you start or what made you start?*"

____

____

____

____

Say, *"How did the use of the substance proceed?"*

Say, *"Was there a particular time that you noticed an acceleration of your use?"*

Say, *"What do you get out of it?"*

Say, *"Do you use just one substance or is there multiple use?"*

Say, *"Did you notice any problems that it causes?"*

Say, *"What are your reasons for quitting?"*

Say, *"How motivated are you to quit?"*

Say, *"What will it get you if you quit?"*

Say, *"Is there any other way to get the same results?"*

___

___

Say, *"How many times have you quit?"*

___

___

Say, *"What worked and what didn't?"*

___

___

Look for possible secondary gain issues that might have to be addressed.

Say, *"Is there anything that you will lose if you quit?"*

___

___

Say, *"What are the types of thoughts that go on in your head about this issue or use?"*

___

___

Say, *"Are there particular ways you think of yourself because of it?"*

___

___

In addition to standard history and cautions, asking open-ended questions such as many of those above will reveal client patterns, communication styles, and decision-making criteria. Listening for key words, phrases, patterns, and belief systems reveals useful insight for metaphors, reframes, and so forth for use in interventions in the therapeutic interweave be it narrative, cognitive, psychodynamic, whatever the therapist's style; this information is useful in maintaining client rapport and for individual therapeutic interventions when nodes open to emerging events relating to core issues.

Step 3: External Support Resources

Say, *"What are the support systems that you have in place?"*

___

___

___

___

Tailor your suggestions to the needs of your clients.

Step 4: Accessing Internal Resource State

Remembering a positive experience supports clients in accessing their strengths and creating a positive forward movement for the rest of your work.

Say, *"Recall a time when you felt resourceful, powerful, in control and focus on those experiences and feelings."*

Say, *"It is helpful to notice the things that you see, hear, smell, taste, and anything else that you were noticing while you were having those experiences. What did you notice while you were in that state?"*

Relate back to clients what they have told you that they see, hear, smell, taste, and so forth, while doing BLS, keeping clients in the positive feelings.

Use BLS (at least 24 rapid BLS) to empower clients and allow the process to move faster.

Say, *"So focus on that time when you were seeing* _______ (state what client is seeing), *hearing* _____ (state what the client is hearing), *feeling* _______ (state what the client is feeling), *smelling* ______ (state what the client is smelling), *and tasting* _____ (state what the client is tasting) *and follow my fingers* (or whatever BLS you are using)."

Do BLS.

Say, *"Now notice all* _______ (repeat their description of what they were seeing, hearing, and feeling) *and think of a word that goes with this. What would that be?"*

Repeat again asking them to assign a word (auditory anchor) to that experience and repeat the word while experiencing that moment. This is an auditory anchor that they can use to bring back those positive feelings.

Say, *"Now repeat that word as you are experiencing that moment."*

___

___

This appears to empower clients and allows the process to move faster.

Test the resource anchor by asking the client to think of a small disturbing experience, notice the emotions, and then speak their resource word and notice the shift to positive feelings.

___

___

Say, *"Now think of a small disturbing experience, notice the emotions, and then say your resource word* ________ (state the resource word). *What do you notice?"*

If clients are only able to momentarily bring up something positive and then immediately the scene shifts to a negative component, have them freeze the experience and only focus on the positive element before doing eye movements.

___

___

Say, *"Okay, let's freeze the experience to right before it became negative. Now focus on that positive element. Go with that."*

___

___

Do BLS.

If clients are not able to think of anything positive in their life to concentrate on, say the following:

Say, *"If it is hard for you to come up with something positive right now, sometimes it helps to think of times when you were involved in sports, or any time you accomplished something no matter how big or small, even times like when you finished washing and shining your car or the feelings you had when your favorite team won an event. Does anything like that come to mind for you now?"*

___

___

Creativity and flexibility are the keys in these difficult situations.

Step 5: Positive Treatment Goal (PG)

A well-formed PG uses positive language, occurs in the near future, is achievable, uses the client's own language concerning coping and functioning successfully, and is attractive, magnetic, and compelling. Guide them through the specifics until they can create a clear image of how they would look being successful, fully functional, and having attained their goal.

Say, *"Imagine seeing a picture of yourself already achieving your goal. Think about what your life would be like after all this is over, without* _______ (list the addiction, or dysfunctional behavior the client would like to be rid of)."

____

____

____

____

Say, *"What will you be doing instead?"*

____

____

____

____

Say, *"What do you want?"*

____

____

____

____

Say, *"What will it get you?"*

____

____

____

____

Say, *"How will you know when you have gotten it?"*

____

____

____

____

Say, *"What would you be seeing?"*

If the response is negative, say the following:

Say, *"If you won't be* _____ (state what the client will not be doing)*, or won't have to* _____ (state what they are moving away from)*, what will you be doing instead?"*

The challenge is to guide them to describe their goals in positive, concrete, sensory-based terms. After they have built the picture, check to see if this is really what they want.

Say, *"Is this what you really want?"*

Say, *"Is it desirable? Does it have a strong attraction or pull to it?"*

Make any adjustments to make it more appealing, does it feel better if they make the picture bigger, clearer, brighter, bring it closer, and add sounds?

Say, *"Does it feel better if you make the picture bigger, clearer, brighter, bring it in closer, or add sounds?"*

Say, *"Go with that."*

Help them make any adjustments to make it more appealing. For example, if the client is a smoker worried about gaining weight, be sure they see themselves looking the way they want to look, perhaps in a special outfit (the same for weight loss clients, inches are more important than pounds). When the picture has the strongest attraction and feels best to them, use BLS to make the goal more compelling and attractive.

Say, *"Are there any other adjustments that you would like to make so that it is even more appealing?"*

___

___

Then do BLS.

Step 6: Associated Positive State

Fully associate a positive state with the positive goal by anchoring and strengthening them.

Say, *"You can build your positive treatment goal. Bring up a clear picture of it. What are the kinds of things that you will be able to do when you have it?"*

___

___

___

___

Say, *"Step into your picture of your positive treatment goal, into that body posture* (as if state). *Notice and experience the positive feelings, breathe into these feelings, move around in them, experience being successful. Notice what you see, hear, feel, smell, and taste. Notice what it's like to function successfully. As you notice and experience those positive feelings, touch your knuckle in this positive state until your positive state is the most desirable. Increase pressure slightly to that same place on your knuckle as your positive feelings peak, strengthening the mind–body link."*

___

___

As you or the client touch the anchor, do BLS.

Say, *"As you make these visual adjustments, notice how you feel inside. You can change the brightness, the focus, the contrast, the tint, the size, the distance, whatever feels right for you. And as you notice the changes that you feel inside, increase the pressure slightly on your knuckle while I do* _______ (state BLS) *with you."*

___

___

This strengthens the mind–body link through touch and the BLS. Repeat the same process using sounds.

Say, *"As you listen to the positive words or sounds that you are saying to yourself and the positive words that others would be saying, adjust the auditory components: the volume, the tone, the tempo, the balance, and so forth and as the positive experience peaks, please touch your anchor and follow my fingers."*

___

___

Apply the anchor touch and the simultaneous BLS to further anchor the feelings of success into their physiology as the association with success peaks. Do BLS.

Test the positive state by having the client touch the knuckle and notice the results. He or she should report a positive experience. It is important for the client to have a strong, positive, sensory-based experience of having successfully achieved his or her goal anchored into his or her physiology.

Say, *"Now touch your knuckle. What do you feel?"*

___

___

Step 7: Identify the Urge Triggers

Identify and make a list of the situations, events, and stimuli that stimulate clients' urges.

Say, *"How do you know when to* ________ (use or do the activity to which you are addicted)? *What prevents you from being in your positive state? These triggers can be a place, person, time, emotion, smell, taste, event, action, or object. Make a list below of all the triggers for use, indicating the level of urge* (LoU) *on the 0 to 10 scale with 10 being the strongest urge. Then rank them based on intensity on the chart below from weakest* (0) *to strongest* (10) *by level of urge."* (Use Trigger List Worksheet below.)

___

___

___

___

___

___

Say, *"Bring up the picture, along with any words, tastes, or smells that go with it. How strong is the level of urge* (LoU), *right now, from 0 to 10, where 0 is the lowest and 10 is the strongest?"* (Use Trigger List Worksheet below.)

Trigger List Worksheet

	Beginning	Ending
t_1:______________________________	LoU =	LoU =
t_2:______________________________	LoU =	LoU =
t_3:______________________________	LoU =	LoU =
t_4:______________________________	LoU =	LoU =
t_5:______________________________	LoU =	LoU =
t_6:______________________________	LoU =	LoU =
t_7:______________________________	LoU =	LoU =
t_8:______________________________	LoU =	LoU =
t_9:______________________________	LoU =	LoU =
t_{10}:______________________________	LoU =	LoU =

Step 8: Desensitizing Each Trigger

Often, it is helpful to give them a metaphor to help explain the process.

Say, *"If strong emotions come up we will keep going. You know how it is when we are driving up a hill, if we take our foot off the accelerator we end up back at the bottom of the hill, but if we keep our foot on the gas we can get to the top and the momentum will carry us forward. Processing is sort of like that."*

Beginning with t_1 (weakest) and proceeding through the final trigger (strongest), repeat the following procedure:

Say, *"Bring up the picture of that trigger along with any words, tastes, smells, or sounds that go with it. How strong is the level of urge* (LoU) *right now, from 0 to 10 where 0 is no urge and 10 is the strongest?"*

0	1	2	3	4	5	6	7	8	9	10
(No urge)								(Strongest urge)		

Say, *"Where are you feeling that number in your body?"*

____

____

Say, *"Hold the picture along with all the associated words, tastes, and smells. Notice what and where you are feeling the urges in your body."*

____

____

Begin using BLS. Use at least 24 passes and watch for changes in the client physiology. As you notice changes,

Say, *"Good"* or *"That's right."*

____

____

After each set of BLS,

Say, *"What are you getting now?"*

____

____

Or say, *"What is coming up now?"*

____

____

Or say, *"What are you noticing now?"*

____

____

Say, *"Go with that."*

____

____

Or say, *"Concentrate on that."*

____

____

Or say, *"Think about that."*

____

____

Resume BLS.
Repeat until the desire drops to 0 (LoU = 0).
When the client reports a LoU of 0,

Say, *"Go with that."*

Do another set of BLS.

Troubleshooting

1. If the client is looping or getting off track, do the following:

   Say, *"Return to the target trigger and what is the LoU? Focus on the body location and go with that."*

   ---

2. If clients report no change, increase the width, distance, speed, number, or direction of the passes.
3. If clients intellectualize, increase the speed.
4. If clients abreact, continue the BLS until they calm down and say the following:

   Say, *"It's in the past, a long time ago…it's old stuff, let it go where old stuff belongs."*

   ---

5. If clients dissociate, keep them in their body:

   Say, *"Notice you are feeling it in your body. Notice any change, even the smallest change."*

Another way to keep clients in their bodies and in present time is to have them process while balancing on a balance or Pilates ball. It is difficult to dissociate while trying to balance yourself on the ball or do the BLS while the client is on a Pilates ball. It is difficult to dissociate while balancing on the ball (Lanius, 2003).

6. If traumatic material or core issues emerge as you address a trigger, you can continue and do another set to see if it processes through or switch to the

standard EMDR protocol and process that material until the SUD is reduced to zero.

Say, *"Go with that."*

___

___

Always go back to the target triggers after long conversations with the client, when lost or confused, or when you feel that the LoU = 0 or is close to 0.

Step 9: Link and Install Positive State

After the LoU for a specific trigger reduces to 0 with BLS, anchor and install.

Say, *"Bring up the triggering incident again and apply slight pressure to your knuckle."*
Do BLS.
Say, *"What do you notice now?"*

___

___

Whatever positive feelings or statement the client reports after the set:
Say, *"Hold that"* (and do another set of BLS).
Say, *"What do you notice now?"*

___

___

If the client's report is negative, usually another channel has opened up and needs to be addressed.

Step 10: Test and Future Check

In this step, it is important to test installations and future check after each trigger is desensitized.

Say, *"Imagine a time in the future when ____* (state the event that triggered the client), *what is the level of urge, with 0 being little or no urge and 10 being the highest?"*

0	1	2	3	4	5	6	7	8	9	10
(No urge)								(Highest urge)		

Say, *"Where do you feel that in your body?"*

___

___

Do another set of BLS along with the anchoring pressure to the knuckle. Say, *"Go with that as you use your knuckle anchor."*

___

___

If there is any remaining urge, work with each trigger until each one is reprocessed. Use Steps 8 to 10.

Step 11: Closure and Self-Work

Remind the client that the process continues after the session is over and that they may or may not experience new thoughts, memories, or experiences, and that they can contact you if necessary. If they notice anything unusual, they must make a note of it for the next session.

Say, *"The process continues after the session is over and you may or may not experience new thoughts, memories, or experiences. Please make note of them for the next session. If you have any major concerns or questions, please call me."*

___

___

To give them more resources, say the following:

Say, *"If you feel any urges, notice what and where you are feeling it or them. If any uncomfortable urges arise, pick a spot on the wall and move your eyes rapidly back and forth until the urge or desire fades and then touch your knuckle* (i.e., anchor the positive state). *If the urge remains, call your sponsor or support group person. If you are unable to prevent the urge and indulge in the dysfunctional behavior, remember that this is new information emerging and make a note of it so we can work on it during your next visit. It is like peeling away the leaves of an artichoke to get to the heart of the matter."*

Step 12: Follow-Up Sessions or Reevaluation

At the beginning of each session, check for the following: new targets or relapse triggers, new information, previously desensitized triggers, or relapse. Do BLS on all successes to build ego strength. This helps build ego strength on the successes noticed to date. If client reports relapse, begin working on the triggers causing the relapse.

Say, *"Okay, let's go over what happened since our last session and if you have learned any new information concerning your urges. What is happening concerning the triggers that we have worked on?"*

___

___

___

___

If the client is successful, say the following:

Say, *"Think about the success that you have accomplished and* _______ (state the BLS)."

___

___

If client reports relapse, work on the newly emerging triggers that brought up the urge to use. See Steps 8 to 10.

DESENSITIZING TRIGGER WORKSHEET

Note: Please refer to troubleshooting tips on the main worksheet if urge is not reducing as planned.

Say, *"What trigger are we working on today?"*

___

___

$t_{\#}$___: ___

Say, *"What is the picture?"*

___

___

To desensitize say the following:

Say, *"Bring up the picture, along with any words, tastes, or smells that go with it. How strong is the LoU right now, from 0 to 10, where 0 is the lowest urge and 10 is the highest?"*

Starting LoU = 0 1 2 3 4 5 6 7 8 9 10

(No urge) (Highest urge)

Say, *"Where are you feeling that number in your body? Hold the picture along with all the associated words, tastes, and smells. Notice what and where you are feeling the urges in your body."*

Begin using BLS. Use about 24 passes and watch for changes in the client's physiology. After each set, ask one of the following:

Say, *"What are you getting now?"*

Or say, *"What's coming up now?"*

Or say, *"What are you noticing now?"*

After the client responds, say the following
Say, *"Go with that."*

Or say, *"Concentrate on that."*

Or say, *"Think about that"* (and resume BLS).

Repeat until the desire drops to 0 (LoU = 0). Use the space below to record what the client says between sets.

When LoU = 0: Say, *"Go with that."* Do another set of BLS.

Install the Positive Internal State With the Triggering Incident

Say, *"Bring up that triggering incident again and apply slight pressure to the knuckle."*

___

___

Do a set of BLS.
Whatever positive feelings or statements the client reports after the set,

Say, *"Notice those positive feelings and go with that"* (do BLS).

___

___

If the client's reports are negative, another channel has likely opened up and needs to be addressed.

Test and Future Check

To test the installations,

Say, *"Bring the trigger up again. What is the LoU right now, from 0 to 10, where 0 is the lowest urge and 10 is the highest?"*

0	1	2	3	4	5	6	7	8	9	10
(No urge)										(Highest urge)

If the LoU is above 0, say the following:
Say, *"Where are you feeling that in your body? Concentrate on that."*

___

___

Do BLS.
If the LoU = 0, do another set of BLS.

Say, *"Imagine a time in the future when you experience the trigger. What is the LoU right now, from 0 to 10, where 0 is the lowest urge and 10 is the highest?"*

0	1	2	3	4	5	6	7	8	9	10
(No urge)										(Highest urge)

If the LoU = 0:

Say, "*Think about it and press your knuckle and follow my fingers* (or other BLS)."

____

____

Refer to main worksheet for session closure and relapse prevention instructions.

APPENDIX C

RESOURCES

These are a few of our favorite resources to use with clients. We find all of the following very helpful:

BOOKS

Cameron, D. (2009). *Why did I do that? How you make sense and why there is hope. An introduction to internal family systems (IFS)*. Natick, MA: Threshold Therapeutics Media.

Fanning, P., & O'Neill, J. (1996). *The addiction workbook*. Oakland, CA: New Harbinger Publications.

Fletcher, A. (2001). *Sober for good: New solutions for drinking problems—Advice from those who have succeeded*. New York, NY: Houghton Mifflin.

Fletcher, A. (2003). *Thin for life: Ten keys to success from people who have lost weight and kept it off*. New York, NY: Houghton Mifflin.

Fletcher, A. (2013). *Inside rehab: The surprising truth about addiction treatment—And how to get help that works*. New York, NY: Viking.

Grand, D. (2001). *Emotional healing at warp speed: The power of EMDR*. New York, NY: Random House.

Leeds, A. M. (2009). *A guide to the standard protocols for clinicians, supervisors and consultants*. New York, NY: Springer Publishing Company.

Levy, M. (2007). *Take control of your drinking and maybe you won't have to quit*. Baltimore, MD: The Johns Hopkins University Press.

Linehan, M. (1993). *Cognitive-behavioral treatment for borderline personality disorder*. New York, NY: Guilford Press.

Linehan, M. (1993). *Skills training manual for treating borderline personality disorder*. New York, NY: Guilford Press.

Luber, M. (2009). *EMDR scripted protocols: Basic and special situations*. New York, NY: Springer Publishing Company.

Luber, M. (2010). *EMDR scripted protocols: Special populations*. New York, NY: Springer Publishing Company.

Najavits, L. (2002). *A woman's addiction workbook*. Oakland, CA: New Harbinger Publications.

Najavits, L. (2002). *Seeking safety: A treatment manual for PTSD and substance abuse*. New York, NY: Guilford Press.

Parnell, L. (2008). *Tapping in: A step by step guide to activating your healing resources through bilateral stimulation*. Boulder, CO: Sounds True Inc.
Shapiro, F. (2001). *Eye movement desensitization and reprocessing (EMDR): Basic principles, protocols, and procedures* (2nd ed.). New York, NY: Guilford Press.
Shapiro, R. (2006). *EMDR solutions: Pathways to healing*. New York, NY: W. W. Norton.
Shapiro, R. (2009). *EMDR solutions II. For depression, eating disorders, performance and more.* New York, NY: W. W. Norton.
Shapiro, F. (2012). *Getting past your past: Take control of your life with self-help techniques from EMDR therapy*. New York, NY: Rodale Books.

HELPFUL WEBSITES

EMDR Institute. This website has information about EMDR training for therapists: www.emdr.com
EMDR International Association. This website has information about the annual EMDR International conference as well as how to find a therapist: www.emdria.org
National Institute on Alcoholism and Alcohol Abuse: www.niaaa.nih.gov
National Institute on Drug Abuse: www.drugabuse.gov
Substance Abuse and Mental Health Administration (SAMHSA): www.samhsa.gov

SELF-HELP RESOURCES

Al-Anon/Alateen
(www.al-anon.org)

Alcoholics Anonymous
(ww.aa.org)

Celebrate Recovery
(www.celebraterecovery.com)

Gam-Anon
(www.gam-anon.org)

Gamblers' Anonymous (GA)
(www.gamblersanonymous.org)

Life Ring
(lifering.org)

Moderation Management
(www.moderation.org)

Narcotics Anonymous (NA)
(www.NA.org)

Overeaters Anonymous and Food Addicts Anonymous
(www.oa.org)
(www.foodaddictsanonymous.org)
(www.foodaddicts.org)

Secular Organizations for Sobriety
(cfi west.org/SOS/index.htm)

Sex and Love Addicts Anonymous (SLAA)
(www.slaafws.org)

SMART Recovery
(www.smartrecovery.org)

Women for Sobriety
(www.womenforsobriety.org)

REFERENCES

Abadkinsky, H. (2008). *Drug use and abuse: A comprehensive introduction*. Belmont, CA: Thomson Wordsworth.

Abel, N. J., & O'Brien, J. M. (2010). EMDR treatment of comorbid PTSD and alcohol dependence: A case example. *Journal of EMDR Practice & Research, 4*(2), 50–59.

Adrian, M., & Barry, S. J. (2003). Physical and mental health problems associated with the use of alcohol and drugs. *Substance Use & Misuse, 38*(11–13), 1575–1614.

Agrawal, A., & Lynskey, M. T. (2006). The genetic epidemiology of cannabis use, abuse and dependence. *Addiction, 101*(6), 801–812.

Allostasis. (2008). *Alcohol Research & Health, 31*(4), 303.

American Cancer Society. (2012). *Guide to quit smoking*. Retrieved November 16, 2013, from http://www.cancer.org/acs/groups/cid/documents/webcontent/002971-pdf.pdf

American Cancer Society. (2013). *Second hand smoke: What is second hand smoke?* Retrieved November 14, 2013, from http://www.cancer.org/cancer/cancercauses/tobaccocancer/secondhand-smoke

American Psychiatric Association (APA). (1980). *Diagnostic and statistical manual of mental disorders* (3rd ed.). Washington, DC: Author.

American Psychiatric Association (APA). (2013). *Diagnostic and statistical manual of mental disorders* (5th ed.). Washington, DC: Author.

American Psychiatric Association (APA). (2004). *Practice guidelines for the treatment of patients with acute stress disorder and posttraumatic stress disorder.* Arlington, VA: Author.

American Psychological Association. (2005). *Policy statement on evidence-based practice in psychology*. Washington, DC: Author.

American Psychological Association Presidential Task Force on Evidence-Based Practice. (2006). Evidence-based practice in psychology. *American Psychologist, 61*(4), 271–285.

American Society of Addiction Medicine (ASAM). (2011). *Public policy statement: Definition of addiction.* Retrieved November 10, 2013, from http://www.asam.org/docs/publicy-policy-statements/1definition_of_addiction_long_4–11.pdf?sfvrsn=2

Andersen, M. L., Sawyer, E. K., & Howell, L. L. (2012). Contributions of neuroimaging to understanding sex differences in cocaine abuse. *Experimental and Clinical Psychopharmacology, 20*(1), 2–15.

Anderson, P., Cremona, A., Paton, A., Turner, C., & Wallace, P. (1993). The risk of alcohol. *Addiction, 88*(11), 1493–1508.

Australian Drug Foundation. (2013). *Fact sheet: Benzodiazepines*. Retrieved November 13, 2013, from http://www.druginfo.adf.org.au/attachments/391_ADF_FactSheet_Benzo.pdf

Back, S. E., Brady, K. T., Waldrop, A. E., Yeatts, S. D., McRae, A. L., & Spratt, E. (2008). Early life trauma and sensitivity to current life stressors in individuals with and without cocaine dependence. *The American Journal of Drug and Alcohol Abuse, 34*(4), 389–396.

Back, S., Dansky, B. S., Coffey, S. F., Saladin, M. E., Sonne, S., & Brady, K. T. (2000). Cocaine dependence with and without post-traumatic stress disorder: A comparison of substance use, trauma history and psychiatric comorbidity. *The American Journal on Addictions, 9*(1), 51–62.

Bae, H., & Kim, D. (2012). Desensitization of triggers and urge reprocessing for an adolescent with internet addiction disorder. *Journal of EMDR Practice and Research, 6*(2), 73–81.

Bailey, K. M., & Stewart, S. H. (2013). Relations among trauma, PTSD and substance misuse: The scope of the problem. In P. Ouimette & J. Read (Eds.), *Trauma and substance abuse*. Washington, DC: APA Books.

Baird, C. (2011). Families and addiction. *Journal of Addictions Nursing, 22*(4), 229–231.

Baker, D. G., Heppner, P., Afari, N., Nunnink, S., Kilmer, M., Simmons, A.,...Bosse, B. (2009). Trauma exposure, branch of service, and physical injury in relation to mental health among U.S. veterans returning from Iraq and Afghanistan. *Military Medicine, 174*(8), 773–778.

Balmford, J., Borland, R., & Burney, S. (2008). Exploring discontinuity in prediction of smoking cessation within the precontemplation stage of change. *International Journal of Behavioral Medicine, 15*(2), 133–140.

Bamatter, W., Carroll, K. M., Añez, L. M., Paris, M., Ball, S. A., Nich, C.,...Martino, S. (2010). Informal discussions in substance abuse treatment sessions with Spanish-speaking clients. *Journal of Substance Abuse Treatment, 39*(4), 353–363.

Barber, C. F. (2008). Domestic violence against men. *Nursing Standard, 22*(51), 35–39.

Bardone-Cone, A. M. (2012). Examining the match between assessed eating disorder recovery and subjective sense of recovery: Preliminary findings. *European Eating Disorders Review, 20*(3), 246–249.

Baz, B., & Wang, N. (2012). Physical abuse of children: Identification, evaluation, and management. *Primary Care Reports*, 82–95.

Beck, J. G., & Coffey, S. F. (2007). Assessment and treatment of PTSD after a motor vehicle collision: Empirical findings and clinical observations. *Professional Psychology, Research and Practice, 38*(6), 629–639.

Begun, A. L., Murphy, C. M., Bolt, D., Weinstein, B., Strodthoff, T., Short, L., & Shelley, G. (2003). Characteristics of the Safe at Home instrument for assessing readiness to change intimate partner violence. *Research on Social Work Practice, 13*, 80–107.

Ben-Ezra, M. (2011). Traumatic reactions from antiquity to the 16th century: Was there a common denominator? *Stress & Health: Journal of the International Society for the Investigation of Stress, 27*(3), 223–240.

Ben-Porat, A., Boaz Yablon, Y., & Itzhaky, H. (2013). Is the development of PTSD blind to differences in social resources? Evidence from high school students facing terrorism. *Journal of Community Psychology, 41*(2), 175–187.

Berman, S., O'Neill, J., Fears, S., Bartzokis, G., & London, E. D. (2008). Abuse of amphetamines and structural abnormalities in the brain. *Annals of the New York Academy of Sciences, 1141*, 195–220.

Bergmann, U. (2012). *Neurobiological foundations for EMDR practice*. New York, NY: Springer Publishing Company.

Bernstein, E. M., & Putnam, F. W. (1986). Development, reliability, and validity of a dissociation scale. *The Journal of Nervous and Mental Disease, 174*(12), 727–735.

Black, D. W. (2013). Behavioural addictions as a way to classify behaviours. *Canadian Journal of Psychiatry, 58*(5), 249–251.

Black, D. W., McNeilly, D. P., Burke, W. J., Shaw, M. C., & Allen, J. (2011). An open-label trial of acamprosate in the treatment of pathological gambling. *Annals of Clinical Psychiatry, 23*(4), 250–256.

Blake, D. D., Weathers, F. W., Nagy, L. M., Kaloupek, D. G., Gusman, F. D., Charney, D. S., & Keane, T. M. (1995). The development of a clinician-administered PTSD Scale. *Journal of Traumatic Stress, 8*(1), 75–90.

Blanchard, E. B., Jones-Alexander, J., Buckley, T. C., & Forneris, C. A. (1996). Psychometric properties of the PTSD Checklist (PCL). *Behaviour Research and Therapy, 34*, 669–673.

Blumer, M., & Murphy, M. (2011). Alaskan gay males' couple experiences of societal non-support: Coping through families of choice and therapeutic means. *Contemporary Family Therapy: An International Journal, 33*(3), 273–290.

Bockting, W. O., Miner, M. H., Swinburne Romine, R. E., Hamilton, A., & Coleman, E. (2013). Stigma, mental health, and resilience in an online sample of the US transgender population. *American Journal of Public Health, 103*(5), 943–951.

Boden, J. M., Horwood, L. J., & Fergusson, D. M. (2007). Exposure to childhood sexual and physical abuse and subsequent educational achievement outcomes. *Child Abuse & Neglect, 31*(10), 1101–1114.

Boriskin, J. A. (2004). *PTSD and addiction: A practical guide for clinicians and counselors*. Center City, MN: Hazelden.

Bowen, S., & Marlatt, A. (2009). Surfing the urge: Brief mindfulness-based intervention for college student smokers. *Psychology of Addictive Behaviors, 23*(4), 666–671.

Brandon, T. H., Herzog, T. A., Irvin, J. E., & Gwaltney, C. J. (2004). Cognitive and social learning models of drug dependence: Implications for the assessment of tobacco dependence in adolescents. *Addiction, 99*(Suppl. 1), 51–77.

Bryant, R. A., & Harvey, A. G. (2000). *Acute stress disorder: A handbook of theory, assessment and treatment*. Washington, DC: American Psychological Association.

Braun, B. G. (1988). The BASK model of dissociation. *Dissociation, 1*(2), 16–23.

Breslau, N. (2002). Epidemiologic studies of trauma, posttraumatic stress disorder, and other psychiatric disorders. *Canadian Journal of Psychiatry, 47*(10), 923–929.

Breslau, N., Chen, Q., & Luo, Z. (2013). The role of intelligence in posttraumatic stress disorder: Does it vary by trauma severity? *PloS One, 8*(6), e65391.

Breslau, N., Chilcoat, H. D., Kessler, R. C., & Davis, G. C. (1999). Previous exposure to trauma and PTSD effects of subsequent trauma: Results from the Detroit Area Survey of Trauma. *The American Journal of Psychiatry, 156*(6), 902–907.

Breslin, M. J., & Lewis, C. (2008). Theoretical models of the nature of prayer and health: A review. *Mental Health, Religion & Culture, 11*(1), 9–21.

Brewer, J. A., Elwafi, H. M., & Davis, J. H. (2013). Craving to quit: Psychological models and neurobiological mechanisms of mindfulness training as treatment for addictions. *Psychology of Addictive Behaviors, 27*(2), 366–379.

Brewerton, T. D. (2007). Eating disorders, trauma, and comorbidity: Focus on PTSD. *Eating Disorders, 15*, 285–304.

Briere, J., & Elliott, D. (2000). Prevalence, characteristics, and long-term sequelae of natural disaster exposure in the general population. *Journal of Traumatic Stress, 13*(4), 661–679.

Briere, J., & Scott, C. (2006). *Principles of trauma therapy: A guide to symptoms, evaluation and treatment*. Thousand Oaks, CA: Sage.

Briere, J., & Scott, C. (2007). Assessment of trauma symptoms in eating-disordered populations. *Eating Disorders, 15*(4), 347–358.

Brown, R. L., Leonard, T., Saunders, L. A., & Papasouliotis, O. (1998). The prevalence and detection of substance use disorders among inpatients ages 18 to 49: An opportunity for prevention. *Preventive Medicine, 27*(1), 101–110.

Buchman, D., & Reiner, P. (2009). Stigma and addiction: Being and becoming. *Neuroscience, 9*(9), 18–19.

Buckley, T. (2007). *Traumatic stress and motor vehicle accidents*. U.S. Department of Veterans Affairs: National Center for PTSD. Retrieved October 6, 2013, from http://www.ptsd.va.gov/professional/pages/traumatic-stress-vehicle-accidents.asp

Budney, A. J., Moore, B. A., Vandrey, R. G., & Hughes, J. R. (2003). The time course and significance of cannabis withdrawal. *Journal of Abnormal Psychology, 112*(3), 393–402.

Butler, J. (2008). The family diagram and genogram: Comparisons and contrasts. *American Journal of Family Therapy, 36*(3), 169–180.

Calderwood, K. A. (2011). Adapting the transtheoretical model of change to the bereavement process. *Social Work, 56*(2), 107–117.

Calhoun, L. G., & Tedeschi, R. G. (2004). The foundations of posttraumatic growth: New considerations. *Psychological Inquiry, 15*(1), 93–102.

Cameron, D. (2009). *Why did I do that? How you make sense and why there is hope*. Natick, MA: Thresholds Therapeutics Media.

Cardove, M. J., Andrykowski, M. A., Redd, W. H., Kenady, D. E., McGrath, P. C., & Sloan, D. A. (1995). Frequency and correlates of posttraumatic stress disorder like symptoms after treatment for breast cancer. *Journal of Consulting and Clinical Psychology, 63*, 981–986.

Carlson, E., & Putnam, F. (1993). An update on the Dissociative Experiences Scale. *Dissociation: Progress in the Dissociative Disorders, 6*(1), 16–27.

Carlson, J. G., Chemtob, C. M., Rusnak, K., Hedlund, N. L., & Muraoka, M. Y. (1998). Eye movement desensitization and reprocessing (EDMR) treatment for combat-related posttraumatic stress disorder. *Journal of Traumatic Stress, 11*(1), 3–24.

Carnes, P. (1989). *Contrary to love: Helping the sex addict*. Center City, MN: Hazelden.

Carnes, P. (1991). *Don't call it love: Recovery from sex addiction*. New York, NY: Bantam Books.

Carnes, P. J. (1998). Editorial: The presidential diagnosis. *Sexual Addiction & Compulsivity, 5*(3), 153.

Carnes, P., Delmonico, D., & Griffin, E. (2007). *In the shadows of the net: Breaking free of compulsive online sexual behavior* (2nd ed.). Center City, MN: Hazelden.

Carney, M. M., & Kivlahan, D. R. (1995). Motivational subtypes among veterans seeking substance abuse treatment: Profiles based on stages of change. *Psychology of Addictive Behaviors, 9*(2), 135–142.

Carroll, K. M. (2005). Only connect? *Addiction, 100*(3), 267–268.

Carroll, K. M. (2012). Dissemination of evidence-based practices: How far we've come, and how much further we've got to go. *Addiction, 107*(6), 1031–1033.

Caselles, A., Micó, J. C., & Amigó, S. (2010). Cocaine addiction and personality: A mathematical model. *The British Journal of Mathematical and Statistical Psychology, 63*(Pt 2), 449–480.

Cerdá, M., Digangi, J., Galea, S., & Koenen, K. (2012). Epidemiologic research on interpersonal violence and common psychiatric disorders: Where do we go from here? *Depression and Anxiety, 29*(5), 359–385.

Chopko, B. A., & Schwartz, R. C. (2009). The relation between mindfulness and posttraumatic growth: A study of first responders to trauma-inducing incidents. *Journal of Mental Health Counseling, 31*(4), 363–376.

Clark, H. W., Masson, C. L., Delucchi, K. L., Hall, S. M., & Sees, K. L. (2001). Violent traumatic events and drug abuse severity. *Journal of Substance Abuse Treatment, 20*(2), 121–127.

Clark, L., Lawrence, A. J., Astley-Jones, F., & Gray, N. (2009). Gambling near-misses enhance motivation to gamble and recruit win-related brain circuitry. *Neuron, 61*(3), 481–490.

Clarke, P. B., & Myers, J. E. (2012). Developmental counseling and therapy: A promising intervention for preventing relapse with substance-abusing clients. *Journal of Mental Health Counseling, 34*(4), 308–321.

Cloitre, M., Courtois, C. A., Charuvastra, A., Carapezza, R., Stolbach, B. C., & Green, B. L. (2011). Treatment of complex PTSD: Results of the ISTSS expert clinician survey on best practices. *Journal of Traumatic Stress, 24*(6), 615–627.

Coleman, E. (1992). Is your patient suffering from compulsive sexual behavior? *Psychiatric Annals, 22*(6), 320–325.

Connors, G. J., DiClemente, C. C., Velasquez, M. M., & Donovan, D. M. (2013). *Substance abuse treatment and the stages of change: Selecting and planning interventions*. New York, NY: Guilford Press.
Connors, G. J., Donovan, D. M., & DiClemente, C. C. (2001). *Substance abuse treatment and the stages of change*. New York, NY: Guilford Press.
Conrad, A., & Roth, W. T. (2007). Muscle relaxation therapy for anxiety disorders: It works but how? *Journal of Anxiety Disorders, 21*(3), 243–264.
Cooper, A. (2000). *Sex and the Internet: A guide book for clinicians*. New York, NY: Brunner-Routledge.
Corrigan, P. W., Mueser, K. T., Bond, G. R., Drake, R. E., & Solomon, P. (2008). *Principles and practices of psychiatric rehabilitation: An empirical approach*. New York, NY: Guilford Press.
Cortina, L. M., & Kubiak, S. P. (2006). Gender and posttraumatic stress: Sexual violence as an explanation for women's increased risk. *Journal of Abnormal Psychology, 115*(4), 753–759.
Côté, D., Caron, A., Aubert, J., Desrochers, V., & Ladouceur, R. (2003). Near wins prolong gambling on a video lottery terminal. *Journal of Gambling Studies, 19*(4), 433–438.
Cottler, L. B., Nishith, P., & Compton, W. M. (2001). Gender differences in risk factors for trauma exposure and post-traumatic stress disorder among inner-city drug abusers in and out of treatment. *Comprehensive Psychiatry, 42*(2), 111–117.
Cotton, M. A., Ball, C., & Robinson, P. (2003). Four simple questions can help screen for eating disorders. *Journal of General Internal Medicine, 18*(1), 53–56.
Cox, R. P., & Howard, M. D. (2007). Utilization of EMDR in the treatment of sexual addiction: A case study. *Sexual Addiction and Compulsivity, 14*(1), 1–20.
Cullen, B. (2011). Treating alcohol-related problems within the Irish healthcare system, 1986–2007: An embedded disease model of treatment? *Drugs: Education, Prevention & Policy, 18*(4), 251–260.
Cullen-Drill, M., & Schilling, K. (2008). The case for mandatory outpatient treatment. *Journal of Psychosocial Nursing and Mental Health Services, 46*(2), 33–41.
Cummings, C., Gordon, J. R., & Marlatt, G. A. (1980). Relapse: Prevention and prediction. In W. R. Miller (Ed.), *The addictive behaviors* (pp. 291–321). New York, NY: Pergamon.
Cyndi, R. (2004). Sex addiction and women: A nursing issue. *Journal of Addictions Nursing, 15*(2), 53–62.
Davis, J. (2004). *Survey: Addiction touches many lives*. Retrieved November 9, 2013, from http://www.webmd.com/mental-health/news/20040514/survey-addiction-touches-many-lives
Dayton, T. (2005). The use of psychodrama in dealing with grief and addiction-related loss and trauma. *Journal of Group Psychotherapy, Psychodrama & Sociometry, 58*(1), 15–34.
Dias, E. (2008, Summer). Trauma: Cultural perspectives and clinical considerations. *Trauma Matters, 6*(4).
Dick, D. M., & Agrawal, A. (2008). The genetics of alcohol and other drug dependence. *Alcohol Research & Health, 31*(2), 111–118.
DiClemente, C. C. (1991). Motivational interviewing and the stages of change. In W. R. Miller & S. Rollnick (Eds.), *Motivational interviewing: Preparing people to change addictive behavior* (pp. 191–202). New York, NY: Guilford Press.
DiClemente, C. C. (2003). *Addiction and change*. New York, NY: Guilford Press.
DiClemente, C. C., & Hughes, S. O. (1990). Stages of change profiles in outpatient alcoholism treatment. *Journal of Substance Abuse, 2*, 217–235.
DiClemente, C. C., & Prochaska, J. O. (1998). Toward a comprehensive, transtheoretical model of change: Stages of change and addictive behaviors. In W. R. Miller & N. Heather (Eds.), *Treating addictive behaviors* (2nd ed., pp. 3–24). New York, NY: Plenum Press.
DiClemente, C. C., Prochaska, J. O., Fairhurst, S. K., Velcier, W. F., Velasquez, M. M., & Rossi, J. S. (1991). The process of smoking cessation: An analysis of precontemplation,

contemplation and preparation stages of change. *Journal of Consulting and Clinical Psychology, 59*, 295–304.

DiClemente, C. C., Story, M., & Murray, K. (2000). On a roll: The process of initiation and cessation of problem gambling among adolescents. *Journal of Gambling Studies, 16*(2–3), 289–313.

Dictionary.com. Retrieved November 10, 2013, from http://dictionary.reference.com/browse/addiction?s=t

Dimeff, L., & Linehan, M. (June, 2008). Dialectical behavior therapy for substance abusers. *Addiction Science and Clinical Practice*, 39–47.

Ditlevsen, D. N., & Elklit, A. (2012). Gender, trauma type, and PTSD prevalence: A re-analysis of 18 nordic convenience samples. *Annals of General Psychiatry, 11*(1), 26.

Doubeni, C. A., Schootman, M., Major, J. M., Stone, R. A., Laiyemo, A. O., Park, Y.,…Schatzkin, A. (2012). Health status, neighborhood socioeconomic context, and premature mortality in the United States: The National Institutes of Health-AARP Diet and Health Study. *American Journal of Public Health, 102*(4), 680–688.

Douglas, E. M., & Hines, D. A. (2011). The helpseeking experiences of men who sustain intimate partner violence: An overlooked population and implications for practice. *Journal of Family Violence, 26*(6), 473–485.

Drug Enforcement Agency (DEA). (2011). *Drugs of abuse*. Washington, DC: Author.

Drugs.com. (2013). *Benzodiazepines*. Retrieved November 13, 2013, from http://www.drugs.com/drug-class/benzodiazepines.html

Eagan Chamberlin, S. M. (2012). Emasculated by trauma: A social history of post-traumatic stress disorder, stigma, and masculinity. *Journal of American Culture, 35*(4), 358–365.

Edmond, T., & Rubin, A. (2004). Assessing the long-term effects of EMDR: Results from an 18-month follow-up study with adult female survivors of CSA. *Journal of Child Sexual Abuse, 13*(1), 69–86.

Edmond, T., Rubin, A., & Wambach, K. (1999). The effectiveness of EMDR with adult survivors of childhood sexual abuse. *Social Work Research, 23*, 103–116.

Edmondson, D., Richardson, S., Falzon, L., Davidson, K. W., Mills, M. A., & Neria, Y. (2012). Posttraumatic stress disorder prevalence and risk of recurrence in acute coronary syndrome patients: A meta-analytic review. *PloS One, 7*(6), e38915.

Edmondson, D., Richardson, S., Fausett, J. K., Falzon, L., Howard, V. J., & Kronish, I. M. (2013). Prevalence of PTSD in survivors of stroke and transient ischemic attack: A meta-analytic review. *PloS One, 8*(6), e66435.

EMDRIA. (2012). *EMDR Institute: Basic training course*. Watsonville, CA. Author.

Evans, K. (2010). *Unfortunate hero: The soldier's path from trauma and addiction*. Author.

Evren, C., & Evren, B. (2006). The relationship of suicide attempt history with childhood abuse and neglect, alexithymia and temperament and character dimensions of personality in substance dependents. *Nordic Journal of Psychiatry, 60*(4), 263–269.

Evren, C., Cagil, D., Ulku, M., Ozcetinkaya, S., Gokalp, P., Cetin, T., & Yigiter, S. (2012). Relationship between defense styles, alexithymia, and personality in alcohol-dependent inpatients. *Comprehensive Psychiatry, 53*(6), 860–867.

Falk, D., Yi, H. Y., & Hiller-Sturmhöfel, S. (2008). An epidemiologic analysis of co-occurring alcohol and drug use and disorders: Findings from the National Epidemiologic Survey of Alcohol and Related Conditions (NESARC). *Alcohol Research & Health, 31*(2), 100–110.

Farlex. (2013). *The free dictionary*. Author. Retrieved May 18, 2013, from http://www.thefreedictionary.com/

Felitti, V., & Anda, R. (2010). The relationship of adverse childhood experiences to adult medical disease, psychiatric disorders, and sexual behavior: Implications for healthcare. In R. Lanius, E. Vermetten, & C. Pain (Eds), *The impact of early life trauma on health and disease: The Hidden Epidemic* (pp. 77–87). New York, NY: Cambridge University Press.

Finkelhor, D. (2009). The prevention of childhood sexual abuse. *The Future of Children, 19*(2), 169–194.

First, M. B., Gibbon, M., Spitzer, R. L., Williams, J. B., & Benjamin, L. S. (1997). *Structured clinical interview for DSM-IV Axis II Personality Disorders (SCID-II)*. Washington, DC: American Psychiatric Press, Inc.
Fisher, C. B., & Oransky, M. (2008). Informed consent to psychotherapy: protecting the dignity and respecting the autonomy of patients. *Journal of Clinical Psychology, 64*(5), 576–588.
Fitzgerald, J. P., & McCarty, D. (2009). Understanding attitudes towards use of medication in substance abuse treatment: A multilevel approach. *Psychological Services, 6*(1), 74–84.
Fleming, T., Anderson, C., Amin, S., & Ashley, J. (2012). Third-hand tobacco smoke: Significant vector for PAH exposure or non-issue? *Integrated Environmental Assessment and Management, 8*(4), 763–764.
Fletcher, A. M. (2001). *Sober for good: New solutions for drinking problems—Advice from those who have succeeded*. Boston, MA: Houghton Mifflin.
Fletcher, A. (2013). *Inside rehab: The surprising truth about addiction treatment and how to get help that works*. New York, NY: Viking Penquin.
Foa, E. B., Keane, T. M., Friedman, M. J., & Cohen, J. A. (Eds.) (2009). *Effective treatments for PTSD: Practice guidelines from the International Society for Traumatic Stress Studies* (2nd ed.). New York, NY: Guilford Press.
Foa, E., Hembree, E., & Rothbaum, B. (2007). *Prolonged-exposure therapy for PTSD: Emotional processing of traumatic experiences*. New York, NY: Oxford University Press.
Forbes, D., Creamer, M., & Biddle, D. (2001). The validity of the PTSD checklist as a measure of symptomatic change in combat-related PTSD. *Behavior Therapy and Research, 39*, 977–986.
Ford, J. D., Hawke, J., Alessi, S., Ledgerwood, D., & Petry, N. (2007). Psychological trauma and PTSD symptoms as predictors of substance dependence treatment outcomes. *Behaviour Research and Therapy, 45*(10), 2417–2431.
Forgash, C. (2008). Integrating EMDR and ego state treatment. In C. Forgash & M. Copeley (Eds.), *Healing the heart of trauma and dissociation*. New York, NY: Springer Publishing Company.
Forgash, C., & Copeley, M. (2008). *Healing the heart of trauma and dissociation with EMDR ego state therapy*. New York, NY: Springer Publishing Company.
Forgash, C., & Knipe, J. (2008). Integrating EMDR and ego state treatment. In C. Forgash & M. Copeley (Eds.), *Healing the heart of trauma and dissociation with EMDR and ego state therapy* (pp. 1–59). New York, NY: Springer Publishing Company.
Forgash, C., & Knipe, J. (2012). Integrating EMDR and ego state treatment for clients with trauma disorders. *Journal of EMDR Practice & Research, 6*(3), 120–128.
Foundation for a Drug Free World. (2013). *Drug facts*. Retrieved November 14, 2013, from www.drugfreeworld.org/drugfacts
Frans, O., Rimmö, P. A., Aberg, L., & Fredrikson, M. (2005). Trauma exposure and posttraumatic stress disorder in the general population. *Acta Psychiatrica Scandinavica, 111*(4), 291–299.
Friedlander, M. L. (1992). Psychotherapeutic processes: About the art, about the science. *Journal of Counseling & Development, 70*, 740–741.
Fuchs, R., Lasseter, H., Ramirez, D., & Xie, X. (2008). Relapse to drug seeking following prolonged abstinence: The role of environmental stimuli. *Drug Discovery Today. Disease Models, 5*(4), 251–258.
Goodman, A. (1997). Sexual addiction. In J. H. Lowinson, P. Ruiz, R. B. Millman, & J. G. Langrod (Eds), *Substance abuse: A comprehensive textbook* (3rd ed., pp. 340–354). Baltimore: Williams & Wilkins.
Gracer, R. I. (2007). *A new prescription for addiction* (Gracer Behavioral Health Services). San Ramon, CA: Author.
Grant, J. E., Potenza, M. N., Weinstein, A., & Gorelick, D. A. (2010). Introduction to behavioral addictions. *The American Journal of Drug and Alcohol Abuse, 36*(5), 233–241.

Grant, J. E., Schreiber, L. R., & Odlaug, B. L. (2013). Phenomenology and treatment of behavioural addictions. *Canadian Journal of Psychiatry, 58*(5), 252–259.

Greene, S. L., Kerr, F., & Braitberg, G. (2008). Review article: Amphetamines and related drugs of abuse. *Emergency Medicine Australasia: EMA, 20*(5), 391–402.

Greenwald, R. (1999). The power of suggestion: Comment on EMDR and mesmerism: A comparative historical analysis. *Journal of Anxiety Disorders, 13*(6), 611–615; discussion 617.

Grinage, B. (2003). *Diagnosis and management of post-traumatic stress disorder* (Adapted with permission from American Psychiatric Association. *Diagnostic and statistical manual of mental disorders*, fourth edition, text revision. Washington, DC: American Psychiatric Association, 2000:467–468. Copyright 2000). *American Family Physician, 68*(12), 2401–2409, 2321–2323.

Guigliamo, J. (2007). Out of control sexual behavior: A qualitative investigation. *Sexual Addiction & Compulsivity, 13*, 361–337.

Gunter, R. W., & Bodner, G. E. (2009). EMDR works. But how? Recent progress in the search for treatment mechanisms. *Journal of EMDR Practice & Research, 3*(3), 161–168.

Handley, R., Salkovskis, P., Hackmann, A., & Ehlers, A. (2009). Travel, trauma, and phobia: Treating the survivors of transport-related trauma. In N. Grey (Ed.), *A casebook of cognitive therapy for traumatic stress reactions* (pp. 31–48). New York, NY: Routledge/Taylor & Francis Group.

Hapke, U., Schumann, A., Rumpf, H. J., John, U., & Meyer, C. (2006). Post-traumatic stress disorder: The role of trauma, pre-existing psychiatric disorders, and gender. *European Archives of Psychiatry and Clinical Neuroscience, 256*(5), 299–306.

Hardi, L., & Kroo, A. (2011). The trauma of torture and the rehabilitation of torture survivors. *Zeitschrift Für Psychologie/Journal of Psychology, 219*(3), 133–142.

Harding, H., & Helweg-Larsen, M. (2009). Perceived risk for future intimate partner violence among women in a domestic violence shelter. *Journal of Family Violence, 24*(2), 75–85.

Hargreaves, A. (2009, September). Children's health. *Education Journal, 118*, 25.

Harrison, L. D., & Scarpitti, F. R. (2002). Introduction: Progress and issues in drug treatment courts. *Substance Use & Misuse, 37*(12–13), 1441–1467.

Hase, M. (2006, September). *Reprocessing of the addiction memory*. Paper presented at the Annual EMDR International Conference, Philadelphia, PA.

Hase, M. (2010). CraveEx: An EMDR approach to treat substance abuse and addiction. In M. Luber (Ed.), *EMDR scripted protocols* (pp. 467–488). New York, NY: Norton.

Hase, M., Schallmayer, S., & Sack, M. (2008). EMDR reprocessing of the addiction memory: Pretreatment, posttreatment and 1-month follow-up. *Journal of EMDR Practice and Research, 2*(3), 170–179.

Hayes, S., Strosahl, K., & Wilson, K. (2012). *Acceptance and commitment therapy: Second edition: The process and practice of mindful change*. New York, NY: Guilford Press.

Heather, N., & McCambridge, J. (2013). Post-treatment stage of change predicts 12-month outcome of treatment for alcohol problems. *Alcohol and Alcoholism, 48*(3), 329–336.

Hensley, B. J. (2012). Adaptive information processing, targeting, the standard protocol, and strategies for successful outcomes in EMDR reprocessing. *Journal of EMDR Practice & Research, 6*(3), 92–100.

Hepp, U., Kraemer, B., Schnyder, U., Miller, N., & Delsignore, A. (2005). Psychiatric comorbidity in gender identity disorder. *Journal of Psychosomatic Research, 58*(3), 259–261.

Herman, J. (1992). *Trauma and recovery*. New York, NY: Basic Books.

Herrero, M. J., Domingo-Salvany, A., Torrens, M., Brugal, M. T., & Gutiérrez, F.; Itinere Investigators. (2008). Personality profile in young current regular users of cocaine. *Substance Use & Misuse, 43*(10), 1378–1394.

Hicks, B. M., Durbin, C., Blonigen, D. M., Iacono, W. G., & McGue, M. (2012). Relationship between personality change and the onset and course of alcohol dependence in young adulthood. *Addiction, 107*(3), 540–548.

Hirvonen, N., Huotari, M., Niemelä, R., & Korpelainen, R. (2012). Information behavior in stages of exercise behavior change. *Journal of the American Society for Information Science & Technology, 63*(9), 1804–1819.
Hiskey, S., Luckie, M., Davies, S., & Brewin, C. R. (2008). The phenomenology of reactivated trauma memories in older adults: A preliminary study. *Aging & Mental Health, 12*(4), 494–498.
Hoek, H. W., & van Hoeken, D. (2003). Review of the prevalence and incidence of eating disorders. *The International Journal of Eating Disorders, 34*(4), 383–396.
Högberg, G., Pagani, M., Sundin, O., Soares, J., Aberg-Wistedt, A., Tärnell, B., & Hällström, T. (2007). On treatment with eye movement desensitization and reprocessing of chronic post-traumatic stress disorder in public transportation workers—a randomized controlled trial. *Nordic Journal of Psychiatry, 61*(1), 54–61.
Holbrook, T. L., Galarneau, M. R., Dye, J. L., Quinn, K., & Dougherty, A. L. (2010). Morphine use after combat injury in Iraq and post-traumatic stress disorder. *The New England Journal of Medicine, 362*(2), 110–117.
Horn, D. A. (1976). A model for the study of personal choice health behavior. *International Journal of Health Education, 19*, 89–98.
Horwath, C. C., Schembre, S. M., Motl, R. W., Dishman, R. K., & Nigg, C. R. (2013). Does the transtheoretical model of behavior change provide a useful basis for interventions to promote fruit and vegetable consumption? *American Journal of Health Promotion, 27*(6), 351.
Houston, J. E., Shevlin, M., Adamson, G., & Murphy, J. (2011). A person-centered approach to modelling population experiences of trauma and mental illness. *Social Psychiatry and Psychiatric Epidemiology, 46*(2), 149–157.
Howard, M. D. (2007). Escaping the pain: Examining the use of sexually compulsive behavior to avoid the traumatic memories of combat. *Sexual Addiction & Compulsivity, 14*(2), 77–94.
Hudson, J. I., Hiripi, E., Pope, H. G., & Kessler, R. C. (2007). The prevalence and correlates of eating disorders in the National Comorbidity Survey Replication. *Biological Psychiatry, 61*(3), 348–358.
Hughes, M., Brymer, M., Chiu, W., Fairbank, J. A., Jones, R. T., Pynoos, R. S., & .. Kessler, R. C. (2011). Posttraumatic stress among students after the shootings at Virginia Tech. *Psychological Trauma: Theory, Research, Practice, and Policy, 3*(4), 403–411.
Iancu, I., Lowengrub, K., Dembinsky, Y., Kotler, M., & Dannon, P. N. (2008). Pathological gambling: An update on neuropathophysiology and pharmacotherapy. *CNS Drugs, 22*(2), 123–138.
Ironson, G., Freund, B., Strauss, J. L., & Williams, J. (2002). Comparison of two treatments for traumatic stress: A community-based study of EMDR and prolonged exposure. *Journal of Clinical Psychology, 58*(1), 113–128.
Iverson, K. M., Gradus, J. L., Resick, P. A., Suvak, M. K., Smith, K. F., & Monson, C. M. (2011). Cognitive-behavioral therapy for PTSD and depression symptoms reduces risk for future intimate partner violence among interpersonal trauma survivors. *Journal of Consulting and Clinical Psychology, 79*(2), 193–202.
Jacobsen, L. K., Southwick, S. M., & Kosten, T. R. (2001). Substance use disorders in patients with posttraumatic stress disorder: A review of the literature. *The American Journal of Psychiatry, 158*(8), 1184–1190.
Jeffries, F. W., & Davis, P. (2013). What is the role of eye movements in eye movement desensitization and reprocessing (EMDR) for post-traumatic stress disorder (PTSD)? A review. *Behavioral and Cognitive Psychotherapy, 41*, 290–300.
Jenkins, I. A. (2011). Tolerance and addiction; the patient, the parent or the clinician? *Paediatric Anaesthesia, 21*(7), 794–799.
Jensen, J. A. (1994). An investigation of eye movement desensitisation and reprocessing as a treatment for posttraumatic stress disorder symptoms of Vietnam combat veterans. *Behavior Therapy, 25*, 311–32.

Johns Hopkins Medical Center. (2013). *Information about caffeine dependence*. Retrieved November 14, 2013, from http://www.caffeinedependence.org/caffeine_dependence.html#tolerance

Jonker, J., De Jong, C. A., de Weert-van Oene, G. H., & Gijs, L. (2000). Gender-role stereotypes and interpersonal behavior how addicted inpatients view their ideal male and female therapist. *Journal of Substance Abuse Treatment, 19*(3), 307–312.

Jovanovic, T., & Ressler, K. J. (2010). How the neurocircuitry and genetics of fear inhibition may inform our understanding of PTSD. *The American Journal of Psychiatry, 167*(6), 648–662.

Juhnke, G. A., & Hagedorn, W. B. (2006). *Counseling addicted families: An integrated assessment and treatment model*. New York, NY: Taylor & Francis.

Kampman, K. M. (2009). Biologic treatments for drug and alcohol dependence. *Primary Psychiatry, 16*(8), 47–52.

Karim, R., & Chaudhri, P. (2012). Behavioral addictions: An overview. *Journal of Psychoactive Drugs, 44*(1), 5–17.

Katsavdakis, K. A., Sayed, M., Bram, A., & Bartlett, A. B. (2001). How was this story told in the mother tongue? An integrative perspective. *Bulletin of the Menninger Clinic, 65*(2), 246–265.

Kausch, O., Rugle, L., & Rowland, D. Y. (2006). Lifetime histories of trauma among pathological gamblers. *The American Journal on Addictions, 15*(1), 35–43.

Kaye, W., Wagner, A., Fudge, J., & Paulus, M. (2011). Neurocircuity of eating disorders. *Current Topics in Behavioral Neurosciences, 6*, 37–57.

Keating, G. M., & Lyseng-Williamson, K. A. (2010). Varenicline: A pharmacoeconomic review of its use as an aid to smoking cessation. *PharmacoEconomics, 28*(3), 231–254.

Kendler, K. S., Jacobson, K. C., Prescott, C. A., & Neale, M. C. (2003). Specificity of genetic and environmental risk factors for use and abuse/dependence of cannabis, cocaine, hallucinogens, sedatives, stimulants, and opiates in male twins. *The American Journal of Psychiatry, 160*(4), 687–695.

Kenji Iwamoto, D., Corbin, W., Lejuez, C., & MacPherson, L. (2014, January). College men and alcohol use: Positive alcohol expectancies as a mediator between distinct masculine norms and alcohol use. *Psychology of Men & Masculinity, 15*(1), 29–39. Doi:10.1037/a0031594

Kessler, R. C. (2000). *National Comorbidity Survey: Baseline*, 1990–1992.

Kessler, R. C., Berglund, P., Demler, O., Jin, R., Merikangas, K. R., & Walters, E. E. (2005). Lifetime prevalence and age-of-onset distributions of DSM-IV disorders in the National Comorbidity Survey Replication. *Archives of General Psychiatry, 62*(6), 593–602.

Kessler, R. C., Sonnega, A., Bromet, E., Hughes, M., & Nelson, C. B. (1995). Posttraumatic stress disorder in the National Comorbidity Survey. *Archives of General Psychiatry, 52*(12), 1048–1060.

Khantzian, E. J., & Albanese, M. J. (2008). *Understanding addiction as self-medication. Finding hope behind the pain*. New York, NY: Rowman & Littlefield.

Killeen, T. K., Greenfield, S. F., Bride, B. E., Cohen, L., Gordon, S. M., & Roman, P. M. (2011). Assessment and treatment of co-occurring eating disorders in privately funded addiction treatment programs. *The American Journal on Addictions, 20*(3), 205–211.

Kilpatrick, D. G., Acierno, R., Saunders, B., Resnick, H. S., Best, C. L., & Schnurr, P. P. (2000). Risk factors for adolescent substance abuse and dependence: data from a national sample. *Journal of Consulting and Clinical Psychology, 68*(1), 19–30.

Kimble, M. (2007). Neurobiological models in post traumatic stress disorder: Effects on public perception and patient care. *Journal of Psychological Trauma, 6*(4), 57–78.

King, L., Pless, A. P., Schuster, J. L., Potter, C. M., Park, C. L., Spiro, A., & King, D. W. (2012). Risk and protective factors for traumatic stress disorders. In J. G. Beck & D. M. Sloan (Eds.), *The Oxford handbook of traumatic stress disorders* (pp. 333–346). New York, NY: Oxford University Press.

Kinyanjui, D. W., & Atwoli, L. (2013). Substance use among inmates at the Eldoret prison in Western Kenya. *BMC Psychiatry, 13*, 53.

Klanecky, A. K., Harrington, J., & McChargue, D. E. (2008). Child sexual abuse, dissociation, and alcohol: Implications of chemical dissociation via blackouts among college women. *The American Journal of Drug and Alcohol Abuse, 34*(3), 277–284.

Koenen, K. C. (2006). Developmental epidemiology of PTSD: Self-regulation as a central mechanism. *Annals of the New York Academy of Sciences, 1071*, 255–266.

Koenen, K. C., Moffitt, T. E., Caspi, A., Gregory, A., Harrington, H., & Poulton, R. (2008). The developmental mental-disorder histories of adults with posttraumatic stress disorder: A prospective longitudinal birth cohort study. *Journal of Abnormal Psychology, 117*(2), 460–466.

Kong, S., & Bernstein, K. (2009). Childhood trauma as a predictor of eating psychopathology and its mediating variables in patients with eating disorders. *Journal of Clinical Nursing, 18*(13), 1897–1907.

Konuk, E., Epözdemir, H., Atçeken, Ş., Aydin, Y., & Yurtsever, A. (2011). EMDR treatment of migraine. *Journal of EMDR Practice & Research, 5*(4), 167–176.

Korn, D. L. (2009). EMDR and the treatment of complex PTSD: A review. *Journal of EMDR Practice & Research, 3*(4), 264–278.

Korn, D. L., & Leeds, A. M. (2002). Preliminary evidence of efficacy for EMDR resource development and installation in the stabilization phase of treatment of complex posttraumatic stress disorder. *Journal of Clinical Psychology, 58*(12), 1465–1487.

Kupchik, M., Strous, R. D., Erez, R., Gonen, N., Weizman, A., & Spivak, B. (2007). Demographic and clinical characteristics of motor vehicle accident victims in the community general health outpatient clinic: A comparison of PTSD and non-PTSD subjects. *Depression and Anxiety, 24*(4), 244–250.

Kuss, D. J. (2013). Internet gaming addiction: Current perspectives. *Psychology Research & Behavior Management, 6*, 125–137.

Landes, S. J. (2013). The case: Treating Jared through dialectical behavior therapy. *Journal of Clinical Psychology, 69*(5), 488–489.

Långström, N., & Hanson, R. K. (2006). High rates of sexual behavior in the general population: Correlates and predictors. *Archives of Sexual Behavior, 35*(1), 37–52.

LaPaglia, D. (2011). Challenges and solutions of adding medication treatment to specialty addiction treatment programs: A review with suggestions. *Alcohol Research & Health, 33*(4), 306–307.

Lasseter, H. C., Xie, X., Ramirez, D. R., & Fuchs, R. A. (2010). Prefrontal cortical regulation of drug seeking in animal models of drug relapse. In D. W. Self, & J. K. Staley (Eds.), *Behavioral neuroscience of drug addiction* (pp. 101–117). New York, NY: Springer Publishing Company.

Lasting, O., & Charles, G. (2008). Crystal Meth. *Relational Child & Youth Care Practice, 21*(2), 10–19.

Lauritsen, J. L., & Heimer, K. (2008). The gender gap in violent victimization, 1973–2004. *Journal of Quantitative Criminology, 24*(2), 125–147.

Ledgerwood, D. M., & Petry, N. M. (2006). Post traumatic stress disorder symptoms in treatment seeking pathological gamblers. *Journal of Traumatic Stress, 19*, 411–416.

Leeds, A. M. (2009). *A guide to the standard EMDR protocols for clinicians, supervisors and consultants*. New York, NY: Springer Publishing Company.

Leeds, A. M. (2011). *Working with personality disorders – defense and affect restructuring in the EMDR approach to psychotherapy*. Advanced EMDR Workshop Madrid, Spain, February 20, 2011.

Leshner, A. I. (2001). Addiction is a brain disease. *Issues in Science & Technology, 17*(3), 75–80.

Leung, L. (2004). Net-generation attributes and seductive properties of the internet as predictors of online activities and internet addiction. *Cyberpsychology & Behavior, 7*(3), 333–348.

Levy, M. (2007). *Take control of your drinking and you may not need to quit*. Baltimore, MD: Johns Hopkins University Press.

Lindauer, R. J., Olff, M., van Meijel, E. P., Carlier, I. V., & Gersons, B. P. (2006). Cortisol, learning, memory, and attention in relation to smaller hippocampal volume in police officers with posttraumatic stress disorder. *Biological Psychiatry, 59*(2), 171–177.

Linehan, M. (1993a). *Cognitive-behavioral treatment of borderline personality disorder*. New York, NY: Guilford Press.

Linehan, M. (1993b). *Skills training manual for treating borderline personality disorder*. New York, NY: Guilford Press.

Linehan, M. M., Dimeff, L. A., Reynolds, S. K., Comtois, K. A., Welch, S. S., Heagerty, P., . . . Kivlahan, D. R. (2002). Dialectical behavior therapy versus comprehensive validation therapy plus 12-step for the treatment of opioid dependent women meeting criteria for borderline personality disorder. *Drug and Alcohol Dependence, 67*(1), 13–26.

Linehan, M., Schmidt, H., Dimeff, L., Craft, J., Kanter, J., & Comtois, K. (1999). Dialectical behavior therapy for patients with borderline personality disorder and drug-dependence. *American Journal on Addictions, 8*(4), 279–292.

Littlefield, A. K., Sher, K. J., & Wood, P. K. (2009). Is "maturing out" of problematic alcohol involvement related to personality change? *Journal of Abnormal Psychology, 118*(2), 360–374.

Luber, M. (2009). *Eye movement desensitization and reprocessing (EMDR) scripted protocols: Basic and special situations*. New York, NY: Springer Publishing.

Luber, M. (2010). *Eye movement desensitization and reprocessing (EMDR) scripted protocols: Special populations*. New York, NY: Springer Publishing.

Luber, M., & Shapiro, F. (2009). Interview with Francine Shapiro: Historical overview, present issues, and future directions of EMDR. *Journal of EMDR Practice & Research, 3*(4), 217–231.

Lundgren, L., Amodeo, M., Krull, I., Chassler, D., Weidenfeld, R., de Saxe Zerden, L., & Beltrame, C. (2011). Addiction treatment provider attitudes on staff capacity and evidence-based clinical training: Results from a National Study. *American Journal on Addictions, 20*(3), 271–284.

Lutz, R., Lochbaum, M. R., Carson, T., Jackson, S., Greenwood, M., & Byars, A. (2008). Are we underestimating the affective benefits of exercise? An experience sampling study of university aerobics participants. *Journal of Sport Behavior, 31*(2), 166–186.

Maccallum, F., & Blaszczynski, A. (2003). Pathological gambling and suicidality: An analysis of severity and lethality. *Suicide & Life-Threatening Behavior, 33*(1), 88–98.

Macklin, M. L., Metzger, L. J., Litz, B. T., McNally, R. J., Lasko, N. B., Orr, S. P., & Pitman, R. K. (1998). Lower precombat intelligence is a risk factor for posttraumatic stress disorder. *Journal of Consulting and Clinical Psychology, 66*(2), 323–326.

Manso, A., & Rauktis, M. (2011). What is the therapeutic alliance and why does it matter? *Reclaiming Children & Youth, 19*(4), 45–50.

Marich, J. (2009). EMDR in the addiction continuing care process: Case study of a cross-addicted female's treatment and recovery. *Journal of EMDR Practice and Research, 3*(2), 98–106.

Marich, J. (2010). Eye movement desensitization and reprocessing in addiction continuing care: A phenomenological study of women in recovery. *Psychology of Addictive Behaviors, 24*(3), 498–507.

Marlatt, G. A. (Ed.). (1998). *Harm reduction: Pragmatic strategies for managing high-risk behaviors*. New York, NY: Guilford Press.

Marlatt, G. A., & Gordon, J. R. (1985). *Relapse prevention: Maintenance strategies in the treatment of addictive behaviors*. New York, NY: Guilford Press.

Marmar, C. R., McCaslin, S. E., Metzler, T. J., Best, S., Weiss, D. S., Fagan, J., . . . Neylan, T. (2006). Predictors of posttraumatic stress in police and other first responders. *Annals of the New York Academy of Sciences, 1071*, 1–18.

Marr, J. (2012). EMDR treatment of obsessive-compulsive disorder: Preliminary research. *Journal of EMDR Practice & Research, 6*(1), 2–15.

Martin, B., Clapp, L., Bialkowski, D., Bridgeford, D., Amponsah, A., Lyons, L., & Beresford, T. P. (2003). Compliance to supervised disulfiram therapy: A comparison of voluntary and court-ordered patients. *The American Journal on Addictions, 12*(2), 137–143.

Martin, P. R. (2013). Hormone treatment for PTSD. *U.S. Naval Institute Proceedings, 139*(8), 79–80.

Martino, S., Ball, S. A., Nich, C., Frankforter, T. L., & Carroll, K. M. (2009). Informal discussions in substance abuse treatment sessions. *Journal of Substance Abuse Treatment, 36*(4), 366–375.

Mason, T., Worsley, A., & Coyle, D. (2010). Forensic multidisciplinary perspectives of Tarasoff liability: A vignette study. *Journal of Forensic Psychiatry & Psychology, 21*(4), 549–554.

Matthews, C. R., Lorah, P., & Fenton, J. (2006). Treatment experiences of gays and lesbians in recovery from addiction: A qualitative inquiry. *Journal of Mental Health Counseling, 28*(2), 110–132.

Maxfield, L. (2009a). EMDR milestones: The first 20 years. *Journal of EMDR Practice & Research, 3*(4), 211–216.

Maxfield, L. (2009b). Twenty years of EMDR. *Journal of EMDR Practice & Research, 3*(3), 115–116.

McBride, D. (2010). Third-hand smoke produces carcinogens. *ONS Connect, 25*(4), 6.

McCauley, J. L., Killeen, T., Gros, D. F., Brady, K. T., & Back, S. E. (2012). Posttraumatic stress disorder and co-occurring substance use disorders: Advances in assessment and treatment. *Clinical Psychology, 19*(3).

McGue, M. (1999). The behavioral genetics of alcoholism. *Current Directions in Psychological Science, 8*, 109–115.

McNally, R. J. (1999). EMDR and Mesmerism: A comparative historical analysis. *Journal of Anxiety Disorders, 13*(1–2), 225–236.

McNally, R. J. (2001). How to end the EMDR controversy. *Psicoterapia Cognitiva E Comportamentale, 7*(2), 153–154.

Medline Plus. (2012). *Nicotine and tobacco.* Retrieved November 10, 2013, from http://www.nlm.nih.gov/medlineplus/ency/article/000953.htm

Mehta, D., & Binder, E. B. (2012). Gene × environment vulnerability factors for PTSD: the HPA-axis. *Neuropharmacology, 62*(2), 654–662.

Merriam-Webster Dictionary. (2013a). *Merriam-Webster Dictionary*. Author. Retrieved June 2, 2013, from http://www.merriam-webster.com/dictionary.htm

Merriam-Webster Dictionary. (2013b). Retrieved January 12, 2013, from http://w-m.com.

Meyer, I. H. (2003). Prejudice, social stress, and mental health in lesbian, gay, and bisexual populations: Conceptual issues and research evidence. *Psychology of Sexual Orientation and Gender Diversity, 129*(5), 674–697.

Miller, R. (2012). Treatment of behavioral addictions utilizing the feeling-state addiction protocol: A multiple baseline study. *Journal of EMDR Practice & Research, 6*(4), 159–169.

Miller, W. (1985). Motivation for treatment: A review with special emphasis on alcoholism. *Psychological Bulletin, 98*(1), 84–107.

Miller, W. R., & Rollnick, S. (1991). *Motivational interviewing: Preparing people to change addictive behavior*. New York, NY: The Guilford Press.

Moak, D. A., & Anton, R. F. (1999). Alcohol. In B. McCrady & B. Epstein (Eds.), *Addictions: A comprehensive guidebook*. New York, NY: Oxford University Press.

Moore, L. E., Tambling, R. B., & Anderson, S. R. (2013). The intersection of therapy constructs: The relationship between motivation to change, distress, referral source, and pressure to attend. *American Journal of Family Therapy, 41*(3), 245–258.

Moore, T. M., Seavey, A., Ritter, K., McNulty, J. K., Gordon, K. C., & Stuart, G. L. (2013). Ecological momentary assessment of the effects of craving and affect on risk for relapse during substance abuse treatment. *Psychology of Addictive Behaviors*. Advance online publication. Doi:10.1037/a0034127

Morales, Z., Pascual, L., & Carmona, J. (2010). The validity of the Transtheoretical Model through different psychological variables. *Health & Addictions, 10*(2), 47–66.

Moran, S., Schmidt, J., & Burker, E. J. (2013). Posttraumatic growth and posttraumatic stress disorder in veterans. *Journal of Rehabilitation, 79*(2), 34–43.

Morin, S. F., & Rothblum, E. D. (1991). Removing the stigma: Fifteen years of progress. *American Psychologist, 46*(9), 947–949.

Morse, S. J. (2004). Medicine and morals, craving and compulsion. *Substance Use & Misuse, 39*(3), 437–460.

Moyers, T. B., & Miller, W. R. (2013). Is low therapist empathy toxic? *Psychology of Addictive Behaviors, 27*(3), 878–884.

Moyers, T. B., Miller, W. R., & Hendrickson, S. M. (2005). How does motivational interviewing work? Therapist interpersonal skill predicts client involvement within motivational interviewing sessions. *Journal of consulting and clinical psychology, 73*(4), 590–598.

Mueser, K. T., Noordsy, D. L., Drake, R. E., & Fox, L. (2003). *Integrated treatment for dual disorders. A guide to effective practice.* New York, NY: Guilford Press.

Muga, R., Sanvisens, A., Fuster, D., Tor, J., Martínez, E., Pérez-Hoyos, S., & Muñoz, A. (2012). Unhealthy alcohol use, HIV infection and risk of liver fibrosis in drug users with hepatitis C. *Plos One, 7*(10), 1–7.

Myers, D. (2013). *Psychology: Tenth edition in modules.* New York, NY: Worth Publishers.

Najavits, L. M., Griffin, M. L., Luborsky, L., Frank, A., Weiss, R. D., Liese, B. S., ... Onken, L. S. (1995). Therapists' emotional reactions to substance abusers: A new questionnaire and initial findings. *Psychotherapy: Theory, Research, Practice, Training, 32*(4), 669–677.

Najavits, L. M. (2002). *Seeking safety. A treatment manual for PTSD and substance abuse.* New York, NY: Guilford Press.

Najavits, L. M. (2011). Treatments for PTSD and pathological gambling: What do patients want? *Journal of Gambling Studies, 27*(2), 229–241.

National Council on Alcoholism and Drug Dependence (NCADD). (2013a). *Alcohol affects far more lives than all other drugs combined.* Retrieved November 13, 2013, from http://www.ncadd.org/index.php/in-the-news/137-alcohol-affects-more-people

National Council on Alcoholism and Drug Dependence (NCADD). (2013b). *Alcohol and drug information.* Retrieved November 13, 2013, from http://www.ncadd.org/index.php/for-the-media/alcohol-a-drug-information

National Gambling Impact Study. (1999). *Commission report.* Washington, DC. Retrieved November 12, 2013, from http://govinfo.library.unt.edu/ngisc

National Institute of Mental Health (NIMH). (2011). *Eating disorders.* Bethesda, MD: Author. Retrieved February 24, 2013, from http://www.nimh.nih.gov

National Institute on Alcohol Abuse and Alcoholism (NIAAA). (2008). *Alcohol alert.* Retrieved November 15, 2013, from http://pubs.niaaa.nih.gov/publications/AA76/AA76.pdf

National Institute on Alcohol Abuse and Alcoholism (NIAAA). (2013). *What's "at risk" or "heavy" drinking?* Retrieved November 15, 2013, from http://rethinkingdrinking.niaaa.nih.gov/isyourdrinkingpatternrisky/whatsatriskorheavydrinking.asp

National Institute on Drug Abuse (NIDA). (2007). *The neurobiology of drug addiction.* Retrieved November 14, 2013, from http://www.drugabuse.gov/publications/teaching-packets/neurobiology-drug-addiction/section-iii-action-heroin-morphine/6-definition-tolerance

National Institute on Drug Abuse (NIDA). (2009a). *Hallucinogens.* Washington, DC: Author. Retrieved November 14, 2013, from http://www.drugabuse.gov/sites/default/files/hallucinogens09.pdf

National Institute on Drug Abuse (NIDA). (2009b). *Principles of drug addiction treatment: A research-based guide* (2nd ed.). Washington, DC: U.S. Government Printing Office. Retrieved September 28, 2013, from http://www.nida.nih.gov/podat/podatindex.html

National Institute on Drug Abuse (NIDA). (2010a). *Drug facts: Club drugs*. Retrieved November 14, 2013, from http://www.drugabuse.gov/sites/default/files/clubdrugs10.pdf

National Institute on Drug Abuse (NIDA). (2010b). *Research Report Series: Comorbidity: Addiction and other mental illnesses*. Washington, DC: U.S. Government Printing Office. Retrieved September 29, 2013, from http://www.drugabuse.gov/sites/default/files/rrcomorbidity.pdf

National Institute on Drug Abuse (NIDA). (2011a). *Addiction science: From molecules to managed care*. Retrieved November 10, 2013, from http://www.drugabuse.gov/publications/addiction-science-molecules-to-managed-care/introduction/drug-abuse-costs-united-states-economy-hundreds-billions-dollars-in-increased-health

National Institute on Drug Abuse (NIDA). (2011b). *Prescription drugs: Abuse and addiction*. Retrieved November 13, 2013, from http://www.drugabuse.gov/sites/default/files/rrprescription.pdf

National Institute on Drug Abuse (NIDA). (2012a). *Drug facts: Cigarettes and other tobacco products*. Retrieved November 14, 2013, from http://www.drugabuse.gov/publications/drugfacts/cigarettes-other-tobacco-products

National Institute on Drug Abuse (NIDA). (2012b). *Drug facts: Inhalants*. Retrieved November 14, 2013, from http://www.drugabuse.gov/sites/default/files/dfinhalants_1.pdf

National Institute on Drug Abuse (NIDA). (2012c). *Monitoring the future. National survey results on drug use 1975-2012*. Retrieved November 10, 2013, from http://www.monitoringthefuture.org/pubs/monographs/mtf-overview2012.pdf

National Institute on Drug Abuse (NIDA). (2013a). *Drug facts: Cocaine*. Washington, DC: Author. Retrieved November 14, 2013, from http://www.drugabuse.gov/sites/default/files/drugfacts_cocaine_final_0.pdf

National Institute on Drug Abuse (NIDA). (2013b). *MDMA (ecstasy/Molly)*. Retrieved November 14, 2013, from http://www.drugabuse.gov/drugs-abuse/mdma-ecstasymolly

National Institute on Drug Abuse (NIDA). (2013c). *Marijuana*. Retrieved November 14, 2013, from http://www.drugabuse.gov/publications/research-reports/marijuana-abuse

Nelson, N. (2012). Diaphragmatic breathing: The foundation of core stability. *Strength & Conditioning Journal, 34*(5), 34–40.

Neuner, F., Schauer, M., Karunakara, U., Klaschik, C., Robert, C., & Elbert, T. (2004). Psychological trauma and evidence for enhanced vulnerability for posttraumatic stress disorder through previous trauma among West Nile refugees. *BMC Psychiatry, 4*, 34.

Nieuwenhuis, S., Elzinga, B. M., Ras, P. H., Berends, F., Duijs, P., Samara, Z., & Slagter, H. A. (2013). Bilateral saccadic eye movements and tactile stimulation, but not auditory stimulation, enhance memory retrieval. *Brain and Cognition, 81*(1), 52–56.

Norcross, J., Krebs, P., & Prochaska, J. (2011). Stages of change. *Journal of Clinical Psychology, 67*(2), 143–154.

Nordfjærn, T. (2011). Relapse patterns among patients with substance use disorders. *Journal of Substance Use, 16*(4), 313–329.

Nordfjærn, T., Rundmo, T., & Hole, R. (2010). Treatment and recovery as perceived by patients with substance addiction. *Journal of Psychiatric and Mental Health Nursing, 17*(1), 46–64.

Nowill, J. (2010). A critical review of the controversy surrounding eye movement desensitisation and reprocessing. *Counseling Psychology Review, 25*(1), 63–70.

Nuttbrock, L., Hwahng, S., Bockting, W., Rosenblum, A., Mason, M., Macri, M., & Becker, J. (2010). Psychiatric impact of gender-related abuse across the life course of male-to-female transgender persons. *Journal of Sex Research, 47*(1), 12–23.

Nygaard, E., & Heir, T. (2012). World assumptions, posttraumatic stress and quality of life after a natural disaster: a longitudinal study. *Health and Quality of Life Outcomes, 10*, 76.

O'Brien, J. M., & Abel, N. J. (2011). EMDR, addictions, and the Stages of Change: A road map for intervention. *Journal of EMDR Practice & Research, 5*(3), 121–130.

Ogden, P., Minton, K., & Pain, C. (2006). *Trauma and the body: A sensorimotor approach to psychotherapy*. New York, NY: W. W. Norton.

O'Hare, T. (1996). Court-ordered versus voluntary clients: Problem differences and readiness for change. *Social Work, 41*, 417–422.

O'Hare, T., Sherrer, M. V., & Shen, C. (2006). Subjective distress from stressful events and high-risk behaviors as predictors of PTSD symptom severity in clients with severe mental illness. *Journal of Traumatic Stress, 19*(3), 375–386.

Olszweksi, T. M., & Varrassee, J. F. (2005). The neurobiology of PTSD: Implications for nurses. *Journal of Psychosocial Nursing, 43*(6), 41–47.

Orman, J. S., & Keating, G. M. (2009). Buprenorphine/naloxone: A review of its use in the treatment of opioid dependence. *Drugs, 69*(5), 577–607.

Oscar-Berman, M., Shagrin, B., Evert, D. L., & Epstein, C. (1997). Impairments of brain and behavior: The neurological effects of alcohol. *Alcohol Health and Research World, 21*(1), 65–75.

Osório, C., Greenberg, N., Jones, N., Goodwin, L., Fertout, M., & Maia, Â. (2013). Combat exposure and posttraumatic stress disorder among Portuguese special operation forces deployed in Afghanistan. *Military Psychology, 25*(1), 70–81.

Ostafin, B. D., & Marlatt, G. (2008). Surfing the urge: Experiential acceptance moderates the relation between automatic alcohol motivation and hazardous drinking. *Journal of Social & Clinical Psychology, 27*(4), 404–418.

Owen, I. (2009). The intentionality model: A theoretical integration of psychodynamic talking and relating with cognitive–behavioral interventions. *Journal of Psychotherapy Integration, 19*(2), 173–186.

Pallanti, S., Bernardi, S., Allen, A., & Hollander, E. (2010). Serotonin function in pathological gambling: Blunted growth hormone response to sumatriptan. *Journal of Psychopharmacology, 24*(12), 1802–1809.

Pallentino, J., & Lang, D. M. (2012). Malpractice chronicle. *Clinician Reviews, 22*(4), 21–26.

Palo Alto Medical Foundation. (2013). *Dimethyltryptamine*. Retrieved November 17, 2013, from http://www.pamf.org/teen/risk/drugs/hallucinogens/dmt.html

Park, J., Park, K., Lee, I., Kwon, M., & Kim, D. (2012). Standardization study of internet addiction improvement motivation scale. *Psychiatry Investigation, 9*(4), 373–378.

Parnell, L. (2008). *Tapping in*. Boulder, CO: Sound True Inc.

Patel, D. A., Grunzweig, K. A., Zochowski, M. K., Dempsey, A. F., Carlos, R. C., & Dalton, V. K. (2013). Human papillomavirus vaccine stages of change among male and female university students: Ready or not? *Journal of American College Health, 61*(6), 336–346.

Peirce, J. M., Kindbom, K. A., Waesche, M. C., Yuscavage, A. S., & Brooner, R. K. (2008). Posttraumatic stress disorder, gender, and problem profiles in substance dependent patients. *Substance Use & Misuse, 43*(5), 596–611.

Pervanidou, P. (2008). Biology of post-traumatic stress disorder in childhood and adolescence. *Journal of Neuroendocrinology, 20*(5), 632–638.

Peterson, C., Park, N., Pole, N., D'Andrea, W., & Seligman, M. E. (2008). Strengths of character and posttraumatic growth. *Journal of Traumatic Stress, 21*(2), 214–217.

Petry, N., & Schneider, K. (2005). Childhood maltreatment in male and female. Treatment-seeking pathological gamblers. *Psychology of Addictive Behaviors, 19*(2), 226–220.

Petry, N. M., & Steinberg, K. L.; Women's Problem Gambling Research Center. (2005). Childhood maltreatment in male and female treatment-seeking pathological gamblers. *Psychology of Addictive Behaviors, 19*(2), 226–229.
Petry, N. M., Stinson, F. S., & Grant, B. F. (2005). Comorbidity of DSM-IV pathological gambling and other psychiatric disorders: Results from the National Epidemiologic Survey on Alcohol and Related Conditions. *The Journal of Clinical Psychiatry, 66*(5), 564–574.
Petry, N. M., Weinstock, J., Ledgerwood, D. M., & Morasco, B. (2008). A randomized trial of brief interventions for problem and pathological gamblers. *Journal of Consulting and Clinical Psychology, 76*(2), 318–328.
Pettinati, H. M., O'Brien, C. P., & Dundon, W. D. (2013). Current status of co-occurring mood and substance use disorders: A new therapeutic target. *The American Journal of Psychiatry, 170*(1), 23–30.
Philip, D. (1996). Eye wash for perverts? *Alberta Report/Newsmagazine, 23*(36), 22.
Phillips, C. J., Leardmann, C. A., Gumbs, G. R., & Smith, B. (2010). Risk factors for posttraumatic stress disorder among deployed US male marines. *BMC Psychiatry, 10*, 52.
Plant, M., & Plant, M. (2003). Sex addiction: A comparison with dependence on psychoactive drugs. *Journal of Substance Use, 8*(4), 260–266.
Platter, A., & Kelley, M. L. (2012). Effectiveness of an educational and support program for family members of a substance abuser. *American Journal of Family Therapy, 40*(3), 208–213.
Plotnikoff, R. C., Lippke, S., Johnson, S. T., & Courneya, K. S. (2010). Physical activity and stages of change: A longitudinal test in types 1 and 2 diabetes samples. *Annals of Behavioral Medicine, 40*(2), 138–149.
Popky, A. J. (1993). *Smoking protocol.* Paper Presented at the EMDR Institute Annual Conference, Sunnyvale, CA.
Popky, A. J. (2005). DeTUR, an urge reduction protocol for addictions and dysfunctional behaviors (pp. 167–188). In R. Shapiro (Ed.), *EMDR solutions: Pathways to healing*. New York, NY: W. W. Norton.
Popky, A. J. (2010). The desensitization of triggers and urge reprocessing (DeTUR) protocol. In M. Luber (Ed.), *Eye movement desensitization and reprocessing (EMDR) scripted protocols: Special populations* (pp. 489–511). New York, NY: Springer Publishing.
Potenza, M. N., Steinberg, M. A., Skudlarski, P., Fulbright, R. K., Lacadie, C. M., Wilber, M. K., . . . Wexler, B. E. (2003). Gambling urges in pathological gambling: A functional magnetic resonance imaging study. *Archives of General Psychiatry, 60*(8), 828–836.
Presley, C. A., Meilman, P. W., & Lyerla, R. (1994). Development of the Core Alcohol and Drug Survey: Initial findings and future directions. *Journal of American College Health, 42*(6), 248–255.
Priester, P., Scherer, J., Steinfeldt, J., Jana-Masri, A., Jashinsky, T., Jones, J., & Vang, C. (2009). The frequency of prayer, meditation and holistic interventions in addictions treatment: A National Survey. *Pastoral Psychology, 58*(3), 315–322.
Prochaska, J. O. (1991). Prescribing to the stage and level of phobic patients. *Psychotherapy: Theory, Research, Practice, Training, 28*(3), 463–468.
Prochaska, J. O., & DiClemente, C. C. (1982). Transtheoretical therapy: Toward a more integrative model of change. *Psychotherapy: Theory, Research and Practice, 19*(3), 276–288.
Prochaska, J. O., & DiClemente, C. C. (1983). Stages and processes of self-change for smoking: Toward an integrative model of change. *Journal of Consulting and Clinical Psychology, 51*, 390–395.
Prochaska, J. O., & DiClemente, C. C. (1984). *The transtheoretical approach: Crossing traditional boundaries of change*. Homewood, IL: Dorsey Press.
Prochaska, J. O., & DiClemente, C. C. (1992). Stages of change in the modification of problem behaviors. In M. Hersen, R. M. Eisler, & P. M. Miller (Eds.), *Progress in behavior modification* (Vol. 28, pp. 183–218). Sycamore, IL: Sycamore Publishing Co.
Prochaska, J. O., & DiClemente, C. (2002). Transtheoretical therapy. In F. W. Kaslow (Ed.), *Comprehensive handbook of psychotherapy: Integrative/eclectic* (Vol. 4, pp. 165–183). Hoboken, NJ: John Wiley & Sons.

Prochaska, J. O., & DiClemente, C. C. (2005). The transtheoretical approach. In J. C. Norcross & M. R. Goldfried (Eds.), *Handbook of psychotherapy integration* (2nd ed., pp. 147–171). New York, NY: Oxford University Press.

Prochaska, J. O., DiClemente, C. C., & Norcross, J. (1982). Transtheoretical therapy: Toward a more integrative model of change. *Psychotherapy: Theory, Research and Practice, 19*(3), 276–288.

Prochaska, J. O., DiClemente, C. C., & Norcross, J. (1992). In search of how people change: Applications to addictive behaviors. *American Psychologist, 47*(9), 1102–1114.

Prochaska, J. O., Velicer, W. F., DiClemente, C. C., & Fava, J. (1988). Measuring processes of change: Applications to the cessation of smoking. *Journal of Consulting & Clinical Psychology, 56*(4), 520–528.

Prochaska, J., Velicer, W., Fava, J., Rossi, J., & Tsoh, J. (2001). Evaluating a population-based recruitment approach and a stage-based expert system intervention for smoking cessation. *Addictive Behaviors, 26*(4), 583–602.

Pruett, J. M., Nishimura, N. J., & Priest, R. (2007). The role of meditation in addiction recovery. *Counseling & Values, 52*(1), 71–84.

Quadflieg, N., & Fichter, M. M. (2003). The course and outcome of bulimia nervosa. *European Child & Adolescent Psychiatry, 12*(Suppl. 1), I99–109.

Ramo, D. E., & Brown, S. A. (2008). Classes of substance abuse relapse situations: A comparison of adolescents and adults. *Psychology of Addictive Behaviors, 22*(3), 372–379.

Raskind, M. A., Peterson, K., Williams, T., Hoff, D. J., Hart, K., Holmes, H.,... Peskind, E. R. (2013). A trial of prazosin for combat trauma PTSD with nightmares in active-duty soldiers returned from Iraq and Afghanistan. *The American Journal of Psychiatry, 170*(9), 1003–1010.

Redish, A. D., Jensen, S., Johnson, A., & Kurth-Nelson, Z. (2007). Reconciling reinforcement learning models with behavioral extinction and renewal: Implications for addiction, relapse, and problem gambling. *Psychological Review, 114*(3), 784–805.

Reid, R. C. (2007). Assessing readiness to change among clients seeking help for hypersexual behavior. *Sexual Addiction & Compulsivity, 14*(3), 167–186.

Resick, P., & Schnicke, M. (1996). *Cognitive-processing therapy for rape victims. A treatment manual*. Newbury Park, CA: Sage.

Reynaud, M., Karila, L., Blecha, L., & Benyamina, A. (2010). Is love passion an addictive disorder? *The American Journal of Drug and Alcohol Abuse, 36*(5), 261–267.

Rhodes, P. (2003). The Maudsley model of family therapy for children and adolescents with anorexia nervosa: Theory, clinical practice, and empirical support. *Australian & New Zealand Journal of Family Therapy, 24*(4), 191–198.

Roberts, A. L., Austin, S. B., Corliss, H. L., Vandermorris, A. K., & Koenen, K. C. (2010). Pervasive trauma exposure among US sexual orientation minority adults and risk of posttraumatic stress disorder. *American Journal of Public Health, 100*(12), 2433–2441.

Robertson, N. (2000). *Getting better: Inside alcoholics anonymous*. Lincoln, NE: iUniverse.com, Inc.

Rosen, G. M., McNally, R. J., & Lilienfeld, S. O. (1999). Eye movement magic. *Skeptic, 7*(4), 66.

Rosen, T. J., & Shipley, R. H. (1983). A stage analysis of self-initiated smoking reductions. *Addictive Behaviors, 8*, 263–272.

Rosenthal, R. N., & Westreich, L. (1999). Treatment of persons with dual diagnoses of substance use disorder and other psychological problems. In B. McCrady & E. Epstein (Eds.), *Addictions: A comprehensive guidebook* (pp. 439–476). New York, NY: Oxford University Press.

Ross, A., & Thomas, S. (2010). The health benefits of yoga and exercise: A review of comparison studies. *Journal of Alternative and Complementary Medicine, 16*(1), 3–12.

Rothbaum, B. (1997). A controlled study of eye movement desensitization and reprocessing in the treatment of posttraumatic stress disordered sexual assault victims. *Bulletin of the Menninger Clinic, 61*(3), 317–335.

Rothbaum, B. O., Astin, M. C., & Marsteller, F. (2005). Prolonged exposure versus eye movement desensitization and reprocessing (EMDR) for PTSD rape victims. *Journal of Traumatic Stress, 18*(6), 607–616.
Rotunda, R. J., & Doman, K. (2001). Partner enabling of substance use disorders: Critical review and future directions. *American Journal of Family Therapy, 29*(4), 257–270.
Rowe, C. L. (2012). Family therapy for drug abuse: Review and updates 2003–2010. *Journal of Marital and Family Therapy, 38*(1), 59–81.
Ruglass, L. M., Miele, G. M., Hien, D. A., Campbell, A. N., Hu, M. C., Caldeira, N., . . . Nunes, E. V. (2012). Helping alliance, retention, and treatment outcomes: A secondary analysis from the NIDA Clinical Trials Network Women and Trauma Study. *Substance Use & Misuse, 47*(6), 695–707.
Schachter, S. (1982). Recidivism and self-cure of smoking and obesity. *American Psychologist, 37*(4), 436–444.
Schaeffer, H. J., & Jones, S. B. (1989). *Quitting cocaine: The struggle against impulse.* Lexington, MA: Lexington Books.
Scheck, M. M., Schaeffer, J. A., & Gillette, C. (1998). Brief psychological intervention with traumatized young women: The efficacy of eye movement desensitization and reprocessing. *Journal of Traumatic Stress, 11*(1), 25–44.
Schimmenti, A., & Caretti, V. (2010). Psychic retreats or psychic pits? Unbearable states of mind and technological addiction. *Psychoanalytic Psychology, 27*(2), 115–132.
Scrimshaw, E. W., Siegel, K., Downing, M. J., & Parsons, J. T. (2013). Disclosure and concealment of sexual orientation and the mental health of non-gay-identified, behaviorally bisexual men. *Journal of Consulting and Clinical Psychology, 81*(1), 141–153.
Schubert, S., & Lee, C. W. (2009). Adult PTSD and its treatment with EMDR: A review of controversies, evidence, and theoretical knowledge. *Journal of EMDR Practice & Research, 3*(3), 117–132.
Schubert, S. J., Lee, C. W., & Drummond, P. D. (2011). The efficacy and psychophysiological correlates of dual-attention tasks in eye movement desensitization and reprocessing (EMDR). *Journal of Anxiety Disorders, 25*(1), 1–11.
Schulz, D., Kremers, S., & de Vries, H. (2012). Are the stages of change relevant for the development and implementation of a web-based tailored alcohol intervention? A cross-sectional study. *BMC Public Health, 12*, 360.
Schumacher, J. A., Coffey, S. F., & Stasiewicz, P. R. (2006). Symptom severity, alcohol craving, and age of trauma onset in childhood and adolescent trauma survivors with comorbid alcohol dependence and posttraumatic stress disorder. *The American Journal on Addictions, 15*(6), 422–425.
Scott, C. K., Foss, M. A., & Dennis, M. L. (2005). Pathways in the relapse–treatment–recovery cycle over 3 years. *Journal of Substance Abuse Treatment, 28*(Suppl. 1), S63–S72.
Scott, S., & Babcock, J. C. (2010). Attachment as a moderator between intimate partner violence and PTSD symptoms. *Journal of Family Violence, 25*(1), 1–9.
Selzer, M. L. (1971). The Michigan alcoholism screening test: The quest for a new diagnostic instrument. *The American Journal of Psychiatry, 127*(12), 1653–1658.
Shafer, D., Telch, C., & Chen, E. (2009). *Dialetical behavior therapy for binge-eating and bulimia.* New York, NY: Guilford Press.
Shaffer, H. (1989). *The nature of substance abuse and the dynamics of addiction.* Harvard Medical School: Center for Addiction studies. Handout.
Shaffer, H. (1994). Denial, ambivalence, and countertransference hate and rage. In J. D. Levin & R. Weiss (Eds.), *Alcoholism: Dynamics and treatment* (pp. 421–437). Northdale, NJ: Jason Aronson.
Shaffer, H. H., & Simoneau, G. (2001). Reducing resistance and denial by exercising ambivalence during the treatment of addiction. *Journal of Substance Abuse Treatment, 20*, 99–105.
Shaffer, H. J. (1994). Denial, ambivalence and countertransference hate. In J. D. Levin & R. Weiss (Eds.), *Alcoholism: Dynamics and treatment* (pp. 421–437). Northdale, NJ: Jason Aronson.

Shaffer, H. J., & Jones, S. B. (1989). *Quitting cocaine: The struggle against impulse*. Lexington, MA: Lexington Books.

Shapiro, F. (January, 2008 & January, 2005). *EMDR Institute Training Manual*. Watsonville, CA: EMDR Institute.

Shapiro, F. (1989). Efficacy of the eye movement desensitization processing in the treatment of traumatic memories. *Journal of Traumatic Stress, 2*, 199–223.

Shapiro, F. (1991). Eye movement desensitization and reprocessing: A cautionary note. *The Behavior Therapist, 14*, 188.

Shapiro, F. (1995). *Eye movement desensitization and reprocessing: Basic principles, protocols, and procedures*. New York, NY: Guilford Press.

Shapiro, F. (2001). *Eye movement desensitization and reprocessing: Basic principles, protocols, and procedures* (2nd ed.). New York, NY: Guilford Press.

Shapiro, F. (2006). *Theory, practice and research*. Presentation at EMDRIA, Philadelphia, PA, Handout.

Shapiro, F. (2007a). EMDR, adaptive information processing, and case conceptualization. *Journal of EMDR Practice & Research, 1*(2), 68–87.

Shapiro, F. (2007b). *Handbook of EMDR and family therapy processes* (pp. 3–34). Hoboken, NJ: Wiley.

Shapiro, F. (2012). *Getting past your past: Take control of your life with self-help techniques from EMDR therapy*. New York, NY: Rodale Books.

Shapiro, F., Vogelmann-Sine, S., & Sine, L. F. (1994). Eye movement desensitization and reprocessing: treating trauma and substance abuse. *Journal of Psychoactive Drugs, 26*(4), 379–391.

Shapiro, R. (2005). The Two-Handed Interweave. In R. Shapiro (Ed.), *EMDR solutions: Pathways to healing*. New York, NY: W. W. Norton.

Siegel, S. (2005). Drug tolerance, drug addiction, and drug anticipation. *Current Directions in Psychological Science, 14*(6), 296–300.

Simons-Morton, B. (2007). Social influences on adolescent substance use. *American Journal of Health Behavior, 31*(6), 672–684.

Skinner, H. A. (1982). The drug abuse screening test. *Addictive Behaviors, 7*(4), 363–371.

Smedema, S. M., & Ebener, D. (2010). Substance abuse and psychosocial adaptation to physical disability: Analysis of the literature and future directions. *Disability and Rehabilitation, 32*(16), 1311–1319.

Smith, D. E. (2012). The process addictions and the new ASAM definition of addiction. *Journal of Psychoactive Drugs, 44*(1), 1–4.

Snow, M., Prochaska, J., & Rossi, J. (1992). Stages of change for smoking cessation among former problem drinkers: A cross-sectional analysis. *Journal of Substance Abuse, 4*(2), 107–116.

Solomon, R. M., & Rando, T. A. (2012). Treatment of grief and mourning through EMDR: Conceptual considerations and clinical guidelines. *European Review of Applied Psychology, 62*(4), 231–239.

Solomon, R. M., & Shapiro, F. (2008). EMDR and the adaptive information processing model: Potential mechanisms of change. *Journal of EMDR Practice & Research, 2*(4), 315–325.

Soule, L. C., Shell, L., & Kleen, B. A. (2003). Exploring Internet addiction: Demographic characteristics and stereotypes of heavy Internet users. *Journal of Computer Information Systems, 44*(1), 64–73.

Sreeraj, V. S., Prasad, S., Khess, C. R., & Uvais, N. A. (2012). Reasons for substance use: A comparative study of alcohol use in tribals and non-tribals. *Indian Journal of Psychological Medicine, 34*(3), 242–246.

Steele, K., & van der Hart, O. (2009). Treating dissociation. In C. Courtois & J. Ford (Eds.), *Treating complex traumatic stress disorders: An evidence-based guide* (pp. 145–165). New York, NY: Guilford Press.

Steenkamp, J. O., van der Walt, M. J., Schoeman-Steenkamp, E. M., & Strydom, I. (2012). Introducing SHIP® as a psychotherapeutic model to access the body memory of traumatised clients: Depathologising expressions of trauma. *South African Journal of Psychology, 42*(2), 202–213.

Steinberg, M. (2000). Advances in the clinical assessment of dissociation: the SCID-D-R. *Bulletin of the Menninger Clinic, 64*(2), 146–163.

Steinberg, M., & Schnall, M. (2001). *The stranger in the mirror: Dissociation-the hidden epidemic*. New York, NY: Harper Collins Publishers.

Stine, S. M., & Kosten, T. R. (1999). Opioids. In B. McCrady & E. Epstein (Eds.), *Addictions* (pp. 141–161). New York, NY: Oxford Press.

Stinson, F. S., Grant, B. F., Dawson, D. A., Ruan, W. J., Huang, B., & Saha, T. (2005). Comorbidity between *DSM-IV* alcohol and specific drug use disorders in the united states: Results from the national epidemiologic survey on alcohol and related conditions *Alcohol Research & Health, 29*(2), 94–106.

Stinson, F., Grant, B., Dawson, D., Ruan, W., Huang, B., & Saha, T. (2006). Comorbidity between *DSM-4* alcohol and specific drug use disorders in the United States (Results from the National Epidemiologic Survey on Alcohol and Related Conditions). Reprinted from *Drug and Alcohol Dependence, 80*(1).

Sturgess, J. E., George, T. P., Kennedy, J. L., Heinz, A., & Müller, D. J. (2011). Pharmacogenetics of alcohol, nicotine and drug addiction treatments. *Addiction Biology, 16*(3), 357–376.

Substance Abuse and Mental Health Services Administration (SAMHSA). (2006). *Definitions and terms related co-occurring conditions*. Rockville, MD: Office of Applied Studies, National Survey on Drug Use and Health. Retrieved November 15, 2013, from http://www.atforum.com/addiction-resources/documents/OP1-DefinitionsandTerms-8–13-07.pdf

Substance Abuse and Mental Health Services Administration (SAMHSA). (2012a). *Results from the 2011 National Survey on Drug Use and Health: Mental Health Findings*. Rockville, MD: Center for Behavioral Health Statistics and Quality. Retrieved September 29, 2013, from http://www.samhsa.gov/data/NSDUH/2k11MH_FindingsandDetTables/2K11MHFR/NSDUHmhfr2011.htm

Substance Abuse and Mental Health Services Administration (SAMHSA). (2012b). *Results from the 2011 National Survey on Drug Use and Health: Mental Health Findings* (NSDUH Series H-45, HHS Publication No. [SMA] 12–4725). Rockville, MD: Author. Retrieved September 29, 2013 from http://www.samhsa.gov/data/NSDUH/2k11MH_FindingsandDetTables/2K11MHFR/NSDUHmhfr2011.htm

Substance Abuse and Mental Health Services Administration (SAMHSA). (2012c). *Mental Health Findings*: Office of Applied Studies, National Survey on Drug Use and Health). Washington, DC:. Author. Retrieved November 15, 2013, from http://www.samhsa.gov/data/NSDUH/2k11MH_FindingsandDetTables/2K11MHFR/NSDUHmhfr2011.pdf

Substance Abuse and Mental Health Services Administration (SAMHSA). (2013a). *Results from the 2012 National Survey on Drug Use and Health: Summary of National Findings* (NSDUH Series H-46, HHS Publication No. [SMA] 13–4795). Rockville, MD: Author. Retrieved September 29, 2013, from http://www.samhsa.gov/data/NSDUH/2012SummNatFindDetTables/NationalFindings/NSDUHresults2012.pdf

Substance Abuse and Mental Health Services Administration (SAMHSA). (2013b). *Results from the 2012 National Survey on Drug Use and Health: Summary of National Findings*. Rockville, MD: Center for Behavioral Health Statistics and Quality. Retrieved September 29, 2013, from http://www.samhsa.gov/data/NSDUH/2012SummNatFindDetTables/NationalFindings/NSDUHresults2012.pdf

Suire, J. G., & Bothwell, R. K. (2006). The psychosocial benefits of alcoholics anonymous. *The American Journal on Addictions, 15*(3), 252–255.

Sullivan, M., & Risler, E. (2002). Understanding college alcohol abuse and academic performance: Selecting appropriate intervention strategies. *Journal of College Counseling, 5*(2), 114–123.

Sutherland, I. (1997). The development and application of a questionnaire to assess the changing personalities of substance addicts during the first year of recovery. *Journal of Clinical Psychology, 53*(3), 253–262.

Talley, A. E., Sher, K. J., & Littlefield, A. K. (2010). Sexual orientation and substance use trajectories in emerging adulthood. *Addiction, 105*(7), 1235–1245.

Tamam, L., Zengin, M., Karakus, G., & Ozturk, Z. (2008). Impulse control disorders in an inpatient psychiatry unit of a university hospital. *Klinik Psikofarmakoloji Bulteni, 18*, 153–161.

Taylor, L. K., & Weems, C. F. (2009). What do youth report as a traumatic event? Toward a developmentally informed classification of traumatic stressors. *Psychological Trauma, 1*(2), 91–106.

Tedeschi, R. G., & Calhoun, L. G. (1995). *Trauma and transformation. Growing in the aftermath of suffering*. Thousand Oaks, CA: Sage.

Ter Heide, F. J., Mooren, T. M., Kleijn, W., de Jongh, A., & Kleber, R. J. (2011). EMDR versus stabilisation in traumatised asylum seekers and refugees: results of a pilot study. *European Journal of Psychotraumatology, 2*.

Tesch, B., Bekerian, D., English, P., & Harrington, E. (2010). Same-sex domestic violence: why victims are more at risk. *International Journal of Police Science & Management, 12*(4), 526–535.

The Free Dictionary by Farlex. (2013). Retrieved January 12, 2013, from http:// http://www.thefreedictionary.com

Tolin, D. F., & Foa, E. (2008a). Sex differences in trauma and posttraumatic stress disorder: A quantitative review of 25 years of research. *Psychological Trauma: Theory, Research, Practice, and Policy* Vol. S, No. 1, 37–85.

Tolin, D. F., & Foa, E. (2008b). Sex differences in trauma and posttraumatic stress disorder: A quantitative review of 25 years of research. *Psychological Bulletin, 132*(6), 959–992.

Tsuang, M. T., Bar, J. L., Harley, R. M., & Lyons, M. J. (2001). The Harvard twin study of substance abuse: What we have learned. *Harvard Review of Psychiatry, 9*(6), 267–279.

Tsui, V., Cheung, M., & Leung, P. (2010). Help-seeking among male victims of partner abuse: men's hard times. *Journal of Community Psychology, 38*(6), 769–780.

Twitchell, G. R. (2003). *Concentrated alcohol consumption by heavy drinkers: Associated risk and costs*. Report developed under contract with the California Department of Alcohol and Drug Programs. Retrieved November 13, 2013, from http://www.adp.ca.gov/rc/pdf/Concentrated_Alcohol.pdf

Tyagi, E., Agrawal, R., Zhuang, Y., Abad, C., Waschek, J. A., & Gomez-Pinilla, F. (2013). Vulnerability imposed by diet and brain trauma for anxiety-like phenotype: Implications for post-traumatic stress disorders. *Plos ONE, 8*(3), 1–12.

U.S. Department of Health and Human Services. Office on Disability. (2010). *Substance abuse and disability*. Retrieved from http://www.hhs.gov/od/about/fact_sheets/substanceabuse.html

van der Hart, O., Groenendijk, M., Gonzalez, A., Mosquera, D., & Solomon, R. (2013). Dissociation of the personality and EMDR therapy in complex trauma-related disorders: Applications in the stabilization process. *Journal of EMDR Practice and Research, 7*(2), 81–94.

van der Berg, D., & van der Gaag, M. (2012). Treating trauma in psychosis with EMDR: A pilot study. *Journal of Behavior Therapy and Experimental Psychiatry, 43*, 664–671.

van der Hart, O., Nijenhuis, E., & Steele, K. (2006). *The haunted self: Structural dissociation and the treatment of chronic traumatization*. New York, NY: W.W. Norton and Co.

van der Kolk, B. (1990). The body keeps the score: Approaches to the psychobiology of post-traumatic stress disorder. In B. van der Kolk, A. McFarlane, & L. Weisaeth (Eds.), *Traumatic stress: The effects of overwhelming experience on mind, body and society*. New York, NY: Guilford Press.

van der Kolk, B. (1996). The body keeps the score: Approaches to the psychobiology of post-traumatic stress disorder. In B. van der Kolk, A. McFarlane, & L. Weisaeth (Eds.),

Traumatic stress: The effects of overwhelming experience on mind, body and society. New York, NY: Guilford Press.

van der Kolk, B. A. (1994). The body keeps the score: memory and the evolving psychobiology of posttraumatic stress. *Harvard Review of Psychiatry, 1*(5), 253–265.

van der Kolk, B. A., Roth, S., Pelcovitz, D., Sunday, S., & Spinazzola, J. (2005). Disorders of extreme stress: The empirical foundation of a complex adaptation to trauma. *Journal of Traumatic Stress, 18*(5), 389–399.

van Veen, T., Wardenaar, K. J., Carlier, I. V., Spinhoven, P., Penninx, B. W., & Zitman, F. G. (2013). Are childhood and adult life adversities differentially associated with specific symptom dimensions of depression and anxiety? Testing the tripartite model. *Journal of Affective Disorders, 146*(2), 238–245.

van Wormer, K. V., & Davis, D. R. (2013). *Addiction treatment: A strengths perspective* (3rd ed.). Belmont, CA: Thomson Brooks/Cole.

VanDerNagel, J., Kiewik, M., Buitelaar, J., & DeJong, C. (2011). Staff perspectives of substance use and misuse among adults with intellectual disabilities enrolled in Dutch disability services. *Journal of Policy & Practice in Intellectual Disabilities, 8*(3), 143–149.

Verdejo-García, A., Pérez-García, M., & Bechara, A. (2006). Emotion, decision-making and substance dependence: A somatic-marker model of addiction. *Current Neuropharmacology, 4*(1), 17–31.

Volkow, N. D. (2007). *Comorbidity: Addiction and other mental illnesses.* NIDA Research Report Series. Retrieved February 26, 2009, from http://www.nida.nih.gov/researchreports/index/html

Wagner, A., Aizenstein, H., Venkatraman, V. K., Bischoff-Grethe, A., Fudge, J., May, J. C., . . . Kaye, W. H. (2010). Altered striatal response to reward in bulimia nervosa after recovery. *The International Journal of Eating Disorders, 43*(4), 289–294.

Warren, J. R., & Hernandez, E. M. (2007). Did socioeconomic inequalities in morbidity and mortality change in the United States over the course of the twentieth century? *Journal of Health and Social Behavior, 48*(4), 335–351.

Wasserman, D. A., Havassy, B. E., & Boles, S. M. (1997). Traumatic events and post-traumatic stress disorder in cocaine users entering private treatment. *Drug and Alcohol Dependence, 46*(1–2), 1–8.

Weathers, F. W., Huska, J. A., & Keane, T. M. (1991). *PCL-C for DSM-IV*. Boston, MA: National Center for PTSD—Behavioral Science Division.

Weathers, F. W., Litz, B. T., Herman, D. S., Huska, J. A., & Keane, T. M. (1993). *The PTSD checklist (PCL): Reliability, validity, and diagnostic utility*. Paper presented at the 9th Annual Meeting of the International Society for Traumatic Stress Studies, San Antonio, TX.

Weaver, M. F., & Schnoll, S. H. (1999). Stimulants: Amphetamines and cocaine (pp. 105–120). In B. McCrady & E. Epstein (Eds.), *Addictions*. New York, NY: Oxford University Press.

Weber, K., Rockstroh, B., Borgelt, J., Awiszus, B., Popov, T., Hoffmann, K., . . . Pröpster, K. (2008). Stress load during childhood affects psychopathology in psychiatric patients. *BMC Psychiatry, 8*, 63.

WebMD. (2013). *Caffeine*. Retrieved November 14, 2013, from http://www.webmd.com/vitamins-supplements/ingredientmono-979-CAFFEINE.aspx?activeIngredientId=979&activeIngredientName=CAFFEINE

Wegscheider Cruse, S. (1989). *Another chance: Hope and health for the alcoholic family*. Palo Alto, CA: Science and Behavior Books, Inc.

Weiss, R. (1994). Countertransference issues in treating the alcoholic patient. Institutional and clinical reactions. In J. D. Levin & R. Weiss (Eds.), *Alcoholism: Dynamics and treatment* (pp. 407-420). Northdale, NJ: Jason Aronson.

Whang, L. S., Lee, S., & Chang, G. (2003). Internet over-users' psychological profiles: A behavior sampling analysis on internet addiction. *Cyberpsychology & Behavior, 6*(2), 143–150.

White, W., & Miller, W. (2007). The use of confrontation in addiction treatment: History, science and time for change. *Counselor, 8*(4), 12–30.

Widyanto, L., & McMurran, M. (2004). The psychometric properties of the internet addiction test. *Cyberpsychology & Behavior, 7*(4), 443–450.

Wikipedia. *List of twelve-step groups*. Retrieved November 9, 2013, from http://en.wikipedia.org/wiki/List_of_twelve-step_groups

Wileyto, P., Patterson, F., Niaura, R., Epstein, L., Brown, R., Audrain-McGovern, J., ... Patterson, F. (2004). Do small lapses predict relapse to smoking behavior under bupropion treatment? *Nicotine & Tobacco Research, 6*(2), 357–366.

Wittchen, H. U., Behrendt, S., Höfler, M., Perkonigg, A., Lieb, R., Bühringer, G., & Beesdo, K. (2008). What are the high risk periods for incident substance use and transitions to abuse and dependence? Implications for early intervention and prevention. *International Journal of Methods in Psychiatric Research, 17 Suppl 1*, S16–S29.

Wohl, M., & Sztainert, T. (2011, March). Where did all the pathological gamblers go? Gambling symptomatology and stage of change predict attrition in longitudinal research. *Journal of Gambling Studies, 27*(1), 155–169.

Wölfling, K., Beutel, M. E., & Müller, K. W. (2012). Construction of a Standardized Clinical Interview to Assess Internet addiction: First Findings Regarding the Usefulness of AICA-C. *Journal of Addiction Research and Therapy*, S6, 003.

Xie, H., McHugo, G. J., Fox, M. B., & Drake, R. E. (2005). Special section on relapse prevention: Substance abuse relapse in a ten-year prospective follow-up of clients with mental and substance use disorders. *Psychiatric Services, 56*(10), 1282–1287.

Yehuda, R., Southwick, S., Nussbaum, G., Wahby, V., Giller, E., & Mason, J. (1990). Low urinary cortisol excretion in patients with posttraumatic stress disorder. *The Journal of Nervous and Mental Disease, 178*(6), 366–369.

York, C., & Leeds, A. M. (2001, June 21). *Gate theory: An accelerated information processing model for developing functional state change*. Paper presented at the EMDRIA Conference, Austin, TX.

Young, K. S. (1998). Internet addiction: The emergence of a new clinical disorder. *Cyberpsychology & Behavior, 1*(3), 237–244.

Young, K. S. (2011). Clinical assessment of internet-addicted clients. In K. Young & C. de Abreu (Eds.), *Internet addiction: A handbook and guide to evaluation and treatment* (pp. 19–34). Hoboken, NJ: John Wiley & Sons.

Zinberg, N. (1984). *Drug, set, and setting: The basis for controlled intoxicant use*. New Haven, CT: Yale University Press.

Zinberg, N. (1986). *Drug, set and setting: The basis for controlled intoxicant use*. New Haven, CT: Yale University Press.

Zweben, J. E., Clark, H. W., & Smith, D. E. (1994). Traumatic experiences and substance abuse: mapping the territory. *Journal of Psychoactive Drugs, 26*(4), 327–344.

INDEX

www.ingramcontent.com/pod-product-compliance
Ingram Content Group UK Ltd.
Pitfield, Milton Keynes, MK11 3LW, UK
UKHW051924100926
8556IPUK00021B/1349

9 780826 198563